ECONOMIC INTEGRATION AMONG UNEQUAL PARTNERS

Pergamon Titles of Related Interest

Balassa The Newly Industrializing Countries in the
World Economy
Fordwor The African Development Bank
Higonnet/Jorge/Salazar-Carillo Foreign Debt and Latin
American Economic Development
Odle Multinational Banks and Underdevelopment
Seiber International Borrowing by Developing Countries
Solis Economic Policy Reform in Mexico

Related Journals*

ECONOMIC BULLETIN
HABITAT INTERNATIONAL
SOCIO-ECONOMIC PLANNING SCIENCES
WORLD DEVELOPMENT

*Free specimen copies available upon request.

ECONOMIC INTEGRATION AMONG UNEQUAL PARTNERS

THE CASE OF THE ANDEAN GROUP

ALICIA PUYANA DE PALACIOS

PERGAMON PRESS

New York   Oxford   Toronto   Sydney   Paris   Frankfurt

Pergamon Press Offices:

U.S.A.   Pergamon Press Inc., Maxwell House, Fairview Park,
                    Elmsford, New York 10523, U.S.A.

U.K.   Pergamon Press Ltd., Headington Hill Hall,
                    Oxford OX3 0BW, England

CANADA   Pergamon Press Canada Ltd., Suite 104, 150 Consumers Road,
                    Willowdale, Ontario M2J 1P9, Canada

AUSTRALIA   Pergamon Press (Aust.) Pty. Ltd., P.O. Box 544,
                    Potts Point, NSW 2011, Australia

FRANCE   Pergamon Press SARL, 24 rue des Ecoles,
                    75240 Paris, Cedex 05, France

FEDERAL REPUBLIC Pergamon Press GmbH, Hammerweg 6
OF GERMANY   6242 Kronberg/Taunus, Federal Republic of Germany

Library of Congress Cataloging in Publication Data

Puyana de Palacios, Alicia, 1941-
    Economic integration among unequal partners.

    (Pergamon policy studies on international
development)
    Bibliography: p.
    Includes index.
    1. Andes region--Economic integration. 2. Acuerdo
de Cartagena. I. Title. II. Series.
HC165.P89   1982   337.1'8   81-21005
ISBN 0-08-028822-7   AACR2

Printed in the United States of America

To my husband

MARCO PALACIOS

for his companionship.

To My Parents

Carlos Cesar Puyana

Graciela Mutis de Puyana

CONTENTS

LIST OF TABLES

xi

LIST OF GRAPHS

LIST OF ACRONYMS

ANDI	Colombian Association of Industrialists
CACM	Central American Common Market
CAF	Andean Development Corporation (Corporacion Andina de Fomento)
CARICOM	Caribbean Community
CET	Common External Tariff
CMEA, COMECON	Council for Mutual Economic Assistance
CMET	Common Minimal External Tariff
COMECON, CMEA	Council for Mutual Economic Assistance
CSSR	Czechoslovakia
DNP	National Colombian Planning Department
EACM	East African Common Market
ECIEL	United Studies on Latin American Economic Integration (Estudios Conjuntos Sobre la Integración Económica en A. Latina)
ECLA	Economic Commission for Latin America
EEC	European Economic Community
EFTA	European Free Trade Area
EURATOM	European Atomic Energy Community
FEDECAMARAS	Federation of Chambers of Commerce of Venezuela
GATT	General Agreement on Tariffs and Trade
GRAN	Andean Group (Grupo Andino)
IDB	Interamerican Development Bank
ILET	Latin American Institute for Transnational Studies
IMF	International Monetary Fund
INCOMEX	Colombian Institute for Foreign Trade
INTAL	Institute for Latin American Integration
JCMS	Journal of Common Market Studies
Junta	Junta of the Agreement of Cartagena
LAFTA	Latin American Free Trade Association

LDC   Less Developed Country
MCET   Minimum Common External Tariff
OAS   Organization of American States
PID   <u>Punto Inicíal de Desagravación</u>   (starting
             point for reduction of tariffs)
SIDP   Sectoral Industrial Development Programme
UNCTAD   United Nations Conference on Trade and De-
             velopment

ACKNOWLEDGMENTS

I am indebted to many members of the technical staff of the Junta de Cartagena for the supply of valuable information concerning the negotiations of the different Cartagena Agreement Programmes and for numerous and patient discussions held during my 1975 stay in Lima. I would also like to thank the many people at different levels within the governments and in the private sector who gave me access to information or provided me with interviews. I am also indebted to the Director and colleagues of the Centro de Estudios Economicos y Sociales del Tercer Mundo for the possibility of updating the initial research; to Miss T. Cooper, Fellow of St. Hugh's College for her extensive understanding and help; and to my supervisor, Mrs. Rosemary Thorp, for her generous friendship, constant encouragement and guidance; she was a constant stimulus to my work.

Finally I wish to thank my husband, Marco Palacios, for his patient effort in making me understand the complexity of the political events, and for his confidence in my work and his generosity.

INTRODUCTION

This book presents a study of the problems of economic integration among a group of less developed countries (LDCs) with small national markets and uneven economic development, where each of those countries has already begun a process of import substitution and has entered the integration program in order to accelerate industrialization.

The study undertakes two main tasks. The first is the quantitative evaluation of the degree of progress and the economic costs and benefits incurred to date in economic integration among the countries of the Andean Group. This analysis concentrates on the dynamic effects of increased trade on growth. Since these effects are extremely limited, the second task is the explanation of this in terms of an examination of the genesis of policies. In this context the central hypothesis explored is that the different levels of industrial development generate national aspirations with regard to integration which are liable to create antagonism. That possibility is further reinforced by the small size of the regional market and by the character of the preexisting development strategy in the countries in question.

Our preoccupation with the second aspect, that of policy making and the genesis of conflict, has grown in the course of the research. We began with the intention of analyzing the effects of integration on development in the terms in which economists usually carry this out. However, we have become increasingly concerned with the discontinuity that exists between the framework typically applied by economists, on the one hand, and political scientists, on the other. Economic analyses have tended to justify and to evaluate integration purely in terms of economic costs and benefits. For this purpose, static indicators are used, such as increases or changes in composition of trade, and, more recently, certain dynamic factors, such as economies of scale, the growth of investment, and growth in factor productivity. Political scientists, on the other hand, when analyzing integration, do take into account factors such as divergent levels of economic development and asymmetrical market size. However, when they focus their attention on economic elements, they concentrate mainly on the distributional consequences of these factors, thereby neglecting other implications that help to explain more fully the political constraints on integration, particularly in the case of less developed countries.

Thus, for economists, it is important to bear in mind that, even after it has been accepted that development combined with integration is a "second-best" solution, several problems have to be solved regarding qualitative differences in the process of import substitution. The analysis must not ignore the political interdependence and conflicts generated by the process of industrialization itself when undertaken by countries significantly different from each other. Through integration new types of political and economic communities are created, for which the governmental and nongovernmental elites have to redefine their interests in regional terms. This process is not free of conflicts, conflicts that may even reverse it. A study of the interests of the different actors involved is crucial to establish the political viability of economic integration. What disagreements arise between the industrialists, legislators, and politicians of member countries? What do they consider are the costs and benefits derived from a changed economic, administrative, and institutional climate and from the extended market?

In a political analysis, in turn, it is important to search for some explanation of the lack of political support in the economic characteristics of the integrating countries. In addition to the scarcity of the resources available for "equitable distribution," the ending of the easy stage of import substitution implies new costs that may affect the interests of the already installed industrialists, as well as the interests of other groups (landowners, importers).

The characteristic neglect by economists of the insights offered by political science has meant, we would claim, that, while the existing economic literature is rich in providing an understanding of the essentials of economic integration, the reasons why countries decide to integrate, and the arguments over planned versus spontaneous integration, it is less useful in other ways. It does not provide a framework within which we may try to understand why it is that, after a short period of very substantial advances, integration schemes among less developed countries have almost always stagnated, or even disintegrated.

In respect of policy making, the different authors writing in the field of economics usually perceive the importance of

avoiding a resort to policies that will weaken the agreement.(1)
The most important aspect of policy harmonization is usually
recognized to be industrial planning, which is aimed both at
greater efficiency and at preventing damaging regional concentration.(2)   The importance of avoiding "incentive wars" is
also recognized.(3)

But the implicit assumption is then made that, once
agreement has been reached on the convenience of integrating
markets and harmonizing policies, conflicts of interest will
disappear since countries will recognize that no one is better
off without integration. At least in the long run, the common
interest is identical with the national interest.(4) From that it
follows that the costs of sacrificing sovereignty are surely
outweighed by considerations of welfare gains. In that sense,
"the constraints of co-operation are less restrictive than those
imposed by the lower level of income and development."(5)

Economists stress two elements which make this outcome
more likely. The first is that integration movements today
typically occur <u>after</u> LDCs have introduced significant elements
of planning into their policy-making processes.(6) The second
is the existence of highly technical studies demonstrating
objectively the costs and benefits of integration, of optimal
allocation of integrated industries, and of harmonizing policies.
On the basis of such studies governments will bargain among
themselves, reach agreements, and then be capable of and
interested in enforcing these agreements nationally.(7)

Should the disagreement turn critical, for example over
allocation of industries,the proposed solution lies in creating
joint enterprises in which all countries have an interest.(8)

Turning to the political theory of economic integration, we
find that political scientists have not arrived at a consensus on
what regional integration is.   Three main lines of thought have
appeared: the federalist approach, which emphasizes the role
of institutions; the transactionalist approach, which stresses
transactions between people; and the neo-functionalist approach, which focuses on the ways in which supranational
institutions emerge from a convergence of interests of various
significant   groups   in   society.(9)   The   neo-functionalistic
approach is generally considered the most convenient for
analyzing common market schemes in which the creation of new
institutions and the liberalization of trade relations are basic.
We will, therefore, refer to it in connection with the analysis
of the Andean Group experiences.

For the neo-functionalist approach a central idea is the
concept of gradual politization or spillover, by which "the
progression from a common market to an economic union and
finally to a political union among states in automatic."(10)

A second important element is the gradual bureaucratiza-
tion of politicians dealing with economic matters, with the
consequence that political ideology recedes. This would allow

the group to advance until the critical point is reached, when it becomes impossible to return to nationalistic positions.(11)

European experiences have led to the revision of the main points of the functionalistic approach, especially those related to the revival of "nationalistic positions," and the change in the priority put on integration due to changes in the international economic and political environment.(12)

Many authors have contributed to the analysis of the applicability of the neo-functionalistic approach to integration schemes among LDCs. The majority of them point to the following characteristics of the integrated LDCs which make the approach inadequate:

- differences in economic development and the size of the union make the distribution problems crucial(13)
- the lack of pluralism and the absence, or weakness, of support from social groups and associations make integration more difficult because it reduces the capacity of leaders to commit their societies(14)
- The lack of support isolates the political leaders and the technocrats, the only actors firmly engaged in integration.(15)

This literature leaves us with a number of the problems, which form the context of this book. First, from it we fail to understand why it is that conflicts became irreconcilable and that, even when reciprocal trade grew and no serious concentration problems were detected (as in the cases of the EACM and CACM), progress came to a halt and countries were reluctant to move into deeper forms of integration. We find that the more serious gap lies in the failure to explain the objective basis of the different national positions; that failure goes back to the philosophy implicit in the import substitution process, which assumes that industrialization is legitimate for the nation and that in pursuing it the state is free of contradictions and has the power to enforce it.

We will argue that there exists a relationship between a country's level of industrial development and its national policies. A country's policies seem to follow the import substitution goal more closely if it is one of the less industrial countries. The relatively more industrialized countries among the LDCs tend toward more liberal models of integration. The more advanced countries obtain immediate gains from the "negative" stage of integration, that is, from freed trade, because they have a greater elasticity of industrial supply. The less developed countries cannot respond so quickly, and therefore their interest lies in "positive" integration, especially in those programs related with the planned allocation of new industries. The problem is not just that diametrically opposed points of view exist concerning the different stages of integration, but that these attitudes tend to manifest themselves in the form of conflicts, the extent and nature of which weaken the political objective of the process.

The small size of the integrated market increases the costs of integration for the wealthier members. This is implicit in the principle of "subregional balance," which sets out to accelerate growth in the less developed member countries. As a consequence their willingness to participate on more complex forms of cooperation such as SIDPs or strict harmonization policies is seriously affected.

One additional element should be taken into account: the constraints of the import substitution model with integration. The only new element is the integration of national markets. We find no other measures that will act upon the supply or demand side such as income redistribution.

A second problem we cannot resolve in reading the current literature is the gap between the official position that strongly favored integration and the passive, sometimes negative, attitude of the national industrial sector. We find no sufficiently clarifying studies about the behavior and objective interests of the Latin American industrial sector and find it difficult to accept that it necessarily will agree on any type of policy that will expand production and lower costs.

It is improbable that industrialists and other pressure groups will accept the goal of regional integration, when they perceive themselves to be assuming the costs of other countries' industrialization.

The third question that emerges is how to explain the impossibility of agreeing on technical planning parameters. The literature does not consider the relativity of concepts such as efficiency, equity, costs, and so on. When starting off from different factor endowments and levels of industrial development, it is entirely possible that countries may reach a different definition of what is "efficiency" and what will be the more "rational" use of resources.

Exploring these questions, we attempt to explain the general lack of political support which may make it impossible to reach the high levels of integration required to fully integrate countries pursuing a more intensive industrial import-substituting development. The model requires a great deal of central planning, state intervention, and the transference of a considerable part of decisions on economic policies to the supranational institutions, which is near to impossible to attain given the present political constraints.

THE PLAN OF THE BOOK

The book is developed in three parts. The first, comprising two chapters, deals first with the historical, political, and theoretical backgrounds that led to integration proposals in Latin America. It reviews the existing literature on integration, with special emphasis on that of Latin American experiences, and shows the need for the kind of approach taken here: namely, one that draws on the perspectives both of economics and political science to evaluate the implications of unequal levels of development in the context of integration.

It then analyzes the economic structure of each country and the national economic development strategies and policies directly linked with integration that may affect the integration process.

The second part, Chapter 3, studies the progress made, up to 1975 in the commercial program. Using primary data we evaluate what are referred to in the economic literature as dynamic effects.

The third part, comprising four chapters, deals with the attitudes of the different actors, internal and external, directly affected by the integration process, and with the program of positive integration, legislation on foreign capital, the establishing of the Common External Tariff (CET), industrial sectoral planning, and the harmonization of macroeconomic policies. We observe that differences in industrial development resulted in differences in the national positions taken with respect to the above-mentioned policies. The countries with a lesser degree of industrial development wish to have a higher and relatively dispersed CET, strong policies of industrial development, and an active public sector planning and investing in industry, which was opposed by the more liberal model of the relatively more developed countries. The contradictions were resolved by eliminating the commitment to establish a CET, the weakening of the intensity of planned industrial specialization, and by the indefinite delaying of the policy harmonization programs.

It is likely that the interest in integration based on expectations of economic gains is satisfied by relatively limited measures. In the Andean Group this point seems to be reached once exports of marginal production are occurring.

A NOTE ON SOURCES

We developed the basic analysis presented in this work and drew out its more important conclusions between 1974 and 1978, during the production of the D. Phil. thesis approved by the Economics Faculty of the Oxford University in September 1980. We considered the period 1966-1976 which includes the negotiations about the Cartagena Agreement, its approval and its operation until its great crisis which led to large reforms of the program and the withdrawal of Chile. Our main preoccupation was to find and explain the causes of this crisis. In our conclusion, we suggested that, far from resolving itself, the nucleus of the crisis was still present after the changes of 1976 and the intensive advance of the integration process was exhausted. Later events have proved our findings. For that reason, we considered it necessary to update this work to include an evaluation of the Cartagena Agreement and to present the chapter about economic structure of each member country and national strategies and politics of economic development in its original version, since they constituted the cause and explanation of the latent conflicts that existed since the sixties; they also led to the crisis of 1976, the subsequent restraint, and the decision of 1981 to reformulate the agreement.

Primary Sources

- records of the discussions held by the national representatives at the technical and political level during the process of negotiating the Treaty of Cartagena
- the records of the Commission of the Treaty of Cartagena 1968-1978, especially the discussions about the main integration programs (CET, SIDPs, freeing of trade and policy harmonization)
- Junta documents evaluating the integration process; interviews made by the author with government representatives responsible for designing national economic policies and for the development of integration agreements in all member countries (these interviews were held during 1975 when the author was a member of the United Nations Development Advisory team to the Junta; simultaneously interviews were made with representatives of the private sector)
- review of ten years (1965-1975) daily publication of the more important Colombian newspapers
- personal interviews in 1978 with politicians, planners, and private sector representatives in Colombia

From January 1979 to November 1981, the author continuously reviewed all the Junta and Commission principal documents, mainly the "Evaluation Studies" and the Commission meetings final reports. She also had numerous interviews with high level Junta officials and with Colombian government representatives.

Secondary Sources

• studies of different integration attempts both in Europe and among LDCs, and finally

• studies carried out by political scientists on economic integration among developed as well as among less developed countries

We found the study of other experiences very useful, especially the analysis of the Council for Mutual Economic Assistance (CMEA) experiences. In the CMEA as well as in the Andean Group the aim was a high level of industrial specialization, through common planning and the transfer of a considerable number of decisions to supranational institutions. In spite of the differences in political organization both groups have passed through crises defined by the divergent position adopted by the less and the more developed countries. In both cases industrial planning and sacrifices in sovereignty caused similar crises that were resolved by the relaxing of the previous targets. In both cases "national interest" and "national state" proved to be stronger than the need and observed utility of integrating.

PART I

HISTORICAL, POLITICAL, AND THEORETICAL BACKGROUND

CHAPTER 1
THE CARTAGENA AGREEMENT

THE INSTITUTIONAL FRAMEWORK AND THE HISTORY
OF THE AGREEMENT

This chapter provides a brief description of two closely related aspects of the Andean Group (Grupo Andino, hereinafter the GRAN), exploring the political and economic ideas, theories, and ideologies that led to the Treaty of Cartagena and the constituent elements of the Treaty, its objectives, and the mechanisms designed to achieve them. To set that description in its context, the institutional framework will be sketched in and the history of the treaty reviewed.

The original members of the GRAN were Bolivia, Chile, Colombia, Ecuador, and Peru. Although Venezuela participated in all the negotiations that took place from 1965 until the treaty was signed in the Colombian city of Cartagena on May 25, 1969 it did not enter the group until February 1973. The total area of the GRAN countries (including Venezuela) is 5.5 million square kilometers, and the population of the area in 1969 was 64,192,000. A population of this size might be considered important in terms of demand; however, as we shall see in Chapter 2, there are several limitations upon the market, including the size and structure of Gross Domestic Product, the structure and distribution of income, and relations with the international economy. At the time the treaty was signed the GDP of the area was US$27.3 billion, similar to that of Brazil or Mexico. However, GDP per capita was considerably lower than that of Mexico or of Argentina, while still higher than that of the Central American Common Market countries. A detailed analysis of the economic structure of the Andean countries is given in Chapter 2 (see especially Table 2.1 at end of chapter); the area is an important source of

3

minerals such as oil, copper, tin, and coal, and of agricultural products such as coffee, sugar, and bananas.

The Institutional Framework

The GRAN is organized on the basis of equal rights for all members and on the principle that each member country has a single vote in decisions and the right to veto; a majority of two-thirds is required for all decisions. The question of voting rights on the Commission was one of the most controversial and most heatedly debated within the Mixed Commission set up to prepare the Treaty as a result of the Bogota Declaration of 1966. Opposition to a majority rule by Peru and Venezuela led to the adoption of a compromise solution by which a two-thirds majority could be overruled by a veto in delicate areas thought likely to provoke controversy, such as the Sectoral Industrial Development Programs (SIDP), the CET, decisions to modify the treaty or accelerate the commercial or agricultural programs, and decisions to reverse proposals made by the Junta. The inclusion of the last point is an indication of the importance ascribed to that body.

Approval of the CET and SIDP was subject to a complex procedure. They would be approved by a majority of two-thirds as long as no veto was cast; if one were cast, the proposal under discussion would return to the Junta for revision, to be voted upon once more after a period of six months. At the second vote the same rule would apply, with a two-thirds majority assuring acceptance as long as no new veto was cast.

As the foregoing account indicates, two different bodies participate in running the GRAN: the Commission - formed by the plenipotentiary presidential delegates of the member countries and generally operating at ministerial level, and the Junta - directly responsible to the Commission, and entirely independent from the governments of the different member countries. Only the Commission has legislative power, and it meets six times each year, three times for ordinary sessions, and three times for extraordinary ones. The Junta consists of three members designated by the Commission for a two-year period and is a permanent body with executive functions and research capabilities. On its own initiative or at the behest of the Commission it produces studies and proposals for the Commission to consider, and for this purpose it has at its disposal a large technical staff which is also independent from the member governments. The Junta is a potentially powerful body, in some ways similar to the Commission of the European Economic Community.(1) It receives advice, as does the Commission itself, from specialized councils, set up on an ad hoc basis to make recommendations.(2)

The Treaty also provides for the creation of a judicial body, the Arbitration Tribunal, charged with ruling on all lawsuits arising out of the implementation or later working of the decisions of the Commission.

Finally, it was agreed that a representative of the Latin American Free Trade Association (LAFTA) should attend the sessions of the Commission as an observer.

The headquarters of the GRAN are in Lima, and all the meetings of the Commission take place there; the composition of national delegations to the Commission depends on the policies of the member countries and the matters being discussed, but in general governments have sought to blend functionaries from state entities with representatives of the private sector.

It could be argued that this organizational scheme gives the Junta informal power that goes beyond its formal limits, first, because its supranational character makes it independent of the different governments, second, because of its permanent activity, and third, because it controls a vast technical staff.

The Junta has adopted the procedure of holding multiple consultations with technical experts from the different nations during the process of preparation of studies leading to formal proposals.   Once basic information has been compiled and a methodology adopted, the Junta sends its technical experts from the relevant field to visit each country for more detailed discussions; these are continued until the Junta is satisfied that the process has yielded all its fruits.   However, while this process is under way the officials of the Junta do not inform the different member countries of the positions taken up by their fellows in the group.   If the members of the Junta consider that the national positions adopted are irreconcilable, they delegate to their own technical experts the task of resolving the problem; thus the final proposal reflects both the technical and regional considerations initially adopted by the Junta and the compromises considered necessary to satisfy the "national aspirations" put forward by individual member countries as discussions proceed.   The final proposals are studied by the technical experts from each nation and thereafter at a political level by the respective ministers, with reference where necessary to the president, and a decision is taken on the position the country will take when the matter comes before the Commission.

As we shall see, it appeared in the early stages of the GRAN that the Junta built up such a position of strength that it functioned as a "sixth government,"(3) and the national governments, becoming aware of the danger, decided upon open opposition to a number of its proposals; since that time the power of the Junta has been somewhat checked.

The History of the GRAN

Six distinct phases may be identified in the brief history of the GRAN. They are outlined briefly below.

i. The period of negotiation, 1965-69

The movement toward the GRAN dates back to the growing wave of criticism of the Latin American Free Trade Association throughout 1965 by the "intermediate countries" within it. This criticism arose out of the frustration of a group of countries in the face of poor results from their trade within the zone and of the failure of the negotiations over the second stage of the LAFTA Common List. The presidents of Chile, Colombia, and Venezuela (respectively, the Christian Democrat Eduardo Frei, the Liberal Carlos Lleras Restrepo, and Raul Leoni of the Democratic Action Party) assumed the international leadership of this group of countries, and on August 16, 1966 they signed the Declaration of Bogota, which laid down the general lines of the "Andean Common Market," conceived explicitly as a means of strengthening LAFTA rather than as an alternative to it. The Declaration of Bogota set in motion an agitated phase of intergovernmental negotiations of a technical and political nature, centered on a specially designated body, the "Mixed Commission," representing the three signatories of the Declaration along with Peru, Ecuador, and later Bolivia.(4) Unlike similar bodies created at the time when LAFTA and the Central American Common Market (CACM) were in the process of formation, the Mixed Commission had from its inception a markedly political character regarding the technical elements of the project for integration; rather than appearing as the idea of a group of technical experts, successfully sold to the politicians, the GRAN would appear as an initiative of the politicians themselves. For this reason among others, an effort was made from the start to involve the private sector in the Mixed Commission, although the response was not enthusiastic.

At the beginning of 1968 the Mixed Commission produced a document that would subsequently serve as the basis for the CAF (Corporación Andina de Fomento, or Andean Development Corporation),(5) an agency charged with financing national development projects in the subregion with funds from member countries and international credit agencies; all six members of the Mixed Commission entered the CAF. At the end of the same year the Commission produced the document that would serve as the basis for the Treaty of Cartagena, which was signed in May 1969 by all the members of the Commission except Venezuela, which left its entry open pending future discussions.

In the earliest debates in the Mixed Commission, positions began to emerge that would polarize with time; Chile and Colombia showed a clear preference for free trade, while Peru and Venezuela favored protectionist policies. Thus, while Chile and Colombia proposed that internal tariff barriers should be removed within six years, considering tariff reductions to be a stimulus to economic development, the other countries sought a minimum period of 12 years, with Venezuela going so far as to propose that tariff barriers should be maintained until regional development plans could be implemented.(6)   Venezuela and Peru placed considerable emphasis on the planning of previously selected new industries and proposed that high tariffs should be maintained to protect existing high-cost production.   Venezuela asked that the CET should not be adopted until LAFTA as a whole took steps toward a common market and instituted such a common tariff; at the same time, both Venezuela and Peru sought exemptions for endless lists of products for an indefinite period from the inception of the commercial program.   The first draft of the Treaty set this period at 11 years, and at 16 years for the relatively less developed countries.   Despite this and other guarantees in view of their lower levels of development, Bolivia and Ecuador adopted positions similar to those of Peru and Venezuela, reducing the Andean common market in effect of complementarity agreements for new industries.

ii.   The period of rapid advance, 1969-72

The first years after the signing of the treaty were marked by rapid advances and by considerable euphoria, as the integrationist rhetoric of the politicians was encouraged by the punctuality with which agreements and decisions were reached in Lima in accordance with the previously established timetable. This was the case of the Commercial Programme, with its different sections, the Minimum Common External Tariff (MCET), and a number of important dispositions, such as Decisions 24 (Common Regime on Foreign Capital), 49 (Policies for Industrial Harmonization), 46 (Policies regarding Treatment of Sub-Regional Capital), and 47 (Andean Multinational Corporations). In fact many of these agreements were only partially implemented or remained in a kind of legal limbo.(7)   Others, such as Decision 24, were to be drastically reformed in subsequent years.(8)

      The active participation of the private sector remained minimal at this stage, as it was to do in the future; where explicit positions were taken up by private associations, they were unreasonably hostile and without exception, protectionist. In the case of Venezuela, the Federation of Chambers of Trade (FEDECAMARAS) raised a series of technical objections to the policies of the government and sought systematically to block entry into the GRAN.(9)   Peruvian industrialists took the same line, arguing that they could not compete with other member

countries. Nor was the hostility of the private sector confined
to major industrial concerns; protests came from the small
Peruvian weavers in 1971, and pressure from the Ecuadorian
hosiery sector forced the government of that country to deliv-
er an ultimatum in the 1970 negotiations, threatening definitive
withdrawal.

Another characteristic that would mark this and subsequent phases was the monopoly by the executive power (the
presidency, planning department, and specialized ministries) of
all political and legal initiatives in relation to the GRAN.
Where national parliaments existed, they were effectively
by-passed, whatever the general degree of participation in the
political process - whether in Chile, where the Popular Unity
coalition, once elected, sought to mobilize the whole population
behind the transformations it proposed; or in Peru, where the
government of General Velasco pursued nationalistic and reformist goals while seeking to keep political participation under
control. The fact was that, as far as the GRAN was concerned, all governments excluded political and trade union
groups from the debate and appeared to seek the participation
of the private sector more to establish an alibi for its own
conduct than as a principle in itself.(10) The legal justification put forward by governments to secure this monopoly was
that the GRAN was a development of the Treaty of Montevideo
which had set up LAFTA.(11) In Colombia, for example, this
legal ploy enabled the government to avoid debate and approval by parliament, and thus circumvent the opposition of the
private sector and its ability to exploit the veto power which
the Colombian parliament still enjoys, despite the fact that the
constitutional reform of 1968 removed from the legislature initiative in economic matters such as the national budget and
overall planning.

This period also saw the emergence of tensions between
the national governments and the technocrats in Lima, the
so-called "sixth government." These technocrats, inspired by
the example of ECLA, took seriously their role as disseminators
of "formal rationality" (to use a phrase Medina Echeverría liked
to use when he spoke of ECLA), with the inevitable consequence that considerations of national sovereignty were relegated to second place. At this stage, however, these tensions
did not emerge in important conflicts between the Junta and
the Commission. On the whole, the rapid pace set by the
bureaucrats in Lima was matched by the member governments,
who saw rapid progress as a source of prestige at home.

iii. The crisis looms: 1972

The first serious clash of opinions came in this year, when the
Commission, and thus the member governments, unanimously
rejected the Junta proposal on the "Petro-Chemicals Program-

me," the result of two years of detailed studies. At the same time the first serious division between member countries occurred, with Chile considering voting against or even vetoing the Light Engineering Programme (Programa Metal-Mecánico). The impasse was resolved when the Popular Unity government, apparently for political and diplomatic reasons, withdrew its objections and voted for the program. In the same year Colombia began to manifest doubts regarding projects for industrial planning and to employ delaying tactics when these came up for discussion.(12)

iv. Progress grinds to a halt: 1973-75

In this period there appeared unequivocal signs that the phase of easy and rapid advance was over, and this despite the belated entry of Venezuela. Paradoxically, the entry of this oil-rich country polarized positions within the Commission, and strengthened and united the Peru-Bolivia-Ecuador front; it also had a considerable effect of the economic dimensions of the GRAN. In general the period was marked by stagnation; the sectoral programs suffered delays, and the Junta was unable to put the whole set of sectoral programs before the Commission as originally planned. Discussion of the industrial programs was linked to that concerning the CET, and no progress was made on either. As a result the target date for approval of the CET and the sectoral programs, December 31, 1975, came and went without any agreement being reached. Nevertheless, defenders of the GRAN could argue that all was not lost, for the Petro-Chemicals Programme had been approved in April 1975. However, numerous and substantial reforms had been introduced into the original proposal, completely subverting the principle of specialization, and the program approved left every member country much as it has been before, with the option of developing an integrated petrochemical industry if it so desired. The period also saw discussions on the harmonization of macroeconomic policies reach an impasse, and representatives of the Junta began to draw attention to a worrying general failure to comply with and implement the decisions of the Commission.(13)

v. The crisis of 1976

The crisis of 1976 reached its peak with the definitive withdrawal of Chile from the GRAN. Nevertheless, we have seen that it would be wrong to see their dramatic event as the only sign of crisis. The malaise created by the failures of previous years was aggravated by the Chilean Junta's Decree 600, which openly violated Decision 24, and the labyrinthine negotiations that ensued led to a serious setback; many of the advances toward political integration and in other fields were

reversed. The curious thing about the 1976 crisis is that the
Commission was prepared to move so far in a liberal direction
in response to the common front presented by Chile and Colombia, despite the political and institutional distance between
Lopez Michelsen's democratic government and the right-wing
dictatorship in Chile. Pressure from Colombia and Chile
effected a number of changes, which together amounted to a
considerable retreat. Decision 24 was liberalized; the attempt
to set up a common external tariff was abandoned and replaced
by a "tariff band" (studied in detail in Chapter 5); the participation of member countries in sectoral programs was made
optimal rather than obligatory as before and a considerable
number of items were removed from the list for inclusion in the
programs; the date for approval of the tariff band and the
modified sectoral programs was moved back two years; and
discussion on the harmonization of macroeconomic policies was
postponed indefinitely. The dream of an "Andean Economic
Union" was shattered.

Chile withdrew in October 1976, after it had achieved
satisfaction through its common front with Colombia on all the
reforms it had sought. It appears therefore that the Chilean
decision to renounce the treaty may have come from reasons of
a diplomatic or internal political nature, rather than from the
grievances expressed throughout the year. In any case, from
the point of view of the history of the GRAN, the crisis of
1976 can be seen as illustrative of the exacerbation of conflicts
between free traders and protectionists which had been present from the beginning.

vi.   The crisis spreads: 1977-78

As a direct result of the traumatic events of 1976, serious
splits developed in the Commission and a mood of weariness
and waning enthusiasm set in. The process of tariff reduction
was halted, for the first time in the GRAN's short history,
and not one single national legislature introduced the modifications necessary for the implementation of the 1976 reforms
known as the Lima Protocol (Decisions 100 and 103).(14) In
the circumstances, the approval of the Automobile Programme
in September 1977 after four years of tortuous negotiations -
hailed as a success by defenders of the GRAN - must be seen
as a face-saving measure, particularly as it ignores the question of specialization, as the Petro-Chemicals Programme did
before it, and refers only to co-production and assembly.

In the economic field, the GRAN began to approach certain developed countries (the United States, the European
Economic Community, Spain, Japan) as well as other Latin
American countries (Argentina, Brazil, and Mexico). In the
political sphere, it moved to consolidate the diplomatic front
for support of Panama's negotiations on the Canal Treaty, it

took an active part in isolating Somoza, and it censured the interruption in Bolivia's democratic process.

vii. 1981, The Turning Point

1981 brought with it a legacy of dissatisfactions and frustrations, a very hard year with the Peru-Equador armed conflict seriously aggravating the situation.   This frontier conflict made the delicate diplomatic situation between the member countries untenable, a situation created by the virtual censure of the Bolivian government; and which practically paralyzed all activity for eight months.

The Thirtieth period of the Commission's extraordinary sessions, convened "to reactivate the Andean integration process," could be celebrated only in September of 1981.

From its final act, the following tendencies in the future activities of the Andean Group can be inferred:

- The trade program which will look for agreement on the national margin of tariff reductions for the consolidation of the "Free Trade Andean Zone" (15) will be reactivated and accelerated.
- Although they promise to "go on studying the problem," they renounce through practice the CET adoption.
- They propose to reduce the sectoral industrial planning to the three programs approved and to revise them fundamentally.   Only the allowances granted to Bolivia and Ecuador would practically stay effective.
- The new definition of the mechanisms and the new formulation of the objectives that take into account the changes in the economic scheme are admitted in the hope that they will lead to further conciliation.

Regarding the harmonization of macroeconomic policies, the absolute stupidity added to the later aspects permit one to think that the Andean Common Market formation was conscientiously and indefinitely postponed.

We have to note that the tendency toward political cooperation did not succeed in creating an atmosphere which would facilitate decision making about integration.   On the contrary, it became a factor of tension which negatively affected the process.(16)

THE EMPIRICAL AND THEORETICAL BACKGROUND

We commented above that, in contrast to the cases of the CACM and LAFTA, the initiative for the creation of an "Andean Common Market" came from national political leaders rather than from bureaucrats with access to political circles.

However, with every birth, especially in the field of ideas, there is always room for dispute over paternity and geneology, and one scarcely needs reminding that the idea of economic integration was enjoying something of a vogue in intellectual and political circles in Europe in the sixties; at the same time the ECLA analysis (described in greater detail below) was gaining ground in Latin America among politicians and technical experts alike, in the face of the problems of depression, chronic inflation, balance-of-payments difficulties, and declining terms of trade.(17)   The ECLA view seemed at the time to provide a coherent alternative to the traditional position of "orthodox" economic thought, as expressed with eloquence in the various reports produced by IBRD missions to different nations.   The question of what contribution if any Prebisch's work has made to economic theory, or of the extent to which his writings provide a "scientific" analysis of Latin American economies, lies beyond the scope of this thesis;(18)   what does seem beyond dispute is that as the sixties advanced these ideas gained more and more adherents in political circles in Latin America.   The Cuban revolution was viewed with apprehension and in some cases with terror; in more general terms, the sixties were marked by an accumulation of social and political problems as a result of depressed economic activity. Governments were open to "heterodox" solutions, and the ECLA view seemed to offer a coherent set of practical recipes, which had the advantage of being based upon a systematization of economic policies sporadically practiced since the depression.   For all its normative loading and political and ideological bias, visible behind its apparently neutral language, the ECLA approach to "structural" problems was accepted by men such as Frei, Lleras, and Leoni as practical and feasible.

It would, however, be an exaggeration to suppose that ECLA had an intellectual monopoly as far as integration was concerned.   The explicit statements of the founding fathers of the GRAN and the evolution of the GRAN itself bear witness to the influence of prevailing ideas concerning integration, derived in the main from the European experience.   The range of professional economists and agencies who contributed to the founding of the GRAN and to the shaping of particular policies is a further confirmation of the eclectic sources on which it drew;(19) furthermore, the neo-functionalist approach was not spurned; it was certainly familiar to men like Lleras Restrepo, who sought to incorporate into the GRAN some of its basic principles, not least that successive stages of economic integration should lead automatically to political agreements, and to a gradual ceding of national autonomy.   This theme will be taken up again in Chapter 4, when we consider some of the political and ideological dimensions of the GRAN.

Import Substitution and Integration in Latin America:
The ECLA View

Up to 1930 the Latin American economies had in general been
linked to the international market by the sale of primary products, whether minerals or agricultural goods, but either in the
wake of the Great Depression or during and after the Second
World War many of them adopted protectionist policies to foster
industrial growth, in the belief that the manufacturing sector
was the motor of development and the means by which chronic
dependence on the external sector could be overcome. Coming
later on the scene, the Untied Nations' Economic Commission
for Latin America (ECLA) sought to provide conceptual analysis and support for the practice of nearly two decades and
attempted to resolve the problems of the acceleration of progress and of the rate of growth, the incorporation of Latin
America into the modern world, and breaking of the strangle-
hold of export and foreign exchange problems.

ECLA's ideas diverged from the prevailing orthodox liberal theory of international trade, which accepts the principle of
comparative advantage in the international division of labor and
analyzes the effect of international trade upon the returns to
productive factors, concluding that trade between countries
leads to specialization according to each nation's resources and
that, in consequence, a relative leveling of returns to factors
will be achieved, thus reducing the differences between countries. ECLA took the opposite point of view, arguing that
economic relations between countries at the center and those
on the periphery tended to breed the conditions of underdevelopment and to widen the gap between the developed and
underdeveloped world, and that market forces aggravated
rather than diminished inequalities. The viewpoint expressed
has aroused and continues to arouse considerable polemical
debate; in the fifties and early sixties Prebisch and his allies
engaged in fierce theoretical skirmishes with the World Bank,
opposing its analysis and its recommendations to Latin American governments. In recent years there has been considerable
support for the liberal position, as witnessed in the orthodox
stabilization policies recommended by the International Monetary
Fund (IMF) among others. As we have suggested, however,
regardless of the final conclusions of that debate, the historical importance of the ECLA approach at the time is clear.

For ECLA, the main explanation for the process of concentration of the gains of growth lay in the retention and
concentration of technological processes in the developed
countries. On the basis of an analysis of trade statistics,
ECLA argued that the terms of trade between primary and
manufactured products tended to deteriorate as a result of the
difference in the rates of growth of productivity for manufacturers and primary goods. This difference was itself

exacerbated by the more developed conditions of production in advanced countries and by high degrees of monopolization of production and effective trade union organization, which increased the level of value-added for each unit of output. The next step taken by ECLA was to identify industrialization as the basic element of development, which, as well as supplying, for example, goods that could not be imported in times of war, could produce domestically those goods that could not be imported for lack of foreign exchange. It would also lead to technological development in underdeveloped countries. The gains from industrialization would be reinforced by the spread of technological advances in primary production, and the ability

> to take economic advantage of the labour force which was being freed from those activities and that coming from natural population growth.(20)

Such considerations set the need to industrialize apart from concentration upon the restrictions and shortcomings of international trade and led to criteria for the full and effective use of human resources:

> Although the productivity of an industrial activity may be lower than in a foreign counterpart, the resources used in it contribute to a greater or lesser degree to the material product, which they would not if they were unemployed or engaged in traditional activities in which their yields would be lower.(21)

It was foreseen, however, that development of the industrial sector would not occur by means of market forces alone. In addition to the slow expansion of the export sector, the smallness of the national markets and the social and economic structures of individual countries hindered the organization and distribution of resources by such forces. There thus arose the need to direct economic growth, that is, to create the conditions under which industry could fulfil its task of reconstruction. If, apart from accelerating economic growth, it was necessary to "correct" it, the state had to intervene in the allocation of resources, to modify commercial mechanisms and any structures that might hinder development. Planned economic development therefore required a system of rationalization of state actions and of private activity and a broader ideology stressing the need for a concerted drive to overcome resistance to change.(22)

However, government intervention of this kind could not offer a viable, long-term solution. It failed because it took the form of control of the use of external resources rather than planning of growth, but also because of inevitable politi-

cal problems from which the planners could not extricate themselves.

Certainly the 1960s were years of expansion for the Latin
American countries. Exports increased, external financing was
abundant, and gross production grew at a greater rate than
previously. But the basic problems still existed. First,
industry based on insufficient markets created internal distortions such as lack of linkages, low levels of specialization, and
small plant size. Given these conditions, it was impossible for
either national or foreign industries to export. Second, underemployment and unemployment, the increasing concentration
of income, balance-of-payments problems, and the backwardness of the agricultural sector continually threatened growth.
Given the difficulties of accelerating exports or of incorporating marginal people of areas into the market,

> integration was put forward as the means to achieve
> the double objective of gaining greater foreign ex-
> change incomes for the countries and reducing their
> vulnerability to high concentration of income.
> Intra-regional integration was proposed for both
> goals, as an indispensable tool and to a large ex-
> tent, an irreplaceable one. It was the only method
> capable of bringing about a qualitative change in the
> situation as it had been analysed.(23)

The novelty of ECLA's concept of integration was contained precisely in what it hoped to achieve: development that
brought with it qualitative changes in a country's socioeconomic structures. Integration was a crucial weapon if such
changes were to be brought about. While the desarrollo hacia
adentro (inward-facing development) model was to be broad-
ened and modified, it was also to be oriented towards the
supranational region. In other words, import substitution was
to be combined with export promotion

> in such a way as to substitute Latin American im-
> ports while its countries would be developing ex-
> ports, which would allow members to expect that
> they would finance and increase their imports from
> within the group.(24)

By the beginning of the sixties, the importance of industrialization, planning, ahd integration had become accepted
without reservation at government levels and in political
circles, and this was reflected in national development plans.
Other goals appeared: social justice and Pan-American solidarity were enshrined in the Punta del Esta Agreement (1961),
and they formed the basis of the Alliance for Progress.

Faced with the Cuban revolution and increased socioeconomic tensions, and encouraged by the Kennedy administration, Latin American governments accepted part of the ECLA view and some of its practical recommendations, but with a shift of emphasis. First, discussions took place on the internal, social, and political obstacles to development, and the need to create "new and more developed forms of co-operation" became the principal goal. The Interamerican Development Bank (IDB) began to finance health projects, agrarian reform, road-building and bilateral frontier schemes. The Organization of American States (OAS) meeting in 1961 at Punta del Este marked the zenith of North American sociopolitical reformist zeal and its flirtation with ECLA's doctrines, and previously dangerous themes such as agrarian and tax reform, cooperativism, planning and regional cooperation became legitimate. In this respect the Declaration of the Presidents of America is perhaps the document most illustrative of the political climate from which the Treaty of Cartagena and Latin American integration emerged, with its statement:

Our purpose in creating the Latin American Common Market is to recover the image and meaning of the Alliance for Progress as a multilateral programme of international co-operation in which all the countries of the inter-American system will assume concrete obligations oriented towards strengthening the process of economic integration of Latin America and towards the creation of more favourable conditions for the social and economic development of the region within a free, just and democratic society.(25)

Previous Attempts at Integration

The previous attempts at economic integration in Latin America, the Latin American Free Trade Association and the Central American Common Market, had proved unable to create the conditions necessary to overcome the problems of development; they had at best stimulated new trade flows. Among other reasons for this failure, the following have been put forward:

i. These models of integration were based in general upon the principle of free trade. They were unable to shape expectations of and possibilities for new investment, and therefore they did not stimulate new activities. Given free trade within an enlarged market closed to third parties, a boom in industrial investment could have been expected. This did not occur, either on the scale or in the sectors expected, among other reasons because the LAFTA countries soon began to show signs of stagnation and of wavering commitment to the agreements reached.

ii. There are inherent limitations to reciprocal concessions. In the case of LAFTA, each step in the commercial
program had to be studied, negotiated, and agreed by all the
member countries.(26)

iii. There was a failure to bring national economic
policies gradually into line to prevent the individual actions of
countries from hindering the fulfillment of essential aspects of
the agreement, such as exchange rate policies or protection
against third countries.

iv. There was a lack of provisions favoring the less
developed countries, to prevent or compensate for the effects
of concentration.

To summarize the problem, LAFTA suffered from a series
of weaknesses that led, in a very short period, to its almost
total demise. The considerable increase in trade was brought
about by the reduction of tariffs on goods previously traded,
and strengthened traditional trade sectors; progress was only
achieved when one country was interested in claiming other
countries' markets for a certain product; the freeing of trade
did not necessarily mean the disappearance of the higher cost
producer.(27)

Under the LAFTA program, new industrialization led to
greater differences in levels of development and to industrial
specialization in some countries and primary production in
others. The acceleration of development in the larger countries meant a considerable rise in the share of returns going
to foreign firms, and there was also a greater degree of
concentration in these companies. Thus part of the benefits of
a wider market went to transnationals and so left the region in
the form of larger transfers to the Centre.

After more than ten years of stagnation and prolonged
renegotiations the Montevideo Treaty expired. Its successor,
the 1980 Montevideo Treaty, was born. This new document
has an essentially free trade orientation. It is the legitimation
and stimulus for bilateral trade agreements, and the factual
renunciation of the treatment of integration as an instrument of
long-term economic policies within a "developmental" framework
and of the creation of the Latin American Common Market.

The Treaty of Cartagena expressed the discontent of the
less developed countries over the limited achievements of
LAFTA, especially over the difficulty of gaining entry to the
Argentinian, Brazilian, and Mexican markets. The Treaty
therefore sought to rectify, at least partially, the shortcomings
of LAFTA and the CACM.

The Theory of Economic Integration

The theoretical framework of studies on economic integration
has its roots in English foreign trade theory and is restricted

to customs unions. Pioneers of this work were Viner, Meade,
and Lipsey(28) whose writings "may be described as an adap-
tation of that traditional foreign trade theory which studies the
effects on welfare following a change from protection to free
trade."(29)   The basic assumptions of foreign trade theory,
such as markets working under perfect conditions, immobility
of productive factors between countries, and the lack of differentiation of products, were fully applied to customs unions.
Also, transport costs and monetary aspects were excluded.
Thus the main concern of classical theory was whether or not
the freeing of trade between members of a customs union can
lead to an increase in the world's welfare when restrictions on
trade are maintained with other countries.

The classical theory of economic integration concentrated
almost exclusively on the problems of integration among industrialized countries.   Therefore its main preoccupation was with
the achievement of adjustments in patterns of production and
consumption by means of geographically discriminating tariff
mechanisms.(30)   It tried to solve two questions, first, what
are the probable effects of a customs union upon the world's
welfare? and second, what factors affect the advantages of a
union?

Viner considered that trade diversion would have a negative productive effect and trade creation a positive one as a
result of a customs union.(31) In general, the world's welfare
would only increase if the creation effects were greater than
the diversion effects.   This could only be achieved when the
customs union operated a system as near as possible to total
free trade.   But, in stating this, Viner limited his analysis to
productive effects because he assumed a zero elasticity of
demand and an infinite elasticity of supply.   Over the long
term, Viner considered that customs unions misallocate resources because they withdraw from the optimum position of
total free trade.   Meade improved on the realism of this analysis by introducing the possibility of price elasticity demand
and concluded that the way to weight the changes in trade
flows was to multiply the money values of trade created and
diverted by the tariffs of the importing countries and take the
net value as a measure of the welfare created.   Even within
the context of the traditional theory of economic integration,
this stance has been criticized.   For example, Lipsey suggested:

When consumption effects are allowed for, the simple
conclusions that trade creation is good and trade
diversion is bad are no longer valid.(32)

In the economic literature on economic integration a different starting point was taken.   Johnson, for instance,(33)
introduced the assumption that governments have moved away

from free trade and instituted tariffs with the objective of overcoming the gap between social and private costs (or benefits). Cooper and Massell developed this line further. They showed under what circumstances a customs union could give sufficient protection to uncompetitive industries (hence allowing industrial diversification), while at the same time bringing about a rise in the level of specialization through free trade among the partners, thereby reducing the costs of diversification.(34) Scitovsky analyzed other effects (with reference to Europe), such as the results of an increase in competition, the use of economies of scale, changes in the volume and location of investments, and changes in the terms of trade. However, he dealt with them within the traditional analytical framework which places great significance upon the effects of changes in the conditions of competition, arguing that

> the main results of integration are shown to be various consequences of the increase in competition which the common market is almost certain to bring about.(35)

In Chapter 3, which deals with the commercial program, we will study in detail the significance of the European approach when dealing with the creation of a customs union in less developed countries. At this point, therefore, we will simply examine the validity of the factors which, according to traditional theory, affect the desirability of customs unions among underdeveloped countries. The factors are: (i) the level of complementarity or competitiveness of the respective economies; (ii) the size of the union; (iii) the level of national tariffs in existence before the signing of a treaty; (iv) the proportion of intra-subregional trade compared with trade with the rest of the world; and (v) transport costs. One author suggests that,

> although these criteria [those that affect the desirability of the customs union] were designed specifically for integration among industrialized countries, they are appropriate for application to less developed areas as well.(36)

We believe, however, that their validity is limited, as will be seen in the following discussion.

i. Competitiveness and complementarity

According to Viner, a customs union will be the more beneficial, the more competitive are the countries concerned. Given competitive rather than complementary structures, the size of the benefits from integration depend upon the extent of differences in production costs.

Because less developed countries specialize in primary products, they tend to be competitive in Viner's sense. But this does not genuinely indicate potential for gains from integration because these goods are exported to third parties, not to the region. Competitiveness and complementarity ought to be given a different meaning to acquire any worth when dealing with lesser developed countries.(37) A dynamic perspective is essential: what is being sought is to develop a complementary structure and to minimize the costs of industrialization.(38)

ii. Size of the union

In traditional economic integration theory, the size of the union is decisive for determining the number of benefits to be gained from it. The size of the union is measured by the proportion of trade that will be created under conditions of universal free trade within the group of countries.(39) If, in general, the member countries are at the same level of development and are geographically close, total population or income can be used as a measure of the potential size.

It is known that intraregional trade among LDCs is small, and this implies that welfare gains will be small. But once again a dynamic perspective may alter our interpretation: here it is important to take into account that trade may increase very rapidly once the factors that limit intraregional trade, such as the low level of development, inadequacy of transport facilities, overvalued currencies, and so on, have been removed.(40)

iii. Previous tariff rates

The higher the initial tariffs are and the lower the common external tariff, the greater will be the welfare gains from economic integration. Here again the relevance looks slight: the majority of less developed countries have relatively high tariff levels, either for revenue or protection purposes. Higher tariffs in LDCs may be established as development instruments to utilize idle resources. Therefore welfare may be increased. The LDCs are interested in expanding protection to the whole integrated region, which may permit a better utilization of resources than would a national autarchic industrialization project. Some authors imply that the external common tariff might have to be higher than the national tariffs of the partners.(41)

iv. External trade and domestic expenditures

The traditional theory accepts that the gains from intraregional trade are likely to be greater, the lower is the proportion of

foreign trade of each member to purchases of domestic commodities.(42) Thus, apparently, the chances for achieving welfare
gains from a customs union among LDCs are very limited because the proportion of foreign trade to domestic expenditure
is high. But, again, that conclusion is not completely valid
because if the LDCs are going to develop on the basis of a
rather slow growth of export proceeds, the foreign trade-to-
domestic expenditures ratio will decline rapidly. "Welfare
gains will be achieved through the creation of regional markets
because they will tend to retard the rate of decline in the
ratio of foreign trade to domestic expenditures."(43)

v. Transport costs

Finally, it is assumed that transport costs tend to restrict the
benefits of economic integration. In East Africa, for example,
the elimination of tariffs did not lead to the integration of
markets because of the lack of a transport infrastructure.(44)
The same conclusion can be extended to Caribbean Community
(CARICOM), LAFTA, or the Andean Group.(45) But the
transport infrastructure is a variable that results from the
export-led type of economic development; it is not predeter-
mined.
     As we show in the following chapter, one result of this is
that the costs of transport are lower between the GRAN countries and Europe or the United States than between the GRAN
countries themselves.
     We see therefore that a relatively strict application of the
traditional theory of economic integration leads to the conclusion that the LDCs are poor candidates for entry into
integration arrangements and that customs unions among those
countries are likely to decrease welfare both to the member
countries and to the world. But we have also seen how a
dynamic perspective, starting from the existing institutional
situation, qualifies this. Another way to make the same point
is to say that the reason why generalizations of traditional
theory have a limited applicability to LDCs is because in their
case integration should be treated as an approach to economic
development rather than as a tariff issue. We may thus consider how membership in a customs union may enable a less
developed country to reach more efficiently the objectives it
seeks to achieve through protection.(46)
     In other words, for economic integration to produce its
effects in terms of economic development, it has to be converted into an integral part of development policies and to seek
the same ends. The emphasis is put on the need to plan
industrial development in order to save productive resources,
to adopt a common external tariff, and to unify macroeconomic
policies, in order to achieve more efficient industrial growth at
regional levels. Further, the best path to economic integration

is to aim for a common market and, later, for an economic union. The need for a more sophisticated model of integration in less developed countries arises from differences in the level of economic development which require measures to prevent concentration effects. It is recognized also that industrialization does require planned allocation of scarce resources and coordinated tax, credit, and foreign trade policies. As well as factors that raise the level of economic development, integration should include those elements that improve the countries' international trade positions. And, in evaluating the desirability of integration for less developed countries, the emphasis has to be placed on effects that have strong implications for the prospects of development. According to writers such as Balassa, Cooper, and Massell,(47) the following conditions must exist for integration to be successful in less developed countries.

    i.   A Common External Tariff (CET). If a common tariff is not adopted, specialization based on differences in internal tariff levels will occur. The preferences agreed between members will depend upon the level of the external tariff. Countries with higher tariffs give greater preference in their markets and get less in the other members' markets.

    ii.   Planning in the industrial sector. If permanent membership is to be attractive to less developed countries, it must ensure the use of economies of scale and prevent concentration effects.

    iii.   Unification of policies. This should create conditions under which agreements become irreversible and stop countries from acting unilaterally and introducing distortions to the attitude toward competition.

We will study these requirements in more detail in the chapters on the CET, sectoral planning, and policy unification.

We shall call the approach described the integrated development model. Its explicit aim is the acceleration of the economic and social development of the member countries,(48) and it is oriented toward the optimization of economic policy as a whole. The process of integration takes a linear form as economic union is reached step by step. As the programmed stages advance, the level and scope of the process become amplified because those activities subject to common treatment spill over into new sectors, or because they are carried out in greater depth in a specific sector.(49) The assumption is that, as the process advances, governments will delegate increasing responsibilities to common institutions. Agreement on delegation has to be reached at the outset to ensure that the requirements for coordination are fulfilled.(50)

This view finds its origin in neo-functionalist theory, according to which a scheme for economic integration which starts with joint ventures in noncontroversial areas may end with the spillover effects mentioned above, because of the dynamic properties of the process.(51)   The neo-functionalists call it the process of "gradual politization" and consider it as inherent in integration and in the recognition of the automatic links between economic and political integration.   The neo-functionalist thesis suggests that,

> under modern conditions, the relationship between economic and political union had best be treated as a continuum.(52)

These principles were widely known and apparently accepted by the leaders and technical experts who founded the GRAN, as may be deduced from the emphasis placed, in the work of the Mixed Commission, on the elaboration of a program of harmonization of macroeconomic policies, always linked to the perfecting of the market, and leading to the creation of Andean economic unity.   It is also implicit in the stages of the integration process elaborated by the Junta and discussed in Chapter 4.(53)

Therefore the process of integrated development presupposes the creation of supranational institutions which will ensure the continuity of the system and attainment of the planned objectives.

The evidence for the concept of political-economic continuum was taken from the European experience, from the setting up of the ECSC and the Schumann plan of 1950 up to the signing of the agreements of the European Economic Community (EEC) and European Atomic Energy Community (Euratom). The development of the EEC has put the functiona'ist theory to the test and has especially called into question the automatic movement toward levels of political integration as a means of resolving conflicts.   Perhaps the most important lesson is that governments are not disposed to give up their sovereignty and undermine national autonomy in important areas of economic policy.

The Treaty of Cartagena was designed on the basis of European and non-European experiences in integration, and its ambitious aims created very high expectations.   Nevertheless, the account given in the first part of this chapter is sufficient to show that continual progress toward political integration (the ceding of sovereignty) was not achieved, and that a series of crises brought about changes in the plan as originally envisaged.(54)

THE TREATY OF CARTAGENA

Compatibility with LAFTA

In Resolutions 202 and 203, approved by the Council of Ministers of the parties concerned in the formation of LAFTA in December 1967, the basis was laid down for the creation of subregional groups between two or more members of LAFTA.(55) The Resolutions determine that such subregional agreements should "establish a programme of freeing of trade more accelerated than that of LAFTA, adopt a common external tariff and measures to intensify industrialization and the manner of bringing into line the legislation of each nation concerned."(56) The only restrictions made related to the timespan of subregional agreements; it was expected that they would expire when LAFTA became a common market and with the opening of the sectoral programs to all members of LAFTA.(57)

Resolution 222 of the Council of Ministers, passed at the seventh meeting of the member countries' Conference, approved and sanctioned the compatibility of the Treaty of Cartagena with the Treaty of Montevideo, as follows.

i. The former emerged out of the juridical structure of the latter, as the signatories declared that they subscribed to it as arising out of Resolutions 202 and 203 of the Council of Foreign Ministers of LAFTA and the Treaty of Montevideo.

ii. The intention of the Treaty of Cartagena was that the signatory countries should continue to broaden the field of their commercial relations with other members of LAFTA, as it did not seek to "create a closed and autarchic organization." Article 59 of the Treaty states that "member countries will seek to reach joint complementarity agreements with the other members of LAFTA in the sectors of production which are susceptible to such treatment, in accordance with the dispositions of the Treaty of Montevideo and the relevant resolutions."

iii. In accordance with the dispositions of the Declaration of the Presidents of America and of the Resolutions of the member countries, the Cartagena Agreement remains transitory until the commitments within the framework of the Treaty of Montevideo are overtaken by those adopted in the Sub-Regional Treaty, as Article 110 disposes.(58)

Nevertheless it is clear that the Cartagena Agreement was more ambitious than the Treaty of Montevideo in its goals and went further in many aspects. The GRAN was conceived as an instrument to accelerate the economic development of its members, and with this objective in view it covered practically every aspect of economic activity - unlike the Treaty of Montevideo, whose objectives were more restricted and largely confined to the freeing of trade. The GRAN contemplated the harmonization of economic policies toward third countries by means of a common external tariff and a common regime for foreign capital and technology, whereas LAFTA lacked policies of this kind and saw the development of a war of incentives to capture foreign investment of the kind experienced by the CACM. Furthermore, the GRAN saw as one of its major objectives balanced regional economic growth, formalized in such norms as preferential treatment for the less developed countries (Bolivia and Ecuador) in all the programs of the Agreement, while LAFTA lacked effective measures in this area, despite its lip service to them. This may have been one of the reasons for the unwillingness of Bolivia and Paraguay to join and may have been one of the arguments put forward for founding the GRAN.

The GRAN's industrial sector program was complex and involved advanced elements of regional integration, very distant from the complementarity agreements of LAFTA. The latter agreements did not cover such a broad range, nor did they constitute an indispensable element in the functioning of LAFTA. There was no timetable or schedule for the conclusion of the complementarity agreements such as there was in the case of the GRAN. The most important difference was that in the LAFTA complementarity agreements there was no requirement that all countries should participate, as there was in the case of the GRAN.(59)

The GRAN introduced the principle that decisions were automatic and irreversible, so that, once a commercial program had been approved, it was not subject to further negotiation until the lowering of tariff barriers was complete; whereas LAFTA introduced a system of periodic negotiations for bands of products, based on the principle of reciprocity, and never advanced beyond the first band.

Institutionally, too, there are a number of differences between LAFTA and the GRAN. In the first, greater power is given to the veto, which makes it very difficult to arrive at decisions, while, despite having a far more complex organization than the GRAN, LAFTA lacks a stable permanent institution such as the GRAN's Junta.(60)

The Basic Elements of the Cartagena Agreement

Having contrasted briefly the two schemes of integration, we shall review the way in which concrete form was given to the guidelines worked out by the political leaders of the member countries;(61) those guidelines may be summarized as follows,

i. Integration is requisite for development, and its form has to comply with the needs of a policy of development.

ii.   Irrespective of their levels of development, all member countries have to participate in the dynamism that may be generated by integration.   For this reason, integration has to be a practicable combination of regional programming and freeing of trade.   Planning is the most appropriate element for overseeing the new industrial base, giving all the members an opportunity to take part in the industrialization process, and guiding activities in those sectors most prone to conflict, such as agriculture.

iii.   The process of integration has to be rapid and its achievements secure enough to induce quick action in the new economic climate.   Above all, in the first stages, it will have to define the rules of the game, the scope of various mechanisms, and the means by which programs should be prepared and policies harmonized.   These decisions have to be made in a short space of time and their effects have to be automatic, that is, they must need no further negotiation and they must create interrelationships that will make the attainment of integration necessary.

iv.   The freeing of trade has to be achieved by lists and must be irreversible.   This removes obstacles that arise out of negotiations on a product-to-product basis.

v.   Integration has to lead to the establishment of a new negotiating authority that will allow common policies on external trade, foreign investment, technology, etc., to be formulated and adopted.

By presenting the objectives and tools of the Treaty, we will be able to appreciate how the original assumptions took juridical shape, how the balance between immediate commercial and political interests was established, and how the market was to be strengthened.   It is useful for this analysis to draw a distinction between purely commercial programs (negative integration) and unifying policies (positive integration); this will be developed in the second part of the book.

Objectives and Tools of the Agreement

According to its second article, the objectives of the Agreement are: to promote stable and uniform development in the member countries, to accelerate growth through economic integration; to aid the countries' participation in the process of economic integration foreseen in the Treaty of Montevideo; and to establish the necessary conditions for LAFTA to join the Latin American Common Market.

The tools created to achieve these objectives are, first, of a commercial character, the dismantling of barriers and obstacles to intra-subregional trade (negative integration) and, second, of a political nature (positive integration), which lead to the setting up of a common market.

i. Commercial tools. Freeing of trade would take place according to the following lists: (a) automatic tariff reduction; (b) a common list with LAFTA countries; (c) goods reserved for sectoral industrial development programs (SIDPs); (d) goods not produced and reserved for Bolivia and Ecuador; and (e) lists of exemptions.

ii. Tools of political economy. (a) a Common External Tariff (CET); (b) sectoral programming; (c) unification of macroeconomic policies; (d) preferential treatment for Bolivia and Ecuador; and (e) rules for the agricultural sector, the physical infrastracture, and standard of origin.

We shall now examine each of these areas in turn in greater detail.

i. Commercial tools (or the program for free, subregional trade)

This envisaged the total elimination of tariffs and other trade restrictions within the subregion by December 31, 1980. It used different methods according to types of groups of products included in the following lists.

a. The list of automatic reductions is made up of 3,470 items(62) (50% of the tariff structure) and is the lynchpin of the commercial program. It operates according to the following standards:

• In 1970 the Punto Inicial de Desgravación (PID, or starting point for reduction of tariffs) was established for each product at the lowest national tariff of Chile, Colombia, and Peru.
• On December 31 of each year, starting in 1971, the PID would be automatically reduced by 10 percent of the initial value.
• Goods produced by Bolivia and Ecuador were to benefit from a process of greatly accelerated access to the markets of the other countries. These goods were to be favored by three consecutive annual cuts in tariffs of 40 percent, 30 percent, and 30 percent of the initial value. Therefore, by December 31, 1973, Bolivia and Ecuador's goods on the automatic reduction list were to be completely free of tariffs.
• From December 31, 1976, these two countries were to begin the process of removing tariffs against other members' products, starting from their own national tariffs, not the PID. The process was to finish by 1985.

b. It was agreed that goods included on the common list with LAFTA were to have tariffs removed completely on February 25, 1970.(63)

c. As far as goods included in the list reserved for sectoral industrial planning (SIDP) were concerned, reduction would be made according to each program.

d. Products not produced in the subregion were to be completely freed by February 28, 1971. Of these, some were reserved for Bolivia and Ecuador to produce. These would benefit from total freedom in the other members' markets.(64)

e. Regarding lists of exemptions, on December 31, 1970, each country presented its lists of goods for which they were demanding the suspension of the program. Specific cases were dealt with, such as where competition would bring about distortions in the country concerned in terms of loss of employment following the close-down of a firm.(65) Exemptions were to last until 1985 and, for Bolivia and Ecuador, until 1990.

ii. Tools of political economy

a. The CET. The Commission proposed that the Junta should approve the CET no later that December 31, 1975, to be applicable to products coming from outside countries. The objectives were: to establish a margin of preference in favor of subregional production; to give adequate protection to subregional goods, and to stimulate efficiency in the group's industries.(66)

As an intermediate step, the Minimum Common External Tariff (MCET), was set up, and also a system to consolidate national tariffs by reducing differences by 20 percent each year, so that the process would be complete by December 31, 1975, the date when the CET was to be adopted. The rules for the application of the MCET and CET did not apply to those products "which are the object of sectoral programmes, for which the norms governing the common external tariff will be established in the said programmes."(67)

b. Sectoral Industrial Development Programmes (SIDPs). Some 2,000 items, or one-third of all goods covered by tariffs, were included on the lists of goods reserved for SIDPs. They were grouped into the following productive sectors: petrochemicals, metallurgy, automotive, pulp and paper, pesticides and fertilizers, iron and steel, pharmaceuticals, industrial and domestic electronics. This policy is a direct instrument for locating industry, independent of market mechanisms, according to the following objectives:

• to achieve greater expansion, specialization, and rational diversification of production, which will expand above the initial rates of industrial development and increase the per capita income of the population

- to take maximum advantage of the area's resources through the careful location of centers of production
- to raise the rate of the incorporation of new technology in order to achieve a higher rate of growth of production
- to raise the level of productive efficiency by taking advantage of new economies of scale
- to guarantee the equitable distribution of benefits so that all the countries can take part in industrial growth

It follows from the list above that the achievement of the fundamental objectives of integration, as set out in political statements and in the Treaty, depend upon industrial programming. Therefore, the SIDP was made the central theme of the agreement, to which all other policies were to be correlated. In principle, the aim of SIDP was to create leading sectors of production that would allow the process of import substitution to advance in those activities that, because of their nature, need high levels of investment, technological advances, large-scale production, and long gestation periods. In general, the national markets are limited and have impeded the development of the projects. The characteristics of these leading sectors justify their being planned (68) and their being given a monopoly for their products.

An important part of sectoral planning is "industrial rationalization," focused on existing industries not included in the program. The Treaty provided that at least annually proposals should be made to the Commission concerning rationalization. The aim of the programs was to help industry and prevent distortions that could arise. Therefore, they ought to raise the capacity to combine, or to facilitate, the transfer of productive resources to other sectors.

c. <u>Unification of macroeconomic policies.</u> The consolidation of a wider market is considered to be the key element for guaranteeing the spreading of the benefits of integration as set out in the programs.

As in the previous sections, the Treaty specified a fixed period for the establishment of the program. It said that the countries should proceed immediately "to adopt a common strategy for the development of the sub-region." In turn, it made the promise "to co-ordinate the various national development plans and harmonize economic and social policies" with a view to achieving "a jointly planned order" (Article 26). The process of unification would be carried out "parallel to and in conjunction with the formation of the sub-regional market," through the following mechanisms:

- a common system for the treatment of foreign capital, trade markets, patents, licences, and royalties, which was to be approved by December 31, 1970.

- a uniform system governing Andean multinational enterprises, to be adopted by December 31, 1971.
- harmonization of member countries' industrial promotion legislation, to be adopted by December 31, 1971.
- a program to unify member countries' methods of regulating foreign trade, which was to be applied by December 31, 1972.
- permanent procedures and mechanisms to be approved by December 31, 1970, as necessary to achieve the coordination and harmonization of exchange, monetary, financial and fiscal policies, industrial programming, agricultural development, and planning of physical and social infrastructure.

After analyzing the contents of the section of the Treaty dealing with harmonization, one can see from the urgency of the time periods laid down that it was intended to be carried out more quickly than the new economic policies demanded - that is, before the strengthening of economic links - and much before the full opening of the market. In the EEC, political integration was considered to be, and foreseen as, a result of economic integration; after each step forward in the latter, a corresponding stage in the former would follow. In the GRAN, the reverse was the case. The precarious nature of economic relations and the weakness of integrationist factors had to be reinforced by accelerated political integration which would induce and make necessary economic integration. Another point that arises is the ambiguity in defining the scope and depth of unification. The commercial program was laid out in detail, with timetables and lists, tariff reduction rates, and levels of protection all specified. On the other hand, the section on unification left open for later negotiation not only the definition of the scope of unification, but even the definition of the concept itself. Although this situation allowed for an element of flexibility, it made the Treaty above all an instrument for the freeing of the market.

d.   Preferential treatment for Bolivia and Ecuador.   The Treaty granted preferential treatment for Bolivia and Ecuador to reduce the gap between them and Chile, Colombia, Peru, and Venezuela: Section III of the Treaty set out the provisions that would permit these two countries "to achieve an accelerated rhythm of economic development through their effective and immediate participation in the benefits arising from the industrialization of the area and the liberalization of trade (Article 91)."

The special provisions and incentives aimed at evening out the structural differences of the two countries had to be made by unifying the social and economic policies of the group in such a way that it would ensure the "mobilization of indispensable resources to achieve the objectives of the agreement (Article 92)."

Dealing with Bolivia and Ecuador's special structure, the subregional industries policy granted them "priority in the allocation of production." The sectoral programs were to include "exclusive advantages and effective preferential treatment," which would enhance their ability to take effective advantage of the subregional market and to guarantee, by special means, the necessary technological, human, and financial resources for the installation of the production assigned to them.

With regard to the CET, the most important provision was that the application of these levels should not cause upsets to Bolivia and Ecuador and that the two countries could establish "exceptions (to be authorized by the Commission) to the process of bringing national tariffs and the CET together, which permit them to continue applying their existing laws of industrial promotion."

e. The agricultural sector, rules of origin and physical infrastructure programs.

1. Agriculture. In Article 69, the countries promised to adopt a plan for developing agriculture with the aim of substituting agricultural imports to the subregion. It was to be based upon joint programs of agricultural development of products or groups of products, common systems of commercialization, the promotion of agreements among the national agricultural agencies for joint planning of applied research, technical and financial assistance, and common regulations on plant and animal health. The objective was to raise production and productivity in this sector and to eliminate the deficit in foodstuffs.

2. Rules of Origin. The Treaty states that the Commission, on the Junta's suggestion, would adopt such special rules as might be necessary for qualifying the origin of goods. Such rules were considered to be a dynamic element in the development of the subregion's industrial structure, in which an exaggerated tendency toward assembly activities was to be avoided. The rules could be modified by the Junta to adapt them to the economic and technological advances made by the group.

3. Physical Integration. Article 87 stated that the Junta should lay before the Commission programs for the development of the physical infrastructure (energy, transport, and communications) no later than December 31, 1972. These should, as far as possible, identify and rank the priority of the projects to be included in the various development plans. They should also evaluate the financial and technical requirements.

Again, in the sections referring to the agricultural sector, physical integration, and rules of origin, the nonspecific nature of the agreements stood out. As with the harmonization of policies, there was no definition of the scope and depth of the programs.

CONCLUSIONS

In summary, we can say:

A.   The Treaty of Cartagena reflected the ideas on economic and social development prevailing in the 1960s. In the declaration of Bogota and in the discussions of the Mixed Commission, the idea was always present of accelerating the economic development of the member countries, for which integration was considered the most suitable means. This acceleration of development was necessary to overcome the economic crisis of the sixties and as an answer to the social agitation provoked by the crisis and stimulated by the Cuban revolution. It is clear from the Declaration of Bogota that integration was seen as a means of strengthening the Alliance for Progress and creating bonds of solidarity that would lead to the formation of a common front. Nevertheless, strictly political goals such as the creation of a power bloc by the United States were never explicit. The GRAN was presented in purely economic terms, as a defense against the domination of the LAFTA market by Mexico, Brazil, and Argentina.

B.   The Treaty of Cartagena set out a model for integrated economic development in which industrial planning (not the freeing of trade) was to be the central mechanism for the advance of import substitution.

> The predominant concern of the Andean Pact is to influence the course of industrial development in the sub-region: what is to be manufactured, where and with how much competition.(69)

This presupposed a strong supervisory state, capable of carrying out reforms affecting the economies at their roots and with an increasing capacity to invest in the productive sector. Industry was given the role of modernizing the economy and permitting participation in the international division of labor which would lead to growing incomes.

C.   It attempted to strengthen balanced subregional development by the central direction of the new manufacturing activities.

D.   It assumed implicitly that there were no differences in definition of the objectives of development and that no conflicts would arise either between or within countries out of the formulation of the policies of subregional import substitution.

E. Possible conflicts of interest would be solved by the creation of an adequate institutional framework, leading to the setting up of the common market.

The following chapter will describe the economic characteristics of the countries to be included in the integration program outlined above. Emphasis will be placed upon those aspects that bear directly on the process of integration and not on an analysis and characterization of the process of economic development attempted by the six countries, because the latter is not the object of this work.

CHAPTER 2
THE ANDEAN SUBREGION

In this chapter we will study the structural characteristics of the six member countries of the Andean Group and their policies and goals. Attention will be first oriented to those elements more directly related with the integration process, such as level and trend in GDP as the first indicator of the economic capacity both of each member country and of the region. Second, we will examine the present industrial structure and the absolute and relative levels of industrial development reached. Those two elements (GDP and level of industrialization) will permit us to give an approximate characterization of the real subregional market for manufactures, which is further reduced by the low level of productivity and income of the high rural sector and by high transport costs. We will then explain the main tendencies in national economic policies, especially those concerned with the industrial, external, and public sectors, which constitute the object of positive political integration. However, as we shall see, the governments shape them in accordance with their national needs, which sometimes go in the opposite direction to that required by the integration programs.

We have defined the central hypothesis that this study will explore as follows: that different levels of industrialization and differences in potential for forwarding the import substitution process generate national aspirations with regard to integration which are likely to become antagonistic. National policies, which up to a point are a variable dependent upon the level of development, allow us to detect the possible antagonisms. The greater the difference in the level of development between member countries, and in our case in industrial development in particular, the greater the gap between national objectives and therefore the greater the urgency for achieving political integration. But the greater this gap between national objectives, the greater also are the political costs of integration. The absolute size of the integrated market is a factor that can increase or decrease the foreseeable costs of political integration. If the integrated market allows a real reduction of the social costs of industrialization, a greater disposition to incur the political costs of integration can be expected. But if the new market is poor or insufficient it is possible that the foreseeable costs of becoming integrated (and of redistributing productive resources) would be considered to be greater than the benefits to be gained from more trade. In the case of the GRAN the two elements come together: a great gap between levels of development of member countries and an insufficient subregional market for the degree of substitution to which they aspire.

STRUCTURAL CHARACTERISTICS

Latin America has experienced a century-old process of disintegration. The colonial era established more or less arbitrary links and frontiers which allowed for nascent economic relations. These links were broken and frontiers strengthened after independence and the advent of liberal ideologies and concepts of the nation, and the national state. The elites looked increasingly toward Europe and the United States for models of political culture and economic organization. The result at present tends to be a strong interventionist state combined with a weak concept of nation. Countries generally express their economic nationalism through models of industrialization and need to integrate the national market.

The process of development in the countries of the GRAN seems to have brought about the reduction of some national differences and to have shaped an economic pattern which basically is the same in all the countries. These economies became more and more open to the United States and Europe and progressively less open to Latin American countries. This opening came with the export of agricultural goods (Colombia and Ecuador) or minerals (Chile, Bolivia, and Venezuela) or relatively diverse primary products (Peru). Whatever the case, similar reactions appeared when confronted by worldwide circumstances; there was a movement away from free trade to import substitution and then to the diversification of exports. While common to all countries, these stages occurred sooner for some than for others. The difference is not merely a question of timing, but implies different capacities to develop economically.

Especially after the Second World War, Latin America experienced higher rates of industrial growth and a diversification of the productive system. In the larger countries complex industries appeared, such as metallurgy, electrical, chemical, machinery, petrochemical, and consumer durables. Physical infrastructure was constructed, the integration of the national market began, and the financial system was modernized. However, the industrialization process did not produce the expected results. Only a part of the population felt the effects of economic growth; the majority was still excluded from industrial consumption. Agriculture fell behind and retained a large mass of underemployed people. The use of new technology had unbalanced results; it was concentrated in those sectors producing goods that were luxuries in terms of the prevailing income levels. Relations with the international economy were changed; foreign capital moved to the dynamic sectors, producing for the internal market, and into financial institutions.

The extreme generality of the typical interpretation of Latin American economic development, as set out in the previous paragraph, means that, by trying to include all the countries in one group and to deal with variables on an aggregate basis, the full range and diversity that exists between countries and areas is by-passed. This analytical discrimination has been exercised especially against the relatively less developed countries (a characterization that can be applied to all GRAN members), with the result that there is still no sufficient basis for defining their pattern of development or for precision as to the circumstances that explain different national performances.(1)

For this reason it is not possible, within the scope of this work, to present anything more than the socioeconomic characteristics of the Andean subregion, without trying to characterize its model of development. The principal factors that can be studied are those most closely linked to economic integration as related in the introduction to this chapter.

Economic Growth

The GRAN covers an area of 5.5 million square kilometers and in 1969 had a population of 64,192,000 people. A population of this size could be considered important in terms of demand. However, as we will see later, there are several limitations upon the market, such as the size and structure of the GDP, the functioning of the economy, relations with the international economy, and the structure and distribution of income.

At the time the Treaty was signed, the Andean GDP was US$27.3 billion, similar to the level of Brazil and Mexico. However, GDP per capita of the group is considerably lower than in Argentina or Mexico, though higher than in the CACM. The GRAN is an important producer of primary, mineral, and agricultural products as shown in Table 2.1 and discussed in the preceding chapter.

Between 1950 and 1968, GDP in the subregion grew faster than the population. Serious annual oscillations were related to prices of export products and specific internal circumstances such as those that occurred in Bolivia at the beginning of the 1950s, in Peru in the late 1960s, and in the 1970s in Chile. The slow growth of the agricultural sector and low rates of savings can be considered as elements impeding the achievement of higher growth rates of GDP. These factors can be even more restrictive upon a model of industrialization at the subregional level because of the extraordinary demand for investment resources in the industrial sector, the resulting process of technology transfer, and the unemployment caused by rural/urban migration.

The differences in total and per capita GDP of the countries are considered as a negative element in economic integration because they constitute the "asymmetry of the group,"(2) which is a negative element when dealing with higher levels of economic union. In the GRAN, this "asymmetry" (the ratio of the highest and lowest values of the GDP) is higher than that encountered in the CACM, COMECON, LAFTA, and of course in the EEC and EFTA. In 1969, Ecuador and Bolivia's GDP accounted for 8.4 percent of the subregional total and 30 percent of Venezuela's share.

In terms of global GDP, the countries in the Andean Group can be divided into two very different groups, the first comprising Bolivia and Ecuador, and the second the other countries. This second group (Colombia, Chile, Peru, and Venezuela) accounted for 89.5 percent of regional GDP in 1950, while Bolivia and Ecuador contributed only 4.8 percent and 5.7 percent respectively. Since 1950 the relatively less developed countries have tended to lose ground, although Ecuador and Bolivia recovered toward 1975 thanks to higher oil prices. Thus the share of total regional GDP attributable to Bolivia fell to 8.6 percent in 1960 from 10.5 percent in 1950, but regained this level in 1975 (see table 2.2).

The ratio of the highest GDP (Colombia) to the lowest (Bolivia) was 5.6:1 in 1950 and 8.6:1 in 1975 (Venezuela and Bolivia), while the figure for the EEC is 1.4:1, that for EFTA 1.8:1, that for the Council for Mutual Economic Assistance (CAME) 2.1:1 that for LAFTA 3.4:1, and that for the Central American Common Market (CACM) 2.8:1.

Table 2.3 shows the evolution of per capita GDP. Once again, the values obtained for Bolivia and Ecuador differ sharply from those for the other countries in the Group, although less so than those for global GDP. The ratio between the highest and lowest GDP per capita (Venezuela and Bolivia, respectively, in each case) was 2.6:1 in 1950, 4.1:1 in 1969, and 3.5:1 in 1975, the latter reduction being due to Bolivia's increased income from petroleum exports.(3)

The changes in the structure of the subregional GDP between 1950 and 1968 were characteristic of underdeveloped economies setting out on a process of industrialization: a reduction in the share of the agricultural sector (especially in Chile and Venezuela), a relative acceleration in industrial activity and even more so in services, construction, and the state sector (see table 2.4).

The agricultural sector is the second most important contributor to GDP and the most important employer. However, its productivity is 42.0 percent of the average level of productivity of the economy.(4) Its stagnation is the cause of very low rural incomes. The increase in agricultural productivity has mainly been achieved by mechanization, that is, increases, in product per man have come, as in industry, through the increased use of capital.

Traditionally, Andean national policies have sought agricultural self-sufficiency without considering the limitations of productive resources. The result is the existence of rather similar production structures, highly protected and with limited possibilities for trade. In 1970, the subregional food deficit was covered by $500 million worth of imports. It has been estimated that by 1980 these imports will rise to account for 47 percent of subregional supply. Integration in agriculture presupposes a movement away from national autarchy toward optimum allocation of subregional resources, the replacement of inefficient producers, the solution of landholding problems, and the creation of a modern productive sector. These goals are of great political and economic complexity, and the various governments have still to speak out on the subject. The Treaty was extremely vague on this point, as was noted in Chapter 1.

The different weights of the rural population vis-à-vis the total gives rise to varying sectoral policies. In general, up until 1974, all the countries except Peru had apparently given up the idea of pushing through agrarian reforms and have since opted for other methods of raising productivity and increasing production. The rural population in Bolivia and Ecuador represents 65.7 percent and 56.2 percent (1970), respectively, of the total. The strategy of these countries seems to be to promote rural out-migration and to accelerate productive employment in the towns. At the same time, they are pushing forward with projects to make new land available and to promote production through credit and technical schemes and by giving protection to national agricultural production. In 1971, the Venezuelan rural population was 21 percent of the total; there is no demographic pressure upon the land. The problem in this country is to raise the rate of growth of agricultural production to meet the level of urban demand, without accelerating migratory movements. The strategy is, therefore, to raise productivity by increasing the use of technology.   The situation is similar in Chile (with a 30 percent rural population), where the policy is to try to raise efficiency by exposing the sector to external competition and by eliminating the discrimination against the sector implicit in the previous national tariff structure (and in that envisaged by the Junta).   In Colombia, which has a 44.4 percent rural population, the tactic is to raise the productivity and income level of the minifundista (very small landholding peasant) by guaranteeing "reasonable" prices for his products and cheaper inputs.(5)   Tariff reforms have reduced discrimination against agriculture, and the National Integrated Rural Development Plan provides sufficient credit and technical assistance to the minifundista sector to improve "native technology."   The objective is to diminish rural-urban migration.

The Manufacturing Sector

We shall study the manufacturing sector in somewhat greater detail, not because we consider it more important than other sectors of the economy, but because the Treaty of Cartagena aimed to promote industrialization, and countries were motivated to enter and remain within the GRAN largely by the prospect of improved rates of growth in manufacturing.   To develop our main hypothesis in this section, we shall examine the regional industrial structure and the levels of industrial development in individual countries.   We shall subsequently be able to establish the extent to which the degree of industrialization and the possibilities of growth in the sector in each country tended to generate different national economic policies and different attitudes toward integration.

The period from 1960 to 1965 saw the greatest growth in the industrial sector.   From 1956 to 1968 the sector's growth was comparable with that of GDP (see Graph 2.1).   However, the growth rate was higher for heavy industry than for light industry, as shown in table 2.7, which gives the different rates of industrial growth for each sector at the national level. The performance of the sector in those years can be explained by the availability of reserves of installed capacity created in the 1950s, the restrictions on imports caused by the fall of export product prices in the 1960s, and the growth of investment in intermediate sectors, which can be seen from the relative increase in the coefficient of industrial imports.

In 1968, the manufacturing sector of the Andean subregion represented 18.6 percent of GDP.   Although growth is relatively rapid in this sector, the generation of employment is insufficient to meet the accelerated process of urbanization experienced by all the Andean countries.(6)   It would be superfluous to repeat here the criticism of the import substitution processes put into operation by the individual countries, using complex regulations on protection, subsidized credit, and multiple exchange rates. The results are well known: the supplying of nationally produced final consumer goods, to a lesser extent intermediate products, and initially no capital goods. National structures are extremely diversified and largely duplicate each other. By using severe import restrictions, the supply of national products has been expanded, at the expense of international producers. Industrialization basically sought saving of foreign exchange rather than productive efficiency. In general, it led to oversized productive units producing the same good in the different countries, disparities in internal prices, and, logically, to the failure to save exchange and to furnish the resources for further industrial expansion.

In such a setting, theory tells us, integration plays a multiple role: it reduces production costs through a wider market. It makes possible the so-called third stage of import substitution. It helps use productive resources better through interindustrial specialization by countries, and it generates additional foreign exchange through regional trade. Nevertheless, we shall see how difficult it is in practice to achieve such "rationality."

i.   The structure of industry in the GRAN

As we noted previously, import substituting industrialization produced duplicate structures at the national level. In theory, the resulting lack of specialization is a strong argument for integrationist policies. Trade creation effects would be obtained in the short term and in the long term. The first would come from the reduction in costs as a result of increased competition, while the second would come as competitive national manufacturing sectors gradually became complementary. In the case of the GRAN, as we shall see in Chapter 3 when we discuss subregional trade, strongly protectionist tendencies were manifested, and these reduced the extent to which these envisaged benefits were in fact obtained.

To illustrate the possible benefits that might have been derived from greater competition between the Andean countries, we have taken data from an ECLA study on prices of industrial goods in Latin America; these are summarized in table 2.5. It is evident that the range of prices for a single article is very wide: for example, refrigerators ranged from US$320 in Venezuela to US$2,000 in Chile. The most efficient country appears to be Venezuela, while the cost of most products appears to be highest in Chile. It should be made clear that the price differences that are quoted in dollars at the 1962 rates of exchange do not reflect costs exactly, because distortions can exist, caused by taxes, subsidies, rebates, etc. These price differences are also a result of differing exchange rate policies. For example, Venezuela maintains an overvalued currency, as Peru did until 1976, and Chile has done on occasions. Salaries in the oil industry in Venezuela have pushed up the general wage levels of the whole economy. Countries with lower coefficients of internal production have lower tariffs for imports than in the more industrialized economies. In the former group, this gives rise to a lower cost structure. Finally, there are different industrial promotion mechanisms, such as the low tariffs on capital goods levied for a long time by Venezuela and more recently by Bolivia and Ecuador. Another element to consider is difference in labor costs. Countries with lower labor costs in manufacturing should in theory have a comparative advantage in exporting, but they suffer a technological disadvantage.(7)

In regional analysis coefficients of location and of specialization are frequently used to study the degree of specialization of regional structures. The first of these illustrates the participation of a country in the industrial production of the region.(8) A coefficient greater than 1 indicates that a country is dominant in a particular regional industry; if it is less, it indicates a less than proportionate participation in the industry in question. The first situation might reflect an export sector, the second a local activity.(9) The measure is normally employed in conjunction with the specialization coefficient to measure the degree of industrial specialization present in a region. The specialization coefficient (10) measures the extent to which the distribution of value added (or of employment) by the industrial sector in a particular country deviates from the same distribution over the region. If the country has a structure identical to that of the region, the coefficient will be zero. If, on the other hand, all the industrial value added (or employment) of a country is concentrated in a single sector, the value of the coefficient will be 1.

From tables 2.6 and 2.7 we have calculated the location quotient and the coefficient of specialization of Andean industry in 1969, and the results are as follows:

Location Quotient and Coefficient of Specialization for
Industry in the Andean Group, 1969

ISIC[1]	Bolivia		Chile		Colombia		Ecuador		Peru		Venezuela	
	a	b	a	b	a	b	a	b	a	b	a	b
3.1	1.6	0.17	0.6	0.11	1.1	0.05	1.5	0.13	1.2	0.05	1.0	0.0
3.2	1.2	0.03	1.3	0.0	1.2	0.00	0.9	0.02	0.8	0.02	0.7	0.05
3.3	0.8	0.01	2.4	0.07	0.6	0.01	1.0	0.03	0.9	0.03	0.8	0.02

(continued)

Location Quotient and Coefficient of Specialization for
Industry in the Andean Group, 1969 (continued)

ISIC[1]	Bolivia		Chile		Colombia		Ecuador		Peru		Venezuela	
	a	b	a	b	a	b	a	b	a	b	a	b
3.4	0.6	0.03	1.1	0.0	0.9	0.0	1.3	0.02	0.8	0.01	0.9	0.0
3.5	1.1	0.02	0.6	0.07	1.0	0.01	1.1	0.07	1.0	0.0	1.5	0.09
3.6	0.7	0.02	0.9	0.0	1.1	0.06	1.0	0.0	1.2	0.01	1.0	0.5
3.7	0.1	0.04	1.2	0.02	0.4	0.02	0.1	0.04	1.4	0.03	0.9	0.0
3.8	0.0	0.13	0.1	0.07	0.1	0.04	0.1	0.08	0.1	0.01	0.1	0.03
3.9	0.8	0.01	1.5	0.0	1.2	0.01	1.7	0.0	1.4	0.0	1.0	0.01

---

a = quotient of location
b = coefficient of specialization

Source: Our tables 2.6, 2.7, 2.8.

Note: (1).   ISIC = International Standard Industrial Classifica-
              tion: see table 2.6 for the divisions.

Examination of the values for the location quotient demonstrates, for example, that five of the six countries would have
export potential in ISIC sectors 3.1, 3.5, and 3.9, and that
four countries could export goods in sector 3.6, as these
countries present values greater than 1 for the relevant sectors.   However, when these values are compared with those
obtained for the coefficient of specialization, it is clear that no
country can be considered as specializing in these sectors, as
in no case does the coefficient approach unity.

The Andean industrial structure does not present any
appreciable margin of specialization or complementarity.   Therefore, trade diversion costs and those of transforming the
present industrial structure into a complementary one will be
extremely high.   Likewise, the long-term benefits to be derived from this process will be considerable.

ii.   The level of industrial development

It is now increasingly accepted that different levels of industrial development generate, in member countries of a region
experiencing integration, diverse possibilities regarding the
siting of industries within the integration scheme, and that the
political evaluation of benefits is made, in the first instance,
with an eye to the capacity of integration to accelerate and
modify industrial growth.

The level of industrial development is significant as an indication of greater or smaller capacity to take advantage of the benefits of integration. These will be assessed in the light of national motives for integration, such as the expansion of trade and changes in the structure of industrial production. These motives are in turn related to the degree of industrial development in the country and the size of the integrated market. We propose the following relationship: the greater the development of the industrial sector of a country, and the larger its domestic market in relation to the regional market, the greater will be its preference for the expansion of trade over changes in the productive structure which are oriented through the central allocation of the new industries. Less industrialized member countries, having a reduced market, would prefer an integration model that included strong planning mechanisms which would guarantee faster growth of their industrial structures.

The concept of "the level of industrial development," then, is a complex one. Furthermore, the composite indicators that are used to measure it, to which we have already referred, include elements of efficiency, of the greater or lesser interdependence of industrial activities (for example, the degree of development of the production of capital goods), and of the greater or lesser complexity and sophistication of incentive policies. In particular, therefore, the concept is an implicit evaluation of the capacity for rapid response to new market conditions.

The composite indicators generally used to measure the degree of industrial development are industrial production per capita, the level of import substitution or of national supply of internal demand, and the concentration of manufacturing production and exports.

Industrial GDP per capita, which Maizels considers to be the clearest indicator of economic development and of the standard of living,(11) is as important as or more important than global GDP per capita. However, it is subject to many of the same difficulties as GDP in making international comparisons, which is why we place more emphasis here on the degree of import substitution and the structure of industry.

Evaluating the COMECON, Kaser found the different levels of industrialization of the countries or the productivity gap, measured in terms of industrial net value per capita, constitute a problem primarily because of the resulting difference in the goals of the member nations. The aspirations of the two poorest members (Rumania and Bulgaria) were concentrated on achieving the level of the industrialized members, who in turn took Western standards as their goal.(12) The ratio between net industrial levels of the most and least industrialized countries of COMECON was 3.5 in 1950 and 3.4 in 1963. This was considerably smaller than the difference in

the GRAN, where by 1969 the ratio between the highest industrial GDP per capita figure (Chile, at US$227.6 p.a) and the
lowest (Bolivia, at US$35.5 p.a) was 6.4:1 (see table 2.6).
This figure was considerably higher than the ratio between the
highest and lowest values of GDP per capita (4.1:1).

By 1975 the ratio of highest to lowest industrial GDP per
capita had fallen to 4.4:1. In this year the greatest value of
output per capita was that of Venezuela, at US$200.2. Again,
we can distinguish two groups of countries in the region: for
Bolivia and Ecuador, industrial GDP per capita barely reached
50 percent of regional industrial GDP per capita in 1969, setting them apart from the other four countries.

From 1960 to 1975 changes in the relative values took
place; although they did not modify the basic division into two
groups, which we have noted, they did reduce the gap, while
Chile lost its first place.

Given the difficulties of measurement and comparison, it
is only the basic division into two groups that we consider
valid. To understand the real differences in the level of
industrial development within those groups, we turn now to
the more complex but more significant indicators.

National Industrial GDP Per Capita, Expressed as a Percentage of Regional Industrial GDP Per Capita

	1960	1969	1975	1979
Bolivia	20.3	31.4	34.9	39.6
Colombia	72.7	73.3	83.2	97.4
Chile	220.1	200.1	92.8	–
Ecuador	33.4	53.2	78.3	82.6
Peru	87.4	98.3	122.9	105.7
Venezuela	148.7	114.8	155.3	138.3

iii. The level of import substitution

The result of the advances made in the 1960s in the manufacturing sector was the raising of the level of import substitution, that is, of the proportion of internal industrial demand
supplied by national production.(13)

The inverse of this measure gives the import coefficient,
which tells us the proportion of internal demand covered by
imports. This coefficient indicates two aspects of industrial
production which are of great value when considering programs
of economic integration, aspects that are interrelated and cannot be discussed in isolation. First, it tells us in which
sectors and in which countries there is still room for further
import substitution, and in which the process is relatively

exhausted.   Second, it indicates the degree of elasticity of
industrial supply: the lower the import coefficient in a given
sector, the greater the elasticity of supply.   This difference is
important because it determines the divergent instances taken
up with regard to the objectives of integration introduced
earlier, expansion of trade or change in the structure of production.   Greater elasticity of industrial supply generates
preferences for the expansion of trade, while lesser elasticity
creates preferences for changes in the structure of production.   This will be seen in the chapters on the Common External Tariff and on Sectoral Planning.

As regards the first aspect, the important coefficient of
the industrial sector on the subregional scale fell to 26.8 by
1960, and to 24 by 1970.(14) This suggests that the scope for
reduction in the global import coefficient is limited; nevertheless, greater possibilities do exist at the subsectoral level, as
in light engineering, for example.(15)

When the import coefficient is examined at the national
level (table 2.10), we see that by 1960 Chile and Colombia had
reduced the imported component of internal demand for manufactures to 24.6 percent, and that their advantage over the
other countries was increased toward 1967.

At the time the Treaty was signed, all the countries
except Bolivia and Ecuador could be said to have practically
exhausted the process of import substitution in traditional
industries and in intermediate goods.   As most of these products had been placed in lists for automatic tariff reductions, it
is to be assumed that increases in production would be local-
ized in those countries that already possess the relevant
facilities, and not in Bolivia or Ecuador, which would import
from within the region rather than from outside it.

In the light engineering sector(16) Chile and Colombia
had reduced their import coefficient by 1967 to 0.476 and
0.470, respectively, while Venezuela and Peru still had considerable scope for substitution (0.625 and 0.758, respectively),
and Bolivia and Ecuador had barely begun production in the
sector.   It was in this sector that significant conflicts
occurred, as Chile and Colombia sought a greater degree of
liberalization of trade in order to take advantage of the
relative advantage deriving from the greater development of
their production.   The other four countries sought sectoral
programming, hoping to set up new industries on their own
soil and transform their structures of production.   It is
important to remember that these positions were taken up while
the Treaty was in its gestation period, and maintained
throughout the period in which implementation took place; they
remained latent until the crisis of 1976 and have not yet been
resolved.(17)

Nevertheless, the relationship between the degree of
industrialization and the preference for a scheme for integra-

tion and development based upon free trade or upon import
substitution is not so simple. It is affected by economic
policies that are in turn frequently a response to specific
situations. Thus, for example, the Popular Unity government
in Chile and the military government in Peru (until 1976)
pursued substitution policies that correspond to particular
political situations and objectives. Venezuela and Peru adopted
protectionist policies and preferred industrial programming in
order to protect their industries from the high costs resulting
from income from petroleum in the first case, and from the
overvaluation of the national currency in the second.(18)   As
we shall see, this was one of the reasons for which Peru and
Venezuela took sides with Bolivia and Ecuador, although their
degree of industrialization was more similar to that of Colombia.

iv.   Concentration of industrial production and exports

The concentration of manufacturing industry in the Andean
region is marked. By 1960, two countries, Chile and Colombia, were generating 57.7 percent of total industrial GDP, and
similar figures are obtained if a distinction between light and
heavy industry is made (see table 2.6). At the other end of
the scale, Bolivia and Ecuador were responsible for only 4.5
percent of total industrial GDP, and only 2.9 percent where
heavy industry was concerned. Peru and Venezuela, taken
together, generated something over 37 percent. By 1969 the
growth of Peruvian and Venezuelan participation is marked, as
is the decline of Chile's share, a decline that shows up even
more clearly in 1975, by which date Chile's participation had
fallen by 50 percent from its 1960 level. We could say that
during the period 1960-1975 the structure of industry at
subregional level saw the following changes: the loss of
supremacy by Chile, a slow relative advance by Colombia, a
rapid relative advance by Peru and Venezuela, and an increase
in Ecuador's participation.
      The export of manufactured goods in 1969 presented a
degree of concentration similar to that in manufacturing production. The greater export capacity of the larger countries,
and particularly of Chile and Colombia after 1975, is significant. Our analysis of subregional trade in Chapter 3 will
demonstrate that manufacturing exports are concentrated in the
countries with greater industrial development. We find that
the greater the degree of complexity, the greater is the
tendency toward the concentration of exports in Chile and
Colombia, which were responsible for 80 percent of reciprocal
exports in 1975. Where relatively complex products are concerned, the participation of Peru and Venezuela is slightly
higher than that of Bolivia and Ecuador.(19)   After 1976,
when Chile left the group, the relative share in the exports of

manufactured goods changed: Venezuela exported 42 percent of
the subregional total, Peru 21.6 percent, and Colombia 17.6
percent.

SIZE AND STRUCTURE OF THE INTERNAL MARKET

It is important to study and classify the populations of the
GRAN countries in terms of their personal income and minimum
levels of expenditure on basic foodstuffs; because the demand
they create is the basis for the Treaty of Cartagena and upon
it depends the success of the subregional industrial policy.
    We will use various ECIEL studies which allow us to see
the comparative distribution of population and consumption
patterns according to income levels. If $300 per capita per
annum is taken as a minimum level for industrial consumption,
the potential market would be 38.5 percent of the total population, or 24 million people (see table 2.11). However, this
limit appears to be too low because within manufactured goods
there are basic products such as flour, bread, coffee, clothing, footwear, and drugs.(20)
    Therefore, it is necessary to raise the income level to
ascertain the demand for manufactures of interest to the
GRAN. If it is set at $500, which is still too low, the Andean
market would be 13.9 million people.(21) The 10.1 million
people whose income varies between $300 and $500 have no real
access to the market for manufactures(22) (see table 2.11).
The population that is really integrated into the market for
modern manufactures, with consumption patterns similar to
those of Europe, and that buys chemical and electrical goods,
for example, is that with incomes above $1,000 p.a.(23) In
the GRAN only 9 percent of the total population (5.6 million
people in 1968 and 6.8 in 1978) has this income level.(24)
    In terms of demand, the Andean population is concentrated
in the urban areas as well as regionally. The average Andean
rural income is $202 p.a. and over the region as a whole, it is
$446 (see table 2.12). The rural population is very concen-
trated in the lowest income levels. Eighty-seven percent have
less than $300 p.a. and 94.3 percent less than $500, which is
considered to be the minimum for industrial demand. This
group represents 42 percent of the total Andean population.
One-hundred percent of the Bolivian rural population earns
less than $300 p.a., which excludes it completely from the
manufactures market. Forty-one point four percent of the
Andean rural population with incomes above $500 is to be
found in Venezuela and 19.4 percent in Chile.
    Taking the region's population as a whole, we find that
45.0 percent of those with incomes above $1,000 per capita
p.a. are Venezuelans; Chile follows with 21 percent, Peru with

15.3 percent, and Colombia with 13.4 percent.(25)   The pre-
dominance of Venezuela as the major national market for the
industrial development of the GRAN is indisputable.   If the
availability of resources for financing development is added to
the size of the market, one can understand the change the late
entry of Venezuela has brought to the previously existing
equilibrium; it may explain in part the new stance assumed by
Colombia and Chile regarding sectoral planning.   Venezuela has
a strong negotiating position because of its national market,
which represented a 50 percent increase in the subregional
demand for manufactures.   Thus it can be understood why
Venezuela concentrates its attention on the sectoral programs,
because in a situation of low competitiveness at the present
time given its high costs structure, it opened its market to the
lists of tariff reduction, hoping for the advantageous allocation
of new industries covering the subregional market.

The two relatively less developed member countries only
represent 4.2 percent of the Andean market for manufactures.
The size of their national markets is very much reduced because of the size of their population and GDP and also the
concentration of income (see table 2.13).   In Bolivia, only 3.7
percent of the population has a per capita income above $500
p.a.; 12 percent of the Ecuadorian population is to be found
in the same range.   In absolute terms, their markets would
only be about 800,000 people.   Thus these figures show the
significance that these two countries have given to Andean
integration in general and to planning in particular.   The
Andean Market is decisive for them if they are to obtain higher levels of efficiency and gain financial resources without
upsetting the balance of payments.   In Bolivia and Ecuador's
industrial development plans, the state has taken the incentive
in investing in Andean industrial projects, and assuring their
competition.(26)

The withdrawal of Chile meant a 14 percent reduction in
the group's population.   However, in terms of the market for
manufactures, its importance was much greater.   This event
represented a 23 percent fall in the population with incomes
over $1,000.   With no prospect of Chile returning, Andean
demand for manufactures by 1975 was to be 5.5 million people
and by 1985 would be no higher than 10 million, which severely
affects the projected use of economies of scale.

The advance of the industrialization process outlined by
the Junta's experts, which is the basis for the drafting of the
sectoral plans, would mean a reduction of the total import
coefficient of industry at least to 13 percent by 1985, in line
with the level in Argentina and Mexico in the 1970s.   Those
sectors singled out for reductions in the coefficient vary from
country to country, but, over the subregion as a unit, they
are mainly in the production of intermediate and "metal mecánico" goods.

Import Coefficient Planned for 1985

	1960	1970	1985
nondurables	8.9%	7.8%	5.0%
intermediate	29.9	26.6	12.9
metal mecanico	66.4	58.2	28.0
Total	26.8	24.0	13.8

Thus the market toward which subregional industrial expansion is directed is made up of higher income groups: the only ones in the Andean group able to buy consumer durables.(27)

The horizontal enlargement of the top range of the national markets only partially resolves the problem of their limitations as a whole, and therefore it only allows for a marginal reduction in industrial costs. Certainly relatively better conditions are created, but the utilization of economies of scale is still very low, even compared to LAFTA. An ECLA study shows that for 10 out of 12 chemical products, the capacity of one plant in developed countries is usually larger than total demand in Latin America (1965), and by 1970 still larger than the demand of the largest Latin American countries. Per capita demand in the GRAN for nonelectrical machinery is 20 times less than that of the United States, 6 times less than in France, and half the Spanish level. The same alarming relationship can be seen in the demand for chemical goods where, for example, per capita demand in the United States is $227: the Andean level is $25.49.(28)

Apart from the limited effective demand in the subregional market, it is worth taking into account the way in which the process of industrial growth functions on the basis of dynamism in the production of consumer durables, the nature and prices of which are in line with patterns of consumption in economies with per capita incomes 5 times higher. This type of growth tends to go through periods of deceleration and to bring about higher social costs and bottlenecks in intersectoral relations. The possibilities for growth in the industrial sector depend upon the creation of sufficient demand. Under normal conditions (that is, without upsets in the trend of growth) three ways of increasing demand can be seen to exist:

- the incorporation of new groups into higher consumption patterns, which attracts part of the increase in incomes
- the transfer of resources from the higher strata to certain middle class groups, and better-paid workers, who use extensive commercial credit to adopt modern consumption patterns,
- the diversification of the upper groups' consumption.

Even when there are no upsets in the growth of global income, the regressive distribution of wealth and the high role of indebtedness of medium-range consumers make the first two ways of increasing demand relatively insignificant. Therefore, the last method is the only one available for the internal growth of demand for manufactures. Thus, by not modifying the structure of the supply of goods, the growth of industry would be limited to 10 percent of the Andean population, and the diversification of its consumption.(29) To overcome the small size of the global market, the Junta proposed drastic reforms in income distribution. It should be noted that only in 1976 was it first recognized that integration alone could not resolve the lack of demand. The Junta affirmed that reforms at the national level were necessary to solve the problem of effective subregional demand, and it said that:

> joint integration and income distribution policies must be put into effect, especially in those countries whose alternatives to development on the basis of international inter-dependence are scarce.(30)

It is worth emphasizing the fact that no politically possible redistribution of income would be sufficient to transform substantially the structure of demand. Further still, demand cannot be isolated from supply, which would have to undergo concurrent changes to prevent the same rigidities occurring in the future on an even higher scale. Considering that employment is an effective means of income redistribution and demand expansion, it is urgent that the types of goods selected for production should be basic items of consumption and that in their production labor-intensive methods should be given priority. In other words, it is necessary to change the composition of supply and consumption patterns not simply in response to a changing structure of demand, but so that re-distribution of income may be effected and consolidated.

The developments in income structure in the last few years do not change the conclusions drawn in 1968 from the ECIEL studies. From the outset, only Peru used a redistributive policy, and some relative improvement for the lower income groups can be expected.(31) In Bolivia, Ecuador and Venezuela, whose national income increased rapidly because of oil exports, the benefits were concentrated among limited groups of the population: those directly linked to the oil industry. In Chile, the redistributive measures of the Popular Unity government were more than cancelled out by the policies of concentration implemented by the new regime. There is a definite tendency toward greater concentration in Colombia, determined among other things by regressive taxation and inflation (which is present in all six member countries), transport costs, and the size of the market.

Transport costs and size of market

However, there is still a further problem that we have not yet touched on. Even a market of 6 million people is an abstraction, because no account is taken of the difficulties put in the way of integration by costs of transport and patterns of consumption.

The GRAN countries cover an area of 5.5 million square kilometers, cut from north to south by the Andean range, which is the cause of most problems in land transport. The population is concentrated in urban centers scattered along the coasts, although some capitals and important cities are situated in the mountains.(32) The interior is made up of mountain, forest, and desert zones that have very low, or in some cases almost zero, population densities.

To date, R.T. Brown's study of the transport system and its costs in Latin America is the most complete. According to his description, the route from Colombia to Ecuador is "relatively good."(33) This is a road with many unpaved stretches over which buses and lorries travel at an average speed of 15 to 20 mph because of the constant climbs and descents from sea level to 8-10,000 meters.

Brown thinks that the railway line between Bolivia and Peru is relatively good, but goods in transit from La Paz to Lima have to be shipped by ferry across Lake Titicaca, then again by train; this incurs high handling costs.(34)

This author classifies as difficult land communications between Chile-Colombia, Chile-Ecuador, Bolivia-Colombia, Bolivia-Ecuador, Peru-Colombia, Chile-Venezuela, Peru-Venezuela, and Ecuador-Venezuela.

The problems relating to land transport do not only refer to the state of roads and the availability of suitable vehicles. In some cases, frontier and customs regulations are equally serious obstacles, further increasing transport costs. A good example is the need to transship goods that are to be transported from one country to another on to nationally registered vehicles.

Air transport is not a viable alternative for international trade, first because high-value, low-bulk goods are only a small part of intraregional trade. The rates are often higher than those to the United States. Morawetz found that, while the distance (in air miles) is only 9 percent greater between Santiago and Bogota than between Bogota and New York, the charges are virtually double. Although Bogota to New York is almost 4 times farther than Bogota to Caracas, the rates for the two routes are practically the same.(35)

The most important means of transporting intrasubregional trade goods is by sea, and it accounts for about 90 percent of the total. However, there are three factors that make this costly in relative terms: (i) internal transport costs(36) from factory to port, (ii) port fees,(37) and (iii) ocean freight charges.(38)

Perhaps a better measure of differences in transport costs is the price per ton-mile, because port costs are standardized and the greater the distance, the less the cost per unit of weight. These rates were consistently higher for intra-Andean transport than for movements from the GRAN to the United States or Europe.(39)

It is worthwhile comparing distances and transport costs between Andean countries and those existing in the EEC in order to get a clearer idea of the obstacle that these factors present for the integration of and the increase in trade between the members of the Treaty of Cartagena. The greatest distance between two capitals (Caracas and Santiago) is 4,480 miles; between Rome and London it is only 1,920 miles. The cost of transporting goods to the interior of the EEC is almost 50 percent lower than in the Andean region. For 1971, Morawetz came to this conclusion by comparing transport costs between some Andean cities and between EEC capitals.(40)

THE AGRICULTURAL SECTOR AND
THE SIZE OF THE MARKET

Another element to be taken into account is the low productivity of the agricultural sector and the low income of the massive rural Andean population. Studies made by FAO-Junta estimate that, in 1970, 50 percent of the Andean rural population was receiving $65 per capita p.a., with variations from $22 in Bolivia and $104 in Colombia. In 1970, Bolivian rural per capita income was $123 p.a., and in Colombia it was $450. With this level of income it is easy to see that the demand from the rural areas for industrial products is virtually nonexistent and is mainly for basic products.(41)

Given this situation, industrialization for export would seem to be a solution that would eliminate the need to introduce drastic and painful agricultural reforms in order to increase the effective rural demand. However, the Andean scheme of integration does not seek to industrialize in order to replace necessary imports from more developed countries and to export to them goods with a high labor content (as W.A. Lewis and the GATT would recommend). This form of development would be in accordance with the theory of allocation of factors in international trade, in which "incremental" comparative advantage of underdeveloped countries would result in the rise of exports of the simplest types of manufactured consumer goods because of the abundance of human resources and the scarcity of natural resources. In the case of the GRAN, one is dealing with a closed economic scheme in which industry is directed toward satisfying the subregional market, which for exports of manufactures can be considered as the internal market. The model rests on the integration of the national markets into a unit that will allow the substitution of imports to be pursued. The CET has to guarantee the protection of the new subregional market:

> The basic requirement for this new style of development [is] the substantial raising of the rate of economic growth, which allows and helps bring about the structural changes. This high rate will have to be sustained fundamentally by a new model of import substitution made possible through integration.(42)

Exports to outside countries would only be considered at a later stage, when competitiveness had been achieved. Thus, it could be anticipated that the productivity and income structure of the primary sector would continue to restrict the possibilities of subregional industry. This is because, first, there is not a sufficient market, due to the lack of purchasing power, that reflects the abovementioned low agricultural productivity; second, the local economy would not be able to supply the necessary foodstuffs at reasonable prices to maintain the new industrial workforce.

For industrial development to satisfy internal markets, it needs an advance on the rural front: an across-the-board increase in the sector's productivity. Given the income structure, according to the income elasticities of demand of the consumer, it is possible that a given increase in industrial productivity in a poor region could require a greater development of agriculture than in a more developed country or region.(43)

The point to be made here is that, given that almost all the economies of the Andean countries still have markedly agricultural and rural characteristics, often with archaic productive structures in the countryside, the rural sector is an important source of potential final demand. The Andean rural population represents 44 percent of the total, and only 5.5 percent of this represents demand for any type of industrial goods, and then mainly for basic consumption (see table 2.12).(44) Those new products that need a widened market, given the economies of scale to be gained, cannot as yet touch the rural sector, and in fact can count only on a part of the urban market.(45)

THE EXTERNAL SECTOR

The Treaty of Cartagena sought to create an industrial market
after the failure of the trade arrangements with the developed
countries showed how difficult it was to enter the world manufacturing market.   Also, LAFTA had not fulfilled the less
developed   countries'   expectations   of   exporting   industrial
goods.   The terms of trade increased the pessimism about any
attempt to modify trade conditions.   "Today, our peoples feel
more clearly than ever that they are on their own.   There is
discontent and frustration but also the feeling that there is an
opening to new opportunities and modes of action which only
we can define."(46)
     It is not an aim of this book to discuss the role of the
external sector as a factor that limits development.   It may be
that this single element is not sufficient to explain the global
behavior of underdeveloped economies and that it is necessary
to consult studies of the internal economic and political
structures whose functions can hardly be explained solely in
economic terms.   However, it can be accepted that the external
sector was a hindrance to development.   According to Prebisch's analysis, from 1960 to 1968, it can be seen that
Colombia and Venezuela (the only two countries with higher
growth rates of GDP than of exports) grew thanks to their
decision to reduce the import coefficient.(47)   The possibility
of this depended upon advances in substitution within each
country, the reserves situation, the size of the market, and
the possibilities for directing internal and external savings.
These two countries started their substitution policies in the
early 1950s.   By the mid-1960s, they had substituted imports
of final consumption goods, especially foodstuffs, and had
reduced their import coefficients.   In Chile the reserves had
been exhausted and any reduction or change in the import
structure meant either a fall in the rate of industrial expansion
or in the total supply of food.   Bolivia and Ecuador lagged
behind because of the limited internal market size and the lack
of productive resources.
     From 1968 onward, and especially from 1970 to 1974, the
tendency for the world market to expand, the improvement in
the terms of trade (see table 2.14),(48) and the intensification
of financial activity allowed the countries to overcome balance-
of-payments problems and to expand imports to cover their
current account deficit, to pay back loans, and even to build
up reserves.(49)
     The accelerated rise in imports meant an increase in the
import coefficient and also changes in their composition or "a
process of import de-substitution";(50) purchases of nondurable consumer goods and food rose, while, in relative terms,
imports of capital goods and intermediate products stagnated.

This suggests that industry was incapable of reacting quickly and of expanding in a situation in which the market was expanding but remained still insufficient. (51)

This behavior in the external sector, especially related to the period of expanding exports and improving terms of trade, seemed to suggest new arguments in favor of the integration of markets, because it was apparent that national markets were not sufficiently dynamic to attract new investment during the bonanza and to reduce the import coefficient. (52)

With greater demand, it would be possible in times of bonanza for policies allocating foreign currency to stimulate a higher degree of capitalization of the resources gained by exporting.

After the favorable movement of balances, there were great amounts of resources available to finance the expansion of the Venezuelan and Ecuadorian economies, without them having to diversify their exports. Colombia's situation improved, but from 1976 it still needed a considerable amount of external savings. Peru, Bolivia, and Chile still had chronic deficits, a tendency which can be observed having even more acute characteristics up to the end of 1981.

Pressure in the external sector is particularly serious in Chile and Peru, where large deficits have been built up on the current account. The other countries have managed to reduce their deficits, with an occasional surplus, which has allowed some degree of investment promotion, and especially helped to improve the public sector financial situation. (53)

The weight of service on the foreign debt and of the profits arising out of foreign investment varies considerably from country to country in the Andean region. The relevant amounts, expressed as a percentage of the value of exports, are relatively low in the cases of Venezuela, Bolivia, Ecuador, and Colombia; for Chile and Peru, they came to 48 and 59 percent, respectively. (54)

THE INFLATIONARY PROCESS AND ITS CAUSES

The experience of the Andean Group has varied from country to country, but in general it can be concluded that the whole subregion has felt strong three-pronged inflationary pressure. First, part of this pressure has been caused by bottlenecks in the agricultural and industrial sectors, which have resulted in distortions in supply. Second, some of the explanation is attributable to inflation imported from developed countries. Finally, but not less important, comes the role of the public spending deficit. The two last-named elements will be examined in some detail.

In the 1970s, in particular, inflation has been a persistent problem as far as the formulation of economic policies is concerned.(55)   Although the general response has been to seek to control it by restructuring and controlling the money supply, variations in policy at national levels have affected the process of integration in a number of ways.

Inflation and the External Sector

Much of the inflation that has been prevalent in Latin America in the 1970s has been transmitted through the external sector of the economies of the region, with rapid price increases of imports and exports.   Fluctuations in import and export prices in the period 1974-78 were so great that no economy could absorb them without major distortions in the internal price structure.(56)   The impact of the external sector appears to be a secondary explanation of inflation in Chile, where the phenomenon was particularly marked, but more decisive in the other cases, where rates of inflation have been more moderate.
     Oil price fluctuations have had a serious impact on the external balance throughout the region.   The global import-export price index, from 1974 onward, shows important changes in the external sector.(57)

The Public Sector

The share of the public sector in economic activity increased rapidly in all the GRAN member countries because of the requirements of industrial development planning, the creation of an adequate infrastructure for import substitution, the setting up of indispensable basic industries, and the need to finance various subsidies and other industrial promotion mechanisms and to subsidize basic consumption and service needs.   The state slowly increased its participation in gross capital formation, which, because of the inelasticity of current government income coming mainly from indirect taxes and foreign trade, had to be financed by domestic and overseas borrowing.   In Peru and Chile the public sector acquired an even more dominant role because it became the principal economic agent in the models for change formulated in 1968 and 1971, respectively. In both cases public investment became the principal element because of the nationalization and state control of key productive sectors.   This was to make up for the reduction in private investment, which was discouraged by the social content of the two models.   If one adds to this situation the fall in the prices of export products and in the supply of many of these (e.g., Peruvian fishmeal), we can understand the acuteness of these two countries' financial positions by 1975.   In fact, all Andean countries have a deficit in the public budget which has not been resolved.

Therefore, countries such as Venezuela and Ecuador increase their public spending while others, such as Colombia and Peru, try to decrease public sector participation in the GNP and to thereby reduce the relationship between public debt and the GNP.(58)

In Ecuador the rate of public spending has been affected by increases in oil revenues. Between 1970 and 1972, current public revenues (in dollars) rose by 49 percent; between 1972 and 1975 this figure was 92.7 percent. This allowed a similar growth in expenditures which maintained a healthy level of public debt. The sectors most favored by this increase were the ministries of the Interior, Defense, and Health. Spending on industry, trade, cattle, and agriculture remained small. In 1976, it was only 10 percent of the total, while defense took 12 percent. Given the healthful state of public finances, no attempt has been made to bring about any drastic changes in investment policy other than the greater emphasis on capital expenditure. Since 1975 this favorable financial condition has changed. In spite of the continued growth in public revenue it became impossible to cover expenditure. Public deficit rose to a spectacular level.

In Bolivia, the favorable movement in the terms of trade meant that, from 1974, there was a notable improvement in public finances. On the other hand, the yield from tariffs and taxes on traditional exports rose, changing the external sector into the principal source of fiscal revenues. The healthful state of public finances allowed for a large increase in budget expenditures, especially on public investment.(59) However, while public investment represented an important share of total investment, it only accounted for 15 percent of public expenditure in 1975. Public finances in Bolivia depend for 30 percent of income upon two enterprises: the Bolivian Mining Corporation and the State Petroleum Corporation. The former has registered a deficit since 1972, and this became acute in 1975 because of the fall in the prices of antimony and copper and the drop in the volume of tin exported as a result of the world recession. Although the latter enterprise was in a better position, the low level of exports was affecting its financial operations.(60)

During the years since 1979, public finances in Bolivia have been going through a crisis which has influenced all economic activity.

The public sector deficit reached unprecedented levels in international terms. Revenues deteriorated due to the problems encountered by the most important public enterprises and the decrease in exports (for taxes on external trade represent over 50 percent of total income). The political crisis makes impossible any attempt to improve public finances.

The Peruvian public sector shows an ever-present and rising deficit, which, by 1975, had risen to about 10 percent of GDP. The cause of this is the lack of dynamism of current incomes, which can be explained by three factors. First, there is a great dependence upon the system of taxing the external sector, mainly the mining and fishery industries. Second, as in all the GRAN countries, in Peru the fiscal incentives created to promote industrial development have also eroded the basis of profit taxes and customs taxes (under these provisions, companies can get up to a 99 percent exemption on profit taxes). Finally, the legislation on industrial communities obliges companies to transfer to the workers part of their profits before tax. This affects tax revenues, not only because the industrial community does not pay profit taxes, but also because the majority of the workers belong to the lowest income groups and, therefore, are not taxed.

Consolidated government finances as a percentage of GDP show a deterioration in public savings, which increases the deficit.(61) This can be explained by the tariff structure of the public sector and the growth of expenditure through state enterprises to finance subsidies on petroleum and some basic food products.

Given continual deficits in the Peruvian public sector, severe stabilization measures were taken. In June 1976, a reduction of 5 percent (6,000 million soles) in current public expenditure were ordered, plus the freezing of all public sector wage and salary spending, and the reduction of central government and public enterprise investment by 14,100 million soles. In spite of these measures, the 1976 deficit was not reduced and Peru was obliged to negotiate with the IMF.(62) To alleviate the continued public sector bottleneck, important reforms were imposed in the public enterprises administrative system by the adoption, in 1981, of a stock company regime with the authorization to seek external financing. Another important measure was the tax reform designed to increase the taxable population, strengthen income tax, and stimulate reinvestment. Despite the foregoing in 1979, public deficit figures remain at around 1 percent of the GDP and the debt servicing 37.5 percent of total exports.

Venezuelan public finances depend upon income from petroleum. In 1971, this source (royalties and profits) represented 65.6 percent of total public income. By 1976, it had risen to 74.6 percent (total income was 22 percent of GDP, approximately US$9,000 million). This high public revenue has allowed Venezuela to undertake ambitious development programs without having to resort to exaggerated indebtedness or to set up heavy profit and inheritance taxes. In Venezuela there are no sales taxes and the marginal rates of tax on profits are much lower than in other Latin American countries.(63)

In 1975 public spending (US$7,500 million) represented 27.5 percent of GDP. Investment was about 45 percent of budget expenditure. This figure excludes the contributions made to the investment funds set up to deal with part of the additional government revenues which had been set aside for large public works and industrial projects, but includes the expenditures made by those funds. Public expenditure doubled from 1973 (US$3,500 million) to 1975 (US$7,500 million). So public debt is not a heavy burden in the budget. Repayments in 1976 accounted for only 1.6 percent of total public expenditure. However, public borrowing has been growing very fast in recent years. As a result of the oil policies, crude exports stagnated during 1975-78, so did public revenues. Consequently, the budgetary deficit multiplied many times and was reduced only in 1980, thanks to the high rate of growth of oil exports which reached 46.6 percent between 1978-80. Public debt grew from 84 million dollars in 1975 to 2,127 million dollars in 1980 representing 4.4 percent of the GNP by the end of 1980.

Therefore, in the case of Venezuela, one is dealing with a consolidated financial position without the limitations of the other countries. However, the very great importance of petroleum income to government finances implies certain drawbacks for some aims of fiscal policy. First, direction of the oil industry is insufficient as a tool of stabilization because it is not a suitable instrument for monetary contraction. Second, it is an inadequate redistributive tool, because it is centered on only a few companies highly intensive in the utilization of labor (which have been nationalized). Finally, an element of instability in development plans is introduced because of the dependence upon external conditions of demand and supply.

POLICY GOALS

During the sixties the goals of the economic policies of the member countries were homogeneous, in the sense that all pursued and implemented the general lines of import substitution. However, by 1974 Colombia and Chile had started a process of liberalization of their economies that soon came into conflict with the economic model followed by the remaining member countries and with the scheme of integrated development itself.

By 1974, in the wake of the effects of the world crisis, reduction in export prices and volumes, and the consequent deepening of traditional internal problems (high inflation, public deficits, unemployment, and so on), Colombia designed a development plan in which the main objectives were stabilization and full employment. In the same year, but more clearly since 1975, Chile formulated the new economic policy which like that of Colombia places emphasis on controlling inflation.

In both cases the "rationalization of the national economy" was the main motive; by that was understood the "dismantling of the mechanisms established for substituting industrial imports," in order to diminish costs of national production to a level comparable with international standards.

The second aim strongly linked with the previous one was the reduction and "rationalization" of public sector expenditure, whose chronic deficits were a permanent source of inflation; the objective in this particular aspect was to reduce the participation of the public sector in GDP.

There are two principal consequences of the new Colombian and Chilean economic policies that matter for integration purposes: the first is the industrial policy and the second is the role of the state. We will examine them in some detail in this section. However, when evaluating the implementation of the Treaty of Cartagena, especially the CET, the PSDI, and the harmonization of macroeconomic policies, we will refer to them again.

The Industrial Policies and the Role of the State

The industrial policies of the member countries have undergone modifications, especially since 1974. These changes are a response to both the need to control inflation and to the external crisis. In some countries these modifications represent a reinforcement of the import substitution process, taking advantage of Andean integration; in others they reflect the greater availability of foreign currencies after the rise in export prices. In certain cases both elements were present.(64)

The main objective of Colombian industrial policy is the radical reduction of production costs, which may be achieved by reduction of tariffs, elimination of subsidies, and stabilizing real interest rates in the capital market. Industrial activity is to be completely within the private sector, which is the one to identify "leading sectors" accordingly to profitability. State actions are to be directed towards creating the "right climate" by eliminating intervention in market mechanisms, and regulating direct and indirect taxation, exchange policies, credit, and tariffs. The latter will be low and nondispersed; they must have the minimum possible number of changes and together they must tend to stimulate the production of those goods that can be more efficiently produced in the country than outside.(65) State intervention would only take place in cases of excessive concentration leading to monopolies, or if environmental damage was being caused. In the future, the state would only develop sources of energy and exploit natural resources. Credit policy is primarily aimed at promoting small and medium-sized industry and agro-industry. This strategy forms part of the plan to raise the income level of the poorest 50 percent of the population throughout the country by increasing employment in small and medium-sized industries and the production of large consumer goods.

The overall implications in terms of trade policy are clear: the exchange rate is unified and devalued so as to reflect the trend in internal prices. It constitutes the main mechanism to promote exports and control imports when the balance of trade is in deficit. Exports therefore will be found in those sectors or products in which the country has clear comparative advantages: agriculture, mining, and labor-intensive manufactures.

In Chile,(66) which has a market-oriented strategy similar to that of Colombia, the basis of policy is to give more responsibility to the private sector for the reactivation of the economy. The state only accepts responsibility for drawing up policy and taking a direct part in those activities that for some special reason the private sector cannot undertake. The policy has two basic elements: to break the stagnation of production and to open the economy to the exterior. The former aims to reduce public spending and to increase market activity. The second seeks to raise productive efficiency in international terms. By February 1975, the sixth tariff reduction had been achieved and the objective of a minimum tariff of 10 percent and a maximum of 35 percent was being approached, but further reductions were still programmed. Chile had decided to cut tariffs to a uniform rate of 10 percent, to be reached by mid-1979.(67)

Since 1976, the prime objective of Chilean economic policy is accelerated economic growth (7% p.a. as a minimum) as the prerequisite for any attempt to improve income distribution. Productive efficiency is measured in terms of international prices. The strategy is simple and direct: a 7 percent annual growth rate requires a further reduction of 15 percent in consumption which in political terms is impossible, "given the sociological conditions of the country."(68) Therefore, the scheme needs extra foreign investment to cover the shortfall in domestic savings. A realistic exchange rate policy means accelerated devaluations by adopting a single rate and a crawling peg as the only acceptable tools for stimulating exports and controlling imports. Other factors are: the elimination of price controls (except on monopolies); increases in credit to the private sector; and the reduction of public spending on production and services. Therefore, the state will only intervene in the sphere of distribution through the management of fiscal resources.

It is possible to conclude that, in relation to integration, the Colombian and the Chilean models of managing the national economy in force since 1974 go completely against the subregional model of substitution. The differences between Chile and Colombia are in the degree of the policies and not in their essence.

Venezuelan industrial policy fits into the import substitution model. Industrialization is relatively recent, with the main effort made after the extinction of the trade treaty with the United States in 1973. In contrast to the Chilean and Colombian industrial policies, Venezuela is increasing the participation of the public sector. The Venezuelan state plays a considerable part in basic industries, not only in the extraction of minerals and oil refining, but also in the steel, aluminum, petrochemical, and automotive industries. State investment for the coming five years in the manufacturing sector is to be US$10,000 million, a figure close to the total Colombian GDP. Industrial investment is 22.3 percent of gross fixed investment; for agriculture it is only 8.8 percent.

Venezuelan industry developed under a scheme of tariff protection, trade quota barriers, and tariff exemptions for imported primary materials, which has permitted expansion in spite of high costs. If there were no tariff protection, high real costs would make it impossible to sustain production in most branches of industry. Tariff protection compensates for the imbalances caused by a rate of exchange that reflects the situation of the oil industry rather than the competitive capacity of the larger part of the industrial sector. The acceleration of industrial growth has to capitalize upon the enormous reserves provided by oil profits, to use the natural resources in which the country is rich (steel, aluminum, and oil), to generate employment on a massive scale in a highly urbanized country, and to make use of the enlarged Andean market that can help to reduce production costs.(69) The advantages Venezuelan industry has over the other member countries are, apart from the high rate of state participation in basic industry which seeks a minimum level of efficiency, the size of the national market, high capital intensity, and high profitability brought about by the strict protection scheme, to which can be added the total exemption from duties, most of which are for inputs and capital goods.

In Peru, entry into the GRAN coincided with the coming of the revolutionary military regime. The new government's industrial strategy aimed to change the production structure by developing basic industries and producing intermediate and capital goods. This new approach implied planning and strengthening of the public sector, which was to take over basic industry to ensure the correct direction of industrial development.(70)

Worker participation in the profits and management of companies through industrial communities and the social property sector were to be the means of integrating industry into the sociopolitical strategy of improving incomes and creating a pluralist society.(71) The scheme foundered on the fall in domestic savings and private investment, which obliged the state to take over the investment shortfall. The limitations of internal and external financial resources, labor troubles, and the crisis of foreign trade gave rise to grave fiscal problems which, added to the fall in foreign reserves, led in 1975 and 1976 to a serious economic and political crisis. A shift in policy followed which meant less state intervention and a greater participation of the private sector.

In 1981, the restructuring of the economic model was perfected by reintroducing trade mechanisms and trade criteria: subsidies for a large list of massive consumer goods were eliminated in order to reestablish real prices; interest rates were increased and devaluation of national currency was accelerated to keep pace with internal inflation. On the other hand, Congress endowed the Executive with extraordinary powers to restructure public administration, especially with regard to state enterprises, which from now on would be ruled by a stock company regime.

The industrial scene in Bolivia and Ecuador has been transformed by the opportunities offered by the GRAN and the flow of external resources coming from oil exports. The GDP and the manufacturing sector have grown beyond any precedent. In both countries, gross capital formation and state participation in total investment have increased.

Given that these two countries have been left behind in the industrialization process, it is understood that, to overcome the limitations of market size and financial resources (a low level of private domestic savings, a weak flow of external savings to manufacturing, etc.), the state has to assume the role of principal promoter of industrial growth.

In the case of Bolivia, a mineral and agricultural economy, the government is trying to change the productive structure into an industrial one. Twenty percent of total investment (public and private) envisaged for 1975 to 1980 is directed to industry.

The 1975–1980 investment plan rose to US$3,500 million. Nine point six percent of this sum was to go to the agricultural sector, 15.8 percent to hydrocarbons, 16.1 percent to transport and communications. Industrial development depends on the Andean market, sectoral allocation, and a CET that may take Bolivia's landlocked position into account.

Because internal saving is only 17 percent of the GDP, external finance is needed to cover the deficit. However, the Bolivian government is in a precarious position for mobilizing resources into investment. In 1969, gross public savings only represented 0.12 percent of GDP and 0.69 percent of gross domestic investment. Private savings represented 12 percent and 67.1 percent, respectively of these totals.

The situation has not had any significant change and has become increasingly critical since the public sector capacity for raising external loans is practically exhausted. In March, 1981, the servicing of foreign debt represented 47 percent of

total exports. Renegotiation of the debt has been hindered by
the impossibility of reaching any kind of agreement with the
IMF and with the 127 private creditor banks. A lessening of
the extremely severe conditions claimed by creditors is not
viable because of the lack of political legitimacy of the present
Bolivian government.

A similar situation is to be found in Ecuador, which has
formulated an industrialization policy aimed at capitalizing on
the oil resources by strengthening the public sector and by
granting preference to sectors producing capital and intermediate goods, financed by state-directed funds. Apart from the
financial stimulus, industry is favored by a highly protective
tariff structure and special regulations for foreign trade. The
state is to increase its role as investor in industrial development in those sectors considered to be strategic: oil refining,
chemicals, iron and steel, motor vehicles, cement, and especially those industries linked to sectors singled out for the
Andean sectoral programs.(72)

Within the management of the external sector there are
two more or less visible tendencies in terms of greater or
lesser openness to the international economy and of greater or
lesser intervention through stimuli or restrictions on exports
and imports that are coherent with the industrial and fiscal
policies pursued by each country.

Chile and Colombia have clearly followed their policy of
greater openness to the international market through reforms
in tariffs, exchange policy, and the treatment of foreign capital. These elements are an important part of their analysis of
how to reverse the previous import substitution process, which
for the external sector had meant overvalued rates of exchange, and deficits on balance of payments. In the case of
tariff policy, besides adopting maximum temporary levels (30%
in Chile and 40% in Colombia), exemptions and rebates were
eliminated from the special regulations laid down to favor some
backward industrial sectors or regions.(73) The crawling-peg
system was adopted as exchange rate policy both to promote
exports and to discourage imports by maintaining an effective
real rate of exchange. Neither the tariffs nor the exchange
rate are considered as mechanisms for resource allocation. In
consequence the former may be nondispersed and tend to be
nil, and the latter is unified. The solution to the need for
external savings to finance the required investment was sought
in eliminating discrimination against foreign capital.(74)

The Chilean government proposed a change in the definition of what are foreign or national companies by replacing the
concept of origin and ownership of capital with the local value
added of an enterprise.(75) The use of this criterion reversed the effect of the rules of Decision 24 of the Andean
Group.(76)

To a greater or lesser degree, Bolivia, Ecuador, Peru, and Venezuela seek foreign financing, but they accept the rules laid down by the Common Treaty, especially those referring to the direction of investment according to national priorities and the reduction of the sometimes negative effects of foreign capital on the balance of payments.

In accordance with their scheme of import substitution, these countries maintain a relatively closed economy, with high tariffs and import restrictions, combined with stimuli in the shape of exemptions and tariff rebates.(77) These conditions are especially important in the case of imports of machinery and inputs and goods purchased by state enterprises.

Obviously the differences in policy orientation are reflected as well in the way the member countries have chosen to handle their exchange rate policy. Until 1975, Bolivia, Ecuador, and Venezuela retained fixed exchange rates, with sporadic devaluations. In 1975 Peru devalued its currency for the first time since 1968; it did so again in 1977, as part of the stabilization measures negotiated with the IMF,(78) but there is no explicit suggestion that Peru will move in the near future to a system of devaluation pari passu with inflation. The same is the situation in Bolivia and Ecuador, but the devaluations made in the last two years have been less severe than those of Peru. In Venezuela, exchange policy seeks to maintain an overvalued currency as a mechanism to increase the country's import capacity for capital goods. It is also a consequence of the high income from the oil sector. Bolivia, Ecuador, and Venezuela all maintain free convertibility of their currency, and none shows any intention of modifying this.

In 1968, Colombia introduced a system of devaluation pari passu with inflation; in balance of trade crises devaluation proceeded even faster than inflation did. The system has proved adequate and is unlikely to change, although during the "Bonanza Cafetera" free convertibility was considered and the rate of devaluation was slowed during the last year. In Chile, the currency had been devalued at a higher rate than inflation during the period 1975-1979.(79) In 1979, the Chilean peso was revaluated.

From 1975, Chile and Colombia began a policy of rationalizing public finances by reducing public spending. The central theme of Colombia's public finance policy was the tax reform of 1974. Its principal objectives were to increase yields, and to reduce the inflationary effects of deficitary budgets and the dependence of these budgets upon foreign credit; it also sought to introduce more progressive customs duties and to prevent evasion. But the modifications introduced to this reform in 1975 and 1976 made it ineffective, and by 1976 the deficit had worsened. The government opted for a severely contractionist policy which, apart from reducing the public deficit, tried to arrest the inflationary effects of the increase in international reserves coming from higher coffee prices. In the medium term, the policy of giving greater priority to price stability was to be maintained, while economic growth and income redistribution through public expenditure was given less importance.(80) Between 1974 and 1975 the investment budget only rose by 10 percent, and between 1975 and 1976 it fell by 35.5 percent.

The contractionist policy continued throughout 1981. However, the public debt kept growing at a faster rate than the revenues. In 1981 the deficit in the public sector represented approximately 1.0 percent of the GNP. As a result the government decided to seek internal and external financing sources for the financing monetary emission. The most important element of the monetary contractionist policy is the reduction of credit to the private sector. The effects on the production and cost structures of such policy are well known. Last year it was impossible to postpone the public investment programs, and the governmental expenditure acted again as an expansionist element.

Similarly, Chilean fiscal policy has sought to stabilize the economy through cuts in public spending, which were meant to eliminate deficits.(81) The basic elements of the strategy were to reduce investment spending (by 20% from 1975 to 1976) and transfers to public enterprises, which were to become self-sufficient (a cut of 60% over the same period), and to freeze health and education expenditures. State investment was to be concentrated upon sectors that had social importance.

In Peru, as a remedy for the chronic deficit in public spending, a policy of restriction and contraction was adopted for 1978. It can be predicted that for the foreseeable future these policies will aim for "greater austerity in public expenditure, realistic exchange policy, contraction of external borrowing, increase in retail prices, stimuli to private productive savings and reductions in public investments, all with the intention of contracting domestic demand."(82) The repercussions of these measures on the political and economic climate can be predicted because the policy necessarily has taken effect through the severe reduction of consumption, employment, and incomes. A continued wave of strikes and confrontations with private sector representatives has sometimes caused drawbacks in the stabilization program, such as a reduction in the interest rates and a slowdown on the devaluating rhythm. Nevertheless the effect of the adopted measures remains the same.(83) The effects that the stabilization policy will have on Peru's role in the development of integration schemes are much less clear. Possibly the same will happen as in Chile and Colombia; that is, Peru may move toward a more liberal economic scheme, shifting the priority given in the past to subregional industrial planning to the amplification of the commercial program.

In summary, by 1976, the year that concludes the period under analysis, the Andean countries found themselves divided into two opposite groups. The divergences among the two groups have been made explicit in the formulation of different economic policies.

Chile and Colombia, the countries that started earlier and advanced more in the import substitution process, turned to coherent liberal schemes. They reduced state activity in redistributive programs, eliminated market controls, and diminished the priority to industrial development. In consequence they established low tariffs and reversed the previous discrimination against agriculture and primary exporting sectors. The final objective was to rationalize national production in international terms with the criterion that one unit of foreign currency earned by exports has the same value as one saved by domestic production.

Bolivia, Ecuador, Peru, until 1979, and Venezuela remain within the import substitution model which implies higher protection for industry and a complex program of subsidies, credit, and price stimuli. The public sector has an active role in economic activity and is an important investor. The market is oriented and controlled in order to channel resources to priority industrial sectors.

It is important to point out that the external sector has been an active agent, although not exclusive, in the changes mentioned above. In Chile, the political change in 1973 and the economic crises stemming from internal and external factors induced the radical changes in the economic pattern and in the integrationist policies. The fall of export earnings and the lack of foreign investment were the factors instrumental in persuading the government to open the Chilean economy. The related experiences of Peru during 1977 and 1978 are also indicative of the strong influence of the external sector upon the countries' possibilities of designing an autonomous model of economic development.

Table 2.15 gives a synopsis of the countries' national policies implicit in their development plans, their trade laws, their industrial promotion initiatives, and credit and exchange regulations. It can be seen that the GRAN was divided into two groups: one that proposed economic liberalism; the other, industrial protectionism. The important determinant of these positions seems to be the degree of industrialization.

The first group was formed by Chile and Colombia, countries that, as we have shown, enjoyed relatively higher levels of industrial development, as they had embarked earlier on a process of import substitution. Thus at the time that negotiations on the Treaty began they had a more than proportional share of industrial production and markets in the subregion and were in general terms advantageously placed as regards expanding their supply of manufactures to the whole Andean

market.   The second group was formed by four countries.
Two of these, Bolivia and Ecuador, had the least degree of
relative development, characterized in the 1960s by incipient
industrial development and financial resources and in particular
by a very limited domestic market, and hence with little
prospect of autonomously advancing the process of industrialization.   The other two countries, Peru and Venezuela, were
closer to Colombia in terms of industrial development, but
pursuing protectionist policies explicable more in terms of the
"quality" of industrial development than the relative stage of
development.

In Venezuela the combination of abundant natural and
financial resources and a sizeable national market makes a
national industry viable.   Protectionist policies are required to
compensate for the disequilibrium implicit in a rate of growth
that reflects the specific situation of the petroleum industry
and not that of the economy in general, which suffers from
high real costs.   In Peru, protectionism was an aspect of the
strategy of the revolutionary military government, which aimed
at changing the structure of production by strengthening basic
and strategic industries.   Here, too, protectionism aimed to
compensate for the overvaluation of the national currency, at
least until 1977, and for the high costs of production arising
out of the different social and economic policies being attempted and of the design of the main investment projects for which
the national market was evidently insufficient.

The objectives of the first group, Chile and Colombia,
were a more efficient production and higher growth rates.
The second group sought to transform their primary producing economies into modern industrialized systems, and to
eliminate disequilibria in the levels of development.   The
differences between the two groups came to the surface on the
issues of the participation of the state as a generator of
economic activity, sectoral preference, the level of protection
and the degree of free trade, and the extent to which the
markets for the factors of production should be controlled and
directed.

CONCLUSIONS

We have analyzed in this chapter the structure of production
in the Andean subregion, the different levels of industrial
development reached by individual countries, and the general
orientation of their economic policies.

We were able to show that industrial production in the
subregion was relatively undiversified, and that production
costs were very high and varied considerably from country to
country.   As a consequence, no member of the GRAN could be

described as a specialist in any particular industrial subsector; in no case did coefficients of specialization approach unity.

Furthermore, only 9 percent of the Andean population proved to have access to the market for manufactures, a market concentrated heavily in particular countries, and essentially urban in nature. Thus Venezuela, for example, contributed 44.2 percent of subregional demand for manufactures, while Bolivia and Ecuador together could account for only 3.8 percent.

On the basis of total and per capita GDP we were able to classify the Andean countries into two groups, those of relatively less development, Bolivia and Ecuador, and those with more advanced economies, Chile, Colombia, Peru, and Venezuela. From this point of view, Bolivia and Ecuador generate only 10 percent of subregional GDP. Furthermore, the ratio of the values of per capita GDP in these two countries to that of Venezuela, which makes the largest contribution to subregional GDP, is greater than 3:1, and this reveals an asymmetry in the GRAN far greater than that observable within the EEC, LAFTA, or the CACM.

The classification of the countries into the two groups mentioned was adjusted when introducing into the analysis the concept of the level of industrialization as measured by the import coefficient and the degree of concentration of the production and export of manufactures. On this measure, Bolivia and Ecuador again emerge as the least developed and the least advanced on the path of import substitution, generating a very low proportion of gross Andean manufacturing production (4.5 percent in 1960 and 9.3 percent in 1975), and contributing only minimally to subregional exports. Chile and Colombia emerge with a greater relative level of development than Peru and Venezuela. Thus in 1960 national manufacturing production in Chile and Colombia supplied a greater proportion of internal demand than in Peru or Venezuela, and the gap between the countries was particularly marked in the production of intermediate goods and in light engineering. Nevertheless, significant changes in the subgroup have taken place. In 1969 Chile and Colombia accounted for more than 50 percent of Andean manufacturing production, while Peru and Venezuela accounted for only 37 percent; by the end of the period examined here the increased production of manufactures by Peru and Venezuela and the rapid decline of Chile's share were evident. Finally, the export of manufactures, particularly where a high degree of technological complexity was called for, was highly concentrated in the two more highly developed countries, Chile and Colombia.

Towards 1975 there were clear signs in Chile and Colombia of a reorientation of economic policy and the introduction of liberal economic models aimed at simultaneously solving three problems: accelerating inflation, a negative trend in the terms

of trade, and a budget deficit, all present to a greater degree
in Chile than in Colombia. This reorientation implied the
dismantling of policies of import substitution and the opening
of the economies in accordance with the criteria of international
efficiency and competitiveness, and this led to open conflict
with the approach adopted in the GRAN. In this period the
relatively less developed countries were moving in the opposite
direction and attempting to perfect economic models based upon
the promotion of industry through import substitution. These
countries were at the time in a far less grave situation than
Chile as regards the national budget, the availability of financial resources, and the state of the balance of payments and
were well placed, in fact, to undertake the massive investments needed to reduce the distance that separated them from
their partners in the GRAN. Thus the policies they followed
centered upon the protection of national markets and on the
planning of investment, measures considered legitimate and
healthy given the incipient character of their industrial sectors
and the limited size of their internal markets. The plans and
programs of Peru and Venezuela rested upon similar economic
policies, although the thinking behind them was not identical.
The protectionism of these two countries is better explained if
we take into account the need they felt to reduce the industrial advantage enjoyed over them by Colombia and Chile, the
high costs induced by the external sector, the overvalued rate
of exchange, and, in particular, in the case of Venezuela, the
possibility of taking full advantage of abundant financial
resources. In Peru the military regime sought also to consolidate basic and strategic industries as a means of ensuring
national independence.

It is difficult to determine the extent to which these
differences in national strategies are of a permanent nature
and correspond to long-term policies, or to which they may
change in response to changes of government or in such areas
as the balance of payments. There can be no doubt, however,
as regards the great differences existing in the level of economic development or the orientation of national policies.
These would justify the adoption of a common frame of reference, and the centralization of decision making on certain
economic issues.

In the following chapters we will analyze the results of
the two levels of integration: (i) the liberation of trade, or
economic integration, and (ii) the unification of policies, or
political integration. The emphasis will be placed on two
aspects: (i) the dynamism of the market measured in terms of
the expansion of reciprocal trade, the promotion of new investments and tendencies toward concentration, and (ii) the
different relative levels of development of the countries,
particularly industrial development, and the effects of these
upon the development of programs for harmonizing macroeconomic policies.

Table 2.1. Andean Group, Basic Data on Andean and Other Latin American Countries
1969

	ANDEAN GROUP	ARGENTINA	BRAZIL	MEXICO
POPULATION (000)	64.0	23.9	90.8	48.9
AREA (000 Km²)	5.5	2.8	8.5	2.0
GDP (US $ BILLIONS)	27.3	21.6	30.7	31.7
GDP (per capita)	480.0	902.0	338.0	649.0
MERCHANDISE EXPORTS	5.4	1.6	2.3	1.5
MERCHANDISE IMPORTS	4.5	1.6	2.3	2.1
INDUSTRIAL OUTPUT AS % GDP	18.7	30.7	23.8	23.8
OUTPUT SELECTED ITEMS				
IRON (000 TONS)	26.8	0.1	18.2	2.1
COPPER (000 TONS)	906.7	–	4.3	66.2
LEAD (000 TQNS)	30.1	1.9	1.6	0.5
OIL (Mil MTS³)	229.8	20.7	10.2	26.8
WHEAT (000 TONS)	1568.0	7020.0	1347.0	2300.0
LIVESTOCK (000 TONS)	960.0	2800.0	1720.0	1440.0
COFFEE (00 TONS)	2319.0	978.0	4550.0	2565.0
SUGAR	6816.0	–	12,835.0	1680.0
CEMENT (000 TONS)	4282.2	4346.8	7173.8	93.5
PAPER (000 TONS)	754.0	579.0	870.0	490.0

Source: N.U., ECLA, Statistical Bulletin for Latin América, Vol. 8, No. 1 (marzo de 1971).

Table 2.2. Andean Group, Gross Domestic Product at Market Prices 1950-1979

	GDP at market prices millions dollars						Regional Structure in percentages						Annual Growth Rates			
	1950[1]	1960[1]	1969[1]	1975[1]	1976[2]	1979[2]	1950[1]	1960[1]	1969[1]	1975[1]	1976[2]	1979[2]	1950-60[1]	1960-69[1]	1969-75[1]	1976-1979[2]
Bolivia	705	723	1,195	1,714	2,892	3,146	4.8	3.0	3.1	3.3	4.00	3.86	0.21	5.7	6.2	2.8
Colombia	3,930	6,120	9,629	13,968	23,876	28,642	26.6	25.2	25.2	27.3	33.04	35.21	5.5	5.2	6.4	6.2
Chile	3,536	5,199	7,780	7,444	-	-	23.9	21.4	20.4	14.6	-	-	4.7	4.6	-0.7	-
Ecuador	849	1,354	2,021	3,423	5,786	6,858	5.7	5.6	5.3	6.7	8.00	8.43	5.9	4.6	9.2	5.8
Peru	2,615	4,275	6,794	9,918	16,513	16,948	17.7	17.6	17.8	19.4	22.85	20.83	6.3	5.3	6.5	0.9
Venezuela	3,122	6,583	10,731	14,694	23,190	25,744	21.2	27.2	28.1	28.7	32.09	31.65	11.0	5.6	5.4	3.6
Total Andean Group	14,757	24,253	38,150	51,161	72,257	81,338	100.0	100.0	100.0	100.0	100.00	100.00	6.4	5.2	5.5	4.0

1. 1968 dollars, parity exchange.
2. 1973 dollars, parity exchange.

Source: 1950-1975: Junta del Acuerdo; Informe de Evaluación 1976, Jun/di 248 Lima 1977, Anexo Técnico.

1976-1978 Junta: Indicadores Socioeconómicos de la Subregión Andina, Jun/di 277 rev. 3, abril 1980

72

Table 2.3. Andean Group, Gross Domestic Product Per Capita at Market Prices
(millions dollars, parity exchange)
1950-1979

	GDP per capita US dollars						GDP per capita as % of subregional GDP						Annual Growth Rates			
	1950[1]	1960[1]	1969[1]	1975[1]	1976[2]	1979[2]	1950[1]	1960[1]	1969[1]	1975[1]	1976[2]	1979[2]	1950-60[1]	1960-69[1]	1969-75[1]	1976-1979[2]
Bolivia	233	191	256	317	576	580	58.5	39.9	43.3	47.5	52.26	50.74	1.8	3.3	3.6	0.1
Colombia	336	385	451	540	978	1091	84.4	78.6	76.3	80.8	88.75	95.45	1.5	1.8	3.0	3.7
Chile	580	685	849	726	-	-	145.7	139.8	143.6	108.7	-	-	1.8	2.4	-2.6	-
Ecuador	263	313	346	483	814	882	66.1	63.9	58.5	72.3	73.87	77.16	1.9	1.1	5.7	2.7
Peru	330	421	515	636	1037	980	82.9	85.0	87.1	95.2	94.10	85.74	2.7	2.3	3.9	-2.1
Venezuela	607	862	1,047	1,203	1771	1781	152.5	175.0	177.2	180.1	160.71	155.82	4.2	2.1	2.3	0.2
Total	398	490	591	668	1102	1143	100.0	100.0	100.0	100.0	100.00	100.00	2.3	2.1	2.6	1.2

1. 1968 dollars, parity exchange.
2. 1973 dollars, parity exchange.

Source: 1950-1975: Junta: Informe de Evaluación 1976, Jun/di 248, Lima, 1977.

1976-1979: Junta: Indicadores Socioeconómicos de la Subregión Andina, Jun/di 277/Rev. 3, abril 1980.

Table 2.4.   Andean Group, Changes in the
Structure of the Gross Domestic Product
Percentage Shares
1950–1975

1950

	Agricul- ture	Mining[a]	Manufac- turing	Construc- tion	Services	Total
Bolivia	25.4	19.7	12.4	1.6	40.9	100.0
Colombia	38.2	2.5	13.7	4.0	41.6	100.0
Chile	11.2	12.5	23.1	4.4	48.8	100.0
Ecuador	24.9	6.5	19.7	6.4	42.4	100.0
Peru	24.6	7.0	13.7	6.5	48.2	100.0
Venezuela	7.7	22.7	9.3	5.4	54.9	100.0
Total	22.0	11.8	15.3	4.7	46.2	100.0

1969

Bolivia	17.5	14.3	12.5	4.8	50.9	100.0
Colombia	29.0	2.7	17.0	5.5	45.8	100.0
Chile	6.9	12.4	26.5	4.7	49.5	100.0
Ecuador	30.3	1.0	17.6	3.9	47.2	100.0
Peru	18.2	8.9	17.7	5.1	50.1	100.0
Venezuela	7.9	20.2	14.9	4.2	52.8	100.0
Total	16.2	11.2	18.5	4.5	49.6	100.0

1975

Bolivia	15.8	10.9	13.1	4.4	55.8	100.0
Colombia	26.4	1.9	18.6	4.6	48.5	100.0
Chile	8.0	11.9	20.9	3.9	55.3	100.0
Ecuador	21.3	5.0	17.3	5.5	50.9	100.0
Peru	14.2	5.6	20.5	7.7	52.0	100.0
Venezuela	7.0	10.0	16.0	6.0	61.0	100.0
Total	15.0	7.2	18.2	5.7	53.9	100.0

1978

Bolivia	17.5	6.4	15.2	5.2	55.6	100.0
Colombia	28.9	0.9	19.2	4.4	46.6	100.0
Ecuador	22.1	6.5	19.3	5.9	46.2	100.0
Peru	13.9	8.3	22.1	3.1	42.6	100.0
Venezuela	5.9	11.2	16.9	7.2	58.8	100.0
GRAN	17.0	6.6	18.9	5.2	52.3	100.0

1978 Junta, Indicadores Socioeconómicos de la Subregión Andina, Jun/di 272/Rev. 2, Abril 1980.

Sources: 1950: ECLA, El Desarrollo Económico y social y las
relaciones externas de América Latina, E/CEPAL/1061
marzo 1979, p. 23.

1969–1975: Junta, Informe de Evaluación 1976, Jun/di
248, Lima, 1977.

Note: (a) Includes oil extraction.

Table 2.5. Andean Group, Prices of Selected Manufactured Goods 1962 Prices (US$)

Product	Unit	Bolivia	Colombia	Chile	Ecuador	Peru	Venezuela	Argentina	Mexico	Brazil
Beer	Ltr.	0.45	0.28	0.44	0.49	0.43	0.51	0.31	0.40	0.47
Footwear	Pair	12.95	10.57	13.67	12.02	18.26	16.42	19.95	21.76	34.00
Textile	m^2	1.23	1.08	2.25	1.19	1.97	1.34	1.46	1.42	1.75
Soap	kg	1.03	0.33	0.67	0.85	0.51	0.56	0.26	0.48	0.23
Refrigerator	per unit	882.38	769.81	2,002.14	953.17	994.68	320.54	663.53	932.80	686.36
Washing machine	per unit	840.36	682.81	889.81	886.94	499.01	400.01	515.75	971.13	630.44
Radio	"	95.24	66.08	133.48	160.82	106.12	41.58	107.14	120.22	113.32
Television	"	560.24	881.04	1,557.22	530.06	465.74	282.17	610.33	458.83	757.21
Drill	"	139.36	127.09	220.24	172.32	165.00	90.10	119.70	177.51	133.57
Plough	"	1,210.10	1,087.64	1,142.33	1,332.36	1,419.04	578.95	1,955.13	1,955.13	1,372.25
Lorry	"	9,114.54	7,387.08	7,222.16	6,702.05	8,259.20	3,681.12	9,920.00	6,658.43	
Car	"	6,325.81	8,814.14	8,956.24	5,787.73	5,645.21	2,704.65	9,633.38	5,169.35	9,866.57
Centrifugal motor	"	442.31	317.17	417.11	449.90	455.62	193.07	326.59	253.32	2,185.70

Source: ECLA, EL Proceso de Industrialización en América Latina, 1965, p. 91.

Table 2.6. Andean Group, Gross Domestic Product of Industry, 1960–1979
(mil. US$ 1968)

International Standard Classification	1960							1969						
	Boli-via	Colom-bia	Chile	Ecua-dor	Peru	Vene-zuela	GRAN	Boli-via	Colom-bia	Chile	Ecua-dor	Peru	Vene-zuela	GRAN
31 Food, drinks & tobacco	17	333	276	69	317	271	1283	76	584	367	145	476	480	2128
32 Textiles, clothing & leather industries	19	216	338	19	129	86	807	33	347	434	49	182	183	1228
33 Wood & its products	4	28	104	2	16	23	177	4	30	150	11	39	39	273
34 Pulp, paper, publishing & printing	7	43	90	8	31	53	232	6	105	134	28	67	97	437
35 Chemical substances, oil, coal, rubber and plastics.	13	198	204	19	131	295	860	35	329	254	63	278	478	1437
36 Nonmetallic products	5	63	66	6	25	50	215	6	99	101	18	60	86	370
37 Base metal industries	1	24	73	-	81	7	186	1	38	126	1	102	75	343
38 Metallic products, machinery, equipment	2	105	299	5	58	68	537	3	201	464	24	196	208	1096
39 Various industries	1	27	49	1	11	8	97	3	45	64	12	43	34	201
Total	69	1037	1499	129	799	861	4394	167	1778	2094	351	1443	1680	7513
Light a)	46	650	841	100	504	436	2577	121	1090	1120	242	809	814	4196
Heavy b)	23	387	658	29	295	425	1817	46	698	974	109	634	866	3317
Industrial GDP per capita in US dollars	18.2	65.2	197.2	30.0	78.3	133.3	89.6	35.8	83.4	227.6	60.5	111.8	161.7	113.7

Notes: a. Light industries include: ISIC divisions N. 31, 32, 33, 39 and 42 (publishing and printing), 355 (rubber products), and 356 (plastic products not previously classified).
b. Heavy industries include ISIC divisions N. 36, 37, 38 and 41 (paper and paper products), 351 trial substances), 352 (other chemical products), 353 (oil refining), and 354 (other coal products).
c. 1979 (millions 1973 dollars, parity exchange).

Table 2.6. (continued)

International Standard Classification	1975						1976c						1979c					
	Boli-via	Colom-bia	Chile	Ecua-dor	Peru	Vene-zuela	Boli-via	Colom-bia	Ecua-dor	Peru	Vene-zuela	GRAN	Boli-via	Colom-bia	Ecua-dor	Peru	Vene-zuela	GRAN
31 Food, drinks & tobacco	111	933	362	274	759	671	169	1666	563	1419	1025	4842	182	2249	677	1300	1297	5705
32 Textiles, clothing & leather industries	47	436	291	83	241	278	98	955	244	682	360	2339	101	1030	285	649	318	2383
33 Wood & its products	6	35	100	21	54	43	14	66	65	117	71	333	18	82	85	94	92	371
34 Pulp, paper, publishing & printing	8	173	111	43	77	135	8	261	68	208	213	758	9	283	76	142	225	735
35 Chemical substances, oil, coal, rubber and plastics	53	518	184	148	534	569	81	903	129	775	1131	3019	105	980	117	717	1213	3132
36 Nonmetallic products	8	158	68	40	115	131	20	224	87	179	175	517	26	265	116	183	188	778
37 Base metal industries	1	109	135	4	156	149	13	124	26	305	251	719	19	141	39	574	274	1047
38 Metallic products, machinery, equipment	4	388	357	62	456	408	14	562	55	648	571	1850	20	690	88	510	609	1917
39 Various industries	5	26	67	44	96	58	14	51	3	55	72	195	11	6	4	43	240	304
Total	243	2776	1675	719	2486	2442	431	4812	1240	4388	3869	14740	491	5726	1487	4212	4456	16372
Light a)	176	1606	865	475	1237	1151	47	910	168	1132	997	3254	65	1096	243	1267	1071	3742
Heavy b)	67	1170	810	244	1251	1291	295	2738	875	2273	1528	7709	312	3367	1051	2086	1947	8763
Industrial GDP per capita in US dollars	45.0	107.3	119.6	101.3	158.5	200.2	576	978	814	1037	1771	1102	580	1091	882	980	1781	1143

Source: Junta, Informe de Evaluacion 1976, Jun/di 248, Lima, 1977, Anexo Estadistico. 1976-1979 Junta: Indicadores Socio-economicos de la Subregion Andina, Jun/di 277/Rev. 3, abril 1980

Table 2.7. Andean Group, Gross Domestic Product of Industry, Regional Structure
(in percentages) 1960–1979

ISIC a)	1960							1969							1975						
	Boli-via	Colom-bia	Chile	Ecua-dor	Peru	Vene-zuela	GRAN	Boli-via	Colom-bia	Chile	Ecua-dor	Peru	Vene-zuela	GRAN	Boli-via	Colom-bia	Chile	Ecua-dor	Peru	Vene-zuela	GRAN
31	1.3	26.0	21.5	5.4	24.7	21.1	100.0	3.6	27.4	17.2	6.8	22.4	22.6	100.0	3.6	30.0	11.6	8.8	22.4	22.6	100.0
32	2.3	26.8	41.9	2.4	15.9	10.7	100.0	2.7	28.3	35.3	4.0	14.8	14.9	100.0	3.4	31.8	21.1	6.0	14.8	14.9	100.0
33	2.3	15.8	58.8	1.1	9.0	13.0	100.0	1.5	11.0	54.9	4.0	14.3	14.3	100.0	2.3	13.5	38.6	8.1	14.3	14.3	100.0
34	3.0	18.6	38.8	3.4	13.4	22.8	100.0	1.4	24.0	30.7	6.4	15.3	22.2	100.0	1.4	31.6	20.3	7.8	15.3	22.2	100.0
35	1.5	23.1	23.7	2.2	15.2	34.3	100.0	2.4	22.9	17.7	4.4	19.4	33.2	100.0	2.6	25.8	9.2	7.4	19.4	33.2	100.0
36	2.3	29.3	30.7	2.8	11.6	23.3	100.0	1.6	26.8	27.3	4.9	16.2	23.2	100.0	1.5	29.6	13.2	7.9	16.2	23.2	100.0
37	0.6	12.9	39.2	--	43.5	3.8	100.0	0.3	11.1	36.7	0.3	29.7	21.8	100.0	0.2	19.7	24.4	0.7	29.7	21.8	100.0
38	0.3	19.7	55.7	0.9	10.8	12.6	100.0	0.2	18.3	42.3	2.3	17.9	19.0	100.0	0.2	23.2	21.3	3.7	17.9	19.0	100.0
39	1.0	27.9	50.6	1.0	11.3	8.2	100.0	1.5	22.4	31.8	6.0	21.4	16.9	100.0	1.7	8.9	22.6	14.8	21.4	16.9	100.0
TOTAL	1.6	23.6	34.1	2.9	18.2	19.6	100.0	2.2	23.6	27.9	4.7	19.2	22.3	100.0	2.4	16.0	16.2	6.9	19.2	22.3	100.0
Light Industry	1.8	25.3	32.6	3.9	19.5	16.9	100.0	2.9	26.0	26.7	5.8	19.3	19.4	100.0	3.2	29.1	15.7	8.9	19.3	19.4	100.0
Heavy Industry	1.3	21.4	36.2	1.6	16.2	23.3	100.0	1.4	20.7	29.4	3.3	19.1	26.1	100.0	1.4	24.2	16.7	5.1	19.1	26.1	100.0

Table 2.7. (continued)

ISIC a)	1975 (cont.) Peru	Vene-zuela	GRAN	1976 Boli-via	Colom-bia	Ecua-dor	Peru	Vene-zuela	GRAN	1979 Boli-via	Colom-bia	Ecua-dor	Peru	Vene-zuela	GRAN
31	24.4	21.6	100.0	3.5	34.4	11.6	29.3	21.2	100.0	3.2	39.4	11.8	22.8	22.8	100.0
32	17.5	20.2	100.0	4.2	40.8	10.4	29.2	15.4	100.0	4.2	43.2	11.9	27.3	13.4	100.0
33	20.8	16.6	100.0	4.2	19.8	19.5	35.2	21.3	100.0	4.9	22.1	22.9	25.3	24.8	100.0
34	14.1	24.7	100.0	1.1	34.4	8.9	27.4	28.2	100.0	1.2	38.5	10.3	19.4	30.6	100.0
35	26.6	28.4	100.0	2.7	29.9	4.3	25.7	37.4	100.0	3.4	31.3	3.7	22.9	38.7	100.0
36	22.4	25.5	100.0	3.8	43.3	16.8	34.6	33.8	100.0	3.3	34.01	15.0	23.5	24.2	100.0
37	28.2	26.9	100.0	1.8	17.2	3.6	42.4	34.9	100.0	1.8	13.5	3.7	54.8	26.2	100.0
38	27.2	24.4	100.0	0.7	30.3	2.9	35.0	30.8	100.0	1.0	36.0	4.6	26.6	31.8	100.0
39	32.4	19.6	100.0	7.1	26.1	1.5	28.2	36.9	100.0	3.6	2.0	1.3	14.7	78.9	100.0
TOTAL	24.1	23.6	100.0	2.9	32.6	8.4	29.7	26.2	100.0	3.0	35.1	9.0	25.7	27.2	100.0
Light Industry	22.5	20.9	100.0	3.8	35.6	11.4	29.4	19.8	100.0	3.6	38.4	12.0	23.8	22.2	100.0
Heavy Industry	25.8	26.7	100.0	1.4	28.0	5.2	34.8	30.6	100.0	1.7	29.3	6.5	33.9	28.6	100.0

(a) Sectoral definition in Table 6.

Source: 1960-1975 Junta, Informe de Evaluacion 1976, Jun/di. 248, Lima, 1976.

1976-1979: Indicadores Socioeconomicos de la Subregion Andina, Jun/di 277/Rev. 3, abril de 1980.

Table 2.8. Andean Group, National Structure of the
Gross Domestic Product of Industry
(in percentages)
1960–1979

Industrial Sector ISIC (a)	1960 Boli-via	1960 Colom-bia	1960 Chile	1960 Ecua-dor	1960 Peru	1969 Boli-via	1969 Colom-bia	1969 Chile	1969 Ecua-dor	1969 Peru	1969 Vene-zuela	1969 GRAN	1975 Vene-zuela	1975 GRAN	1975 Boli-via	1975 Colom-bia	1975 Chile	1975 Ecua-dor
31	24.7	32.1	18.4	53.5	39.6	45.5	32.9	17.5	41.3	33.0	31.5	29.2	26.6	26.3	45.7	33.7	21.6	38.8
32	27.5	20.8	22.5	14.7	16.2	19.7	19.5	20.7	13.9	12.6	10.0	18.4	10.9	16.3	19.3	15.7	17.4	11.5
33	5.8	2.7	6.9	1.6	2.0	2.4	1.7	7.1	3.3	2.7	2.7	4.0	2.3	3.6	2.5	1.2	6.0	2.1
34	10.1	4.1	6.1	6.2	3.9	3.6	5.9	6.4	8.0	4.6	6.2	5.3	5.8	5.8	3.3	6.2	6.6	6.0
35	18.8	19.1	13.6	14.7	16.3	21.0	18.5	12.1	18.0	19.3	34.3	19.6	28.4	19.2	21.8	18.7	11.0	20.6
36	7.2	6.1	4.4	4.7	3.1	3.6	5.6	4.8	5.1	4.2	5.8	4.9	5.1	4.9	3.3	5.7	4.1	5.5
37	1.5	2.3	4.9		10.2	0.6	2.1	6.0	0.2	7.0	0.8	4.2	4.5	4.6	0.5	3.9	8.1	0.6
38	2.9	10.2	19.9	3.9	7.3	1.8	11.3	22.2	6.8	13.6	7.9	12.2	12.4	14.6	1.6	14.0	21.2	8.6
39	1.5	2.6	3.3	0.7	1.4	1.8	2.5	3.2	3.4	3.0	0.8	2.2	2.0	2.7	2.0	0.9	4.0	6.2
TOTAL	100.0	100.0	100.0	100.0	100.0	100.0	100.0	100.0	100.0	100.0	100.0	100.0	100.0	100.0	100.0	100.0	100.0	100.0

Table 2.8. (continued)

ISIC a)	1975 (cont.)			1976						1979					
	Peru	Vene-zuela	GRAN	Boli-via	Colom-bia	Ecua-dor	Peru	Vene-zuela	GRAN	Boli-via	Colom-bia	Ecua-dor	Peru	Vene-zuela	GRAN
31	30.5	27.4	30.1	39.2	34.6	45.4	32.3	26.5	32.8	37.1	39.3	45.5	31.0	29.1	34.8
32	9.7	11.4	13.3	22.7	19.8	19.7	15.5	9.3	16.0	20.6	18.0	19.2	15.4	7.1	14.6
33	2.2	1.7	2.5	3.2	1.4	5.2	2.7	1.8	2.3	3.7	1.4	5.7	2.2	2.1	2.3
34	3.1	5.5	5.3	1.9	5.4	5.5	4.7	5.5	5.1	1.8	4.9	5.1	3.4	5.1	4.5
35	21.4	23.3	19.4	18.8	18.8	10.4	17.7	29.2	20.5	21.4	17.1	7.9	17.0	27.2	19.1
36	4.6	5.4	5.0	4.6	4.6	7.0	4.1	4.5	3.5	5.3	4.6	7.8	4.3	4.3	4.8
37	6.3	6.2	5.4	3.0	2.6	2.1	7.0	6.5	5.0	3.9	2.5	2.6	13.6	6.1	6.4
38	18.3	16.7	16.7	3.3	11.7	4.4	14.8	14.8	12.6	4.1	12.1	5.9	12.1	13.6	11.7
39	3.9	2.4	2.8	3.3	1.1	0.3	1.2	1.9	1.3	2.1	0.1	0.3	1.0	5.4	1.8
TOTAL	100.0	100.0	100.0	100.0	100.0	100.0	100.0	100.0	100.0	100.0	100.0	100.0	100.0	100.0	100.0

(a) ISIC: International Standard Industrial Classification; see Table 6 for divisions.

Source: Junta, 1960-1975 Informe de Evaluacion 1976 Jun/di 248, Lima 1977, Anexo Estadistico. 1976-1979: Indicadores Socio-Economicos de la Subregion Andina, Jun/di 277/Rev. 3, abril de 1980.

81

Table 2.9. Andean Group, Gross Domestic Product of Industry Annual Growth Rates, 1960-1979 (in percentages)

ISIC	1960-1969						1969-1975						1976-1979				
	Boli-via	Chile	Colom-bia	Ecua-dor	Peru	Vene-zuela	Boli-via	Chile	Colom-bia	Ecua-dor	Peru	Vene-zuela	Boli-via	Colom-bia	Ecua-dor	Peru	Vene-zuela
31 Food, drink & tobacco	18.1	3.2	6.4	8.6	4.6	6.6	6.5	-0.2	8.1	11.2	8.1	5.7	2.5	10.5	6.3	-2.8	8.1
32 Textiles, clothing & leather	6.3	2.8	5.4	11.6	3.9	8.8	6.1	-6.4	3.9	9.2	4.8	4.8	1.0	2.5	5.3	-1.6	-4.0
33 Wood & its products	0.0	4.2	0.8	20.8	10.4	6.1	7.0	-6.5	2.6	11.3	5.6	1.7	8.7	7.5	9.3	-7.0	9.0
34 Pulp, paper, publishing & printing	-1.7	4.5	10.4	14.9	8.9	6.9	4.9	-3.1	8.7	7.4	2.3	5.7	4.0	2.7	3.7	-11.9	1.8
35 Chemical substances, oil, rubber and plastics	11.6	2.5	5.8	14.3	8.7	5.5	7.2	-4.4	7.9	15.3	11.5	3.0	9.0	5.7	-3.2	-2.5	2.3
36 Nonmetallic Products	2.1	4.9	5.2	13.0	10.2	6.2	4.9	-6.4	7.4	14.3	11.4	7.3	9.1	2.8	10.0	-15.6	2.4
37 Base metal industries	0.0	6.3	5.3	—	2.6	30.1	0.0	1.2	19.2	26.0	7.3	12.1	13.4	4.4	14.4	23.4	2.9
38 Metallic products, machinery, equipment	4.6	5.0	7.5	19.0	14.5	13.2	4.9	-4.3	11.6	17.1	15.1	11.9	12.6	7.0	16.9	7.6	2.1
39 Various industries	13.0	3.0	5.8	31.8	16.4	17.5	8.9	0.3	-8.7	24.8	14.3	9.3	-7.7	-51.0	10.0	-7.8	49.3
Total	10.3	3.8	6.2	11.8	6.8	7.7	6.5	-3.7	7.7	12.7	9.5	6.4	4.4	6.1	6.2	-1.3	4.8
Light a)	11.3	3.3	5.9	10.4	5.4	7.2	6.5	-4.2	6.6	11.9	7.3	6.0	1.8	7.1	6.2	-2.8	8.4
Heavy b)	8.0	4.5	6.6	15.9	8.9	8.2	6.4	-3.0	9.3	14.4	12.0	6.9	11.4	6.3	13.0	3.8	2.4

Source: Junta, Informe de Evaluacion 1976, Jun/di 248, Lima, 1977

1976-1979: Indicadores Socioeconomicos de la Subregion Andina, Jun/di 277/Rev. 3, abril 1980

Notes a and b, see notes a and b to Table 6.

Table 2.10.   Andean Group, Import Coefficient
of Industry 1960-1977

	Import Coefficient[a] Year	A	B	C	D	TOTAL
Bolivia	1960	0.365	0.490	0.810	0.810	0.545
	1967	0.369	0.538	0.849	0.759	0.588
	1970	0.288	0.473	0.791	0.714	0.538
	1977	0.513	0.751	0.861	–	0.729
Colombia	1960	0.046	0.254	0.570	0.130	0.246
	1967	0.019	0.210	0.470	0.123	0.176
	1970	0.018	0.233	0.503	0.159	0.192
	1977	0.056	0.274	0.359	–	0.182
Chile	1960	0.071	0.273	0.527	0.225	0.246
	1967	0.067	0.306	0.476	0.274	0.252
	1970	0.072	0.257	0.471	0.293	0.244
Ecuador	1960	0.063	0.520	0.956	0.498	0.330
	1967	0.056	0.439	0.935	0.324	0.296
	1970	0.065	0.482	0.911	0.278	0.349
	1977	0.126	0.481	0.782	–	0.426
Peru	1960	0.099	0.269	0.723	0.251	0.281
	1967	0.104	0.292	0.758	0.393	0.341
	1970	0.050	0.188	0.432	0.225	0.188
	1977	0.066	0.304	0.528	–	0.249
Venezuela	1960	0.129	0.328	0.777	0.496	0.343
	1967	0.048	0.297	0.625	0.209	0.223
	1970	0.042	0.258	0.608	0.352	0.246
	1977	0.190	0.406	0.591	–	0.391

Notes: a) Import coefficient: share of domestic demand supplied by imports = Imports/ (Production - Exports +
Imports).

A = Traditional Industries
B = Intermediate Industries
C = Light engineering
D = Others.

Source: 1960-1970, ECLA, El Proceso de Industrialización en
America Latina, Santiago, 1970.

1977   Nuestro Calculo en base a Junta, Indicadores Socio-económicos. Jun/di 277, Mayo
1981, cuadros No M7-M19 y Junta, Estadisticas de Comercio Exterior del Grupo
Andino 1969-1979. Jun/di 499, Lima, Sep.
1980, Cuadros 83-90.

Table 2.11. Andean Group, Population According to Annual Income Scales in 1968
(thousand inhabitants)

Scale	U.S. 1968 dollars	Bolivia		Chile		Colombia		Ecuador		Peru		Venezuela		Andean Group	
		Inhabitants	%	Inhabitants	%	Inhabitants	%	Inhabitants	%	Inhabitants	%	Inhabitants	%	Inhabitants	%
1	0-300	3,776	82.8	3,921	43.4	15,252	73.8	4,244	75.2	7,836	62.7	3,302	33.2	38,331	61.4
2	301-500	609	13.3	2,226	24.6	3,188	15.4	652	11.6	1,896	15.2	1,538	15.4	10,109	16.3
3	501-1000	125	2.7	1,954	21.6	1,647	8.0	596	10.6	2,100	16.8	3,190	32.0	9,612	15.5
4	1001-1500	46	1.2	483	5.3	306	1.5	92	1.6	322	2.5	1,034	10.4	2,283	3.6
5	1501-2000	1	-	145	1.6	229	1.1	49	1.0	90	0.9	493	4.9	1,007	1.6
6	2000 and more	-	-	302	3.5	45	0.2	8	-	246	1.9	405	4.1	1,006	1.6
TOTAL		4,557	100.0	9,031	100.0	20,667	100.0	5,641	100.0	12,490	100.0	9,962	100.0	62,348	100.0

Source: Junta, Grupo Andino: Estructura del Ingreso y su Capacidad de Compra, J/PR 70, April 1976.

84

Table 2.12. Andean Group, Rural Population (1968) According to Annual Income Scales (thousand inhabitants)

Scale	U.S. 1968 dollars	Bolivia		Colombia		Chile		Ecuador		Peru		Venezuela		Andean Group	
		Inhabitants	%	Inhabitants	%	Inhabitants	%	Inhabitants	%	Inhabitants	%	Inhabitants	%	Inhabitants	%
1	0-300	2,994	100.0	8,438	92.0	1,947	70.0	2,884	91.0	5,880	89.0	1,988	67.0	24,131	87.1
2	301-500	-	-	642	7.0	528	19.0	158	5.0	331	5.0	326	11.0	1,985	7.2
3	501-1000	-	-	92	1.0	185	6.7	127	4.0	396	6.0	594	20.0	1,394	5.0
4	1001-1500	-	-	-	-	121	4.3	-	-	-	-	59	2.0	180	0.7
5	1501-2000	-	-	-	-	-	-	-	-	-	-	-	-	-	-
6	2000 and more	-	-	-	-	-	-	-	-	-	-	-	-	-	-
TOTAL		2,994	100.0	9,172	100.0	2,781	100.0	3,169	100.0	6,607	100.0	2,967	100.0	27,690	100.0
Average rural income		72		148		374		183		189		389		202	
Average national income		206		310		597		308		426		800		466	

Source: Junta, La Población Andina y su Capacidad de compra, J/PR 70, April 1976.

Table 2.13. Andean Group, Internal Industrial Demand, 1970

Sector	Bolivia	Chile	Colombia	Ecuador	Peru	Venezuela	Total	Major Lafta Countries
Traditional industries	107.3	941.6	175.4	360.8	1064.3	638.9	3288.3	15,875.1
Intermediate industries	57.9	648.6	872.0	177.6	711.2	1173.9	3641.2	14,624.3
Light engineering industries	113.8	878.9	880.2	143.6	582.5	396.7	2995.7	18,329.8
Others	11.2	126.0	169.1	27.7	128.8	237.5	700.3	2,179.8
Total industrial demand	290.2	2595.1	2096.7	709.7	2486.8	2447.0	10625.5	51,009.0

Source: ECLA, El Proceso de Integración, la Sustitución de Importaciones en América Latina, Santiago, 1974, Anexo, p. 51.

Table 2.14. Andean Group, Terms of Trade, 1968–1978

Countries	1968	1969	1970	1971	1972	1973	1974	1975	1976[1]	1977[1]	1978[1]
Bolivia	100.0	105.2	128.1	96.2	89.2	84.2	135.8	111.0	114.2	120.9	123.1
Colombia	100.0	95.8	113.5	100.6	101.9	111.2	110.3	91.5	130.8	188.5	147.0
Chile	100.0	125.2	132.0	99.7	73.0	87.3	79.1	–	–	–	–
Ecuador	100.0	98.5	122.5	100.3	84.3	83.3	128.6	132.9	143.9	158.3	137.4
Peru	100.0	105.5	110.0	97.6	87.4	98.2	84.9	105.1	158.3	103.8	92.3
Venezuela	100.0	96.6	90.9	112.2	123.5	147.7	369.8	283.2	137.4	279.7	254.3

Note 1: Basis year 1970 = 100; Chile left the Group in 1976.

Source: 1968–1974 Junta, Departamento de Programación Global, Grupo Asesor UNDAT, La Subregión Andina, Lima 1976, Volume 1, page 32.

1975–1978 Estadísticas de Comercio Exterior de los Países del Grupo Andino 1969–1979. Jun/di 499, 9 de Septiembre de 1980.

Table 2.15. Andean Group, Comparative Analysis of the Development Strategies of the Andean Group Countries

	State Share of the Economy	Planning versus Market Forces	Sectoral Preference	Priority within the Treaty	Decision 24	External Credit	Exchange Rate	State Purchase	Industrial Policies
Colombia	Limited	Market forces	Neutral	Commercial program and application of harmonized instruments	Treaty of Sochagota[a] and value added criterion(b)	Restricted to certain activities	Planned moderate fluctuations	Elimination of exemptions	Very limited
Chile	Limited	Market forces	Neutral	Harmonized Application of instruments	Revision of basic points	Important	Accelerated planned fluctuations	Elimination of exemptions	Very limited to nonfulfillment
Bolivia	Rising	Planning	Industry	Sectoral programming	Treaty of Sochagota[a]	Important	Fixed	Free of duties	Not applied
Ecuador	Rising	Planning	Industry	Sectoral programming	Treaty of Sochagota[a]	Quite important	Fixed	Free of duties	Full import substitution
Peru	Rising	Planning	Industry	Sectoral programming	Treaty of Sochagota[a]	Important	Fixed	Free of duties	Full import substitution
Venezuela	Rising	Planning	Industry	Sectoral programming	Treaty of Sochagota[a]	Little importance	Fixed	Free of duties	Full import substitution

Notes: (a) A treaty signed in 1976 in Colombia, by which Decision 24 was reformed.

(b) It uses value added and contribution to GDP to establish the national or foreign character of capital.

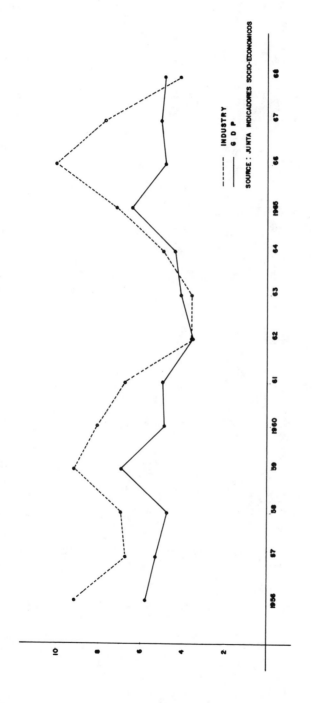

Graph 2.1 ANDEAN GROUP: Annual Growth Rates of GDP, Global and Industrial 1956-1968.

Source: Junta Indicadores Socio-economicos.

89

PART II
PROGRESS

CHAPTER 3
THE COMMERCIAL PROGRAM

This chapter will study the dynamic effects that can result from economic integration. We will study the significance of the enlarged market in regard to the expansion of trade in new and more sophisticated products, and the promotion of new investment. We will also measure how far the commercial preferences that were established were sufficient to arrest the effects of regional concentration coming from more liberal trade relations.

From the extensive literature produced by the Junta, it can be seen that the program for freeing trade is not viewed as the most important element in the process of integration. On the contrary, because the program tends to concentrate economic activity as between countries, it is presented as a generator of contradictions, which in the long term could reverse integration.

In the early stages, and in the interpretation given by the Junta, the potential conflict between free trade and the planning of industrial production was resolved in favor of the latter, to be complemented by measures to harmonize policies. The freeing of trade was relegated to second place because the increase and rationalization of production through market forces could bring with it undesirable effects such as geographical concentration, overlapping investments, the loss of advantages of scale, and the inefficient use of productive resources. The formula for integration for the Andean countries should be one that

> makes development feasible and which needs more complex tools than the freeing of markets. These methods would be deliberately designed to compensate for effects of concentration. In general, they would have a more profound and rapid effect in overcoming the timidity of investors, for example.(1)

It seems that those who drafted the text of the Treaty (who were later elected as members of the first Junta) envisaged a planned industrial development that would create a web of interdependencies. These would oblige countries to stay in the GRAN. It was only the practical difficulty of planning the whole production system that led to the commercial and agricultural programs.

> In any case, it is obvious that this instrument [freeing trade] was set up in the Agreement in the face of the impracticality of making the whole productive system submit to a plan.(2)

In fact, the limiting of the scope of the commercial program, and the reduction of the level of competition, seem to be a compromise with the policies of restriction and control of the market to which the countries subscribed before the Agreement. The result is that potential increases in trade did not occur, increases that could have interested already established industries, in particular those trying to move from a protected substitution stage to a more efficient exporting activity, thereby eliminating inefficient industries.

The commercial program, as we have described it in Chapter 1, contains the following lists: list of products to be subject to immediate and total elimination of duties; lists of those subject to automatic reductions; lists of products reserved for the sectorial programs; list of "exceptions" and list of goods not produced in the group.(3) The details of products of the whole customs union are set out according to their respective lists in table 3.1. This table corroborates our preceding statement as to the limitations imposed upon the commercial program. Suffice it to say that 37 percent of items were reserved for the SIDPs and were therefore outside the scope of the free-trade program. The list of exceptions included 39 percent of the products included in the customs tariff and about 60 percent of the goods on the trade lists.

THE EFFECTS OF THE COMMERCIAL PROGRAM ON A PROCESS OF INTEGRATION AMONG UNDERDEVELOPED COUNTRIES: GENERAL CONSIDERATIONS

According to the classical theory of economic integration, countries which subscribe to a scheme for integration hope for two types of effects:

A. Static effects: that is, losses or gains coming from short-term marginal changes in production and consumption caused by the reduction in tariffs. They include:

- production effects, from intercountry substitution of trade (divided into trade creation and trade diversion)
- consumption effects or intercommodity substitution due to changes in relative prices
- the terms of trade effect

B. Dynamic effects: that is, the various methods by which integration can affect the rate of growth of participating countries and can generate new economic enterprises at a higher level of efficiency. It is hoped that, over a long period, these effects will bring increases in growth throughout the region, increases accompanied by a more efficient allocation of resources, over and above the reallocation of what already exists, which is the aspect dealt with under static effects. The dynamic effects, which overlap each other to some extent, include:

- a widening of demand that will allow a better use of productive resources, especially by taking advantage of economies of scale and externalities in existing plants - this would mean a reduction in costs
- effects on the size and siting of new investments
- polarization effects, that is, the tendency to worsen both the relative and the absolute economic position of the lesser developed member countries or areas
- effects upon economic efficiency coming from changes in the degree of competition and of uncertainty

Static Effects

The international theory of economic integration, developed for the European case, concentrates its analysis on the effects on welfare. In spite of the important contribution made by Meade, Johnson, Lipsey, and Scitovsky, this theory continues to consider economic integration as consistent with the theory of international trade, and as a branch of the science of tariffs. It measures marginal adjustments in production and consumption caused by geographically discriminatory tariff changes, leaving aside problems of economic development.(4) Viner, for example, confined his analysis to production effects only, assuming demand curves of zero elasticity and supply curves of infinite elasticity.

How significant are the static effects in the Andean case? When one is dealing with the integration of underdeveloped countries, the production effects have limited importance. It is even debatable whether or not one can use the typical European distinction between the creation and diversion of trade. These limitations arise because of the following reasons.

1. The alternative to integration (integration constitutes the diversion of trade to regional producers) is to divert trade to national producers who are probably less efficient than regional producers would be, because they have been limited in practice to the national market and have already started the industrialization process protected by high tariffs. In contrast, economic integration, by extending markets, allows companies to lower their production costs over a shorter period. In the absence of an integration policy the rate of growth of domestic demand is low and does not allow a great reduction in production costs in the short term. This is most evident in the case of consumer durables. Economic integration will make the process of trade diversion more efficient in terms of reducing real costs over a shorter period.(5) In other words, the only way to make sense of the trade diversion effects is to consider them in dynamic terms. The dynamic trade-creating comes from the increase in income in the integrated area and through the foreign trade multiplier.

However one looks at it, a productive structure based upon regional specialization seems likely to be more efficient than one directed toward national markets alone. Although the optimum relationship will not be achieved between the price of regionally produced goods and those that would be imported under total free trade, the integrated area will tend toward a "second best optimum," because patterns of prices and production will be improved by regional specialization.

ii. If the diversion of trade means that the labor force is moved to more productive activities, it will produce increases in welfare. This is left out of account in the static analysis. This point is even more important if there is under- or unemployment. In the case of countries with an excess supply of labor, economic calculations ought to balance the loss of economic efficiency, which may come from diversion of trade, against the increase in the net social product, coming from the use of more labor or from more productive employment.(6)

iii. The effect of setting up a customs union between underdeveloped countries is, in the long run, to increase rather than decrease their trade with the outside world. This is because, first, by stimulating the regional economy, more capital goods will need to be imported from outside the group. Second, the group will import industrial goods which before were only marginal to international trade.(7) So the short-run horizon of the static analysis is again inappropriate.

iv. Also, the effects on the terms of trade of the region vis-à-vis the rest of the world are not important because these countries are not major buyers on the world market of those goods that will be the subject of intraregional trade. Changes in the terms of trade within the region are more important. The relatively less developed countries within the region will export goods and manufactures at high prices.

Precisely because of this imbalance within the region
many of the least developed parts of the region have
not looked with favor either upon trade creation at
the expense of their limited manufactures or upon
more costly import substitution.(8)

v. Estimates of the "before and after" effects of trade
creation and diversion (in terms of growth of GNP based on
elasticities of supply and demand of the goods given preference by tariff costs, and taking account of the substitution
of former suppliers) conclude that for EFTA and EEC countries
there is little direct quantitative effect from trade. Benefits
as measured in terms of GNP and of other welfare measure-
ments of a customs union yield an even more pessimistic
picture of the EEC and EFTA performances: according to Johnson, for EEC countries the benefits represent 0.05 percent.
Updating the 1967 calculations, Balassa corroborated this
conclusion in 1974, saying that trade creation meant an increase in GNP of 0.09 percent. As Scitovsky suggests, to
continue with the basic approach of quantitative results would
lead to limited conclusions.(9) He thinks that studies will
have to be orientated toward the ways in which customs unions
affect productive efficiency in terms of economies of scale,
increased competition, and widening of markets. (Table 3.2
presents some of the results of different empirical studies on
the production effects of various integration schemes.)

Dynamic Effects

Given that the basic objective of economic integration among
underdeveloped countries is to accelerate economic growth, the
medium- and long-term contribution of the commercial program
to this process has to be analyzed.(10)

In the case of the GRAN the overall objective will be
achieved through the joint action of trade policy, SIDPs, and
the CET. The last two elements, especially sectoral planning,
bear the major responsibility for increasing the growth rate,
because the final goal cannot be gained automatically by
freeing trade. It is considered necessary to affect the
productive sector in order to change the composition and
volume of investments.

By setting out on a course of integration, a country does
not depart from a situation of general equilibrium nor from
worldwide free trade. In fact there are tendencies which
suggest that the world in general is moving toward greater
distortions in price structures. Less developed countries have
industrialized and developed production at the expense of
specialization. Therefore they attempt to change it by using

integration to increase the volume of trade in manufactures.
The result will be long-term movements in the volume and
structure of trade and investment. This is the most important
relationship between trade and economic development.(11) By
freeing trade, certain intermediate and final consumption goods
can be traded within the subregion, thus freeing hard currencies for importing capital goods from outside.

In general terms, economic development is a function of
capital formation; the supply of capital and capital goods are
the determinants. The rate of capital formation is affected by
(i) the capacity to import, (ii) the possibility of either
substituting imported consumption and capital goods or of
expanding exports, and (iii) by the flow of internal savings.
This is where the trade program is important in the long term
- in expanding the rate of capital formation.(12) Therefore
the trade effect is more than just one that acts on the trade
balance; it encompasses the expansion of the manufacturing
sector and it can stimulate a change of attitude in foreign and
national investors. Therefore, permanent effects can only be
expected in the long term, because disequilibrium in the
external sector is of a structural nature in the sense that
underemployment and the underutilization of resources combine
with external deficits. These bring about the introduction of
controls and other trade restrictions.

To sum up, when one analyzes the effects of wider trade
potential, attention should be concentrated on the expansion of
the availability of foreign exchange to finance growth of GNP
and on its effects on income and demand. These positive
effects may occur even when the net effect is trade diversion.
The question that arises is whether or not the new flow of
trade will be sufficient to increase and maximize the supply of
capital equipment in such a way that dynamic effects may come
into force. In other words, will greater rates of investment
and growth be achieved? Studies made of LAFTA conclude
that the net expansion of trade is slight and that the probable
effects on the rates of growth of GNP are reduced by the
limited ability of the respective systems to react in the short
term.(13) Studies of the Central American Common Market
(CACM) arrive at the same conclusions, in spite of the fact
that increases in reciprocal trade have been very high.(14)

EVALUATION OF SUBREGIONAL TRADE, 1969-75

Having made these general observations on the significance of
the trade effects, we will move on to analyze the results of the
commercial program, referring to the majority of the dynamic
effects listed under item B at the beginning of section 1. It

has to be noted, however, that the results obtained up to 1975 do not represent the full potential of the market, since the trade program is only partially operating. The automatic tariff reductions should be completed in 1980; Bolivia and Ecuador have not opened up their markets and all the countries make full use of their lists of exceptions.

The dynamic effects to be studied are as follows.

i.   The increase in demand for manufactures measured in terms of the total expansion of trade, and the extent to which it leads to a better utilization of productive resources, to economies of scale for those plants producing below their capacity, to economies gained from externalities, to fuller use of human resources; the way in which these induce greater growth by increasing employment, per capita income, and so on, and effects upon efficiency which come from the increase in the level of competition and the reduction of uncertainties

ii.   The effects upon the volume and placing of new investments, especially in those enterprises for which the national markets are insufficient

iii. The results of the tendency toward polarization, that is, the worsening of the relative position of the lesser developed member countries.

The study and measurement of these dynamic effects are possible thanks to the way in which lists were prepared, permitting us, for example, to ascertain the level of trade in those goods that were not produced before the agreement was signed, those that do or do not enjoy tariff reductions, or those that come from Ecuador and Bolivia with or without the benefit of the freeing of trade.

The Increase in Demand

Before analyzing the growth of trade, it is worth making some general comments on the global external trade of the subregion. The period under consideration (1968-1979) was one of rapid growth in external trade, stimulated by the rise in prices of the member countries' exports, especially after 1972-75. In spite of the increase in imports, reserves were accumulated and the balance of payments improved. In tables 3.3 and 3.4 we can see the rates of growth of imports and exports.(15) At this point, attention should be drawn to two factors. First, over the period 1965-1979, the petroleum-exporting countries have experienced much greater rates of growth than other countries. Second, these countries have accounted for a greater share of external trade. For example, Venezuela exported 50 percent of the group's total.

Within this context, the share of intrasubregional trade in the total exports has increased from 4 percent of total imports in 1969 to 6 percent in 1975, but decreased to 3.7 percent in 1979. The share of exports grew from 4 percent to 5 percent in the same period. It is interesting to see that over a longer period (1948 to 1968, see table 3.5) there has been a weakening of commercial links. This can obviously be explained by the import substitution policies applied the last two decades and by the return to trading with the United States and Europe after the interruption of the Second World War. This tendency was reversed after 1969 when the GRAN was set up. The change in the relative weight of international trade is more important when analyzed at individual country level. Ecuador and Colombia are the largest exporters, and Peru the larger importer (until 1976 when Chile left the GRAN Chile was the largest importer).

In terms of dollars at current values, intrasubregional exports increased during the period by 29 percent per annum (from US$171 million to US$880 million). However, using the figures in footnote 15 page 302, the increase in real terms reached an annual rate of 12 percent. Bolivia and Ecuador were the two countries that most notably increased their exports to the GRAN, because of the rise in their petroleum sales.

It is important to illustrate that no important change has taken place in the geographical distribution of intrasubregional trade. The destination of exports of the 1975 trade matrix is the same as in 1969. The increase in transactions has come through the intensification of sales between countries which have always traded (usually those countries with common borders). Trade flows between, for example, Bolivia and Colombia, Bolivia and Venezuela, Venezuela and Ecuador are still very limited.

About 35 percent of the subregional sales in 1975 were fuels and another 15 percent was accounted for by meat and sugar. If these items are excluded, the rate of growth in trade decreases but it has a more consistent character, because the huge increase of 1974 was due to purchases of petroleum. In 1978, oil, refined oil, and other by-products represented 26 percent of the total. Trade in manufactures in 1975 represented about 30 percent of the total, an amount which tends to increase, reaching 57 percent in 1978.

Table 3.6 shows the rate of growth of reciprocal exports and its composition (agricultural, mineral, or industrial). Within these three groups, products that were traded for the first time after the Treaty was signed have been considered as new (though they may have been produced before). The result is that increases in trade have occurred in both new agricultural and new mining products. The growth rate of industrial exports is lower. Bolivia and Ecuador are exporters of primary products. This tendency changed in 1975-78 when the rate of industrial exports exceeded that of oil exports. By 1975, as can be seen in table 3.8, Peru had fallen back as an exporter of manufactures, perhaps because of the problems caused by its overvalued currency.(16) Between 1975-78, it became the most dynamic exporting member country, perhaps due to its new exchange policy.

In this section, we conclude that during the period 1969 to 1978 there was a great expansion of subregional trade (44.3 percent annual growth rate from 1969 to 1975),(17) which meant that each country's exports to the subregion came to represent a larger proportion of their total sales. New agricultural and mining exports grew faster than industrial exports (128.2 %, 127.2 %, and 68.7 %, respectively).

However, in spite of the accelerated growth of manufactured exports, more than 65 percent of trade within the group is made up of agricultural and mineral products. The leading exporters of manufactures are Colombia, Chile, and Peru, but Chile and Colombia alone controlled 62.1 percent of the total (see tables 3.7 and 3.8).

Having established that intrasubregional exports expanded rapidly, we will move on to determine how far that growth can be explained by the different systems of reducing commercial barriers and to what degree it results from factors other than those created by the Agreement.

In the first place, we will try to discover how far markets have been stimulated by tariff reduction programs, to what degree exports are really elastic to these stimuli, and how far they have produced real increases in competition between member countries. We will exclude those products that have demand curves which are relatively inelastic to the type of tariff stimuli given in the Agreement that already represented important traded commodities. In general, the group has a comparative advantage which allows them to sell such goods on the world market. Such products include sugar, meat, and oil. We have also excluded products included in the common list of LAFTA because they already had tariff preferences, and goods on the lists of exceptions are not included because they have no tariff reduction (when it is a question of exports to Colombia, Chile, Peru, and Venezuela). Neither will goods reserved for the SIDPs be considered, nor exports to Bolivia and Ecuador because they are not subject to the process of tariff reduction. We are left with trade in goods on the automatic reduction list; the list of trade which creates openings for Bolivia and Ecuador; the list of goods not produced in the group, and the list of the metallurgical and petrochemical sectors (because after the approval of the respective sectoral plans, a separate process of tariff reduction was set in motion for each one). The results shown in table 3.10 and 3.11* suggest the following conclusions:

i. That trade included in the list of automatic reduction of tariffs (line 1A, table 3.9 and 3.10) which was the principal list of the commercial program, with a 50 percent tariff reduction until 1975, increased by 28.9 percent; this growth was smaller than the change in total trade, which rose by 44.3 percent, (or 29 % if Venezuela is included in 1969). Trade under that list fell from 16.6 percent of the total trade in 1969 to 8.4 percent in 1975. The participation of the exports benefited by the automatic reduction of tariffs (a reduction of 50 % until 1975), decreased from 16.6 percent of the total in 1969 to 8.4 percent in 1975. Between 1976 and 1978 this tendency was reversed, a more accelerated growth can be seen and the participation reached in 1969 was recovered by 1978.

It seems that the full potential of this mechanism has been reduced by the number of products on this list which have been included on lists of exceptions, the latter growing at an annual rate of 46.3 percent (line 2A, table 3.11). This rather extensive use of the exceptions was a result of the following elements: First, Andean industrial structures are currently relatively self-sufficient in consumer goods. Second, preintegration tariffs were high and dispersed(18) and a diffuse system of nontariff barriers was used (as we will see in Chapter 6). And third, prices for similar goods vary by as much as 100 percent from one country to another.(19)

ii. The list of goods where immediate elimination of tariffs were made in favor of Bolivia and Ecuador (line 3, table 3.10 and 3.11) is the most dynamic; trade in these, rising over the period by 115.2 percent. However, the weight of this section is still comparatively slight. (It rose from 0.3% in 1969 to 3.7% of total exports in 1975 and to 8.5% in 1976.) As we shall see later, the acceleration of these exports has not compensated for the concentration effects coming from the relatively low level of development of this trade. Comparing lines 3 and 8 in table 3.10 we see the imbalance in trade suffered by Bolivia and Ecuador. To study 1976-78, compare lines 3 and 9 in table 3.11.

iii. With regard to the lists of goods not produced and that of goods not produced but reserved for Bolivia and Ecuador (line 6, tariff reduced to zero), trade has only reached 0.01 percent of total intraregional trade in 1975 and 1.3 percent in 1978.

---

*Table 3.11 has a different presentation due to the changes in the Junta's report. The differences in the lists in 1976 can be explained by a decrease in oil sales and the absence of Chile.

iv) Metallurgical program (line 7, table 3.10 tariff reduced to zero): by 1975, hardly any exports had been registered because the program was only agreed to in 1972. The small amount of trade(20) which took place came almost totally from Colombia in goods already being produced before the signing of the program. By 1975, exports rose to US$7 million similar to that of 1978 (see table 3.10). In contrast, products reserved for SIDPs not approved so far were traded without any reduction. In line 5 table 3.9 and 3.10, we see that the annual growth rate of their exports was 57.2 percent and in 1975 it represented 7.9 percent of total trade. During 1976-78 the rate of growth of exports of products reserved to SIDP not approved was again superior to the rate of total exports; consequently participation increased.

To summarize, trade covered by tariff reduction programs of the Treaty (table 3.9 lines 1A, 3, 6, 7) fell in proportion to total trade. The rate of growth for the preferred goods was 38.2 percent per annum over the period despite the greater tariff reductions (60%), while the total increased at 23.9 percent per annum. In 1976-78, this rate was higher than the increase in total trade and lower than that of the products without tariff reductions (see the final lines of table 3.10). However, the effect of the program was even weaker than this suggests, for not all the growth of trade in these goods can be attributed to tariff reduction. All countries have schemes for promoting exports of manufactures to third parties as well as to the GRAN. According to industrialists, it is these measures that are decisive for the success of export activity.

Studies made of Colombian manufactured exports show that they are relatively inelastic to tariff reductions because the rate of growth of sales of goods covered by the program and going to the GRAN is no higher than that of the same products going outside the group.(21) This conclusion is supported by a study carried out by the Junta on the performance of manufactured exports. Starting from the nominal margins of preference for goods that have tariff reductions, it calculated the coefficient of the Spearman correlation and the volume of exports. The results show that only in the case of Bolivia is there any significant positive correlation between the two variables (0.74). It is nonsignificant in the case of Colombia (0.16), Peru (-0.074) and Ecuador (-0.54).(22) This evidence leads one to think that other types of incentive are influencing more strongly the performance of manufactured exports.

The following figures show the rates of growth of Colombian exports of goods subject to tariff reductions, before and after the initiation of the policy. They confirm our earlier conclusion that this part of trade has not been the most dynamic and that they are relatively inelastic to tariff reductions.

Growth of Colombian Exports (Subject to Reduced Tariffs) to the Andean Group (% of annual growth rates)

	Before GRAN 1968-70	After GRAN 1971-76	Average
Bolivia	35.86	39.86	39.29
Chile	146.81	42.76	57.63
Ecuador	30.75	16.10	18.19
Peru	130.64	-6.52	13.06
Venezuela	58.01	60.94	58.85

Source: Calculated from Fedesarrollo, "El Comercio Exterior de Colombia en el Marco del Acuerdo de Cartagena, 1969-1978," mimeo., Bogota, May 1978.

If we turn to look at the reasons for these limited results, interviews with industrialists held by the author in 1975 suggest that the great majority considered that the tariff reductions were not sufficient incentives to stimulate trade within the group. This conclusion is clearly supported by an inquiry made by the Junta covering the six countries. Of 110 companies exporting to the GRAN, only 12 said that tariff reductions represented a real incentive. For the rest, foreign exchange, fiscal, credit, and administrative methods were more decisive.[23]

The explanation may lie in the lack of interest in the Andean market due to the failure to fulfill the agreements,[24] and perhaps in the fact that the subsidies and the rate of exchange favor all exports to all countries without discrimination, making it possible to export to third countries as well as to the Andean Group. Another reason suggested by industrialists, is that the majority of tariff reductions have been absorbed by importers, who in the case of final consumer goods are not producers.

Detailed studies of Colombian exports analyzing elasticities of goods in relation to different promotion policies for the period 1958-68 indicate the following conclusions:

i. They are highly sensitive to the effective rate of exchange. The elasticity of the value of manufactured exports with respect to the real rate of exchange is 2.43 at the time of a change, and 1.82 a year after the change.[25]

ii. Another element that promotes exports is the Plan Vallejo, which includes drawback and certificated tax bond systems. These two elements notably increase the profitability of exporting, changing the sign of effective protection granted to various sectors.[26]

Apart from the relatively higher elasticity of exports with regard to the exchange rate and to other stimuli than to tariffs, there are other reasons explaining the limited achievements of the freeing of trade within the Andean Group. Obviously these vary from country to country, but in general, they are as follows:

i. The careful construction of reserved and exempted lists, which has the effect of slowing or obstructing the opening of markets and of retaining opportunities for later negotiation. About 50 percent of the 5,800 items in the customs tariff appear on at least one list of exceptions, if not more. Many, but not all, of those included, are goods efficiently produced and having real potential for export even after the payment of the full tariff. In some cases, all countries include the same goods in their lists, evidently for fear of competition. From line 2A of table 3.9 it can be seen that important trade is carried on in exempted goods, the annual growth rate being 46.3 percent. Therefore, restriction of tariff reductions was not out of fear of disruptions, but to contain competition, with a resulting decrease of the potential gains from trade creation.

ii. The inefficient application of agreements on tariff reductions, especially of automatic reduction lists. In effect, only one country complied with the starting date for the PID. The first four tariff reductions, each of 10 percent, were applied up to 15 months late. In 1980, there was an equally serious example of nonfulfillment regarding the restrictions on trade defined in Article 42 of the Agreement as expressed in the "Cumplimiento de los compromisos," (Jun/Di 478, Jun 1980). In most cases, these restrictions arise from balance-of-payments problems, protection of national industries, the demand for export finance, or from bureaucratic procedures which delay the granting of import licenses.(27) They may take the straightforward form of rules which discriminate against subregional production.(28) The lack of fulfillment in these areas has strengthened the skepticism of entrepreneurs. They feel justified in remaining passive vis-à-vis the new market conditions. Manufactured exports are marginal to production and in many cases are not permanent,(29) a fact which in some part explains why the 100 percent tariff reductions for some products made on February 28, 1971 have not brought any new investment.(30)

iii. The lack of a clear definition of export promotion policies to the subregion. Those that exist stimulate exports in general and tend to strengthen the traditional links with the markets of the United States and Europe.

iv. The lack of stimulus given to exports of products needing higher levels of processing, especially intermediate and capital goods. The low efficiency of the group's production and the lack of confidence demonstrated by the subregion's buyers make imports from outside preferable even when the full duty has to be paid.(31)

v. The conflict of the free trade policy with national policies, sometimes in the short run and sometimes in the long term. An example of short-term problems is the Chilean balance-of-payments situation. The Popular Unity government resorted to a very complex system of multiple exchange rates, advance deposits, allocation of foreign currency by quotas, and so on, which administratively limited the effects of tariff cuts upon demand for imports. Under the present administration, between 1975 and 1976, the periodic devaluations ahead of the rate of inflation made imports from the subregion unable to compete with national production, especially manufactures. For an example of long-term conflicts, one can look at Peru. Because of its rigid exchange system, it was a net importer. Between 1969 and 1974, while imports rose by 46 percent, exports could only manage a rise of 34 percent. Under the heading of luxury articles alone, it imports US$1.5 million in one year from Colombia, which contradicts its policy of restructuring consumption patterns.

vi. The conservative attitude of industrialists, who prefer to remain within the framework of protectionism and to export surplus production only.(32)

In conclusion, then, we may say that the increase of 12.6 percent in intraregional trade attributable to the free trade program, is not very substantial, considering the circumstances and the structure of the Treaty. The result is limited if compared with the achievements between EEC and EFTA countries.

The explanation for the lack of dynamism of the market may be found in the inclination of the countries in question to avoid a real increase in competition by exempting products from the process of tariff reduction, by applying different administrative restrictions to intraregional imports, or by delaying the fulfillment of the agreement. The result is obviously a reduction in the scope of increased competition, which means a weakening in the trade creation effect and in the possibilities of reallocation of resources via industrial specialization, both intraindustry and interindustry.

We conclude that the potential increase in demand was prevented by the action of governments and industrialists, which made it difficult if not impossible to achieve the full functioning of the free trade program and the realization of positive dynamic effects derived from trade, as we will see in the next section.

The Increase in Demand and the
Use of Productive Resources

Accepting that the impact of the free trade program has been
very limited in terms of trade, we shall now try to discover
the effects of the policy on the use of productive resources.
In this section no distinction will be made between manufactured exports that do or do not enjoy tariff reductions and
those going to GRAN countries or outside the area.   This
methodology has been adopted because, as we have shown, the
proportion of exports with lowered tariffs going to member
countries is small, and diminished in the period analyzed.
Intraregional trade of manufactures is a relatively small part of
the total(33) and in general the member countries export the
same or similar products to the rest of the world.   Therefore,
it would be very difficult to isolate the effects of freed
exports to the GRAN on one sector or company when those
same productive units are exporting goods with and without
reductions to the group and to third parties.   On the other
hand, all exports benefit from the indirect effects of the
establishment of the Treaty and from national policies promoting manufactured exports.

If the impact of total manufactured exports on the use of
productive resources is considerable, we must necessarily
resolve the problem of isolating the effect attributable to the
integration mechanism.   If on the contrary effects turn out not
to be important we can avoid such complications and extend
the conclusion drawn from the analysis of total trade to the
impact of trade resulting from integration.   We shall show that
the latter is in fact the position.

We will analyze in more detail the Colombian case, because
it is the country with the longest experience in manufactured
export promotion policies and because its performance in this
area is remarkable among the Andean countries.   In 1975 Colombian manufactured exports to third countries represented 30
percent of the total of such products exported from Andean
countries, and about 50 percent of the intraregional exports of
manufactures were Colombian made.   A second element is the
availability of more detailed data on Colombia.   But, even
given the success of Colombian exports, the effects on growth
will still be shown to be extremely limited; therefore we are
able to argue that our conclusions are equally valid for the
other member countries.

The hypotheses that this section will try to verify refer
to the limited effect that the promotion of manufactured
exports has had on the movements of indicators such as the
export coefficient of industrial production, the use of economies of scale, the greater use of installed capacity, the
generation of industrial employment, and income distribution.

Methodological difficulties cannot be escaped when analyzing the effect of export promotion policies on total employment
and income distribution. We would need far more detailed data
than we have on the demand for direct and indirect inputs for
natural   resources,   skilled   and   unskilled   labor,   imported
machinery, equipment, and other capital goods in order to
establish accurately the links between the marginal productivity of exports and agricultural and manufacturing production.
Data at this level do not exist in the Andean region.   Apart
from this, the demand for productive factors varies according
to company size,(34) in such a way that the results would be
altered according to the degree of exports in large firms.
They would also change according to the degree of connection
with foreign capital.   The question of causality is therefore
also extremely problematic.

i.   Exports and the Volume of Production

The increase in manufactured exports has brought about no
great change since 1950 in the relationship between the gross
value of industrial production and of total exports. Table 3.11
shows that in 1975 there were only two cases in which total
manufactured exports rose above 15 percent of the value of
output: Colombia and, especially, Chile.   Only a small proportion of these exports went to member countries: 2.8 percent
from Chile and 1.4 percent from Colombia.(35)

ii.   Manufactured Exports and the Use of Capacity

Many of the arguments in favor of economic integration of
underdeveloped countries center on the possible advantages
that can be gained from economies of scale, that is, the
reduction in input coefficients that results from an increase in
the size of the market.   Such savings can take the form of
internal and external economies.   They can be related to the
intensification of competition, lessened uncertainty and the
reallocation of investment funds.(36)   In order to obtain these
economies, producers of one country have to expand their
markets by selling in member countries, thus displacing national producers or imports from third parties.   It is held
that, in most integration experiences, advantage has not been
taken of economies of scale if replacement of previous suppliers
at a lower price level does not come about, even though there
may have been a large amount of trade in certain products.(37)   In general, it is accepted that the smaller the
integrating nations and the lower the transport costs between
them, the larger is the scope for obtaining economies of
scale.(38)   However, other authors are more skeptical of the
possibility of achieving economies of scale under schemes for
integrating countries like those of the Andean group which

have a very limited market even after becoming integrated.(39)
Their level of development is low and uneven and intraregional
trade in manufactures is still very limited, as we saw in the
previous section.(40)

Even accepting that for many products there are flat
production curves, less developed countries tend to operate at
the extreme left end of the scale where costs decline significantly because of capital charges.   In these cases, integration
can reduce production costs.   However, the economies tend to
be marginal and come mainly from the use of underemployed
installed capacity and not through the relocation of resources
as a consequence of greater competition.

In this section we shall deal with the greater use of
capacity already in production.   The case of new investments
will be analyzed in Chapter 7 dealing with the SIDPs.(41)

Table 3.12 shows the impact of manufactured exports on
the use of installed capacity in Colombia.(42)   For this we
have used the results of the Fedesarrollo report on manufacturing which covers ISIC sectors 31 to 39.(43)   As we can
see, there is no direct relationship between the growth of
exports in real terms and the trend in the use of installed
capacity.   Apparently there is a short-term link between
internal demand, exports, and employed capacity.   Exports
reduce the negative effect of falls in internal demand in
1973-75, and vice versa in 1974-75.   But there is no evidence
of a positive long-term trend.   The great increase in exports
in real terms in 1975-76 made utilization of capacity rise by 33
percent, but this was well below the levels of 1972.   In
1976-77 internal sales and not exports explain the improvement
in the index of utilization of installed capacity.(44)   In fact,
to assume that there is a clearly defined relationship between
the use of installed capacity and demand would be to cover up
those structural and institutional relationships that contribute
to explaining the installation of excess capacity.   These
structural problems are long term and trade policies only affect
them indirectly.   Stop-go cycles linked to foreign exchange
bottlenecks affect attitudes toward building up stocks or
machinery.   In 1972 a detailed study was undertaken in Colombia of 290 industrial firms which sought to establish what
were the variables determining the use made of industrial
capacity.   It concluded that demand was the most important
factor only in the cases of tobacco, petroleum, and basic
metals.   In that year, the main problems for other industries
were obtaining primary materials, financing, and availability of
labor.(45)   Therefore, it seems that the level of utilization is a
long-term decision (industrialists prefer to lose sales rather
than increase employment or start night shifts).   In such
circumstances a demand-pull strategy would not be completely
successful, because it does not take account of the fact that
many companies only work a single shift in the long term.

The well-known Rosenthal Report on the CACM concluded that
the utilization of installed capacity, far from improving,
actually worsened, in spite of the large increase in the market
and the total elimination of internal tariffs. The relationship
of installed capacity to internal demand remains at 1.5 percent.(46)

iii. Manufactured Exports and Employment

In accordance with the "vent for surplus" theory, we can hope
that the opening of the economy as a consequence of integration will increase the demand for labor, which is in the
case of the Andean countries a surplus resource. However,
there are circumstances that impede the channeling of this
surplus into export activities, circumstances such as the
reluctance of the countries to accept greater competition in
labor-intensive sectors. This tendency is also apparent in
developed countries in their trading relations with underdeveloped countries. Another obstacle is that, in those sectors,the
firms able to compete in external markets are those using
highly technical processes. These sectors are usually the ones
that have the highest margins of underutilization of their
machinery and can export at prices below marginal cost.
       Although it is difficult to establish the relationship
between manufactured exports and total employment, the link
is clear between the former and employment in manufacturing
industry. Over the long term, we would hope to see that
export activities changed the ratio between the economically
active population (EAP) and industrial employment. A decrease in that ratio can be considered as a gain in terms of
GDP because it is assumed that it would shift the un- or
underemployed in less productive sectors to industry. Obviously this is a very clumsy measure, because not all industrial
activities are necessarily more productive, nor is each sector
homogeneous. But, under conditions of extreme unemployment
and surplus labor, as in the case of the GRAN, it is surely
legitimate to assume that to accelerate the absorption of
manpower by industry means an increase in productivity for
the economy as a whole.
       As a basis for analysis we shall use the data in table
3.13. Between 1960 and 1969, manufacturing industry absorbed 7.7 percent of the increase in the EAP of the subregion. This rose to 10 percent from 1970 to 1974. The rate of
growth of industrial employment was 3.3 percent per annum
but decreased to 2.3 percent in 1970 to 1974. The weight of
industrial employment in the total of the EAP has remained
fairly constant: 5.0 percent in 1960 and 5.7 percent in 1974.
The gross value of manufacturing output grew by 5.5 percent
for the whole region, while employment generation only rose by
2.3 percent. The difference in these two rates proves that

growth in industrial production was achieved fundamentally by greater productivity.

Linder's hypothesis that underdeveloped countries export those manufactured goods which they produce in a well-protected national market(47) seems to be borne out by the tendency to reciprocal trade for refrigerators, washing machines, medicines, and relatively sophisticated chemical products in the GRAN. But they sell to the developed countries the largest part of the total exports of manufactured goods. So, we can find here new arguments for the theoretical discussions between Linder and F. Stewart. The demand for productive factors which this type of export generates does not change the internal cost pattern substantially, that is, the demand for skilled labor and capital-intensive processes.(48) This result is intensified when export promotion brings about a freeing of import restrictions on machinery and equipment. This can be taken advantage of even by small and medium companies which under stricter commercial conditions cannot afford the high import prices of capital goods. In other words, the reciprocal trade intensifies technological dependency rather than weakening it.

As with import substitution, it seems that growth of manufactured exports in fact puts pressure on scarce factors: skilled labor, entrepreneurial and professional skills, and capital, all of which are used in place of labor.(49)

iv. Effect of Manufactured Exports on Income Distribution

The effect of the increase in exports upon income distribution is a result of a combination of policies directed at promoting those exports and depends upon the nature of those policies. Thus, ad hoc incentives (according to type of activity or company) can, for example, have more pronounced concentration effects than general incentives. Fiscal and credit promotion measures tend to have a different distributive effect: they lead to more concentration than does the rate of exchange.(50) The effect varies according to the source of the revenue used to subsidize exports, since this may imply for instance reductions in other government redistributive expenditure or in the rate of profits tax.

We also need to examine effects on the distribution of income, via the degree of concentration of exportables, the intensity of labor utilization, the demand for national inputs, and the origin, national or foreign, of exporting companies. In the past there has been a tendency toward the use of more modern technology in "traditional" activities, and it is the more modern companies that are in the best position to export.(51)

Finally, general economic policies have to be taken into account: taxation, customs, employment generation, and agricultural promotion, all of which have direct bearing on the income structure.

Studies on income distribution in Colombia(52) show that in the 1930s a process of greater concentration of income began, which slowed down in the mid-1960s. Between 1967 and 1973, a period of large increases in manufactured exports, the situation of industrial workers worsened. The movements in labor's share of GDP provide a crude but useful index of recent changes in income distribution. These can be seen in table 3.14. It shows that, starting in 1971, labor's share began to fall, first because more capital was used, and, second, because real wages fell. From 1970 until 1978, this process accelerated in the manufacturing sector, coinciding with the period when those exports stimulated by integration grew.(53)

Exports to the GRAN and other countries were stimulated by exchange rates and subsidies as well as by the reduction of tariffs. The effects upon income distribution of such policies are typically expressed as:

a. a consumption effect: when the prices of exportable goods rise, consumption is reduced
b. a redistribution effect: consumers transfer income to producers when higher prices (equal to the subsidy) are paid for a smaller volume purchased domestically; this effect is similar to the raising of tariffs on imports and the resulting tax on consumption(54)

These effects could be counteracted if there was an expansion of employment and a consequent increase in the wage bill. However, given the characteristics of industrial production in the Andean countries, the impact on the demand for labor is low, even if it is assumed that it is labor-intensive exports that expand most rapidly. This is because the value-added of these exports in proportion to GDP is very slight. As we have remarked before, we lack trustworthy data for the value-added content of manufactured exports from Andean countries; nevertheless the evidence from the weight of subregional trade in GDP is very clear.(55)

The types of companies exporting manufactures also influences the effect of those sales on employment and income. If exports come from a highly concentrated source, then the generation of employment and the redistributive effects are small. Our hypothesis is that intraregional manufactured exports are made by large industries with a high coefficient of concentration, and linked to foreign capital in such a way that they use more imported inputs than national enterprises.

According to a document of the Junta,(56) the average size of exporting firms in the GRAN is as follows:

	Average number of workers
Bolivia	57
Colombia	1,884
Ecuador	237
Peru	245
Venezuela	593
GRAN	1,362

According to the manufacturing studies of the Departamento Administrativo Nacional de Estadística de Bogota (DANE),(57) the average size of Colombian firms is 70 workers and only 7 percent of firms have more than 200 employees. Thus, it is possible to deduce that the exporting firms are to be found in the large company group, which operates under conditions of monopoly.

The Colombian exporting companies produce with high levels of concentration. By examining manufactured exports, at the three digit ISIC level of the classification, we can say with some accuracy under what conditions they are producing. An accurate list of principal manufactured exports can be constructed from four different sources,(58) all of which agree upon the identification of the main exports which are shown in table 3.15. The information in DANE's investigation into production has been used to determine the degree of concentration of output compared with their data for the period 1960 to 1973.(59) The data in table 3.15 show that the majority of Colombia's manufactured exports are produced under highly concentrated conditions (in 8 out of 13 of the main export products there is concentration degree A), allowing us to conclude that the handling of these exports is equally concentrated, given the lack of commercial intermediaries. This backs up the findings contained in the Evaluacion de las empresas exportadoras a los paises de Grupo Andino,(60) a study which shows a high correlation between levels of concentration and exports.

Another factor that indicates the limited effects of exports upon income is the high level of participation of foreign-financed companies in manufactured exports. Foreign companies in Colombia make up 83 percent of exporting firms and have retained a leading position. In 1975, they exported 44.5 percent of manufactured exports, while accounting for 43 percent of total production. The relationship of total exports to exports from foreign firms (that is, those with more than 49 % foreign capital) is more important in intermediate and capital goods sectors (see table 3.16). These companies with over 80 percent foreign investment exported about 70 percent of the goods traded by foreign-financed firms.(61)

However, in sectors that may be considered as intermediate, exports of foreign companies account for more than 52 percent of the total exported, while they represent less than this proportion of total output. This fact suggests that those foreign companies producing intermediate goods have greater surpluses and they direct themselves more flexibly towards external markets.(62)

The same study by the Junta suggests a number of other characteristics of the firms exporting to the GRAN, which we have compared with the Colombian case. Using data from surveys of the manufacturing sector, we can establish the main characteristics of the average Colombian firm. We find that there is a very sharp difference between these figures and the typical firm exporting to the GRAN, as can be seen in the following figures:

	Colombian exporting company, according to the Junta's study	Average Colombian company (DANE)
Gross value of production per worker (US $)	12,000	9,000
Real wage per worker (US $)	1,500	500
Imported inputs as % of total inputs	52.7	20.0(63)
Capital/Labor ratio	8.9	4.9

To summarize section 2, we want to stress the fact that exports of manufactured products have had very little effect upon the utilization of productive resources: there is still underutilized installed capacity, a relatively slow increase in absorption of the economically active population by industry, and a relatively static export coefficient of industrial production. Exports are made by big companies working under concentrated conditions and closely tied to foreign capital. These factors give little room for any important employment and income redistribution effects. Next we will examine the effects of exports on industrial investment.

THE INCREASE IN EXPORTS AND
INDUSTRIAL INVESTMENT

In this section, we shall study how the increase in manufactured exports has stimulated investment and whether or not the latter has been encouraged by new criteria of efficiency stemming from greater competition and subregional specialization. Our first conclusion, as reported above, is that no effect of trade on investment was detected. At first glance, the major macroeconomic indicators seem to allow very few conclusions to be drawn. The size of gross capital formation varies greatly but shows no major changes in the subregion as a whole, gross capital formation as a percent of GDP rose slowly between 1969 and 1974, coming to represent 21.2 percent of GDP. In 1975, it decreased, mainly due to the fall in Chilean investments. In 1978, it represented 25.6 percent of the GDP.

Andean Group: Total Investment

	As Percent of GDP		Annual Growth Rate		
	1969	1975	1960-69	1969-75	1975-77
Bolivia	17.5	16.1	9.7	4.7	10.0
Chile	16.4	10.5	5.5	-7.9	-
Colombia	20.5	27.9	3.8	12.2	7.9
Ecuador	15.7	27.5	6.3	19.8	3.0
Peru	13.7	21.4	2.4	14.7	9.1
Venezuela	28.1	33.0	6.2	8.2	3.0

Source: Junta, Documento de Evaluación 1976, Jun/di 248, June 1977.
1975-1977: Indicadores socio-económicos de la Subregion Andina. Jun/di 272 rev., 3 abril 1980.

Between 1960 and 1974, the group's investment growth rate was above the growth of GDP. For the years 1969 to 1975, when integration was set in motion, all countries except Chile had greater investment growth rates than for the prior period, and very much greater than those for the GDP.(64) This tendency was fully corroborated during 1975-77.(65) To determine to what degree investment expansion can be attributed to exports, the Colombian case will be examined because we have rather full data from 1956 to 1975, and because, as we have said, if there is an effect to be seen anywhere it will be seen in Colombia.

We will analyse for the 1956-74 period the behavior of investment and the variables which determine it: the availability of foreign exchange, imports of capital goods, internal sales, and exports of manufactures.

The participation of industrial investment in the formation of gross domestic fixed capital rose from 0.12 percent in 1956 to 0.22 percent by 1967, that is, at an annual rate of 6.9

percent, while GDP rose at 6.0 percent per annum. During the operation of the GRAN (1969-75) and the peak period of Colombian manufactured exports, the relationship between these two factors (annual rate of growth of industrial invest- ment within capital formation and of GDP) was 18 percent compared with 6.5 percent. In the second period, it was to be noted, however, that the weight of gross domestic fixed capital formation within GDP fell from 24.8 percent in 1970 to 19.8 percent in 1975.(66) Therefore, over the period, indus- trial investment increased more quickly than total gross capital formation.

We will analyze the degree of correlation that exists between industrial investment, total and by sectors(67) and the most relevant variables that explain that correlation: availability of foreign currency imports of intermediate and capital goods, exports, and internal sales. For the purposes of analysis, the industrial sector has been divided into three subsectors: traditional, intermediate, and metal mecánico in- dustries.(68)

In our analysis we take as the dependent variable y, industrial investment total and by subsectors as defined here. The independent variables, X, considered one at a time are: internal sales, exports, and import capacity (availability of foreign currency). For total industrial investment we also tested for a correlation with imports of intermediate goods and capital goods. Throughout a time-lag of one year in the independent variable performed best, so that in each case we have a fitted model

$$y_t = a + bX_{t-1}$$

where a and b are unknown parameters to be estimated. The index t runs from 1957 to 1975. In table 3.17 we have summa- rized the result of these regressions by quoting the correlation coefficient r, for each pair of X and Y variables considered. With 19 observations, coefficients greater than 0.38 are significantly non-zero at the 10 percent level, those greater than 0.45 at the 5 percent level, and those greater than 0.58 at the 1 percent level of significance.

In the long term, total Colombian investment is explained in the first place by the behavior of investments in traditional industries. In some periods (1962-68 when import substitution policies were fully applied) investment in intermediate indus- tries is the main component. Investment in capital goods is relatively constant (see Graph 3.1).

The relationship between global exports and investment is modified both by policies of economic stimulation, which can, at a given moment, promote investment beyond the limitations of the balance of payments, or of the size of the market, and by the management of foreign exchange under favorable or unfavorable circumstances. In times of an external trade bonanza, there is typically an apparent liberalization of trade controls which leads, in the first place, to an accelerated growth in the imports of final consumption goods, and, second, of primary materials. Imports of capital goods rise proportionately more slowly than before. Under the reverse conditions, in order to maintain an adequate level of economic activity, imports of consumption goods are reduced first, and finally intermediate products. The considerations of the economic cycle clarify the relationship between the availability of foreign currency and investment. They also show why there is not, in the short and medium term, a greater relation between total exports and GDP, or between the former and industrial production.(69) Governmental policies ensure a minimum level of activity during crises (so do entrepreneurs who accumulate stocks and in-stalled capacity) and in the periods of growing reserves, they prevent excessive capitalization. For this reason, the corre-lation between total industrial investment and the availability of foreign currencies is $r = 0.85$: column d, table 3.17. The respective values fall when dealing with intermediate or capital goods industries.

    In analyzing the relationship between the different variables and industrial investments, we found that the best single determinant of investment behavior is internal sales ($r = 0.92$, columns a and g, in table 3.17 and Graph 3.2). Table 3.17 and Graph 3.3 shows that manufactured exports do not appear to explain and stimulate investment, which backs up the previous hypothesis that exports are still marginal in industrial activities and in investment decisions, as we concluded from the evaluation of the trade program (section 2B in this chapter).

    The correlation coefficients for total investment against total exports ($r = 0.68$, columns e, f, g, and h) fall when considering investment in intermediate or metallurgical indus-tries and their respective total exports. The lowest figures correspond to intermediate industries. These relationships support our earlier findings that it is unlikely that intra-subregional exports will change the rate of growth and the pattern of industrial investment, and that there will be a stimulus to investment in sectors producing intermediate and capital goods, for which the integration was intended in the first place. Investments in those sectors are more sensitive to other types of promotion policies than to the demand push policy. This is coherent with our findings on the lack of trade in products not produced before the signing of the Treaty, which were completely freed by February 28, 1971.(70) The results of the total and immediate tariff reduction up to February 28, 1971, for products listed as "not produced and not reserved for the SIDPs," is an indicator of the lack of dynamism of the subregional market. Line 6 of tables 3.9 and 3.10 shows that trade in these products has not been affected, whether it comes from the lesser or more developed member countries.(71)

The Junta's analytical studies take up the subject of anxieties over the absence of investment in new products covered by Article 49 of the Treaty, and those included in the sectoral programs already approved (automobile and petrochemical).(72) The Junta has proposed the setting up of a detailed study over the whole subregion to find out why these new investments have not been forthcoming.

We can say in summary that perhaps it is the combination of the two schemes, import substitution and export promotion, within a framework of a closed economy and a still-limited market, which explains why the expected changes in investment behavior have not been achieved. The Andean Group economic model still remains completely within the old import substitution scheme. The only one new element is the aggregation of the national elite markets, without any action upon the supply side (the production process and the structure of supply); nor has action been attempted on the demand side (e.g., increase of agricultural productivity, income redistribution, or employment policies), where the positive effects were more likely to happen.

Analyzing the effect of total manufactured exports upon the Colombian economy, we did not find any change in the behavior of investment, the use of installed capacity, the export coefficient, the trend in absorption of labor, or the participation of labor in national income. Despite the high annual growth rate of manufactured total exports, 16.6 percent during 1969-75 (30.3% to the region), and 28.6 percent during 1975-78 we found the trends which had emerged in the previous decade still prevailing.

An explanation of the lack of significant effects on economic growth may lie in the fact that in Colombia (and also in Chile) the export promotion policy was based either on a "real" rate of exchange, or on a time when undervalued rates prevailed. Many studies suggest that, at least in the short term, devaluation can have a deflationary character, especially if at the start there is a deficit in the commercial balance.(73) Income redistribution in favor of profits may be another deflationary aspect of devaluation.(74) Recent studies suggest that devaluation may have a deflationary effect even when there are unemployed resources, in so far as it generates a transfer of purchasing power towards that part of the population with a high propensity to save.(75)

Even the freeing of trade had proved to be affected by the conservative attitude both of governments and entrepreneurs, who prevented the full opening of the market and the abandonment of the protective practices behind which the Andean national economies have been developing during the last three decades.   Many political constraints made the change almost impossible.

THE REGIONAL POLARIZATION EFFECTS

The need to give special protection to new industries because of their weaknesses is an accepted part of the classical theory of free markets.   Over time, the "infant industry" exception has been applied to all industry in underdeveloped countries. But the idea that the dynamic effects of free trade can slow the growth of a backward region has been less studied in economic theory.   This is, among other reasons, because the theory of growth has concentrated on problems of growth at the national economic level while ignoring backward regions within countries.   This is analagous with the problems of growth and the balance of payments in less developed countries or zones in an integrated region.(76)

According to general equilibrium arguments, the spread effects of development in the more advanced areas bring development to the less advanced onces.   The latter will attract productive resources such as capital, because of the comparative advantage to be gained from cheaper labor.   In order to compete, the weaker regions have to devalue their currency progressively.   However, if they are areas within a national economy or an integrated group, their situation is exacerbated because they probably cannot devalue.   Therefore, capital flows to the more developed zones, where, even if labor is more expensive, the social infrastructure, technological development, and the business environment are more conducive to enterprise and allow for greater profits.   We refer in more detail to the meaning of concentration effects in an integration scheme among less developed countries in Chapter 7, section 1.

Within the Andean Group the disparities in levels of economic development are considerable, as was shown in Chapter 1.   It is sufficient to note here that, for example, the ratio of GDP per capita between Bolivia and Venezuela is 3:7 or that Venezuela accounts for 65.1 percent of all the subregion's exports.   Bolivia and Ecuador's share together accounted for only 8.82 percent.   If the possibility of integrating the region were not to be lost, some kind of preference for the less developed countries had to be given.

The commercial program of the Cartagena Agreement gave preferences to Bolivia and Ecuador.(77)   These were:

i.   an accelerated opening of the more developed countries' markets for those products from Bolivia and Ecuador that were included in the automatic reduction list

ii.   total and immediate reduction of tariffs for goods on the "immediate opening" lists in favor of these two countries only

iii.   total and immediate reduction for nonproduced goods that were to be reserved for production in Bolivia and Ecuador

iv.   a ruling that the automatic opening of the markets of the less developed countries was not to take place until December 31, 1976 (for the more developed, it was December 31, 1971)

THE EVOLUTION OF THE
LESS DEVELOPED COUNTRIES' TRADE

In this section we shall examine the global trade of the two least developed countries according to types of goods, and the level of manufacturing or processing. The hypothesis we are setting out to explore is that tariff advantages are not sufficient to counterbalance the effects of concentration of economic activity. These countries tend to be net importers and to specialize in the export of primary goods or of manufactures with low levels of processing, while they import more sophisticated manufactures.

Evolution of Global Trade

Bolivia's and Ecuador's exports rose from US$16.2 million in 1969 to US$180 million in 1975 and decreased to US$124.5 million in 1979. Over this period, their share of intrasubregional trade increased from 10 percent to 25 percent decreasing 15 percent in 1978. Cumulative sales until 1978 amounted to US$602.5 million and purchases US$549.9 million, that is, a considerable balance in their favor. However about 88.7 percent of these exports were products such as petroleum, tin, cacao, and cacao paste. If these items are deducted, a deficit of US$680 million, will result.

Structure of Trade

Bolivia and Ecuador, especially the former, are primary goods exporters and importers of industrial products. The structure of Bolivia's exports has barely changed since 1969. Ninety-six point two percent of its exports were basic products and only 3.8 percent were manufactures, with a low level of processing. Because Ecuador has been an oil exporter since 1973, the proportion of manufactures in its exports has fallen. In 1978, sales of manufactures from Bolivia and Ecuador represented 5.7 percent of subregional trade in those products. Table 3.18 distinguishes between intrasubregional exports that are primary products (coffee, cotton, oil, sugar, meat, and manufactures with low levels of processing, such as cacao paste or fishmeal), and those manufactures with higher level of processing. The former group has been called type A products, and the latter, type B. The table suggests the following conclusions:

i.   the less developed countries are net exporters of type A goods and importers of type B, for which they have an accumulated deficit of about US$150 million

ii. the exports of type B products from Bolivia and Ecuador continue to be limited, especially in the case of Bolivia

iii. until 1975, only Colombia and Chile have positive balances for type B products; in 1975 Colombian exports of type B goods to the GRAN represent 30 percent of the total trade of these products; Chile's share was less, but at 18.9 percent was still important

Trade in Industrial Goods, According to the Degree of Technological Complexity

If a greater disaggregation is made of type B industrial goods traded in the subregion, this provides stronger evidence of the level of the effects of concentration coming from the freeing of the Andean market and the inability of the less developed countries to take advantage of concessions to their industry.

To make this disaggregation, we have taken the classification used by the Junta when drawing up the CET and the criteria for technological contribution. This method groups products from 1 to 9 in ascending order of the technological complexity of production.(78)

Table 3.19 shows that, in spite of the apparent diversification of all countries' sales (especially those of the less developed countries), exports of group 7 to 9 goods are concentrated in the more developed nations, particularly in Chile and Colombia, which account for 80.4 percent of this trade. Peru and Venezuela lead the less developed countries, but only just. If we analyze each country's structure of manufactured exports, we get the following results.

i.   Bolivia sells some whiskey, preserved fruit and tin manufactures.

ii. Ecuador has diversified its sales to a greater extent. However, the recorded increase of 72.8 percent in sales of products such as sardines, cacao cake and paste, medicines, and tinned tuna is largely accounted for by the legalization of goods previously smuggled to Colombia. In 1975, Colombia accounted for 87.4 percent of Ecuador's sales of these products. Ecuador has combined the advantages given by the Treaty and its industrial promotion laws to begin assembling and selling to the subregion refrigerators, electric cookers, and, to a lesser degree, synthetic fibers. The low tariff duties on the necessary inputs have aided this process, where Ecuador has been the most efficient producer.

iii. Peru (the second country ranked by the proportion of its industrial exports in total exports) sells a great number of new products. However, the proportion of low technology goods (fishmeal and fish oil and semimanufactured metal products) continues to be high. The increased weight of new products does not permit us to arrive at any definitive conclusions on the structure of Peru's manufacture trade because many sales are marginal. For example, more than 70 new products were exported, but many of them were valued at less than US$5,000.

iv. Chile is the only country in the GRAN with strong trade links with the large LAFTA members with which it has a significant trade in industrial products. Its sales to the GRAN do not reflect fully its productive structure because about 70 percent of its exports to the group are mainly those with low levels of processing (wine, timber, fruit and preserves, and cellulose).

v. Colombia is the principal beneficiary from sales of manufactures to the subregion and also to the rest of the world. Perhaps this success can be explained by the combination of export promotion policies and the application of the subregional margin of preference which made exports possible, even for products in which Colombia would not be the most efficient producer. It exports many products in fluctuating and insignificant quantities.(79)

CONCLUSIONS

The following conclusions about the effects of reciprocal trade upon the countries' economies were formulated on the basis of a very detailed analysis of reciprocal trade as it evolved from 1969 until 1975 and were totally ratified by the information covering the period 1976-78.

A. There has been a large increase in trade, but much of this has come from products of agricultural and mineral origin.

B. The increase in intrasubregional sales of manufactures can be attributed only partially to tariff stimuli. Trade favored by reduction grew more slowly than total trade and total trade net of sugar, petrol, and meat.

C. The previous point suggests that there was a tendency to limit the attainment of greater competition which, in turn, indicates a lowering of the possible effects of trade creation by means of replacing national firms that are import-substituting and protected, with more efficient, subregional, exporting companies. The fear of the effects of trade creation is one of the obstacles put in the way of free trade and the extension of competition. In the short term, trade creation incurs costs in terms of the dislocation of labor and the reallocation of capital because of the expectation that import-competing companies will not be able to resist competition. The risk of competition is avoided rather than confronted.

D. The new market has not been sufficient to stimulate the production of goods not made before, or to increase and transform the pattern of investment. This proves the hypothesis that the subregional market size is still very limited for advancing the import substitution process further than has been done by countries acting on their own, if industrialists are not guaranteed the advantages of the type to be gained from import substitution policies, plus those derived from the wider market.

E. Manufactured exports have had a small positive effect in reducing the underutilization of capacity. However, the margins of underutilization can also be explained by elements other than demand. Long-term structural factors also have to be taken into account. Exports only partially reduce underutilization.

F. The effect of manufactured exports on employment (and income distribution) are still small and do not allow us to assume that they have facilitated a rise in internal demand or the growth of GDP. The explanation was found in the type of good exported, which tended to be produced largely by foreign and by highly concentrated firms.

G. It is not possible to draw out any direct relationship between manufactured exports and the rate or composition of industrial investment. These factors seem to be determined more by the availability of foreign exchange and, above all, internal sales. The industrial sector considers exports to be a marginal activity. We may conclude that integration schemes that rely only upon free trade do not, in the short or medium term, radically change the patterns of investment. More positive and direct actions upon the productive structure is required.

H. The trade stimuli given to the less developed countries have not been sufficient to prevent the effects of concentration. These countries are net importers and have not been able to mobilize resources to improve their industrial situation nor to raise investment in the goods reserved for them on the list of nonproduced products.

The conclusions derived from the performance of intraregional trade are in accordance with those drawn from much writing on the theory of integration, namely, that in the case of integration among LDCs more advanced forms of cooperation have to be agreed on if the developmental objectives aimed at through integration are to be achieved. The introduction of trade incentives alone has failed to induce changes in the rhythm of industrial investment. It fails also to bring about needed change in the pattern of investment. It could be concluded, therefore, that regional economic activity must be planned in order to create the environment in which those changes may occur.

In the following chapters we will examine the different elements of political integration designed in the Treaty to complement the commercial program. We will examine the progress in and effects of such policies and explore how political constraints affected the realization of the goals of harmonization of economic policies.

Table 3.1. Andean Group, Trade Program

Lists	Regime of Liberalization	Liberalization to be Completed by	No. Items	% of Tariff Nomenclature
Products covered by sectoral programs	Reserved	by the particular program schedule and not later than 1990	1,680	37.0
Products included in the LAFTA Common List	Immediate and total	180 days after the signature of the Treaty of Cartagena	132	2.9
Products not yet produced in any country and not covered by S.P.	Immediate and total	February 28, 1971	144	3.2
Products covered by the automatic tariff reduction system	Automatic	December 31, 1971	2,496	55.1
Products not produced and reserved to be produced by	Immediate and total	January 31, 1971		
a) Bolivia			38	0.8
b) Ecuador			42	0.9
Products exempted from	Exempted	December 31, 1985 Bolivia and Ecuador December 31, 1990	1,778	
a) Trade lists			430	
b) Reserve lists			2,311	

Source: Elaborated on the basis of various Decisions of the Commission.

Table 3.2. Static Gains from Economic Integration: Empirical Evidence

Study	Case	Tariff Change	% Increase in Trade of Goods Covered by Study	% Gain of GNP
1. Scitovsky	Effects on the pattern of trade of C.U. among EEC countries, Scandinavia, and Britain based upon their 1952 trade	to nil	+ 19	0.005 of GNP
2. Johnson	Britain with Western Europe	to nil	Exports + 160 Imports + 75	0.001 of British GNP
3. Welmelsfelder	German imports	by 50%	+ 100	0.0018
4. Balassa	EEC	by 70%	+ 13	0.009
5. Singh and Leibenstein	Gains from trade among LAFTA countries using Scitovsky method	to nil		0.00008

Sources: 1. Scitovsky, Economic Theory, pp. 64-70.

2. Johnson, for Economists' Intelligence Unit, pp. 247-55.

3. Welmelsfelder, "The Short-term Effect of the Lowering of Import Duties in Germany," Economic Journal, Vol. LXX, March 1960.

4. B. Balassa, NASA study, "Trade Creation and Trade Diversion in the EEC," Economic Journal, Vol. LXXVII, March 1967.

5. A. Singh and H. Leibenstein, "Allocative Efficiency versus Efficiency," American Economic Review, 1966, pp. 392-415.

Table 3.3. Andean Group, Total Imports, Growth Rates and % Structure

	Annual Growth Rates %						Mil. US$	% Structure						
Year	Boli-via	Colom-bia	Chile	Ecua-dor	Peru	Vene-zuela	TOTAL	Boli-via	Colom-bia	Chile	Ecua-dor	Peru	Vene-zuela	TOTAL
1965	-	-	-	-	-	-		3.72	12.61	16.78	4.56	20.26	42.07	100
1966	0.75	48.46	24.34	4.88	12.07	-7.33	9.81	3.42	17.05	19.00	4.35	20.67	35.50	100
1967	11.85	-26.26	-3.86	23.26	0.24	9.48	-0.38	3.84	12.62	18.34	5.38	20.80	39.01	100
1968	1.32	29.38	2.91	20.75	-23.08	15.49	6.65	3.64	15.31	17.69	6.10	15.00	42.25	100
1969	7.84	6.53	22.07	-5.47	-4.76	-13.92	-1.74	4.00	16.60	21.98	5.87	14.54	37.01	100
1970	-3.64	23.07	2.65	13.22	3.67	0.04	8.92	3.54	18.76	20.72	6.10	13.84	37.05	100
1971	6.92	10.20	5.26	24.09	20.58	28.11	17.98	3.21	17.52	18.48	6.41	14.15	40.23	100
1972	1.76	-7.53	-3.98	-6.18	6.13	16.92	5.28	3.09	15.39	16.86	5.71	14.26	44.68	100
1973	17.92	23.63	16.68	24.45	28.64	14.19	18.83	3.08	16.01	15.55	5.99	16.44	42.94	100
1974	91.18	25.89	73.95	141.56	49.51	51.47	57.41	3.74	12.81	18.29	9.10	14.66	41.32	100
1975	43.08	12.42	-29.95	-1.67	55.85	34.68	20.08	4.45	11.99	10.67	7.52	19.03	46.34	100
1965-69	5.3	10.8	10.7	10.2	-4.7	0.2	3.4							
1969-75	22.5	13.9	6.7	25.4	25.7	24.9	20.3							
1976[1]	5.37	32.91	23.69	4.17	-12.13	24.14	-21.07	4.54	15.39		8.09	16.23	55.74	100
1977	13.26	33.90	35.58	29.86	3.04	43.35	32.89	3.87	15.50		7.91	12.58	60.13	100
1978	27.32	28.01	40.73	-3.37	-26.01	6.60	5.83	4.65	18.75		7.23	8.80	60.57	100
1979	19.22	35.65	40.69	25.09	30.60	-2.93	10.31	5.04	23.06		8.19	10.42	53.29	100
1976-78	14.7	49.9	-	35.1	-15.3	38.2	29.8							
1976-78[2]	4.0	33.3	-	22.8	-20.8	22.7	15.5							

Source: 1965-75: Junta, Informe de Evaluación 1976, Jun/Dic. 248/1977 Anexo Técnico.
1976-79: Naciones Unidas, Comisión Economica para América Latina – Estudio Económico de América Latina 1979.

1. In 1976, Chile left the Andean Group.
2. Growth rates in dollars of 1970.

Table 3.4. Andean Group, Total Exports-Growth Rates and % Structure

Year	Annual Growth Rates %							% Structure						
	Boli-via	Chile	Colom-bia	Ecua-dor	Peru	Vene-zuela	TOTAL	Boli-via	Chile	Colom-bia	Ecua-dor	Peru	Vene-zuela	TOTAL
1965	10.4	28.0	5.7	4.5	14.5	3.4	4.1	2.49	14.88	11.66	2.86	14.43	53.69	100
1966	18.1	3.7	0.4	13.7	-0.9	5.6	4.2	2.64	18.29	10.55	2.87	15.86	49.79	100
1967	1.3	0.0	9.4	24.2	17.4	0.2	4.5	2.99	18.21	10.16	3.13	15.08	50.44	100
1968	13.1	14.2	8.9	-21.5	0.0	5.2	5.5	2.90	17.93	10.63	3.71	16.88	48.33	100
1969	10.4	14.7	21.0	24.1	21.0	3.4	11.0	3.10	19.40	10.97	2.76	15.63	48.13	100
1970	-4.7	22.0	-6.2	4.7	-14.8	22.3	2.3	3.09	20.05	11.96	3.09	17.03	44.78	100
1971	11.0	11.1	25.5	63.8	5.7	12.1	10.7	2.87	15.28	10.96	3.16	14.18	53.55	100
1972	29.8	43.9	35.9	63.2	11.2	45.3	39.7	2.88	12.26	12.42	4.67	13.54	54.23	100
1973	113.0	101.5	14.8	98.3	44.8	166.6	121.8	2.68	12.63	12.08	5.46	10.77	56.39	100
1974	-20.3	-33.0	8.3	-20.4	-13.5	-27.2	-24.1	2.57	11.48	6.25	4.88	7.04	67.78	100
1975	10.5	3.0	11.8	3.6	6.7	1.8	4.6	2.70	10.13	8.94	5.12	8.02	65.09	100
1965-69	17.1	15.8	7.5	32.8	7.2	26.0	19.8							
1969-75														
1976[1]	-22.95	25.40	28.73	19.40	5.34	4.07	-12.61	4.01		13.16	8.12	8.40	65.21	100
1977	14.43	5.13	30.2	5.24	26.9	3.41	9.75	4.18		15.61	7.78	10.98	61.44	100
1978	-2.58	9.95	25.85	23.85	12.5	-5.05	4.04	3.92		18.88	9.27	11.86	56.07	100
1979	21.53	56.27	14.3	40.76	79.0	55.77	47.97	3.22		14.59	8.82	14.35	59.03	100
1976-78[2]	5.4	-	38.5	9.4	54.2	-0.9	10.1							
1976-78[2]	-7.2		15.6	3.3	49.6	-6.2	9.6							

Source: 1965-75: Junta, Informe de Evaluación 1976, Jun/Dic. 248/1977, Anexo técnico.
1976-79: Naciones Unidas, Comisión Económica para América Latina. Estudio Económico de América Latina, 1979.

1. In 1976, Chile left the Andean Group.
2. Growth rates in dollars of 1970.

Table 3.5. Andean Group, Reciprocal Trade as % of Total Trade, 1948–1978

Year	Bolivia		Chile		Colombia		Ecuador		Perú		Venezuela	
	X	M	X	M	X	M	X	M	X	M	X	M
1948	0.7	15.6	2.3	14.1	0.5	4.3	16.3	3.8	29.4	4.6	0.1	0.7
1960	0.6	7.5	1.5	5.4	1.4	1.3	7.7	2.7	5.5	2.6	0.7	0.6
1969	2.4	3.0	1.2	7.3	7.3	4.4	7.5	11.0	3.1	5.2	2.3	1.1
1970	2.6	4.0	1.8	4.9	9.2	4.7	7.7	10.7	2.5	7.9	1.2	1.1
1971	9.5	3.5	2.8	5.9	11.1	5.6	9.6	12.7	3.0	8.2	1.7	0.8
1972	8.0	4.3	2.4	5.2	10.0	4.5	9.3	8.6	3.4	10.1	1.6	1.0
1973	7.7	4.5	1.9	5.7	7.5	4.9	14.5	9.2	4.3	8.8	1.6	0.9
1974	9.4	2.0	2.7	9.2	10.4	5.9	16.3	6.9	4.5	10.4	1.7	1.3
1975	5.4	2.8	6.4	16.1	13.0	7.0	18.3	8.1	9.9	11.4	1.6	2.2
1976	3.4	3.9	–	–	10.6	5.4	18.4	5.3	3.9	15.7	1.4	1.9
1977	1.6	3.1	–	–	12.2	8.4	12.4	5.1	4.3	20.2	2.8	1.8
1978	2.2	3.4	–	–	11.9	7.6	6.7	5.8	5.7	5.7	1.3	2.0

Source: 1948–60: Calculated on the base of national statistics.
1969–75: Junta, Evaluación del Proceso de Integración, 1976, Jun/Dic. 248, 1977, Anexo Estadístico.
1976–78: Junta, Comercio Exterior de los países del Grupo Andino 1969–1979, Jun/Dic 449, 9 de septiembre de 1980, pp. 23–61.

Table 3.6. Andean Group, Structure of Principal Intraregional
Exports 1969–1978
000 US$

Products	Value of Exports					% Structure					Annual Growth Rates				
	1969	1973	1975	1977*	1978	1969	1973	1975	1977	1978	1969-70	1973-74	1975-76	1969-75	1975-78
Agriculture	32,085	62,218	215,355	110,851	132,460	20.2	20.2	29.0	13.0	17.0	33.8	40.7	-65.42	37.3	14.1
New	297	16,676	41,972			0.2	5.4	5.6			-16.1	-107.9		128.2	
Traditional	31,788	45,542	173,383			20.0	14.8	23.4			34.3	15.9		32.7	
Mining	81,219	132,217	289,824	322,947	193,667	50.9	43.0	39.0	48.0	26.0	-16.9	226.2	-89.55	23.6	-4.1
New	45	5,400	6,192				1.8	0.8			4.49	51.0		127.2	
Traditional	81,174	126,817	283,632			50.9	41.2	38.2			-17.0	233.7		23.2	
Industrial	40,029	113,238	236,908	322,243	428,580	28.9	36.8	31.9	39.0	57.0	32.7	95.4	-13.6	34.5	56.9
New	5,744	58,775	132,213			3.6	10.1	17.8			38.4	121.3		68.7	
Traditional	40,285	54,463	104,695			25.3	17.7	14.1			12.1	67.5		17.3	
TOTAL	159,333	307,673	742,087	873,367	757,980	100.0	100.0	100.0	100.0	100.0	2.6	140.5	-17.3	29.2	12.79
Excl. Oil	83,056	198,416	486,172	467,093	623,639						30.3	92.9	-37.3	34.2	41.3

Source: Calculated from Junta del Acuerdo de Cartagena, Informe de Evaluación 1976, Jun/Dic.
248/1977, Table 13, Anexo Tecnico.
1976-1977: Anexo Técnico No. 9, Estadísticas de Comercio Exterior para el Grupo Andino:
1969-1977, Jun/Di 365, 30 March, 1979.

* In 1976, Chile left the Andean Group.

130

Table 3.7. Andean Group, Principal Exports, National Structure and Growth Rates, 1969-1975

Products	National Structure %												Growth Rates 1969-75					
	Bolivia		Chile		Colombia		Ecuador		Peru		Venezuela		Boli-via	Chile	Colom-bia	Ecua-dor	Peru	Vene-zuela
	1969	1975	1969	1975	1969	1975	1969	1975	1969	1975	1969	1975						
Agriculture	2.21	11.30	17.09	15.75	23.57	46.29	78.12	19.22	43.79	70.65	0.03	0.03	74.34	39.06	46.33	21.82	41.33	17.61
New	1.25	10.34	1.04	3.52	0.05	12.82	0.45	8.79	0.14	0.26	-	-	89.04	72.79	228.18	152.35	45.60	-
Traditional	0.97	0.96	16.05	12.22	23.52	33.47	77.67	10.43	43.65	70.39	0.03	0.03	32.63	34.71	38.69	10.13	41.31	17.61
Mining	97.79	83.56	0.32	0.50	40.43	0.05	2.96	72.55	0.06	0.93	94.22	91.37	29.41	52.33	56.51	162.28	103.95	16.83
New	0.62	15.51	-	0.45	-	-	-	0.15	0.06	0.82	-	0.32	127.01	-	-	-	99.56	-
Traditional	97.17	68.05	0.32	0.05	40.43	0.05	2.96	72.40	-	0.11	94.22	91.04	25.19	3.97	56.51	162.18	-	16.76
Excl. petrol	100.00	35.90	100	100	59.57	100	100	28.28	100	100	5.78	14.56	11.99	41.00	42.59	24.69	30.50	37.00
Industrial	-	5.14	82.59	83.75	36.00	53.65	18.91	8.23	56.15	28.42	5.75	8.50	-	41.30	39.76	33.98	16.50	25.58
New	-	5.14	1.31	31.94	7.47	35.64	3.05	7.29	1.71	10.61	0.69	8.19	-	139.93	69.68	77.95	76.82	77.41
Traditional	-	-	81.28	51.81	28.54	18.02	15.86	0.94	54.43	17.81	5.06	0.41	-	30.77	21.12	3.86	8.33	22.68
TOTAL	100	100	100	100	100	100	100	100	100	100	100	100	-	40.97	30.77	53.90	30.50	17.43
Countries share in intraregional exports of manufactured goods a	-	0.5	20.2	33.6	29.8	39.6	5.3	5.2	35.2	14.8	9.5	6.3						
b	-	1.0	12.7	22.9	44.5	47.5	6.0	8.3	28.9	9.9	7.9	10.4						
c	-	-	24.6	46.7	33.3	29.2	4.4	1.3	29.4	22.1	8.3	0.7						

Source: Calculated from data of Junta del Acuerdo de Cartagena, Documento de Evaluación, Jun/di 248/1976, Table AT 13, Anexo Estadístico.

Notes: (a) Total, (b) New, (c) Traditional

Table 3.8. Andean Group, Principal Exports-National Structure and Growth Rates, 1976-1978

| Products | National Structure | | | | | | | | | | Growth Rates Annual % | | | | |
| | Bolivia | | Colombia | | Ecuador | | Peru | | Venezuela | | Bolivia | Col. | Ecua. | Peru | Venez. |
	1976	1978	1976	1978	1976	1978	1976	1978	1976	1978					
Agriculture	0.3	–	27.0	25.0	8.0	25.0	14.0	4.0	1.0	–	-35.9	29.5	19.8	48.6	-28.2
Mining	22.7	80.0	–	–	–	–	17.0	23.0	8.0	7.0	53.8	47.9	–	164.6	– 7.3
Oil and derivates	73.8	–	4.0	–	83.0	27.0	2.0	7.0	79.0	81.0	–	74.6	-42.7	372.9	– 1.6
Industrial	3.0	20.0	73.0	74.0	9.0	45.0	66.0	61.0	12.0	12.0	126.1	34.1	52.8	92.5	– 0.9
Total excl. petrol	100.0	100.0	100.0	100.0	100.0	100.0	100.0	100.0	100.0	100.0	-25.8	32.9	-28.2	102.5	– 2.0
Countries share in intraregional exports of manufactured goods	0.3	0.7	65.4	63.0	11.1	10.6	16.2	22.0	7.2	3.4	–	32.9	41.8	95.9	– 0.1

Source: Junta: Estadísticas de Comercio Exterior de los países del Grupo Andino 1969-1979; Jun/Di 499, September 9, 1980, pp. 141-145.

Table 3.9. Andean Group, Total Intraregional Exports by Liberalization Program, 1969-1975 (000 US$)

Liberation Program Lists	1969[a]	1970[a]	1971[a]	1972[a]	1973[b]	1974[b]	1975[b]	% Annual growth rate 1969-75	Absolute growth 1969-75	% Structure 1969	% Structure 1975
1 Automatic (not including exemptions lists)	25,259	43,041	64,774	63,743	139,919	322,081	331,225	53.5	305,966	29.3	42.5
1A Net of meat, sugar, & oil	14,332	166,610	23,148	20,817	44,228	63,269	65,665	28.9	51,333	16.6	8.4
2 Automatic (included in exception lists)	6,576	13,898	11,688	17,334	34,366	122,827	177,366	73.2	170,790	7.6	22.8
2A Net of meat, sugar & oil	3,871	3,519	4,431	8,343	19,084	41,683	37,970	46.3	34,099	4.5	4.9
3 Immediate total reduction of tariffs	291	541	3,891	7,375	13,683	23,889	28,900	115.2	28,609	0.3	3.7
4 Common List of LAFTA	27,293	30,486	32,928	32,515	33,951	71,815	60,619	14.2	33,326	31.7	7.8
5 Reserved for SIDP	4,098	7,364	9,336	12,846	25,872	48,614	61,803	57.2	57,705	4.7	7.9
6 Goods not produced	9	5	5	52	212	153	39	27.7	30	0.0	0.0
7 Metal mecanico program	-	-	-	-	1,603	3,716	7,332	-	7,332	-	0.0
8 Exported to Bolivia & Ecuador without preference	25,576	26,762	32,045	32,797	68,876	172,695	110,304	30.3	87,728	26.2	14.2
8A Net of meat, sugar, & oil	17,219	17,075	23,502	28,083	41,862	66,978	88,798	31.4	71,579	20.0	11.4
9 Others	63	63	89	76	165	570	1,323	66.1	1,260	0.1	0.2
TOTAL	86,165	122,160	154,756	166,738	323,647	766,367	778,971	44.3	692,806	100.0	100.0
Total net of sugar, meat, & oil	67,176	75,653	97,330	110,107	185,660	320,693	352,449	31.8	285,273	77.96	45.3
Total freed trade 1A+3+6+7	14,632						101,936	38.20	87,304	16.9	12.1
Total unfreed trade 2A+4+5+8A+9	52,444						250,513	29.7	198,069		

Source: Calculated from trade data from Junta del Acuerdo de Cartagena, Documento de Evaluación 1976, Jun/di 248, Lima, 1976.

Notes: (a) Venezuela not included.
(b) Venezuela included.

133

Table 3.10. Total Intraregional Exports by Liberalization Program, 1976-1978

Liberation Programs	Millions of dollars		Percentages changes	Structure %	
	1976	1978	1978-1976	1976	1978
1. Automatic (not including exemptions lists)	391.1	340.8	-12.9	63.77	44.96
A	341.0	215.6	-36.8	55.60	28.44
Oil	288.9	130.8	-54.7	47.11	17.26
Others	52.1	84.8	62.8	8.49	11.19
B	50.1	125.2	149.9	8.17	16.52
2. Automatic (including exemptions lists)	42.8	124.3	190.4	6.98	16.40
A	0.9	1.7	88.9	0.15	0.23
B	41.9	122.6	192.6	6.83	16.17
3. Immediate total reduction of tariffs	28.3	64.5	127.9	4.61	8.51
A	20.9	32.1	53.6	3.41	4.23
B	7.4	32.4	337.8	1.20	4.27
4. Common List of LAFTA	17.4	38.7	122.4	2.84	5.11
A	12.2	21.9	79.5	1.99	2.89
B	5.2	16.8	223.1	0.85	2.22
5. Reserved for SIDP	35.9	45.8	27.6	5.85	6.04
A	9.8	6.8	-30.6	1.60	0.90
B	26.1	39.0	49.4	4.25	5.14
6. Goods not produced	0.2	1.3	550.0	0.03	0.17
A	-	-	-	-	-
B	0.2	1.3	550.0	0.03	0.17
7. Metalmecanico programme	5.8	7.5	29.3	0.95	0.99
A	-	-	-	-	-
B	5.8	7.5	29.3	0.95	0.99
8. Petrochemical programme	10.3	16.7	62.1	1.68	2.20
A	-	-	-	-	-
B	10.3	16.7	62.1	1.68	2.20
9. Exported to Bolivia and Ecuador without preference.	81.5	117.4	44.0	13.29	15.49
A	20.8	11.0	-47.1	3.39	1.45
Oil	19.4	6.5	-66.5	3.16	0.86
Others	1.4	4.5	221.4	0.23	0.59
B	60.7	106.4	75.3	9.90	14.04
10. Others	-	1.0	(.....)	00.0	0.13
A	-	-	-	-	-
B	-	1.0	(.....)	00.0	0.13
TOTAL	613.3	758.0	23.6	100.0	100.0
Total freed trade	94.7	182.8	46.5	15.4	24.1
Total unfreed trade	156.8	327.2	54.3	25.6	43.2

(...) Not calculated because no data in one of the compared periods.

- No trade.

Products A: numeral ones, petrol, oil and gas, coffee, bananas, sugar, meat, cotton, meal and fish oil, natural wool and cacao.

These products are generally very important for Latinamerican countries and they are not elastic to the tariffs reductions.

Products B: Other products generally more processed than products A.

Source: Calculated from trade data from Junta del Acuerdo de Cartagena, Estadisticas de Comercio Exterior de los Paises del Grupo Andino 1969-1979 Jun/di 499, September 1980, Tables 107-118.

Table 3.11. Andean Group, Share of Total Manufactured Exports in
Gross Industrial Product, 1950-1977

Country	1950 %	1960 %	1967 %	1970 %	1975 %	1970[a] %	1975[a] %	1977	1977[a]
Bolivia	1.75	1.5	0.9	1.8	1.0	0.3	0.5	1.54	0.1
Chile	2.60	1.3	2.3	2.9	15.2	1.0	0.8	--	-
Colombia	0.68	2.08	5.9	3.3	4.8	1.08	1.45	0.7	0.1
Ecuador	0.66	1.50	5.1	8.3	3.8	0.5	1.25	0.3	0.1
Peru	5.3	8.02	2.95	9.37	2.43	0.5	1.02	1.0	0.9
Venezuela	0.13	0.22	1.2	1.9	2.6	0.6	0.6	0.1	0.1

Sources: 1950-70: CEPAL, Integración Económica, Sustitución de Importaciones y Desarrollo Económico en America Latina 1974.

1975 and 1970: our calculations on the basis of Junta, Documento de Evaluación
1976, Jun/di 248, 1977, Tables II 4.5 to II 4.7.

1977=Indicadores socioeconomicos de la Subregión Andina. Jun/di 277 rev. 3
April 1980.

Note: (a) Exports to the GRAN as a percentage of gross industrial product

Table 3.12. Colombia , Industrial Production and Utilization of Installed Capacity

Sectors	Production Change in real terms(a)				Domestic Sales Change in real terms(a)				Export Change in real terms(a)				Use of capacity change in real terms(a)				Utilization of installed capacity in %					
	1974	1975	1976	1977	1974	1975	1976	1977	1974	1975	1976	1977	1974	1975	1976	1977	1972	1973	1974	1975	1976	1977
31	-0.4	5.6	4.6	5.5	4.4	30.0	9.9	10.2	-73.2	138.9	-77.1	-506	-7.3	0.7	-5.8	-6.4	78.6	86.8	79.5	80.2	69.7	65.2
32	-2.0	-20.0	20.0	0.1	11.8	2.6	24.1	1.3	9.1	-35.7	23.2	-32.8	-15.8	5.0	19.4	4.7	85.3	91.4	75.6	76.1	87.5	91.6
33	27.8	-16.9	-4.9	-6.3	1.9	-12.5	-22.0	9.9	29.1	-30.8	119.9	71.7	-43.3	-4.3	-19.1	17.3	71.2	96.8	53.5	49.2	51.4	60.4
34	10.4	-7.0	3.6	-2.7	4.1	27.5	6.3	3.3	15.4	76.9	-18.1	1.6	7.2	11.1	2.4	-6.3	96.3	80.4	87.6	76.5	72.9	68.3
35	10.8	-19.6	-9.8	10.9	23.4	-1.4	-15.7	20.1	-18.7	-60.0	10.5	-13.9	-17.9	4.9	-16.1	3.9	92.1	81.2	63.3	68.2	87.4	90.8
36	15.1	-27.5	25.1	12.6	12.9	6.9	3.1	23.9	26.2	-31.4	167.5	-31.1	-5.4	-20.1	8.1	8.5	83.8	98.2	92.8	72.7	86.2	93.5
37	7.2	-5.5	19.2	7.1	1.3	12.2	6.5	37.5	-90.0	-75.9	-	-50.0	6.6	-17.5	-5.4	-2.0	94.4	92.9	98.8	81.3	83.1	81.4
38	-6.8	-11.2	18.7	8.5	14.6	26.6	14.4	5.2	-17.9	130.9	-23.0	127.8	3.4	-13.8	27.4	17.0	66.6	67.0	70.4	56.6	61.3	71.7
39	24.1				27.9				30.9													
TOTAL	2.4	-9.3	7.2	7.0	6.3	14.9	8.1	10.4	0.7	-18.3	23.7	-13.7	-8.9	-2.9	3.3	1.5	86.1	84.3	75.4	72.8	76.5	78.0

Source: <u>Coyuntura Económica</u>, Dic 1972, 1973, 1974, 1975, 1976, 1977.

Note: (a) The change is calculated from January 1 to December 31.

Table 3.13. Andean Group, Economically Active Population and Industrial Employment (000 persons)

	Economically Active Population				Absolute Growth		Growth Rates	
	1960	1969	1970	1974	1960-69	1970-74	1960-69	1970-74
Bolivia	1,310.0	1,640.9	1,731.6	1,871.4	330.9	139.8	2.53	0.87
Colombia	4,794.0	6,338.5	6,554.6	7,565.5	1,544.5	1,010.9	3.15	1.61
Chile	2,495.0	2,869.0	2,943.6	3,243.7	374.0	300.1	1.56	1.08
Ecuador	1,390.0	1,844.2	1,906.7	2,189.3	454.2	282.6	3.19	1.55
Peru	3,145.0	3,736.9	3,856.0	4,356.9	591.9	500.9	1.93	1.37
Venezuela	2,458.0	2,850.5	2,946.2	3,417.1	392.5	470.9	1.66	1.66
TOTAL	15,592.0	19,280.0	19,938.7	22,643.9	3,688.0	2,705.2	2.39	1.42

Employment in Industry (000 workers)

	Employment in Industry				Absolute Growth		Growth Rates	
	1960	1969	1970	1974	1960-69	1970-74	1960-69	1970-74
Bolivia	12.4	21.5	21.0	21.9	9.0	1.0	6.24	0.52
Colombia	254.1	326.8	338.7	416.9	72.7	78.2	2.84	2.33
Chile	175.2	214.6	243.4	253.4	39.4	9.9	2.28	0.44
Ecuador	31.2	44.2	47.3	65.6	12.9	18.3	3.93	3.71
Peru	128.6	157.4	193.9	257.5	28.8	63.6	2.27	3.20
Venezuela	148.6	233.9	210.0	284.3	85.3	74.3	5.17	3.42
TOTAL	750.1	998.4	1,054.3	1,299.6	248.1	245.3	3.23	2.35
Industrial Employment	4.8%	4.9%	5.3%	5.7%				

Source: ECLA, Economic Survey of Latin America, various issues.

Table 3.14.   Colombia Returns to Labor as a
Percentage of GDP at Factor Costs
1950-78

	Agriculture	Industry	Total
1950-54	35.9	29.2	35.9
1963-67	33.2	35.6	39.3
1970	30.1	41.8	41.2
1971	29.7	40.8	41.5
1972	27.1	40.2	40.0
1973	23.9	35.2	37.6
1974	25.5	30.4	36.3
1975	25.5	31.2	35.5
1976	21.1	31.6	34.7
1977	22.9	31.6	35.0
1978	25.3	30.9	36.6

Source: Calculated from Banco de la República, Cuentas Nacionales 1970-1975, Bogotá 1977, and Cuentas Nacionales 1970-1978, Bogotá, 1980.

Table 3.15. Colombia, Principal Export Products: Degree of Concentration and Nationality of Ownership of Producing Companies, 1974

Export Products	Degree of Concentration(1)	Nationally Owned(2)	Foreign Owned(3)
Food-processing industries	B=3 firms 70% production		3
Cement	B=4 firms 71.2% production		
Cotton cloth	A=2 firms 82.0% production	2	
Cotton thread	A=2 firms 90% production		2
Cardboard boxes	A=1 firm 80% production		1
Medicines (antiacid and antisiphilitic products)	A=1 firm 72% production		1
Glass containers	A=1 firm 90% production		
Glass	B=2 firms 70% production		2
Basic chemicals	C=4 companies 50% production	1	3
Paper	A=2 firms 85% production		2
Electrical cables	A=3 firms 95% production		
Electrical Domestic Products a) grills b) cookers	A=1 firm a) 97% b) 59%		
Chemicals (ammoniac and nitric acid)	A=2 firms 100%		2

Sources: DANE, Boletín de Estadística, Nos. 266 and 203; Banco de la Republica, Revista Mensual, January 1974; Fedesarrollo, Coyuntura Económica, January 1974.

Notes: (1) Degree of concentration: A: from 75% to 100% of production by 3 firms
B: from 50% to 75% of production by 4 firms
C: from 25% to 50% of production by 4 firms

(2) National capital more than 50%

(3) Foreign capital more than 50%

Table 3.16.   Colombia, Share of Foreign and Mixed
Manufacturing Companies in Production and
Exports of Manufactures, 1974

Industrial Division		In Production %	In Exports %
Total		43.3	44.5
31	Food, drinks, and tobacco	6.1	16.4
32	Textiles, clothing, and leather goods	50.0	54.7
33	Wood and furniture	23.2	32.2
34	Paper and publishing	55.8	57.5
35	Chemicals and oil, coal, and rubber derivatives	62.2	86.9
36	Nonmetallic minerals, except oil and coal	58.4	84.9
37	Basic metals	54.6	54.8
38	Metal machinery and equipment	58.3	61.5
39	Others	23.4	15.7

Source: DANE, Boletín Mensual, No. 266, Tables 2 and 5.

Table 3.17. Colombia, Correlation Coefficients of Industrial Investment, with Exports, Domestic Sales Imports, and Import Capacity (availability of foreign currency)

Independent variables, x		Imports				Exports		
Dependent variables, y	(a) Domestic sales	(b) Intermediate goods	(c) Capital goods	(d) Availability of foreign currency	(e) Total	(f) Traditional Industries	(g) Intermediate Industries	(h) Light engineering
Total investment	0.92	0.62	0.84	0.85	0.68	0.47	0.63	0.68
Investment in traditional industries	0.91			0.85		0.69		
Investment in intermediate industries	0.69			0.54			0.40	
Investment in light engineering	0.76			0.54				0.67

Source: Correlations based on unpublished figures from DANE.

Table 3.18.   Andean Group, Growth Rates of
Intraregional Exports, 1969-1978

EXPORTS

		To the GRAN Annual Growth Rates		To third Countries Annual Growth Rates		Accummulated Balance	
		1969-75	1975-78	1969-75	1975-78	1969-75	1975-78
Bolivia	Type A	131.137	-15.87	2.6	- 0.4	109.7	39.9
	Type B	-17.800	42.86	12.3	26.0	43.1	- 50.8
	TOTAL	32.069	- 3.64	2.9	- 0.4	66.6	- 10.9
Colombia	Type A	23.582	- 7.63	1.2	1.1	30.7	-287.9
	Type B	30.287	23.41	15.7	2.0	146.9	629.4
	TOTAL	27.448	15.83	4.5	1.4	177.6	332.5
Chile	Type A	26.66				468.8	
	Type B	41.994				145.6	
	TOTAL	41.392				-323.2	
Ecuador	Type A	57.247	-28.24	15.0	5.6	196.0	456.5
	Type B	38.769	37.54	19.7	10.7	-103.1	135.8
	TOTAL	54.215	- 2.60	15.6	6.4	92.9	320.7
Peru	Type A	30.275	8.69	- 5.9	24.2	-237.4	565.0
	Type B	29.208	62.94	10.2	44.5	- 54.1	73.9
	TOTAL	30.061	45.95	- 5.1	26.1	-291.5	-486.1
Venezuela	Type A	15.582	3.19	10.4	- 5.9	360.8	287.0
	Type B	21.791	7.81	3.6	14.3	- 92.2	513.0
	TOTAL	16.355	4.67	-10.0	- 4.5	-277.6	-226.0
GRAN	Type A	26.69	- 7.91	- 5.8	3.7	---	
	Type B	33.006	30.87	12.9	11.9	---	
	TOTAL	28.802	15.76	- 4.4	4.8	---	

Source: 1969-75, Documento de Evaluación, 1976/di 248, Anexo
Técnico.   Tables AT 10; AT 11; AT 12; AT 101; AT
113 and AT 114.

1975-78:

Notes: 1.   Type A: Primary products (coffee, cotton, oil,
sugar) and manufactured products with low levels
of processing (such as fishmeal).

2.   Type B: Manufactures with higher levels of processing.

Table 3.19.   Andean Group, Percentage of Exports of Group B to the
Subregion by Degree of Technological Complexity, 1969-1975

Scale[1]	1969				1975			
	1-3	4-6	7-9	TOTAL	1-3	4-6	7-9	TOTAL
Bolivia	n.a.	n.a.	n.a.	100%	5.6	69.8	24.6	100%
Colombia	15.2	78.2	6.6	100%	22.3	63.2	14.5	100%
Chile	70.9	28.5	0.6	100%	70.7	26.3	3.0	100%
Ecuador	7.2	92.8	n.a.	100%	10.9	75.5	13.6	100%
Peru	31.2	68.8	n.a.	100%	46.6	46.9[b]	6.5	100%
Venezuela	4.0	92.0	4.0	100%	3.3	93.4	3.3	100%

Source: Calculated from Tables AT 115-117 of Junta, Document Jun/di 248 1977, Anexo Tecnico.

Percentage of Exports of Group B to the Subregion According to the Degree of Processing

Scale[1]	1969			1975		
	1-3	4-6	7-9	1-3	4-6	7-9
Bolivia	n.a.	n.a.	n.a.	0.1	0.7	1.5
Colombia	24.5	51.9	28.7	23.1	49.0	68.2
Chile	64.6	10.6	1.3	65.5	18.1	12.2
Ecuador	1.3	6.8	n.a.	1.5	8.0	8.6
Peru	9.2	8.3	n.a.	9.0	6.8	5.7
Venezuela	0.4	22.4	70.0	0.8	17.4	3.8
TOTAL	100.0	100.0	100.0	100.0	100.0	100.0

Source: Calculated from Tables AT 118-120 of Informe de Evaluación 1976 Jun/di 248/1977, Anexo Técnico.

Notes: (a) The classification used by the Junta when drawing up the CET and the criteria for technological contribution. It grants products from 1 to 9 in ascending order of the technological complexity of production. In groups 1 to 3 there are goods such as vegetable products, oxides, and oil; in 4 to 6, alcohol and its derivatives, simple manufactures, and yarn; in 7 to 9, woven goods, complex glass products, consumer durables, and capital goods

(b) This figure is affected by some occasional exports of Venezuela to Colombia.

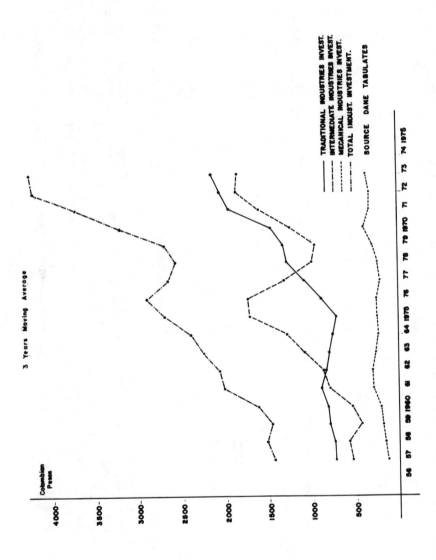

Graph 3.1 COLOMBIA: Industrial Investment 1957–1974.

144

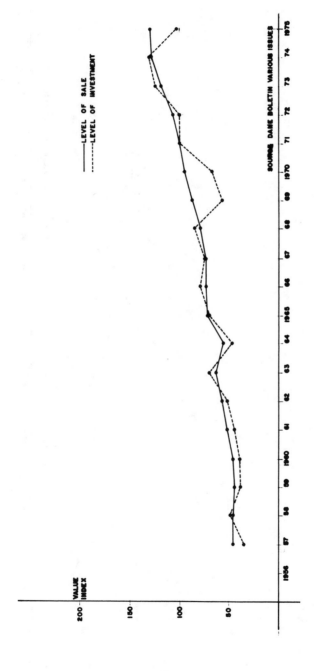

Graph 3.2 COLOMBIA: Evolution of Internal Sales and Investment Industry 1957–1975.

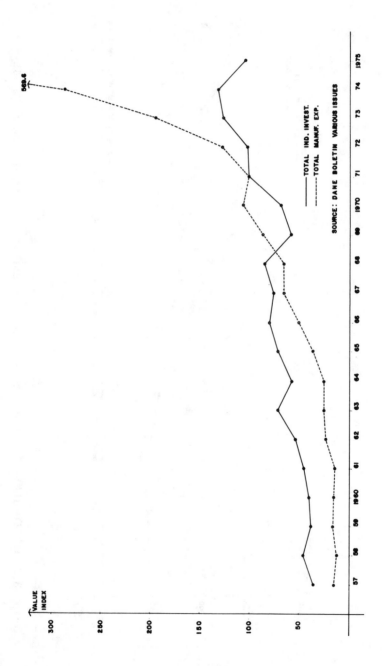

Graph 3.3. COLOMBIA: Manufactures Exports and Investments 1957-1975.

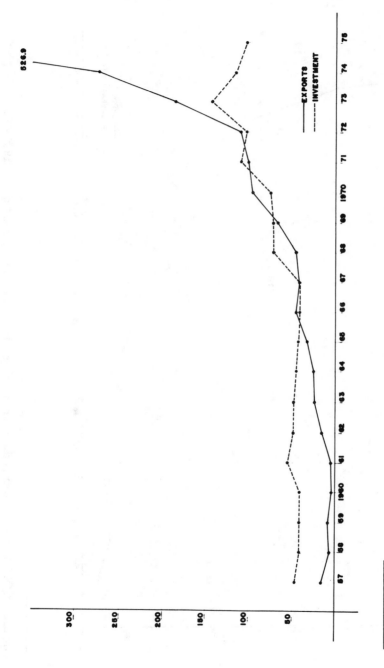

Graph 3.4 COLOMBIA: Traditional Industries, Exports, and Investments 1957-1975.

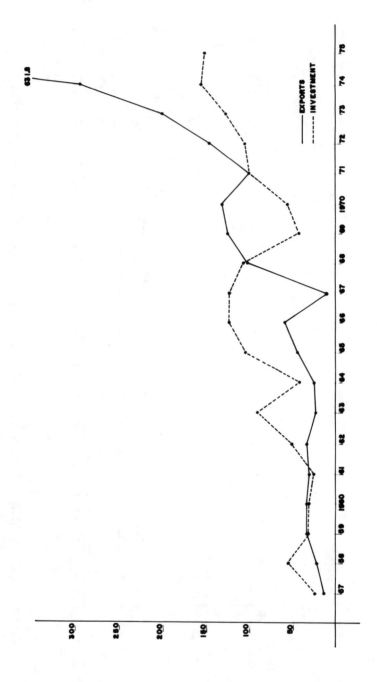

Graph 3.5   COLOMBIA: Intermediate Industries, Exports, and Investments 1957-1975.

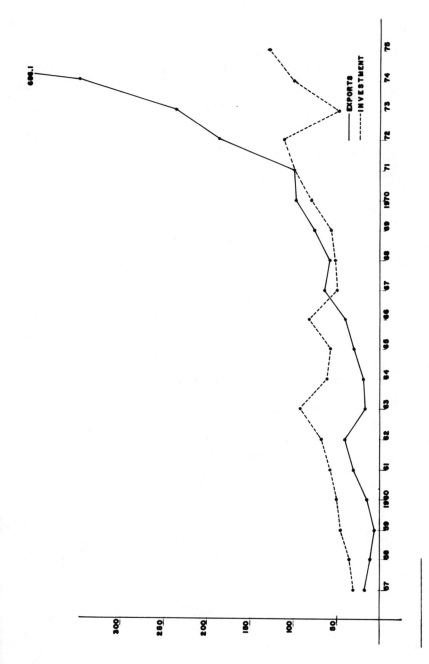

Graph 3.6 COLOMBIA: Metallic Industries, Exports, and Investments 1957–1975.

PART III
ATTITUDES

CHAPTER 4

THE POLITICS OF HARMONIZING
NATIONAL ECONOMIC POLICIES

SOME GENERAL CONSIDERATIONS

Part III of this book deals with the problems which arose with the program for the harmonization of divergent national economic policies. Chapter 4 will study the harmonization program itself, the theoretical basis upon which it was established, and the political difficulties that have so far prevented any real progress. Chapters 5, 6, and 7 will look in greater detail at the problems faced in three particular areas, over common rules for the treatment of foreign capital, sectoral industrial planning, and the Common External Tariff.

The program of harmonization of economic policies sought to make the integration agreements irrevocable: individual countries would not be permitted to reimpose tariffs or quotas, except in specific and exceptional circumstances; they would not be able to resort to measures such as fiscal concessions and preferential credit which would indirectly affect trade between countries; and exchange rates would be coordinated in order to prevent distortions in the ability to compete and in redistributive policies aimed at achieving an equilibrium.

The effect of tariff and promotion policies upon the relative capacity of the countries to compete is very clear. For example, by adopting a CET and the elimination of various subsidies, those countries that previously had lower tariffs and subsidies will gain relatively, because they will benefit from the greater changes in other member countries and lose less by withdrawing support from exports. Theoretically then, they will be more inclined to accept such policies.

With regard to exchange rate policy, problems can be reduced by establishing freely adjustable rates. However, the relative competitiveness of member countries' industries will vary if the rate of inflation differs in each country, and if monetary devaluations occur intermittently. Such variations take place during the inflation-devaluation cycle. Modifications to the exchange rate according to changes in relative prices have the same effect as changes in tariffs and export subsidies. These changes affect flows of intrasubregional trade and create uncertainty regarding the value of national currency and the selling price of foreign competitors. These effects are accentuated if countries "undervalue," or devalue, their currency more than is demanded by changes in internal prices and by the balance-of-payments position. However, these effects can be prevented if member countries adopt a policy of devaluing pari passu with internal inflation, which means maintaining the real rate of exchange constant. Thus, to eliminate those distortions which make economic integration difficult, it is necessary in the first place to adopt a CET, to reject the use of tariff and nontariff barriers to intra-subregional trade, and to eradicate variations in the real rates of exchange.(1)

Balassa states that if similar levels of industrialization exist among member countries, these measures would be sufficient to achieve an equitable distribution of the benefits of integration and to ensure the stability of the group, as all member countries would benefit. But when dealing with countries which have dissimilar levels of industrialization it becomes necessary to harmonize industrial policies. In this connection a distinction has to be made between existing and new industries. For the former, the requirement is that integration should lead to interindustrial specialization by initiating a process of selection in each country; this should lead to the contraction or closure of certain industries. The experience of the EEC, the CACM, and LAFTA suggests that the process leads to intraindustrial specialization, achieved by the increase in trade in consumer goods and specialization within companies on a smaller variety of goods. In the CACM, for example, the growth of trade in textiles and footwear has been considerable, without there being any adverse effects upon the national industries.(2) For new industries, a harmonized industrial policy should plan their location in order to guarantee an equitable distribution of benefits; this is the more urgent the greater is the gap in levels of industrial development.(3)

The relevance of these arguments to the GRAN is clear: there were considerable differences in levels of industrialization, rates and rhythms of inflation, and exchange rate, monetary, tax and promotion policies, as we have seen. Common planning systems and long-term joint development plans would therefore be needed to ensure continuity and rational harmonization.

The argument that such a level of integration was viable, implying as it did at least the partial ceding of national policy management, was based upon the European experience and upon European theories - perhaps more on the latter, for the former was seen in part in political terms, as a move from economic integration to political union. The history of the European integration movement seemed to suggest, at least in the 1960s, that progressive economic integration would inevitably lead to political integration, and possibly to political union or federation. The European experience and the theoretical contributions that emerged from it were familiar to the founders of the GRAN and colored much of their thinking. As in the European case itself, however, political difficulties emerged that at least delayed progress toward more complex forms of integration. We therefore turn here to a detailed analysis of the political and ideological constraints to fuller economic integration.

THE POLITICAL AND IDEOLOGICAL CONSTRAINTS
ON THE PROCESS OF ECONOMIC INTEGRATION

In Chapter 1 we gave a brief account of the theories and ideologies that lay behind the creation of the GRAN, referring in particular to certain currents of European economic thought, to the ECLA doctrines, and to the politically oriented approach of the neo-functionalists. We now turn again briefly to the neo-functionalist approach, as a prelude to a detailed analysis of the political difficulties experienced within the GRAN.

The central emphases of the neo-functionalist approach were drawn almost exclusively from the post-World War II experience of Western Europe, characterized by a movement toward economic cooperation and eventual integration on the part of countries whose history had been one of periodic and bloody conflict. The approach lays particular stress on the gradual evolution of economic integration by stages and on the close relationship between the phase of economic integration and the political integration this produces. The neo-functionalist position - accepted by the founders of the GRAN(4) - is that economic integration is a continuum that passes through stages from the simplest of beginnings to the more complex processes of political integration.(5) This is not defined in the first instance as the total disappearance of national states, but as a very slow process of gradual and progressive ceding of sovereignty. Such a process is inevitable if passage from one stage of economic integration to another is to be made. For the neo-functionalists, the goal of economic integration is political union, which is achieved when national states become obsolete and wither away.

For the founders of the GRAN this approach was appealing because it offered a possible explanation for the failure of

LAFTA, as it could be argued that the weakness of the scheme was that no political mechanisms had been developed to build upon the initial creation of a free trade zone. The liberation of trade should have been followed by a political commitment to negotiate a common external tariff, and so on successively.(6)

The acceptance of the neo-functionalist principle of a gradual movement towards more complex forms of integration was implicit in the periodization of the process suggested by the Junta. The Treaty was to be implemented in four successive stages, each one taking the liberalization of trade a step further. The stages proposed were as follows:

Stage One: the harmonization of policies regarding the
1969-70   treatment of foreign capital. This stage would
               last one year, during which time the programs
               for trade liberation and sectoral development
               would be prepared
Stage Two: five years were allowed for the approval of all
1970-75   sectoral programs and of the common norms for
               commercial exchange which would establish a
               unified market
Stage Three: over a period of five years (and ten in the case
1975-80   of Bolivia and Ecuador) the sectoral programs
               would be launched; the commercial program
               would proceed until the markets of Colombia,
               Chile, Peru, and Venezuela were completely
               open; a common external tariff and common
               norms regarding competition would be adopted;
               and resources for long-term development would
               be assigned
Stage Four: the final stage would see the perfecting of the
1980-85   economic union through the total liberation of the
               products on the list of exceptions, the harmo-
               nization of major economic policies, and the
               adoption of the Common Development Strate-
               gy.(7)

The final stagnation of the Andean Pact was a result not of a lack of economic coherence or rationality, but of a failure of political will; in this respect the neo-functionalist approach offered little guidance regarding the political difficulties that arise when integration is undertaken by countries which could be classified as less developed and which are at different stages of the import substitution stage. While in Europe integration could be seen as an end in itself, or at least as a primarily political goal,(8) in Latin America and in less developed countries in general, whatever their social and economic systems, integration is seen as an instrument of economic policy, capable of accelerating development, reactivating, and extending economic activity - and above all hastening the process of import substitution. It is because integration is seen primarily as a means to accelerate economic modernization that severely limiting constraints of a political and ideological nature arise.

The different political and ideological responses to economic integration and the problems experienced within the GRAN can best be understood not by placing the different political actors along a left-right spectrum (an undertaking that would in any case present serious problems of definition and interpretation), but by taking economic nationalism as a point of reference. The history of the GRAN provides ample evidence that attitudes to the Andean Pact do not correlate with political positions along a left-right spectrum, and this is a characteristic the GRAN shares with other economic communities, particularly the EEC.(9)

In the case of the GRAN, there are a number of reasons why this should be so. Intrasubregional trade constitutes only a very small proportion of the total trade of the GRAN countries, and the GRAN itself has never really been a political issue stricto sensu.(10) Where conflicts have arisen, they have frequently taken place entirely outside the party political arena, as was the case for example with the dispute between FEDECAMARAS in Venezuela and the successive governments of Leoni and Caldera. Furthermore, the GRAN, unlike the EEC, does not impinge massively and directly on internal policies. In the circumstances groups who are directly affected by the policies of the group - such as industrialists - have little to gain by mounting public campaigns and tend to work through official or associational channels. Finally, the GRAN itself can scarcely be described as "leftist" or "rightist." Its developmentalist aims and ideology can embrace specific policies and goals cutting right across the political spectrum, and even in the case of such items as Decision 24 an explanation in terms of economic nationalism alone is perfectly satisfactory.

The characteristics of the phenomenon we call economic nationalism, as described in the following pages can be observed in such things as: (a) the controls leveled upon foreign capital, (b) the prominence given to state direct investment, and (c) the commitment to industrialization. But it could equally be argued that given the circumstances of the member countries, economic integration is a safer and more palatable option than more radical policies such as a significant redistribution of income. And, while one could point to the GRAN's welcoming of Allende's election in Chile as evidence of its commitment to the principle of ideological and political pluralism, a commitment the GRAN members themselves proclaimed in 1971,(11) the same acceptance of "ideological diversity" was equally extended to President Pinochet and to Banzer, the successor to Torres, so that no easy political lessons can be drawn.

Temporary neglect of the principle of pluralism when García Mesa took office in Bolivia does not invalidate our previous hypothesis of a lack of correlation between integration and right- or left-wing political attitudes, for two main reasons: First, incompatibility with the Agreement was not declared by the Bolivian government, and second, the criticizing attitude of the governments of Ecuador, Colombia, and Peru may be explained by domestic reasons: the attempt to discourage and avoid in their countries military actions such as that taking place in Bolivia. Furthermore, entities like the EEC have exercised evident pressure, upon the GRAN member countries' governments, for the diplomatic isolation of García Mesa's government by conditioning the signing of an EEC-GRAN cooperation agreement.

It is important to point out that the policy of isolating a member country, under the pretext of defending and promoting democratic changes in the Continent, have worsened the critical situation the GRAN experienced since 1975 and constituted a determining factor for the stagnation of the last two years. "All attempts to enhance political cooperation have had repercussions in the economic integration process, because from the start it failed to reach the general objective of improving the diplomatic and political climate for economic integration."(12)

The lack of correlation between political attitudes in left-wing terms and attitudes to economic integration and the GRAN can be seen if we examine in greater detail particular national responses to these issues. In this context the Bolivian case is particularly striking. Paz Estenssoro's center-right civilian government, apparently under some pressure from industrial groups, especially those with interests in tin mining, held back on entry into LAFTA,(13) and Bolivia remained outside it until 1966, when it was taken in by the rightist General Barrientos, who subsequently participated in the Bogota Declaration and the formation of the Mixed Commission. However, both the formerly leftist MNR (National Revolutionary Movement) and the rightist Falange Boliviana opposed Bolivian entry to the GRAN on the grounds that the country should not take part in international agreements with Chile if Chile would not guarantee a Bolivian outlet to the Pacific.(14) Bolivian entry was nevertheless ratified in September 1969 by General Ovando, and subsequently by both radical leftist General Torres and his extreme right-wing successor General Banzer, who defeated Torres in a bloody coup. In fact both Torres and Banzer followed a line of strong support for the policies on foreign capital and particularly on sectoral development proposals, with Banzer going as far as to threaten Bolivian withdrawal if the latter were not approved by the GRAN.(15) Governments of an entirely contrasting political stripe were thus able to follow identical policies within the GRAN. It would appear that Bolivia entered the group to escape from diplomatic isolation among the Andean countries and to benefit from the economic advantages offered - although the potential of the larger market was preached more by government officials than by the industrialists who would supposedly stand to gain themselves.(16)

This raises the question of the extent to which other participants were moved by diplomatic or political considerations. In the Chilean case, particularly under the government of President Allende, there was a clearer connection with domestic politics. Changing the emphases of Frei's earlier commitment to the scheme, Allende sought within the Commission to win priority for the adoption of nationalist policies and initiatives that would give the state greater participation in industrial development. The approval of Decision 24 and the adoption of industrial development programs were used by Allende to support and enhance the legitimacy of his domestic policies of nationalization and protectionism, although it is difficult to assess either the real effect of this tactic vis-à-vis a hostile congress, or the true importance that the issue had for Allende. For all this apparent commitment, however, it was Chile that of all the member countries was most frequently accused of violating or failing to implement the decisions of the GRAN.(17)

Peru's record under General Velasco in particular was not dissimilar to that of Chile under Allende. Peru pressed within the Commission for more nationalist and interventionist measures and used those that were forthcoming to legitimize its domestic policies; it also frequently violated clauses of the Commercial Program, as well as others concerning industrial policy and the treatment of capital. In the case of Decision 46, for example, regarding common treatment of subregional capital and Andean multinational corporations, Peru supported the measures actively within the Commission but paradoxically failed to implement them subsequently. It is reasonable to suppose that the Peruvian government was reluctant to do so because, given the restrictions facing capital in Peru, in the form of legislation concerning "social property" and the "industrial community," some capital flight to other Andean countries might have occurred. It may have been for similar reasons too that the Chilean government did not implement the measures in question.

Diplomatic considerations seem to have played a major part in Venezuela's decision to join the GRAN. Presidents Leoni and Caldera both based their case for joining, when facing the opposition of FEDECAMARAS, on the need to escape from diplomatic isolation, perhaps especially with an eye to the rise of Brazil to international prominence.(18) The oil crisis of 1973-74, which had a severe impact on Andean net importers, must have increased the desirability of adherence to the GRAN as a demonstration of solidarity with the rest of the region and neutralized FEDECAMARAS.

The best argument for a left-right polarization within the GRAN would appear to be the Chilean and Colombian reform campaign which ended with the withdrawal of Chile. But, as we saw in Chapter 1, Chile in fact withdrew after it had obtained all the reforms it needed to remain within the group, while continuing at home to pursue the liberal policies inspired by Milton Friedman.(19) The complexities of the case can be better appreciated if we turn our attention more particularly to the shift in Colombian policy that brought it into alliance with what was after all a political regime of an entirely different stamp.

As it has been pointed out in Chapter 2, López Michelsen pursed a program of economic stabilization, following, although with a different intensity, the same neo-liberal strategy as that applied in Chile since 1974. López Michelson had come to power after the greatest electoral victory recorded in a country with a long electoral tradition, but he nevertheless found it necessary to govern with an eye to the demands of the center-left. The first act of his government was to push through a progressive tax reform, although this was later dismantled by Congress and by the Liberal government that succeeded his own. Subsequent policies included severe restrictions on foreign investment in the banking sector, and a scheme to "Colombianize" industry.(20) In labor affairs, the government was the first since 1946 to recognize a trade union federation oriented by the Communist Party, the federation in question being the Confederacion Sindical de Trabajadores Colombianos (CSTC), with the second largest number of affiliates in the country relatively short-lived since its legal status was suspended in October of 1981 by the liberal President Turbay. Lopez also resisted pressure from the army for measures to increase its legal competence to "fight for the maintenance of public order." His government adhered to the principle of press freedom and on the international front reestablished diplomatic relations with Cuba, supported General Torrijos regarding the new treaty with the United States over the Panama Canal, and joined the group of countries attempting to isolate both politically and diplomatically the Somoza dictatorship in Nicaragua. At the same time, and in line with its domestic economic policy, Lopez's government acted in Lima in support of all the Chilean proposals for reform of the GRAN. The withdrawal of Chile while Colombia remained within the organization must therefore be explained by wider political and diplomatic considerations.(21)

It is difficult to argue then that economic integration has been held back by polarization of an elementary left-versus-right nature. On the other hand, it does seem possible to approach a clearer understanding of the problems that have arisen by ascribing them to narrow nationalism.(22) The political leaders and technical experts who worked in the Mixed

Commission and later promoted the GRAN did so almost exclusively with an eye to the economic gains for their own countries, seeing the creation of a common market of accelerating their own industrial development.(23) Given this narrow commitment on all sides, growth in the subregion as a whole was never really accepted as an overriding priority. This approach could not fail to have negative consequences; evidently, the major subregional goals of balanced development and equitable distribution of benefits were not compatible either with the blinkered pursuit of national economic objectives or with the political and diplomatic preoccupations of individual countries. Not all members could expect accelerated growth; some would have to sacrifice national goals if coordinated policies for the whole region were to be achieved. Those countries with more advanced industrial sectors would have to sacrifice a part of their own potential growth on behalf of the less developed, and this fact and the conflicts it created were brought to the fore in the discussions over the protection of industry within the subregion, the common external tariff, and the sectoral programs, as we shall see in subsequent chapters.

In any case, the difficulties of harmonizing major aspects of economic policy, even given the will to do so, should not be minimized: intrasubregional trade was marginal for all member countries in economic terms,(24) and it would have been impractical to expect any government to renounce control over its own economy in strategic areas such as exchange control in order to further the long-term objectives of the GRAN when this was the case, and when it would reduce their ability to react to specific situations affecting for example a single commodity in which the rest of the group had little interest, such as tin (Bolivia), fish meal (Peru), copper (Chile), or coffee (Colombia). The political will for integration did not emerge automatically as the successive stages of economic integration were reached, because of the interplay of long-term political and economic costs with short-term benefits such as increased exports.

Our insistence that it was preoccupation with national economic development that prejudiced the plans for economic integration of the GRAN may seem a little paradoxical in view of the fact that the GRAN itself could be considered nationalist to the extent that it would tend to give the member countries greater strength and autonomy in formulating economic policies relating to the world market, multinationals, and other international economic organizations. But, despite these potential gains, the record shows that no member country was prepared at any stage to cede its sovereignty by allowing the responsibility for economic decisions to be vested in the Commission.(25) Given the lack of congruence between the rhetoric of integration and the actual marginal nature of the GRAN as far as each member country was concerned, the concept of

"Andean nationalism" was clearly utopian. The sum of the different individual nationalisms of member countries would not add up to "Andean nationalism" but annul it.

The impact of nationalism on the GRAN was not, however, confined to economic issues, for other aspects of nationalism emerged as even greater obstacles to integration. Unfortunately narrow nationalism within Latin America has not been studied in any depth, and it will not be possible here to do more than suggest that among the member countries of the GRAN there exist tensions between nations that are the product of history, geography, and even ethnic diversity. These tensions should not be lightly dismissed; all the member countries have been involved in frontier wars at one time or another, and many problems remain unresolved. Colombia and Venezuela have been negotiating for the last 15 years over the frontier in the petroleum zone in the Gulf of Venezuela; Peru does not yet recognize the boundary lines imposed by Chile after the War of the Pacific a century ago, and Bolivia's own position regarding an exit to the Pacific coast is well known. In the thirties and forties Colombia, Ecuador, and Peru were involved in military confrontations over the delimitation of frontiers in the Amazonian region. At the beginning of 1981 we witnessed a military confrontation between Ecuador and Peru; the crisis paralyzed all activity within the GRAN for over eight months and made it impossible to convene any meeting of the Commission. The extent to which these conflicts affect national attitudes and prejudice the prospects for economic integration is a theme for future research and entirely escapes the terms of this book, but they cannot be ignored, if only because of their practical effects. No research has been carried out into the impact of this heritage of unstable frontier regions (to take one example, it is calculated that one million Colombians work illegally in Venezuela) on such things as military spending. And the failure to implement such simple measures as the elimination of the need to present passports within the GRAN is an eloquent testimonial to the utopianism of schemes of "Andean citizenship."

In the end then, in a world in which nation states seek to exercise sovereignty to their maximum advantage and pursue economic growth as a fillip to their self-esteem and their international prestige, the GRAN has not seemed the most adequate mechanism for accelerating the economic development of all member countries.(26)

THE HARMONIZATION OF POLICIES IN THE GRAN

The harmonization of economic policies was clearly conceived in order to condition the reciprocal and dynamic nature of internal policies and those of integration in such a way that the former could not be exercised in favor of national autarchy.(27) Harmonization means the adoption of a common development strategy that aims to achieve balanced growth, employment generation, the strengthening of negotiating capacity(28) through sectoral programs and the harmonization of policies in specific fields.(29) It is a force for overcoming the precariousness of cooperation and integration, which derives, among other things, from differences between the economic units being integrated, low global and per capita GNP, and the wide range of dispersion of these indicators among the members, the low level of previous transactions, the lack of transport infrastructure, sentiments of independence, and the difficulty governments have in formulating long-term policies.

The possibility of achieving political integration was expressed in the term "la vocación integradora" (the vocation for integration) of the Latin American countries, which existed in the 1960s, when the three Latin American cases of integration were being created. This spirit is embodied in the preparatory documents of the Treaty and in presidential statements;(30) economic integration was seen as indispensable for development. It would not just achieve greater rates of growth, but set into motion a planned process for the solution of internal structural problems, to close the gap between developed and Latin American countries, and to consolidate the political ideal of a united Latin America. The central idea was that the solution of a country's development problems was not the responsibility of each one separately but of the Latin American community. But this "vocation" was in fact shared only by the small political and technocratic elite committed to pursuing politicoeconomic reforms, and backed and financed by the United States.

However, the determination to assume collective responsibility for the development of the Andean countries was weakened when abstract principles had to be transformed into concrete agreements and when it became clear that the joint assumption of the ideal meant that some countries would bear a high proportion of the costs.

The loss of momentum of the integrationist idea is to be found during the negotiation and signing of the Treaty, in the political implications deriving from the proposed economic model, the contradictions between and within national groups, and the relations with foreign capital.

We will now study those relations briefly, without trying to be exhaustive. However, as we have asserted, we believe that it is necessary to make a greater connection between economic and political analyses in order to understand better the scope and limitations of the integration process.

Our hypothesis is that the GRAN arose as a political response to socioeconomic problems, without the backing of the groups that would be the subject of integration, partly because it was not clearly foreseen who would benefit, and what the costs of integration would be. These groups did not mobilize until the intensification of the process affected specific areas of vital interest: the common treatment of foreign capital, the CET, sectoral programming of the harmonization of policies. Mobilization tended to move to oppose rather than to support integration. But the whole thrust of parts I and II of this book has been to demonstrate that the Andean group, in order to work, should have enjoyed a great degree of political integration, because of the differences in the level of economic development among member countries and because of the divergent economic policies followed by each of them.

However, it will be our argument here that precisely the same factors that made political integration so necessary also made it less likely: the great differences in economic development and the character and scope of the regional import substitution proposed by the Treaty reinforced the nationalistic positions of the countries for various reasons; in particular, because, when income is low, welfare limited, and resources scarce, distribution problems are likely to be more hotly contested. In addition, it is more likely that backwash effects and the clustering of industry, in order to take advantage of external economies, will be more politically apparent and more difficult to resolve in smaller and poorer economies with fewer poles of growth.

The process of harmonizing policies was conceived as a way to induce and maintain economic integration, not as a result of it. In this way, a premature politization occurred, limiting the power of the technical experts before large groups could give their support.(31) In fact, measures such as Decision 24, the CET, and the sectoral programs, to mention only a few, should have been approved before the commercial program was fully implemented, and long before subregional trade became important.

THE ACTORS IN THE ANDEAN INTEGRATION PROCESS

National Politicians

The GRAN was conceived by a more or less closed group of reformist politicians, who were conscious of the need for reforms in order to alleviate the problems of underdevelopment. These politicians were aided by technocrats, who wanted to take part in the task of achieving higher economic growth rates.

There was a new reformist elite, which had economic growth as its goal, and which understood the consequences of limited national markets for a country's welfare. Nevertheless, in the light of what has already been said, the term "reformist elite" should be somewhat qualified.

Given the incongruence noted between the formal economic objectives ascribed to integration, and the practical political and diplomatic problems that arose, it is clear that not all the politicians who directed the integration effort were part of this "reformist elite" in their own countries; this was especially not the case of the presidents of Bolivia and Ecuador. The term should also be limited in time; it is applicable to the founders of the GRAN, who, as we saw, sought the support of their national technical experts, but can scarcely be applied to later governments, despite their lip-service to the GRAN. Finally, the term "elite" should be understood most emphatically to contain the implication of reform "from above," which marked the GRAN from its beginnings, as it marked all the reforms associated with the Alliance for Progress. No importance was attached to Andean integration by any political or trade union movement or by any industrial association; public feeling was not behind it, nor was it promoted by any political party. The initiative came from an "enlightened group" which, to borrow an example very dear to Max Weber,(32) felt that structural reforms could be achieved by way of institutional reforms, which by their nature tend to be imposed from above. But we will see the incongruency between the structures and the institutions, the gulf between rhetoric and practice, and the presence of governments with little reformist zeal within the GRAN.

The politicians went ahead with integration then without notably increasing their political support. In this case, the politicians were not seeking legitimacy for their programs through the traditional channels: the party apparatus, public debate, and the ballot. Here one is dealing with the personal actions of Andean presidents (especially those of Chile, Colombia, and Venezuela) who were trying to strengthen their national leadership by increasing their prestige internationally.(33)

The Treaty of Cartagena was not widely debated and its legitimation was effected automatically once it was recognized in Montevideo, as it was a development of the Treaty of Montevideo. Thus, the legislators of each member country were technically excluded from integration.

In Colombia, for example, Lleras assumed the leadership of the integrationist movement and presented it in terms of increased industrial and general growth. However he identified the campaign with himself personally and therefore limited the possibilities of continuity. For the new president, Pastrana, a member of the Conservative party who succeeded Lleras in 1970, to continue with the same policy was of little value, because to recognize and accept the leadership of a

predecessor would be to lower his own prestige and to suggest
that he had no alternative programs. Equally, because neither
he nor his party had been included in the negotiations, it was
easy to justify a change in the Colombian position on key
matters such as the common approach to foreign capital or
sectoral programming.(34)   The problem for Lopez, Pastrana's
successor,(35) was made worse by the struggle for leadership
within the Liberal party.   This is the most plausible of the
reasons usually given as to why Lopez was more opposed to
integration than Pastrana, despite the fact that Lleras was a
fellow liberal.(36)

A similar process occurred in Chile, with Frei taking
upon himself the entire leadership role in integration.   But
there the change of regime strengthened the prointegrationist
orientation for external and internal reasons.   Among the
former was Chile's desire not to become isolated from its
neighbors and to prevent the creation of a blockade such as
had been imposed on Cuba under similar circumstances.   Second, the agreements coming from the Treaty granted the necessary institutional base for advancing the nationalistic
change of policy under the Popular Unity administration.
Later, though, because integration was identified as an element
in the Unidad Popular Programme, the Pinochet government
tried from the beginning to disassociate itself from it.   But
this does not explain the Chilean position, as we show in
Chapters 2, 6, and 7.

Perhaps for the same reason as Chile, the Peruvian revolutionary military government reversed the negative stance of
the previous groups in power.   There were elements in the
Treaty that could be developed into nationalistic policies which
would reinforce the nation's negotiating position with the
transnational corporations.(37)   There was another reason why
the government was anxious to join the GRAN: the nationalization of a subsidiary of Exxon and the confrontation between
the government and the United States meant that Peru could
become economically isolated; membership would give it some
sense of solidarity and security.(38)

When, in 1967, Leoni, the Venezuelan president, imposed
the country's entry into LAFTA, the FEDECAMARAS opposed
integration in general, and with the Andean countries in
particular.   The negotiations were undertaken unilaterally
without the full consultation of his party or of other social
groups (professionals, trade unions, etc.).(39)   Leoni held the
debate against the opposition of the powerful FEDECAMARAS,
which weakened his position to the point that Venezuela's
entry into the GRAN was prevented until 1973, when President
Caldera, who had not committed himself or his party in the
previous debates on integration, mobilized some groups disposed to listen to the technocrats and weakened the position of
FEDECAMARAS somewhat.   Both presidents saw the value of

supporting integration in terms of the political leadership that Venezuela could command in Latin America, in place of Brazil, if it were able to count on the support of the other countries and on long-term industrial growth. However, the benefits were presented to public opinion in terms of long-term commercial gains. This made presentation of the argument very difficult for the technocrats, as Venezuela's special economic conditions created serious doubts regarding the benefits that could be obtained. Nevertheless, only the government itself and the FEDECAMARAS took part in the debate. Neither Leoni nor Caldera made any attempt to broaden the debate by bringing in the political parties of the opposition, or civic, professional or trade union groups.

In the case of Bolivia, the government's motives were above all political. Many of the arguments in favor of membership revolved around the desire to gain access to the Pacific and the repercussions that cooperation within the GRAN might precipitate regarding the tense relations with Chile. Vaitsos suggests that for Bolivia, Ecuador, and Peru, the initial interest in the GRAN was of a historical, military, and political rather than economic nature and that, within its framework, they (especially Bolivia and Ecuador) would try to obtain greater economic concessions.

The way in which integration was generally legitimized, in terms of accelerated industrial growth(40) and, because of the very nature of integration, progress in the substitution of imports,(41) meant that the ability of politicians to promote the scheme was fragile. Integration was seen in terms of national advantage. Given the severity of the economic problems of underdeveloped countries, there is a need to secure immediate benefits for industrial sectors in order to legitimize the process. Hence the awareness that it is necessary to distribute the benefits equitably, a point emphasized within the GRAN.

However, the benefits can be neither immediate nor dramatic, because of the existing productive and commercial structure of the member countries, as we have shown in Chapter 3. This factor weakens the sphere of action of the leadership, because there will be high prices to pay for the change in traditional flows of trade from the implementation of the CET, with these changes probably being concentrated on the less developed member countries, with the more developed assuming the costs of distributing the benefits equitably: somebody will be sacrificing national interests in favor of the industrialization of others.(42) As we shall see later in this chapter, the emphasis on industrialization made it impossible for other economic sectors to support the program; there was therefore a repetition of the experience of import substitution policy, which failed to gain widespread support although it was presented as being of "national interest."

Thus we have a situation in which not only were the possibilities for the political leaders to gain support for the GRAN limited by the nature of integration, but the leaders varied in their stance from country to country. Therefore, there was missing one component of the "integrative potential"(43) stressed in neo-functionalist thought, the functioning of which is important for the realization of the movement towards political integration - that is "elite complementarity," which means more than the homogeneity of political regimes. It is perfectly possible, as we have seen, to have military regimes side by side with elected governments, as happened in the CACM and in the GRAN. Complementarity means similar views towards the most important regional issues.

In general, if Nye's criteria are applied to the GRAN, it could be said that its potential for integration was limited because there was a great asymmetry, and therefore the equity of distribution of benefits was not perceived and the visible costs were high. Furthermore, one is dealing with societies that are not pluralist, and with states that do not have a high capacity to respond.(44)

The "Técnicos"

The idea of integration arose among the technical experts (técnicos) in ECLA; Hirschmann says that in this way the men in ECLA were able to soothe frustrations arising from the breakdown of their recommendations and planning.(45) ECLA found allies among national technocrats, especially the planners who helped to advance this integrationist "conspiracy."(46)

The preponderant role of the técnicos in the setting up of the LAFTA and the CACM has been fully recognized. The same participation was decisive in the case of the GRAN, which drew on the LAFTA experience.(47)

In each case, the técnicos were convinced of the need to industrialize and to bring about reforms. They often worked with presidents and planned agrarian, tax, and administrative reforms. These men were capable of giving directions and recommending the more efficient use of scarce resources or ways to achieve a greater flow of external resources.(48) However, their power was very limited because they depended wholly upon the politicians in power; in many cases the planning departments depended directly upon the presidential office, and plans tended to be changed on the arrival of a new president.(49)

Also, in the case of some Andean countries, the possibilities for the technocrats to act independently were limited by the fact that the costs of integration (or the results of tax, agrarian, and administrative reforms) too soon became apparent, and the external pressure that had pushed the countries toward integration subsided. By the beginning of 1974 the fear of the revolution had almost disappeared and the United States and international agencies were interested in pushing "rational economic policies." Thus the technocrats shifted to more conservative positions and began to present solutions that avoided confrontation with opposing interest groups.

Some authors suggest that the limited scope of technocrats is due to the fact that in societies undergoing modernization, the economy and politics are intricately linked; there is a continual switching from one level to another. Each step up the ladder of integration involves greater ceding of sovereignty from existing national units, in policy areas touching more and more closely upon central questions of national prestige or economic welfare. The Latin American experience shows that problems arise very quickly that have to be resolved at a higher political level.(50) The explanation is that economic problems in underdeveloped countries contain a large political element and have governmental priority. Thus what is often considered in the EEC to be a question of welfare politics often becomes associated with national economic and security policies in underdeveloped countries. All this is related, in the final analysis, with the problems of redistributing the benefits of integration and of placing limits on the resources to be distributed.(51) The latter means that "equitable distribution" involves the ceding of sovereignty. All this leads to "overpolitization" of the process,(52) and restricts the scope of action at a technical level.

Added to this are the costs of imports substituted at regional level and the problems derived from the controversial identification of industrialization as the "national aim." The nature and timetable of the Treaty of Cartagena made the phenomenon of overpolitization even more acute. As we saw in Chapter 1, the agreements on positive integration were conceived as antecedents and creators of the institutional framework which would accompany the new economic order. Thus, the field of action and the period of influence of the technocrats and bureaucrats was further limited.(53)

The experience of the CACM was the reverse. The planners set out a low-cost integration strategy for the first stages. Agriculture was excluded. Economic problems that related to specific economic ministers were kept out of the hands of politicians in the Foreign Office. Also, the industrial planning element in the Treaty was eliminated in order to assure external financing. These are the factors to which the great rise of Central American integration is attributed.(54) However, they also created crisis conditions, because they avoided embarking on the task of preventing the concentration of industries and failed to satisfy the need to distribute the benefits of integration.(55)

The Industrial Sector

Nor did the industrial sector, for which the integrationalist plan was primarily designed, act on its own behalf to accelerate the completion of the agreements and to secure a wider market for itself. This sector secured a wider market simply by virtue of the definition of the political leadership and the identification of national interests with that of constructing a modern industry. It was not required to fight for it; for that reason it did not feel committed to accept any costs of integration that might entail the reduction or limitation of its privileges.

For LAFTA several authors have found that the industrialists of the three largest countries - Argentina, Brazil, and Mexico - were in frank opposition to the idea of a free trade zone, as were those of Peru and all the industrial sectors of Uruguay and Paraguay.(56) The industrial sectors of the larger countries were afraid that their higher labor costs would spoil their chances in competition. Within their relatively extensive protected markets they enjoyed satisfactory levels of earnings and profitability. These fears have proved unfounded since they have been the net beneficiaries. Perhaps their reluctance was due to the fear that the agreements could result in a higher level of government intervention, which they did not wish to encourage.(57)

The industrial sectors of the Andean Group - their interests, attitudes, and relations with other groups, with the state and with the external sector - have not yet been studied in sufficient detail to determine their role in the process of policy formation. We have explained their attitudes ourselves through press articles, the official documents of industrial unions, and interviews(58) and conclude that in the majority of cases the industrial sectors of the six Andean countries remained watchful, trying to obtain the highest possible degree of protection within the free trade agreements.(59)

In the Colombian case we can illustrate the lack of mobilization through the analysis of the press during the period 1965 to 1975. A study of the information published by the Colombian newspaper with the highest circulation reveals that during the years in which the agreement was being negotiated, from January 1966 to March 1969, no fewer than 400 informative accounts, articles, and editorials on Latin American integration appeared. Of those only two came from the National Association of Colombian Industrialists (ANDI), and then only after the signing of the Agreement.(60)

Between May 1969 and December 1975 no fewer than 500 news items, articles, and editorials on the Andean Group were published by the same newspaper. Only one was from ANDI and it was a defense of the pact. Two are declarations by the Asociacion Colombiana de Pequenos Industriales (ACOPI) which can be considered as favoring trade in general and not specifically the Cartagena Agreement. During the same period there were 21 declarations by the private sector opposing the progress of the Agreement. The points of opposition were Decision 24,(61) the admission of Venezuela,(62) and sectoral planning.(63)

We are inclined to think that the Colombian industrial sector preferred to adopt a passive attitude during a time when government activity in favor of integration was particularly intense, 1966-1970. This sector firmly supported changes in the Cartagena Agreement proposed by the new government when elements obviously opposed to the plan of Andean integration entered the presidency in 1970. During the 1971-75 period the Colombian private sector attempted to prolong discussion and to avoid making decisions upon matters which could affect it: sectoral planning, CET, and the harmonization of policies.(64)

We considered that the industrialist groups in ANDI were the ones from among whom support for GRAN could be expected because they represented those who could benefit by exporting. ACOPI represents small industrialists less concerned with export opportunities.

Thus we are inclined to disagree with the conclusions of Vaitsos that during the period 1965-68 the endeavors to integrate into what later became the Andean Pact corresponded clearly to the interests and expectations of the industrial bourgeoisie of Colombia and Chile, interpreted and expressed by the political leaders of these countries. The lack of support from Colombian industrialists can hardly be explained by identity of interests among the political leaders and industrialists. We would prefer to suggest that they chose not to oppose the "idea" of integration, accepting the widening of the market, but at the same time assuming protectionist positions.(65)

It would seem that ANDI adopted a strategy that was different from that of the active FEDECAMARAS, but nonetheless had the same context, which we will analyze later. ANDI would be interested in the benefits from an Andean Group without the costs of sectoral planning, and especially without the equitable redistribution of the profits of integration, always provided that some elements of the substitution policy were retained. It would be necessary to analyze the reason for the initial passivity of the industrial sector and to identify clearly what its real interests were. Recent studies show that in Colombia the state has been less firmly based on industrial interests than is generally assumed.(66)

The reason why the Bolivian and Ecuadorian industrial sectors were opposed to the Andean Market is clear; their weak industrial sectors would be seriously threatened by competition.(67) But, unable to resist the governments who were forcing participation, they attempted to gain the greatest possible number of concessions. Even now they remain skeptical and lacking in motivations,(68) but on no occasion have they formed a front of open opposition.(69)

The Peruvian private sector was against entry to the Andean Group, because of the social and economic interest of the hegemonic agroindustrial group.(70) Immediately after the 1968 change of government the private sector altered its position, apparently to avoid being left out of the negotiations. It supported sectoral planning and the role in industrial development granted to the state.(71) The shift in opinion of the private sector Peruvian managers, as radical as that of the government shortly after the military coup, commands one's attention. It would be worthwhile inquiring whether, at bottom, the reasons for this preference are to be found in the possibility of profits and investments realizable in other member countries whose legislation was not aligned with the new industrial regime in Peru.

To turn to the Venezuelan case, it is perhaps paradoxical that FEDECAMARAS, the pressure group which showed greatest interest in the problems of integration, both promoting and developing the debate at national and international levels, always maintained a critical attitude to Venezuela and opposed the entry of Venezuela. FEDECAMARAS succeeded in postponing the entry of Venezuela to the GRAN on two occasions (1968 and 1969), and in obtaining certain favorable concessions, such as the establishment of the power of veto over CET and SIDP, agricultural safeguard clauses, possibilities for countries to take unilateral action to improve safeguard measures taken as a consequence of the reduction of trade barriers, some additions to the list of 200 exceptions for goods produced in Colombia, Chile, and Peru, and modifications to the Capital Statute.(72) It is interesting to note that, at the time when Venezuelan government representatives were criticizing the commercial nature of the Agreement and emphasizing the need for sectoral planning and policy harmonization, its private sector was, above all, protectionist.

The Junta has carried out a study of 110 Andean companies exporting to the GRAN.(73) It is a striking comment upon the concept of the private sector in relation to the GRAN, and our suggestion that there was a lack of support from the private sector. If some support was to be expected, it was precisely from industrialists that were benefiting from the free market.

General Views of the Managers of Exporting Companies

	Positive View		Negative View		No View Given		Total	
	Number	%	Number	%	Number	%		
Bolivia	1	10	6	60	3	30	10	100
Colombia	14	44	8	25	10	31	32	100
Ecuador	9	30	10	33	11	37	30	100
Peru	9	37	8	33	7	29	24	100
Venezuela	6	42	4	29	4	29	14	100
GRAN	39	35	36	33	35	33	110	100

But 33 percent of companies exporting to the Andean Group declared themselves against the Andean Group, 33 percent preferred not to give any opinion, and only 35 percent were in favor, so that the atmosphere was scarcely a favorable one. It is interesting to note that the smaller countries were the most stubbornly opposed, and that the industrialists of Venezuela were most in favor.

This negative, or at least skeptic situation prevails to date with sporadic reappearances. In 1981 large business circles in Ecuador, Bolivia, Venezuela, and even Colombia expressed their doubts with respect to the benefits of integration and considered the advisability of retiring.(74) During 1981 the author held interviews with Panamanian industrialists on the possibilities of trade relations with Lain American countries. The author found identical attitudes to the GRAN industrialists. Panamanians will accept bilateral trade arrangements which will not change the economic domestic atmosphere and will oppose more complex schemes.(75)

In spite of the above, the governments of the GRAN member countries have intensified their activities, as of July 1981, in an effort to find the formulas which will make possible the reactivation of the Andean integration process, contemplating reforms in all critical areas, such as AEC, SIDP, the harmonization of policies, etc.(76)

It is important to have clear explanations for the lack of mobilized support for the Andean Group among the managerial sector. We suggest the following without pretending to be exhaustive. First, the experience of CACM and LAFTA demonstrated that foreign rather than national companies would benefit most from the process, because their readily available

financial and technological resources would allow them to gain
control of the new market. We have shown that this was so in
the Andean Group.(77) Second, the two cases mentioned gave
rise to doubts concerning the positive results and permanence
of the agreements. Third, the relatively good conditions of
the 1960s allowed domestic industry, in which the greater
proportion of national industrial capital was invested, to
expand in the wake of the rise of internal demand under cap-
tive market conditions.(78) Fourth, given the diversity of
regimes and the suspected instability of member countries,
they seemed inclined to give up the possibility of extraordinary profits rather than to enter and establish very close ties.
Nor did they wish to accept the long-term harmonization of
social politics, the systems of economic planning,(79) nor the
formation of a strong state sector and of an interventionist
state that might develop in unforeseeable and perhaps undesirable directions given the internal and external political
milieu.(80) Fifth, the low, and, given the economic and political instability of the countries, precarious level of real
demand of the Andean market was not sufficient to justify the
radical changes agreed in the Cartagena Agreement. In the
sixth place, the entry of Venezuela changed the conditions of
the Agreement. Apart from the undeniable expansion of the
subregional market and the heightening of the disequilibria
between countries, there was a change in political leadership
(third world country, member of OPEC) and a shift in perception of the balance between immediate and future benefits on
the part of Colombia and Chile, for whom Venezuela's financial
potential and industrialization programs induced a shift to a
preference for a more liberal trade regime.(81) Since Venezuela, by entering, had greatly increased the market, her
perfectly legitimate demands for greater participation in new
industries would inevitably reduce the participation of the two
countries.(82) This change in political and economic centers
of activity is a factor that has not been mentioned or studied
in the specific case of the Andean Group and suggests many
analytical possibilities.(83)

The legitimacy of the proposal that integration is a
catalyst to development depends, in the eyes of the groups,
upon the speed with which it is seen to further national
objectives. The slowness of the process and its limited results
create frustration, lack of confidence, and skepticism, which
in turn affect the process of development itself. However, the
achievement of the objectives of integration is now restricted
by present production and trade structures and by a tendency
towards the accentuation of inequalities between countries. As
a consequence of low speed in achieving results, some sectors
that were initially indifferent or passive now urge the governments to abandon the Treaty if negotiation procedures are not
accelerated.(84)

Many groups, after all, accepted integration as an alternative to internal reforms. The opening of the market, for example, allowed countries to increase effective demand horizontally, thus avoiding a vertical increase by means of the redistribution of national income. One would expect these same groups to oppose any integration strategy that required or contained any type of economic or social reforms. Such is the position of the agriculturalists, who saw integration as a means to divert pressure for agrarian reform or income redistribution; but those same agriculturalists may be worried by the potential effect upon the prices of inputs or salaries when, for example, regulations and facilities for the migration of labor appear.(85)

National Regional Pressure Groups

Neither were the backward regions of different countries able to mobilize themselves regarding the Treaty of Cartagena. Distrust arose from the proposed development model and from the experience of import substitution, which worsened regional inequalities within individual countries. The Treaty revealed a great deficiency by only taking account of the effects of the concentration of the profits of integration among the countries and ignoring, at national level, the strengthening of national growth poles and the relative deterioration of the depressed areas. The Treaty of Cartagena watered down the few points in favor of border interchange (border zones can usually be considered as depressed areas) included in the Montevideo Treaty;(86) Decision 49, on the harmonization of industrial promotion policies, placed a upper limit on regional promotion policies in the countries.

Workers' unions and associations were noticeably absent from the process. In spite of the fact that their right to participation was established by the Economic and Social Advisory Council, they were never represented in the relevant delegations.

Unequal levels of economic development make a high level of political harmonization indispensable. In the case of the Andean Group this was assumed to be obtainable because integration was seen as the logical next step towards industrialization, and because the "will to integrate" existed in all countries and was accepted by all national actors. But, in fact, we suggest that at the national level only a number of reformist political leaders and developmentalist technical advisors were interested in integration. Neither group expanded the circle of discussion because of difficulties arising as much from the character of integration as from the fact that not all groups accepted national industrialization objectives and the costs of integration. In the early stages the support of

appropriate social groups was not needed, and the centralization of authority allowed the decision makers to progress.
However, integration is only successful if it can rely upon the
support of producers. The absence or weakness of support
from social groups and associations make integration more
difficult, if not impossible, because it reduces the capacity of
leaders to commit their societies.(87)

It may be surprising that, given the lack of political
support we have shown, the Treaty of Cartagena was even
signed or that any progress was made. It is important to bear
two points in mind: first, integration was part of the package
promoted by the "Alliance for Progress"; second, there are
immediate gains from trade in which some industrialists are
indeed interested. As we show in Chapters 3 and 7, those
interests seem to be satisfied by exports of chance surpluses.

The External Actors

The contribution of the external actors and their interests in a
fixed type of integration has been extensively studied in the
cases of LAFTA, CACM, and the various integration schemes
in Africa.(88)

In the case of Latin American integration the determining
external factor has been the attitude of the North American
government and private sector, and it continues to be so in
the case of the Andean Group.

The attitude of the United States, which was traditionally
opposed to integration and favored bilateral relations, under-
went a change in the early 1960s.(89) If indifference or hostility in the 1950s allowed the preparatory work of the CACM
to develop autonomously,(90) the Cuban Revolution made it
necessary to alter the United States' foreign policy by introducing notions of development in order to avoid the spreading
of revolutionary movements and the deterioration of continental
relations. On the other hand, American transnational corporations had substituted finished export products with direct
investment and capital goods.

In the case of the CACM, the United States forced the
replacement of the scheme proposed by CEPAL and Central
American technical advisors, which included the reduction of
trade barriers and industrial policy, by one of total free trade
based on principles laid down and approved by GATT.(91)
Direct measures were used to gain approval to set up a "true
common market." First, the United States campaigned to eliminate the intellectual influence of CEPAL.(92) Second, it
constantly intervened in opposition to the "plans for the
industries of integration" included in the CACM general agreement. The Central American Investment Bank (BCIE) was
prohibited from funding these industries because they were

"arbitrary, liable to create monopolies . . . unnecessary, and would inhibit industrial investment."(93) The American private sector also opposed the plan for the industries of integration because they "limited the rights and investment opportunities of the companies as well as their freedom of location, and unnecessarily restricted the free play of the market."

The aforementioned experienced led Vaitsos(94) to conclude that a hegemonic power that gains control of an integration movement restructures it and renders it unviable, because this means abandoning the scheme of industrial integration originally intended to act as a balancing factor. He is assuming, perhaps, that such a system would not provoke conflicts between the interests of national industrial groups, like those developed in the Andean Group, because of the SIDP.

After the purging of the CACM, foreign investors made the greatest profits. Prior to integration, foreign investment was concentrated almost exclusively in primary export sectors. Subsidiary companies were practically nonexistent and finished manufactured goods were imported. They eventually controlled 60 percent of intraregional trade and in ten years tripled the book value of investments, concentrating upon industry.(95) Faced with the lack of regulations governing foreign investment the countries began an incentives war, with obvious effects upon their balance of payments.(96)

In the case of the Andean Group, official North American intervention was less overt than in that of the CACM. However, the first official reactions were negative. Opposition became more active and was openly aggressive when the common plan for dealing with foreign capital, known as D24, was negotiated and approved in December 1970.(97) The first institutional conflict of the Agreement arose when the constitutional legality of the Agreement was challenged in the Chilean parliament and in the Colombian Supreme Court of Justice, an incident that will be dealt with later.(98)

It may appear contradictory to assert on the one hand that the United States and international development agencies supported and financed integration in Latin America and, on the other that, especially in the case of the United States, they resisted it, or sought to change its course. In fact their interest was in the creation of subregional groups based on free trade, and with the least possible degree of discrimination with regard to their countries. Nevertheless, in an embryonic form in LAFTA (in the complementarity agreements), more clearly in the Central American Common Market (the CET and the Industrial Integration Programs), and definitively in the GRAN (the CET, the Sectoral Development Programs, Decision 24, etc.), integration took directions very different from those initially formulated and provoked the negative reaction which we discuss in greater detail in Chapter 5.

Regarding the disposition of foreign enterprises toward the integration of the markets of underdeveloped countries, a different approach is needed to improve our understanding of the behavior of transnational corporations. Some have argued that transnational corporations should almost by definition be in favor of or even promote integration. Vaitsos queries this,(99) suggesting that, if transnational corporations operate in underdeveloped countries with a medium-sized or large market, and have developed a local productive capacity, even if it is minimal, they are not interested in effective integration. Conversely, in the case of very small countries in which transnational corporations have not begun parallel production through subsidiary companies, there is some interest on the part of the transnational corporations in "integration."

The logic of this behavior is that transnational corporations are not concerned simply with minimizing their production costs at world level.(100) Their strategy seeks to maximize surplus in the long term, and this can be achieved not only by minimizing costs, but also from the difference between costs and sales. The transnational corporations also seek to maintain an increasing share of the market, which can be achieved by avoiding the risks of government policies and of competition.

Continuing this line of analysis, we conclude that in the case of the Andean Group, the transnational corporations could not have an interest in integration for the following reasons.

i. The production of manufactured goods in the countries of the Group has been achieved by means of parallel investments in subsidiaries in each one of them.(101)

ii. The Treaty of Cartagena included industrial nationalization and specialization programs and granted a degree of protection that was lower than that already existing in the countries of the Group. This meant that some companies could be excluded from the market or could only expand according to common rules. In the case of sectoral planning, there was great pressure from the transnational corporations to "increase the flexibility of programmes"(102) in the petrochemical and automobile sectors. The lower degree of protection could mean lower profits and reduced control over prices.

iii. The Treaty paved the way to greater state intervention in the management of the economy (and of industrial policy, technology, foreign capital, and taxation), to the elimination or harmonization of production incentives affecting competition, and to the importation of the factors of production, all leading to the rationalization of economic activity and to greater participation in the direct production of goods and services. The transnational corporations have reacted energetically to this, through both legal and illegal channels.(109)

CONCLUSIONS

The Andean Group requires a high level of political integration because of the differences in economic levels and in national economic policies. In the Treaty of Cartagena an important program of political integration was devised, aimed at creating a new and stable economic union through industrial planning, a common external tariff, and policy harmonization. To reach such a high level of political integration an even higher level of political decision was needed, along with strong support from national and external actors.

However, at the national level only a very selective group of politicians and technocrats was interested in integration. In all member countries the national industrial sector was at its best passive. In some countries its attitude was negative or supported only the free trade element of integration. Industrialists were not convinced of the virtues of an agreement that implies far-reaching institutional changes and reinforces state intervention.

External actors were opposed to the idea of a common market that aimed to change their traditional relations with the Andean countries. Integration, aimed at reinforcing import substitution processes, reinforces as well the economic functions of the national state, and makes improbable the establishment of supranational institutions.

There were considerable distribution and political costs involved in integrating uneven less developed countries that made it impossible to develop real and effective support for integration when it was required.

It was in the atmosphere of skepticism or rejection by national producers, of foreign opposition, of silence on the part of trade and professional associations, and of the isolation of political and technical leaders who promoted and supported integration, that the rough and hasty policy harmonization program was drawn up for the common market and for a later Economic Union.

The main areas covered by harmonization as indicated by the Agreement were:

A. The management of foreign capital, and rules governing Andean multinational companies, subregional capital, and technology policy
B. The harmonization of major economic policy directives in the following areas: the harmonization of fiscal, monetary, and exchange rate policies, external trade; agricultural programs; infrastructure programs. Mechanisms regulating subregional trade, including CET, rules governing competition, the standardization of the movement of commodities, the unification of planning systems, and the adoption of a subregional development strategy

C. The establishment of regional and sectoral industrial plans.

The elements covered in A will be studied in Chapter 5, while those under B and C will be pursued in Chapters 6 and 7.

CHAPTER 5

HARMONIZATION OF POLICIES TOWARD FOREIGN CAPITAL

In this chapter we will examine the process of establishing common legislation for foreign investments and the conflicts that led to its subsequent reform. After analyzing the convenience of adopting common rules we concentrate on the evaluation of some of its economic effects in order to establish how far the main objectives of Decision 24 were achieved.

LEGISLATION ON FOREIGN CAPITAL: GENERAL CONSIDERATIONS

We discuss this subject in some detail, both because of the important part foreign investments have been shown to play in any type of market integration, and because, in promulgating policies in this field, the Andean Group set itself up as a pioneer.

Decision 24, as the Law for Foreign Capital is called, is considered to be the crucial factor which imbued GRAN with a new character by strengthening the nationalist position of the member countries vis-à-vis multinational companies.(1) Decision 24 articulates the lengthy discussions of the 1960s on the need to regulate foreign investment in such a manner that, with the establishment of a firm and clear set of rules, it would comply with the growth requirements of developing countries. It also incorporates the valuable Latin American experience in foreign capital expropriation and nationalization, particularly with the definition of long-term policies.

Mention must be made of the climate of economic nationalism that prevailed in Latin America during the sixties. Several countries formed part of a wave of nationalizations that created a climate of uncertainty and insecurity which discouraged the foreign investment and imports required by the substitution model of the Treaty of Cartagena. To harmonize the interests of foreign investors with the development interests of Andean countries(2) is a real and basic objective of Decision 24. But it certainly is not a very attractive subject for the diverse social science analysts and critics of Decision 24. They, while discussing Decision 24, centered their approach on the identification of antagonisms and clashing interests. The economic theory behind a Common Statute is neither new nor heterodox and has been expounded by numerous Latin American theoreticians. They view foreign investment as the basic element in the creation and perpetuation of dependency, because of the pressures it generates for technological as well as institutional modernization. This, in turn, aggravates the social problems arising from a growing technological duality.(3) However, the central idea of Decision 24 was to attract foreign capital in such a way as to overcome the insufficiency of internal savings, mobilize national capital, and maintain harmony with national development plans and with economic integration programs. It was important because the projected industrial program constituted a financial burden of unwanted proportions by aiming, over a period of ten years, to surpass the investment capacity of the subregion.(4) It was therefore necessary to attract resources and to channel them in such a way as to adjust them to the requirements of the model; that is to say, to make them flow into particular countries and sectors and make use of appropriate technology, and to prevent them from becoming a contributing factor to balance-of-payments problems. For their part of the bargain, the countries would guarantee a stable climate for investment, an important consideration given that the wave of nationalizations during the 1960s, as well as the Cuban Revolution, had worried foreign investors.

The signatories were very conscious of the need to resolve the contradiction between nationalist policy and the need for external resources.(5) With this in mind they drew up a set of standards which, while gathering together the nationalistic aspects of legislation already found in Latin America (the reserving of certain sectors for national capital, whether public or private, such as mining, transport, and services), took into account the experiences of other integration schemes with multinational companies (especially the CACM, in which foreign capital dislodged national capital from traditionally national sectors(6)) and more general experiences of the distortions caused by the indiscriminate flow of foreign capital into underdeveloped economies.

In the case of the GRAN there was a consensus regarding the convenience of having a single set of regulations. Discrepancies arose because of certain standards that were considered very restrictive by some countries. The case for the

consensus rests on the argument that the absence of regulations would lead to incentive struggles or conflicts between
foreign companies. These would be located in those countries
offering the greatest advantages and would have access to the
entire common market. Thus the countries would reduce rather than increase their powers of negotiation. This would
produce an uncontrolled distribution of the profits of integration, not only between the member countries as a whole and
the foreign investors, but also between the member countries
themselves, and would surely generate greater inefficiency of
production since, in the absence of common standards, the
siting of plants would depend more upon the concessions
granted to companies.

    In addition to the above arguments, other considerations
justified the adoption of rules to control foreign investment:
the nature of the modern transnational company, the position
of transnational corporations in common markets, and the
interest of foreign companies in investing in integrated
markets.(7)

    In examining the nature of transnational companies, we
are dealing with a very imperfect foreign capital market, in
which capital has no "price." Thus the receiver countries are
in a position to obtain better conditions in proportion to the
rate at which they increase their powers of negotiation.

    Another factor that makes the free market unsuitable for
controlling the activities of foreign companies is the advantageous position these have with respect to national companies.
Once "integrated," foreign parent and subsidy companies between them can benefit even more from the integrated market
by producing in low-cost countries and selling in those where
prices are higher. This factor is also linked to the degree of
affiliation and participation of foreign companies in the
markets. Between 1969 and 1971 in Colombia, Chile, and
Peru, around 40 percent of sales were made by transnationals,
a percentage that was greater than their share of production.(8)

    The third reason, the interest of foreign companies in
investing in integrated markets, derives from the movement of
capital promoted by the opening of internal trade and from the
type of external tariff adopted. The greater the common
protection, the greater will be the profitability of investments
in the common market for a transnational company compared to
that of exporting from a parent or subsidiary company. Thus
the protection of industry becomes a subsidy financed by
unprotected companies and consumers to benefit protected
companies; in effect, a form of international redistribution of
income. This consideration justifies discriminatory measures in
the form of higher taxes on profits, forcing companies to have
a mixed character, and other compensatory measures.

The Andean Capital Statute

The above considerations led to the promulgation of the Andean Capital Statute, the basic points of which were designed to:

- guarantee planned growth in selected economic sectors
- guarantee the gradual, progressive conversion of foreign companies into national or mixed concerns
- guide and control the transfer of technology
- limit the access of foreign enterprises to national sources of finance
- avoid the negative effect on the balance of payments of the influx of foreign capital by controlling the transfer of profits and the repatriation of foreign capital.(9)

This radical policy, transforming the relations between foreign investors and the national economies of the member countries, has had to be enforced in an atmosphere of indifference or hostility on the part of national groups. As we saw in Chapter 4, section 4, at the national level there were some political leaders and technocratic groups engaged in the integration task, but their legitimacy was weakened by the definition of the objective of integration, the very contradictions inherent in the substitution process, and the difficulty in assessing what the gains would be and who would benefit. As a consequence the industrial sector was passive in some cases or actively opposed in others. But in general its attitude was to aim to obtain the enlarged market, while sacrificing as little as possible of the privileges of protection. However, the reforms implicit in the Treaty of Cartagena seriously worried the industrial sector, which preferred to close ranks with the external sector that opposed the philosophy of the Treaty, especially those aspects relating to the control of foreign investments, state intervention, and planning. The signing of Decision 24 was chosen as the moment to oppose the Treaty openly.

In effect, when the plans for the formulation of Decision 24 were in their early stages, North American companies began intelligence activities in order to discover which course the legislation would take, and pressured governments, particularly those of Peru, Colombia, and Ecuador.(10) The most active were the senior executives of North American petroleum companies.

During the second stage after the signing, the task of directing the opposition fell to the Council of the Americas, over which David Rockefeller presided. In February 1971 the Council produced a lengthy critical document which was sent to the president and ministers of the member countries, and to influential figures in the American Congress. Immediately after this, Colombia was singled out for more direct pressure. A letter was sent to the conservative President Pastrana which made apocalyptic forecasts about the results of staging an application for capital control regulations, and threatened to suspend investment. A similar letter was sent to the Minister of Economic Development. At the same time Colombian private sector industrialists and financiers made known their serious criticisms of the Statute and, as we showed in Chapter 4, section 4, for the first time became active over the integration issue.(11)   The large corporations attacked, one by one, all the major points of the Statute (i.e., state preference in buying shares from foreign companies, state control of the transfer of profits, and the negotiation and payment for technology), and the establishment of sectors in which new foreign investments were not accepted. ANDI petitioned for the system of privileges for foreign investment established in 1967. FEDEMENTAL and ACOPLASTICOS expressed their opposition to Decision 24 placing their repeal before the public officers responsible for the design of Colombian foreign policy.(12)

For its part FEDECAMARAS in Venezuela was always opposed to any kind of common rules on foreign capital, using the argument that it should be a discretionary policy autonomously decided upon by each country.(13)

In Colombia,(14) and less obviously in Chile and Venezuela, the national producers' associations and financial institutions emulated the active opposition of foreign investors, producing a serious institutional crisis that affected the implementation of Decision 24 in the whole region. In Colombia not only did ANDI start its public opposition, union groups such as ACOPLASTICOS, FEDEMENTAL, and others notified the Colombian government of their repeal to the principle of foreign investment control at diverse meetings of the National Economic Policies Council. Criticism lead to crisis when some prominent Colombian lawyers, in December of 1970, presented to the Supreme Court a petition claiming that Decision 24 was unconstitutional; that plea was accepted by the authorities, who on January 20, 1972, abolished the statute. The impasse was resolved by the ratification of the Treaty in Parliament only when the Congress granted extraordinary powers authorizing the president to enact the Treaty by decree. Colombia remained without valid legislation on the matter until September 1973.

It is interesting to note that at the same time that private researchers(15) and members of the National Planning Department(16) were reaching the conclusion that Decision 24 did not in fact discourage foreign investment, Colombian industrialists, almost without exception, were rejecting it on the grounds that it would discourage such investment and worsen the associated problem of scarcity of capital.

We see therefore that the behavior of the national private sector is consistent with the conclusions formulated in our Chapter 4 when discussing the participation of the different actors involved in the integration movement, and gives us reason to doubt Vaitsos's conclusions regarding the positive interest of the industrial groups of Colombia, Chile, and Venezuela in the regulation and restriction of foreign capital. The law implies a certain degree of control also over the national sector in vital aspects such as the selection of technology or the utilization of the surplus generated. Vaitsos presupposes a nationalist attitude on the part of Andean industrialists, which in fact failed to manifest itself.

The events mentioned above and the special laws governing investment and exchange standards in Venezuela, Ecuador, and Bolivia have prevented the statute from prevailing in the same form throughout the region. In fact, it is possible to suggest that, until the reform by Decision 103 in November 1976, the statute was not generally in effect, for the following reasons:(17)

i. regulations: these were nonexistent in Colombia, and Bolivia, partial in Venezuela and Ecuador, and in violation in Peru.

ii. doubtful effectiveness because of different completion dates: June 1971 in Bolivia, Ecuador, and Peru; September 1973 in Colombia; and January 1974 in Venezuela - in consequence it was not known when the transference of foreign capital should begin; also, the free exchange operative in Bolivia, Venezuela, and Ecuador made it impossible to control regulations governing the transfer of capital abroad

iii. different interpretations and degrees of application: Peru was strict, enacting an industrial law; Bolivia, was on the contrary very lax, and in Decree 10045/71, did not discriminate between foreign and national investors, or place limits on profit transfer or internal and external credit

iv. the lack of a systematic register of investments, reinvestments, and technological contracts makes control of the activities of foreign investors and fulfillment of the provisions of Decision 24 impossible

Almost ten years after it had been approved, implementation of Decision 24 was still being delayed by problems similar to those pointed out in 1975. The Evaluation Document published by the Junta on the first anniversary of the signing of the Cartagena Agreement notes that "several relevant aspects were still pending common interpretation; there lacks the required consensus in deciding the common rules which should harmonise the application of Decision 24 without any further modifications or additions." Subsequent reports for the years 1979 and 1980, as well as the documents submitted to the 1981 Commission that were realized in September for the purpose of "reactivating" the Andean integration process, failed to produce an evaluation or any policy suggestions regarding Decision 24.(18) It is therefore reasonable to assume that the conditions prevailing up to 1979 are maintained and that Decision 24 nonimplementation does not constitute an obstacle for "reactivation" of GRAN.

The Impact of the Statute on the Flow of Foreign Capital

To attempt to measure the effect of the Statute on foreign capital is difficult, in the first place because, as we have shown, it would be untrue to say that the Statute was uniformly effective or generally applied. But a more significant factor affecting such an evaluation is the political climate prevailing in each of the countries.

Another factor making the study of foreign investment behavior within the Andean Group an extremely difficult task is the lack of internationally comparable systematic statistics. Administrative problems can often reflect other differences in the qualification or interpretation of what constitutes a direct foreign investment.(19)

A sustained trend can be shown for the long-term flow of direct foreign investment into the Andean Group (see table 5.1). Graph 5.1 shows the relevant investment instances there: a net disinvestment of 300 million dollars in 1972, which can be explained by the nationalization of foreign investment in the Venezuelan petroleum industry, and the withdrawal of considerable investments in Chile and Venezuela for the period 1974-76. Neither of the two can be attributed to Decision 24.

The aggregated amount of direct foreign investment in the GRAN represented 31 percent of the total for Latin America in 1967 (71% of the total for Argentina, Mexico, and Brazil) and by 1977 the flow into the Andean Group had greatly decreased. It would be unwarranted to attribute this downfall to the Andean Capital Statute in force. In fact, the biggest decrease was registered for the period 1967-1971 prior to Decision 24. Direct foreign investment growth rates registered for the GRAN in the period 1971-77 are inferior only to those of Mexico and Brazil. Foreign investors prefer these two countries because of their large internal markets and their political stability (see Graph 5.1).

Up to 1967 the bulk of FDI in the GRAN was concentrated in Chile and Peru,(20) (about 75 percent of total regional foreign investment) and was mainly oriented toward mining, smelting, and oil (60 percent of the total in 1967). During

1957-67 the flow of foreign capital to the Andean countries grew more slowly than in Mexico, Brazil, Argentina, and Central America.(21)   The explanation is that during the sixties the Andean mining industry, with the exception of Peru, was not particularly attractive, because of international market stagnation and because new supply sources were appearing. The growth of foreign investment in that period was especially important in the manufacturing sector, from US$117 million in 1957 to $369 million in 1967.   Colombia was the recipient of more than 50 percent of the total.   This change in the orientation toward industry affected especially those countries whose market was not sufficient.(22) After the signing of the Agreement and the adoption of Decision 24 (December 1971), only Chile (up until its withdrawal) and Venezuela had their participation reduced, but all the other member countries registered increased direct foreign investment growth rates, in comparison to the preceding period. In spite of this, criticism for Decision 24 kept a steady flow from both the private and the public sectors of member countries. Bolivian government officials and industrialists blame Decision 24 for discouraging foreign investment (see table 5.2). But the factors mentioned above and the political instability experienced in Bolivia, especially in the early seventies, should also be taken into account. It should be remembered that the Statute has only been effective in Bolivia since 1974, and that, even before Decision 24, this country was not very attractive to the foreign investor.(23)   However, two companies have already been installed with foreign capital to produce goods assigned to Bolivia under the light engineering program.

Between 1971 and 1973 in Chile, total foreign investment was only $160 million.(24)   American assets in manufacturing decreased.   It would be difficult to attribute this, at least exclusively, to Decision 24.   It can largely be explained by the existence of the Popular Unity government and the hostility this provoked.   There were earlier symptoms and changes indicating that Chile had ceased to be attractive to foreign capital.

Between the enactment of Decree 600 and May 1975, US$124 million of investment were approved by the Chilean authorities, of which $100 million were assigned to projects in the mining sector.   In spite of the very liberal Decree 600, foreign capital did not flow into industry, or at least not as much as was expected.   It should be remembered that the mining sector could be exempted from the common ruling on capital at the discretion of each country.   The reason for the lack of interest in Chile on the part of foreign investors should be sought in the internal situation of Chile rather than in commitments made in the Treaty of Cartagena.   Chile's extreme stabilization policy, the reduction of internal effective demand, and political tension are hardly stimulants to either national or foreign investment.

Ecuador would seem to be a country of great opportunity for the foreign investor. Besides having a free exchange policy, it is an economy that is expanding on the basis of new petroleum resources. There are many applications to finance industrial projects, some of them of subregional character.

The drop in total investment in Peru in 1969-72 can largely be explained by the nationalist character of the government, its policy of nationalization (Peruanización) of the major companies in strategic sectors, and by its decision to approve new foreign investment only in association with state enterprises. In spite of this policy the minus sign was reversed into a plus sign in 1972, maintaining a constant increase of investments up to 1977. In fact there have been various joint projects, such as the Massey-Ferguson tractor project, and the improvement of acrylic fiber plants by Bayer. American-owned assets in the Peruvian manufacturing sector grew from $97 million in 1969 to $159 million in 1974.

Venezuelan government documents, and those of the Junta, contain statements to the effect that no great change in the attitude of foreign investors to the country has been noted since its admission to the Andean Group and the adoption of Decision 24.

Colombian experiences with legislation on foreign capital are illuminating. The country approved Decree 444 on foreign investment and technology in 1967. It is considered to be in some aspects even more restrictive than Decision 24.(25) After the decree on average the same amount of foreign investment was registered.(26) But, during 1972 and 1973 the inflow of foreign investment considerably decreased. But it would be a mistake to attribute that to the enforcement of Decision 24. As we saw above, in 1972, the Colombian Supreme Court declared Decision 24 to be unconstitutional. In consequence, from that day until September 1973, Colombia was without any effective law on foreign capital. In September 1973 the president, using extraordinary powers, issued Decree 1900, by which Decision 24 was declared again to be constitutional. The lack of legislation affected not only the effective inflow of investment but also the inflow of applications at the National Planning Department, as we can see from the following figures:

Foreign Direct Investment Approved by the National Planning Department
(US$ million)

i. From the approval of Decree 444

1967	1968	1969	1970
18.4	20.0	27.4	39.3

Foreign Direct Investment Approved by the
National Planning Department (continued)

ii. Impact of Decision 24 (July 1971)

   a.   Investment 1st Semester 1971   = 9.4
   b.   Investment 2nd Semester 1971   = 23.4

iii. Impact of Supreme Court Decision

   a.   January 1972–July 1972 investment = 3.4
   b.   July 1972 temporary legislation
        applications for investment
        approval   13.4

Source: National Planning Department, and Junguito and Caballero, Situacion, pp. 5–7.

The Colombian case would seem to indicate that foreign
investment is not discouraged by normalizing legislation, but
that, on the contrary, lack of stimulus is a result of a lack of
legislation and the atmosphere of uncertainty that ensues. It
is significant that Colombian representatives gave definite
support to the Chilean position and endorsed their reform
proposals.

Sectoral Structure and Origin of Direct
Foreign Investment in the Andean Group

The most remarkable thing is not only that foreign capital
should have continued to pour into the country as it did
previously, but also that it did so in traditional sectoral and
geographical patterns, as can be noted in table 5.2 where the
only significant change in mining and hydrocarbon investments
began to show in the year 1973. In the manufacturing sector,
the recipients par excellence are chemicals, refining, rubber,
and plastics. These sectors, being strongly oriented toward
import substitution, have continued to attract about one-third
of total direct foreign investment.(27) The Junta in its evaluation report in 1975 also concluded that up to that year no
important change in the behavior of foreign investors attributable to Decision 24 was observed.(28) These conclusions are
confirmed in the very detailed study prepared by the Junta
for the Evaluation Document on occasion of the tenth anniversary of the GRAN.(29)
Equally unnoticeable are the changes in the origin of
direct foreign investment, in spite of the criticism and fears
expressed by foreign investors. It must be admitted that

"newcomers" such as Japan, Italy, Switzerland, and the Federal Republic of Germany were willing to pay the surcharge for
accepting Decision 24 in order to displace the traditional
investor: the United States. The structure was not appre-
ciably modified, however, since U.S. direct foreign investment
represents over 50 percent of the total amount.

The Fadeout in the Andean Group

Having shown the relative nonenforcement of Decision 24
at least as a regional ruling, and having shown that Decision
24 has not had a considerable negative impact on the inflow of
foreign capital, we now turn to discuss two further elements
considered very important in the philosophy of the Foreign
Capital Law. These are, first, the obligation on foreign firms
to transform themselves into mixed or national companies if
they want to take full advantage of the free market and,
second, the limit on profit remittances.

The Junta made very clear in its own analysis how difficult is the evaluation of these elements. The problems arise
because of the nonexistence in five countries of appropriate
registers of foreign investment, so that it is almost impossible
to know the real value of assets and especially the form of the
contracts on royalty payments. Another point emphasized by
the Junta is the reluctance shown by national authorities to
provide any kind of information.(30) We would add the problems derived from practices such as overpricing, that make
accurate estimates near to impossible. Another element is the
existence of free exchange systems in Bolivia, Ecuador, and
Venezuela.

We will examine the Colombian experience because even
with these two aspects of the Law, given the institutional
problems we have referred to, it is the country with the
longest experience in regulating foreign capital and the one
with relatively more accurate information.

In regard to the obligation on companies to transform
themselves into mixed or national enterprises, it is important
to make clear that as a consequence of the different dates on
which Decision 24 was ratified by the different countries
(especially in Colombia and Venezuela), it was not clear when
the process of transfer was to be initiated. The impasse was
resolved by Decision 103 (December 1976), by which January
1974 was established as the initial date (and not July 1971).
The first 25 percent of foreign capital should be transferred to
national investors in December 1977.

In Colombia, 27 firms in productive sectors (and three in
consultancy) have signed, with the National Planning Department, the "Convenio de transformacion en Empresas Mix-
tas."(31) This figure appears relatively low given that the

number of exporting enterprises is considerably higher. The Banco de la Republica has on its register 760 foreign firms, of which at least 300 have been exporting regularly to third countries or to the Andean Group. Unfortunately, we have no clear idea as to the number of Colombian firms involved or interested in exporting activities.

The second point we want to make is the absence from the joint venture list of the very big exporting firms, such as Propal, Hilos Cadena, La Roche, Abbot Colombiana, Peldar, General Electric, Icasa, Dow Chemical, and many others. This perhaps suggests that firms (or their parent companies) are not interested in transforming themselves into joint ventures because they already control the market. This is especially true when a case of "closed technology" is in question.

The Colombian government, as a part of its program of investing the resources of the "Bonanza Cafetera" or "coffee boom," approved in 1976 Resolution 11 on "Colombianización de la industria Extranjera." This created a fund to provide long-term loans to Colombian industrialists interested in investing in foreign firms already working in Colombia. The fund was provided with US$150 million and up to June 20, 1978 the Banco de la Republica received 31 applications amounting to US$13.8 million; it approved all of them to a total of US$12.0 million.(32)   A comparison of the two lists, the one with firms that signed the Contrato de Intención and the one with those endorsing Colombianización, reveals that only very few of the firms interested in exporting to the Andean Group and transforming themselves into mixed companies are also in the list of candidates for Colombianización. The reason why is not clear, because the Colombianización program is the obvious and cheap way to finance the "convenios de transformación." Another point to be clarified is the extent of the so-called Colombianización. Are Colombian investors buying at least up to 49 percent of the share capital in order to transform the foreign firms into mixed ventures? If so, we would be able to conclude that 57 foreign firms out of at least 300 exporting firms are on the way to being transformed into mixed or national companies.

The lack of information concerning the fadeout at the subregional level prevents evaluation of the foreign capital transfer to domestic investors in all member countries. The Junta has not prepared (or published) the corresponding survey, and it was not possible to obtain domestic data for the remaining four member countries.

On the control of profit remittances, there are two main elements to be considered.(33)   First, we want to know the amount of profits that have actually been remitted; second, we must consider the "Capitales en el limbo,"(34) or immobilized profits. Decision 24 allows the repatriation of profits equal to 14 percent of registered capital and allows reinvestment up to 5 percent.

The Colombian Planning Department estimates that from 1967 (Decree 444) up to 1976 the following were the profits generated and repatriated.

Profits of Foreign Investment in Colombia
(Million pesos)

	1967-74	1975	1976	1967-76
Profits	6,357.9			
Profits remitted	3,550.5	1,100	1,500	
Balance	2,804.7	800	800	
Total balance remaining (approximate)	2,804.7			4,407

Source: DNP, 1.466-S6, January 27, 1978.

The result of the control of profits remittance is obviously the relief of the balance of payments. During the 1967-76 period, about US$115 million was not remitted,(35) and was restricted from reinvestment. That amount represents about 30 percent of all US assets in the Colombian manufacturing sector up to 1974. The total of U.S. investment in manufacturing during 1970-74 amounted to US$155 million, an amount very close to the profits not remitted.(36)

The study on royalty and profit remittances prepared by the Junta and included in its "Evaluación del Proceso de Integración 1969-1979" (Evaluation of the Integration Process 1969-1979) is the only one available for the region. The conclusions derived from this study would suggest that the adverse foreign investment impact on the balance of payments has been reduced by the contracted amount of remittances abroad (see table 5.3). However, this reduction cannot be attributed to Decision 24 entirely, in view of the fact that the total amount of exportable profits has been necessarily reduced by subregional nationalizations. From 1973 on, the total amount of profits has been permanently reduced. As a result, the ratio between total profits and total direct foreign investment in the subregion had been reduced to 8.4 percent in 1972. We agree with the Junta in that this does not represent the full impact of Decision 24 on the balance of payments(37) since the existing drawing rights of the countries, in addition to transnational corporation practices of utilizing diverse means of profit remittance, cause the calculations of transferred capitals to be undervalued.

Decision 103 of December 1976 reformed Decision 24 and solved the problem of those profits that were restricted not only from being remitted but from being reinvested as well (the restriction applied both to the same sector and to others). Decision 103 raised the limit on the percentage to be exported to 20 percent and authorized the reinvestment of profit that exceeded the 20 percent but had already been distributed. The reinvested profits are considered as direct foreign investment. This means that the basis for calculating the 20 percent remittance limit was enlarged. In the Colombian case, if we make the extreme assumption that the whole amount of US$115 million would be reinvested, the additional profit remittance permitted would be US$25 million, which represents approximately one-third of the previous level of remittances.

To sum up, we may conclude that little interest has been shown on the part of foreign investors in being transformed into national or mixed enterprises in order to export freely to the Andean Group. Only 27 foreign firms out of the 761 registered have already signed the "Convenio de Transformación."

Decision 24's control of profits remittances reduced the rate of outflow of profits but at the same time created a vacuum. About 44 percent of profits could neither be remitted nor reinvested. These "profits in limbo" either created new pressures upon illegal transfer practices, went into the extraofficial finance system, or were utilized by the firms concerned as short-term credit resource.

The Reforms to Decision 24

The analysis we have made up to this point shows that reforms to the Decree were virtually inevitable. The story of these reforms provides a further illustration of the conflicts we have emphasized.

The crisis due to the imperfect enforcement of Decision 24 was finally precipitated when, with the dispatching of Decree 600 by the Chilean government in 1974, Decision 24 was definitely and openly violated.(38) The present Chilean government openly declared its intention not to apply the communally agreed-upon foreign capital policy. The most critical items of Decree 600 are concerned with eliminating de facto the obligatory sale of foreign capital to national investors, with authorizing and acquisition of national companies by foreign investors, and with extending unlimited internal credit to foreign enterprises.

During negotiations to resolve the crisis provoked by Chile, Colombia closed ranks with Chile and together they succeeded in reforming important aspects of the Statute by means of Decision 103 as follows.

i. Control of the effects of foreign investment on balance of payments

Decision 24 gave the foreign investor the right to annual profit remittance worth up to 14 percent of the value of direct foreign investment. At the request of the country concerned, the Commission could authorize higher percentages for a limited period.(39)
    Decision 103 raised the limit of profit remittance, with provision for each country to authorize higher percentages at its own discretion.(40)   This virtually eradicates the application of a common standard governing the transfer of profits and paves the way for the aforementioned incentives war. If the new ruling can solve the problem of "capital in limbo" it also burdens the balance of payments perhaps to a considerable degree.(41)   In addition, Decision 103 broadened the definition of FDI with the right to transfer, by including the reinvestment in national currency of these profits without right to transfer, invisible technological contributions and imported primary materials and inputs, which were excluded in the Decision 24 definition of FDI.(42)   It can be assumed that this would encourage the overpricing of imported components and give them preference over national products in order to broaden the base of registered capital with transfer rights.

ii. Restriction of the acquisition of national companies by foreign investors

As a concession to Chile, which wished to denationalize companies nationalized during the Unidad Popular government, Decision 103 made provision for foreign investors to acquire national companies, provided that they retained a mixed character. In other words, foreign investors were allowed to own up to 49 percent of the capital of completely national companies.

iii. Authorization of annual reinvestment

Decision 103 raised the limit for reinvestment without authorization for foreign companies from 5 percent to 7 percent. The limit imposed by Decision 24 was considered to protect the national investor, since foreign investors had ample motives for raising their capital (overpricing, royalties, right of transfer). It also permitted the reinvestment of "capital in limbo."

iv. Internal credit

While under Decision 103 foreign investors were still denied access to long-term internal credit, short- and medium-term credit policies were liberalized, and each country was granted control of terms and conditions.(43)

v. Sectors exempted by Decision 24

Tourism and the agricultural sector were included in the exempted group, and consequently there was no obligation to convert FDI into national or mixed companies.

Finally, the starting date for initiating the transference of property was fixed at January 1, 1974, and not June 1971.

Conclusion

Our analysis of the modus operandi of the Common Statute for the Management of Foreign Capital and events since its implementation lead us to the following conclusions.

i. The first institutional conflict within the Cartagena Agreement in the subregion occurred because of this ruling. This suggests that external actors were prepared to intervene in the integration process as soon as their interests were affected.

ii. The Statute was not, strictly speaking, uniformly implemented, since it was not applied in all countries as required; therefore we cannot attribute to it changes in foreign investment trends. Changes in the rhythm of investment in Chile, Peru, and Colombia are more connected to specific internal situations. In Ecuador the rise in investment has been because of new petroleum resources, the overall growth thus induced, and existing liberal legislation.

iii. Resistance to the Statute, from the external sector and supported by the national private sector, was due to the rejection of its doctrine, to the wishes of companies to negotiate independently with investors and manage their surpluses independently. This is illustrated by the reforms introduced in Decision 103.

iv. The countries could have applied the exceptional rulings designed for special cases under Article 40. However, they chose to modify the Statute, thus adopting a more liberal position by not discriminating between national and foreign capital and weakening both the principles of the regulation of capital and their bargaining position.

REGIONAL RULINGS COMPLEMENTING THE FOREIGN CAPITAL LAW

There are some very important fields that are related to foreign investment and where harmonization is important. These are: rulings on Andean multinational companies and on subregional capital, rulings on mixed companies, subregional technological policy, and rulings on industrial property. Although the corresponding Decisions were approved, none is actually in effect, as we shall see.

Decision 46:   Common Rules for Multinational
Corporations and Treatment Applicable to
Subregional Capital

The decision, approved in December 1971, defines Andean
multinationals as those whose principal location is in a member
country and whose regional capital comes from more than one
member country, each shareholding country owning not less
than 15 percent of the shares.   Under Decision 24, capital
from one member country invested in another affords multinational status to the company so created and will be managed
under the subregional system regulating capital flows, through
which it will receive the same treatment granted by this system
to national capital.   As suggested by Kuczynski,(44) the general rules of Decision 24 and the concept of the Andean multinational company should be seen as elements of subregional
industrial policy and constitute a serious effort to promote
industrial expansion on a planned basis.   The Junta has made
the first attempt in Latin America to correlate regional industrial planning, regulation of foreign capital, and the removal
of trade barriers.   These elements are not to be found in
LAFTA, which provides exclusively for the removal of trade
barriers and for industrial development.   The CACM provides
for the establishment of integration industries in certain sectors, with rights to enter the integrated market, but there is
no legislation on foreign capital and no careful selection of
industries eligible to be considered as regional.(45)
    The Andean Multinational Companies allow countries to
invest in other countries' projects.   These provisions were
considered as an instrument to overcome concentration problems by allowing less efficient countries to invest in the more
efficient.   But it appears probable that the inflow of capital
will aggravate the problems it is intended to solve.   The
Andean Multinational Companies are in fact the type of joint
companies that Hazlewood considers are the solution to the
equitable efficient location contradiction.(46)   However, here
again the Andean Group experiences are not very encouraging.
Decision 46 was not enforced regionally because member countries did not ratify it in time.(47)   Chile did so in June 1972,
Venezuela and Colombia in September 1973, Bolivia a year
later, and Ecuador in June 1975.   Peru had not yet ratified
Decision 46 in December 1977.   The reason for the Peruvian
government's delay may be fear of stimulating an outflow of
domestic capital to other member countries not subject to the
restrictive Peruvian rules.   Furthermore, so far no document
creating Andean Multinational Companies has been registered in
any country.(48)   Junta evaluation documents come to the same
conclusions.   It is evident that the stimuli to subregional investments in Andean Multinational Companies were insufficient.
For this reason the instrument is now substantially revised.(49)

Decision 84: Bases for a Regional Technological Policy

This outlines "Andean Plans for Technological Development and the Tasks of Supporting the Sectoral Programmes for Industrial Development." This decision establishes the bases of regional technological development, defines the Andean Programs of Technological Development, and establishes how the principles should be introduced in the SIDPs.

Decision 84 was not legally in effect up to 1976, because Colombia and Chile considered it as a political document and therefore refused to incorporate it into the corresponding laws and regulations. Venezuela took a similar position. Nevertheless the Junta continued to develop studies in the agriculture, mining, and steel sectors, whose results may be accepted by all countries but which will not be compulsory while the Colombian-Chilean stand continues.

Decision 85: Rules Governing Industrial Property

This was approved in June 1974 and establishes regulations for the application for patents in the areas of investment, factory brand names, industrial services, designs, and models. It legislates for procedures and for the rights and obligations attached to patents and brands. For obvious reasons it is a very important statute. But its very importance and the advanced ideas incorporated made its enforcement almost impossible. By December 1975 no country had incorporated Decision 85 into its legislation.(50) It is legitimate to conclude that also in the case of the Decisions complementing the Foreign Capital Law there is an absolute gap between formal approval and effective enforcement, conclusions that are important to the understanding of the process of creating intranational policies and institutions.

CONCLUSIONS

The Andean Group experiences in unifying regulations on foreign investments show that neither foreign investors nor national entrepreneurs were interested in the enforcement of rules that were intended to transform the character of their relations. They were prepared even to create an institutional crisis to prevent enforcement. A crisis was provoked, the only possible solution to which appeared to be the liberalization of the principal elements of the law, such as the control of remittances and the widening of the sectors excluded from its application. The important complementary Decisions on transfer of technology, Andean multinationals, industrial property, and subregional capital were all approved on schedule but were not implemented effectively.

It is important to ephasize especially the lack of progress in aspects such as the transformation of foreign into national or mixed companies as well as in the creation of multinational Andean enterprises, which should have been by now an important element within the development of regional industrial strategy.

Table 5.1.   Andean Group, Foreign Direct Investment
Stocks, 1957-77
(millions US dollars)

	Bolivia	Colombia	Chile	Ecuador	Peru	Venezuela	GRAN
1957[1]	30	396	666	30	396	–	1518
1967[1]	60	597	879[1]	55	660	–	2251
1967	144	728	963 a	82	782	3495	6194
1971	75	900	850 a	300	880	3000	6005
1973	85	950	643[1] a	400	990	3100	6168
1975	100	1208	400 a	830	1692	3397	7627
1977	120	1400	1215 b	880	2000	3600	9215

% of GRAN

1957[1]	1.97	26.08	43.87	1.97	26.08	–	100.0
1967[1]	2.66	26.52	39.04	2.44	29.3	–	100.0
1967	2.32	11.76	15.55	1.32	12.62	56.43	100.0
1971	1.25	14.96	14.16	5.01	14.66	49.96	100.0
1973	1.38	15.41	10.42	6.48	16.06	50.25	100.0
1975	1.31	15.83	5.24	10.89	22.19	44.54	100.0
1977	1.31	15.19	13.18	9.54	21.71	39.07	100.0

---

[1]U.S. Direct Investment.

Source: Junta: Evaluación del Proceso de Integración (1969–
1979), Anexo Tecnico 4, Tables II-2, II-3.

a)   Tendencias y Cambios en la Inversión de las
Empresas Internacionales en los países en desarrollo particularmente en América Latina, September 1978.

b)   OECD: Estimations du Secretariat du CAD (1981).

Table 5.2. Andean Group, Foreign Direct Investment Stocks by Economic Sectors, 1967-1977

SECTORS	1967	1971	%	1973	%	1975	%	1977	%	Growth Rate 1971-1977 %
AGRICULTURE	–	40.0	0.8	43.1	0.8	47.0	0.6	54.4	0.7	5.3
MINING & OIL FUELS	55.2	2618.2	50.8	3215.5	52.2	4805.5	66.5	4978.5	62.2	11.3
LIGHT INDUSTRY	21.8	1150.0	22.3	1378.2	24.9	1416.2	19.6	1858.1	23.2	8.3
TRADE AND FINANCE	9.2	510.9	9.9	548.5	9.9	622.0	8.6	773.4	9.7	7.2
OTHER	13.8	475.9	9.2	264.7	4.8	256.3	3.6	335.6	4.2	5.7
TOTAL		5155.0	100.0	5225.0	100.0	7227.0	100.0	8000.0	100.0	7.6

Source: Junta, Documento de Evaluación 1969-1979, Lima, March 1979, Anexo IV, Jun/di 360, table No 11 14

Table 5.3. Andean Group, Outward Remittances
as Dividends and Utilities
(millions current US dollars)

COUNTRIES	1971	%	1973	%	1975	%	1977	%
BOLIVIA	9.9	0.9	0.1	0.0	1.0	0.1	2.0	0.3
COLOMBIA[1]	77.0	7.3	77.0	6.7	80.0	10.8	120.0	17.9
ECUADOR	25.2	2.4	124.8	10.8	57.5	7.8	90.0	13.4
PERU[2]	81.8	7.7	100.2	8.7	48.7	6.6	128.5	19.2
VENEZUELA	868.0	81.7	852.0	73.8	552.0	74.7	330.0	49.2
TOTAL GRAN	1061.9	100.0	1154.1	100.0	739.2	100.0	670.5	100.0

[1]It includes the interests of the public and private debt.
[2]It includes the interests of the private debt.

Source: Balance of Payments elaborated by Central Banks of each country.

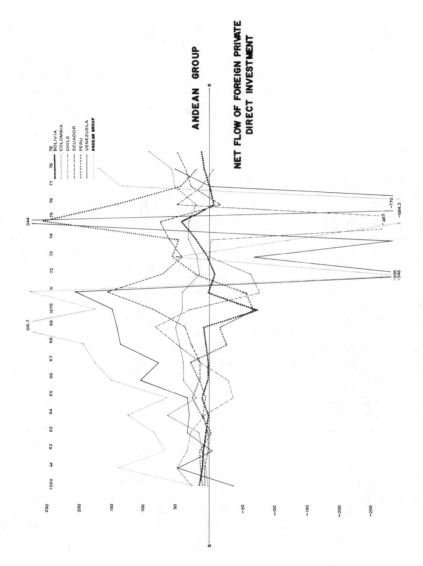

Graph 5.1 ANDEAN GROUP: Net Flow of Foreign Private Direct Investment.

203

CHAPTER 6

THE COMMON EXTERNAL TARIFF (CET)

This chapter will study the process of defining the scope of the Common External Tariff (CET), as a means of protecting subregional production and producing a given allocation of productive resources between both sectors and countries. This process emerges as a particularly clear case study of our underlying hypothesis as to the significance of the different levels of development of the industrial sector in explaining the conflicts that emerged between those countries that granted a greater degree of protection for industry and those that hoped for more efficient industrial development. On a second level, these contradictions appeared as conflicts over whether or not a tariff structure would discriminate in favor of industrial sectors and those countries that were relatively less developed.

We will also study here how much progress was made in the harmonization of fiscal, monetary, exchange, industrial, and foreign trade policies, because these aspects are closely linked with the tariff policy. If not appropriately designed they can even annihilate the effect sought through a particular tariff structure.

We end the chapter with a review of the attempts to establish a regional development strategy, which was considered crucial for the long-term orientation of the economies of each member country in a way consistent with the integration program.

SOME CONSIDERATIONS ON THE NEED TO
ESTABLISH THE CET

The need to establish a common tariff became clear during the negotiations setting up EFTA and, later, with the experiences of LAFTA. If countries in a free-trade zone maintain their national tariff levels levied on third parties, this could encourage trade to be diverted from the group toward importing inputs which are then processed in those countries that have lower duties.

In EFTA, the problem was solved by adopting rules of origin. A good was given the right of entry if at least 50 percent of its final value added was attributable to a member country. Moreover, the use of rules of origin in underdeveloped countries is questionable because of the large differences between the various national customs duties. In such a case, the standards have to be much stricter and will tend to be more "trade diverting."(1)   Also, a great tariff difference for the same inputs and finished products can lead to a specialization on the basis of those disparities rather than according to comparative advantage.(2)   When the differences in national tariffs are retained, preferences agreed between member countries will depend, after reciprocal trade has been freed, upon the level of duties on imports from third countries. Those countries that have higher tariffs will grant greater preference, while they receive less protection in member countries that maintain a lower tariff. This situation appears even more serious if one takes account of the distortions in competition brought about by the differences in subsidies and exchange rates that are so prevalent in underdeveloped countries. As was noted in the first chapter, these disparities are very extensive in the Andean Group countries. Among the causes of the stagnation of LAFTA, Balassa singles out as of particular importance the differences in subsidies and exchange rates, which distorted competition, and the preferences that were granted.(3)

Morawetz summarizes the four conditions that make the introduction of a CET advantageous, so that the risks of misallocation of resources can be prevented after trade has been freed between member countries. The need to introduce a CET is greater, and its costs lower, when (A) the differences in previous tariff levels are great, (B) transport costs are low, (C) national tariff structures are widely dispersed, and (D) there is a high degree of similarity between the various countries' development goals.

A. In relation to the first of these conditions, the following data give us some idea of the dispersion of the previous national tariff levels in the GRAN of 1969, when the Treaty of Cartagena was signed. The unweighted average nominal tariff in Bolivia was 54 percent, in Colombia 70 percent, in Peru 90 percent, in Ecuador 106 percent, and in Chile 172 percent.(4) Therefore, Chile, Ecuador, and Peru would automatically grant preference to Colombian and Bolivian goods, that is, to the countries with the lowest average nominal protection. When protection is broken down by sector, one sees that the highest level in Bolivia was charged on drinks at 95 percent, and in Peru and Colombia on drinks, clothing, and shoes. On some specific articles, the level could vary much more. For example, some chemical products in Chile had a nominal protection of 1,008 percent.(5)

Effective protection is much higher, as it is affected by factors other than the mere duty, such as the enforcement of import licenses and quotas. The obvious result of such acute differences in national tariff levels is a gap between countries' prices of manufactured goods, such as was shown to exist in the second chapter of this work. For example, in international prices, at the end of the 1960s, the domestic price of Chilean bicycles was 4 times the world level. Similar relationships of domestic to world prices can be found for certain products in Colombia, Peru, Venezuela and Ecuador.(6)

B. Transport costs, the second of the conditions, are much higher than in the EEC (see Chapter 2). This tends to reduce the risk of misallocation of resources if a common tariff is not adopted after reciprocal trade has been free.

C. A strong argument that favors the adoption of a CET is the difference that exists in tariff structures. In the GRAN the general pattern of "high-lower-lowest" nominal duties on finished, intermediate, and capital goods, respectively, is common to all member countries. However, broken down into smaller groups of goods, the differences are very important, as was noted earlier. NAB division 93, for example, has a tariff of 52 percent for Colombia and 38.9 percent for Venezuela.(7)

D. With regard to the fourth condition, it has to be asked first whether or not the political objectives that lay behind the various national tariff structures were the same. Second, even if they were, we have to take into account that recently measures have been introduced in certain countries to counteract some of the negative effects of substitution upon the export sector, such as export subsidies, drawback schemes, and crawling-peg exchange rates. In Chile and Colombia, for example, these measures make up part of a co-herent set of policies aimed at forming a liberal model. This package of policies indicates a change in the concept of the state as an economic factor, and implies a rethinking of the role of industry. It means that social efficiency is now to be measured in terms of production costs.

Today, therefore, the cost of adopting a CET is much greater and its usefulness less clear than in 1968, because only two of the four conditions (differences in tariff levels and structures) favor the adoption of uniform levels of protection against third parties.

What is the aim of the CET? In theoretical terms, the "optimum CET" would be defined as that which guarantees more or less equal nominal and effective protection to all economic activities. It would allow for adjustments to take account of monopolies in a given market, infant industries, and other instances that tend to militate against the operation of perfect competition. An "optimum CET" would not be obtained if, for example, it were based upon the averaging out of previous national tariffs, product by product. In either the perfect or imperfect cases put forward above, the word "common" can only be applied when all quantitative and nontariff obstacles to trade have been abolished and export subsidies, which have similar effects on resources as do tariffs, are brought into line with each other. It is assumed that internal taxes are very low or, at least, that they differ less between countries than do tariffs. Michel Bruno has shown, however, that even a less than "optimum" tariff can be a better situation than that prevailing before, if on average it is lower and less fragmented than the old national structure.(8) This hypothesis is very important when dealing with real situations in which there are no "optima" but only a series of "second-best" arrangements.

THE MINIMUM COMMON EXTERNAL TARIFF (MCET)

Because tariff levels were so disparate, a piecemeal approach had to be adopted, so that the adjustment from national to subregional tariffs could be smooth and more or less continual. Decision 30 of the Treaty, approved by the five member countries, provided for an intermediate step towards the CET. This was the Minimum Common External Tariff (MCET), which was to be in operation by December 1971. The MCET was to remain in force until December 31, 1975, and would apply to the countries with a relatively greater level of development, which were to be the only ones having to bring their tariffs into line. The MCET differs from the CET; the former is designed as a commercial mechanism that creates margins of preference for subregional production linked to the program of reducing duties. The latter is a long-term tool of subregional economic development. The approved MCET ranged from 0 to 120 points and gave an average nominal protection of 40 percent, while allowing a standard deviation from the average of 53 percent (see table 6.1). All of these values represent an improvement over previous national levels. Therefore, it agreed with Bruno's hypothesis mentioned earlier. Given that on average, the MCET was below national tariffs, the condition that had to be fulfilled by all countries was to raise those tariffs that were below the new levels. If they wanted, these countries could maintain their uppermost national duties, thus giving extra protection to subregional production over and above the minimum of the MCET. Colombia was 12 months late with its first adjustment. Chile needed five months extra. Peru was 37, 25, and 13 months late with the first, second, and third stages, respectively.

The Operation of the MCET

An analysis of how the MCET might affect the creation of the new economic area has to take into account the accomplishment of the necessary requirements for granting the name "common" to a tariff, that is, the eradication of obstacles to trade and the bringing into line of production and export subsidies. Decision 49, "On the harmonization of industrial promotion policies," approved in December 1971, stated that by December 31, 1975, all measures that in any way affected the operation of the MCET were to be eliminated. In no country has that provision been put into effect. The usual national modes of trading continue - altering, decreasing, or completely negating the agreed margins of preference.

In studying the different systems of external trade and industrial promotion laws (see Chapter 2), we saw the widespread use of rebates and exemptions, which altered the level of nominal protection. The application of the laws of industry, agriculture, fisheries, and telecommunications reduced the level of protection agreed in the MCET. The general average rebate given by the commercial and industrial laws in Bolivia was 18 percent, in Colombia 19 percent, in Chile 28 percent, in Ecuador 29 percent, in Peru 31 percent, and in Venezuela 22 percent. The result of deducting such rebates from the nominal tariff is what is called "liquid protection." The differences between nominal and liquid tariffs, by countries and by NAB sections, at the beginning of 1975, can be seen in table 6.2. This takes account of the tariff reforms in Colombia and Chile (but not the Chilean Reform of September 1975) - which notably reduced both the average levels of protection and the dispersion of national tariffs in those two countries. This meant that more was done there than was stipulated in the MCET. The application of the exemptions and rebates in 1975 constituted a reduction of 11 percent in nominal protection for the subregion as a whole.(9) The most pronounced effects of the rebates appear in Peru and Chile and are more marked in those sectors having the lowest nominal tariffs, which really means an increase in the dispersion of customs duties. The figures in brackets in table 6.2 show those cases where liquid protection is lower than that given by the MCET.

Secondly, the efficacy of the MCET as a regulator of competitiveness between regional and external production is limited because of the statutes that, in general, exempt government agencies from paying duties on their purchases (as was noted in Chapter 2). No studies have been made at the subregional level of impact of state purchasing on total imports. However, figures for Colombia, Peru, and Venezuela indicate that it represents 23 percent, 26 percent, and 16 percent, respectively, of total imports. Apart from the distortions this creates in the ability to compete, it represents a selective reduction in the effective market.(10) A large proportion of state purchases consists of construction plant, motor vehicles, some raw materials, and foodstuffs.

The failure in some cases to raise national tariff levels, to eliminate exemptions and subsidies, and to stop special customs concessions for state purchases hindered the setting up of margins of preference for subregional production. If all the agreements had been rigorously applied, by 1975 there would have been average margins of preference equal to 25 percent (see table 6.3), with higher margins for manufactured, intermediate, and capital goods.

The structure of the CET was to have been agreed upon by December 31, 1975. Because this goal was not fulfilled, the MCET was extended until 1979. At the same time, changes were made in the structure and levels of the MCET, which, as table 6.4 shows, resulted in the following.

i. There was a reduction of ten points from the previous level. More important, there was a greater concentration of goods given between 0 percent and 50 percent nominal protection, a reduction in the average nominal protection from 40 percent to 28 percent, and also a decrease in the dispersion of tariffs measured by their standard deviation.

ii. There was a reduction in the differences between the CET and official liquid tariffs. Table 6.2 compares liquid tariff levels and the customs duties of Decision 104. This shows that the Colombian and Venezuelan levels of the liquid tariff became more similar. However, Peru still has higher levels, even though the difference has been reduced.

iii. There was a 50 percent decrease in the margin of preference given to subregional production (see table 6.3). In principle, this reduction can be viewed as a positive movement toward greater efficiency. But it adversely affects production in Bolivia and Ecuador in particular, and obliges the subregion to be more selective in its industrial development.

The following conclusions can be put forward regarding the intermediate stage of the CET. First, it is hard to believe that the MCET could ever have worked, because of the distortions created by exemptions, by rebates granted by national trade legislation, and by state purchasing practices. All such distortions were supposed to have been eliminated by Decision

49, which it was impossible to implement (see section 5, below). Second, none of the four countries committed to the MCET (that is, those with relatively greater levels of development) carried out the unification of their tariff levels in the required time span, when this process meant an increase in duties in order to obtain the minimum agreed rate of protection. The nonreduction of higher national tariffs was not considered as nonfulfillment because there was extra protection granted to subregional production, putting the country that gave higher protection than the MCET at a disadvantage. Nevertheless, it is still possible to conclude that both the original MCET and its modified form represent a step towards greater productive efficiency at the subregional level, because the level of protection has fallen and the dispersion of tariffs has been reduced. However, the modifications of Decision 104 mean an average reduction in the margin of preference from 25 percent to 13 percent, which can seriously affect the competitiveness of the relatively less developed countries, and reduces the scope of subregional import substitution.

THE SUBREGIONAL TARIFF POLICY

Having surveyed the workings of the MCET, we can now study the drawing up and negotiation of the CET, and we will see how this led to the most serious crisis experienced to date in the GRAN.

The principal elements needed for the CET to work are outlined in Chapter 4, articles 61 to 68 of the Treaty. They define the tariff as a tool of planning which provides the protection necessary for industrial growth, establishes the margin of preference, and encourages productive efficiency. The remaining chapters of the Treaty, and the Bases para una Estrategia Sub-Regional de Desarrollo (Bases for Sub-Regional Development), set out other objectives related to the CET and the other tools of integration. However, in the talks held by the Commission or by government and subregional experts, other goals have been added one by one. These new aims break up the basic objectives and make points more specific, thus turning the CET into a tool for allocating productive resources by sector and using it to affect the structure of relative factor prices, fiscal incomes, the balance of payments, consumption patterns, income distribution, and employment.

Obviously, the CET could not affect all of these variables simultaneously and effectively. Therefore, it was necessary to choose one central objective:

the search for a rational allocation for productive resources, which accords with the common aims of economic development in the subregion.(11)

Here it was assumed that there exists a common objective and a common model of development and necessities and priorities common for all countries, and that these could be achieved through a given tariff structure, with no contradictions arising during the process. It was implicitly assumed also that it was possible to satisfy (without contradiction) the demands of each member country, and thus to satisfy the position of the region as a whole.(12) The formula for achieving this expansion of the area of the CET rested upon the choice of the following objectives: to promote industry, to increase Andean productive efficiency at the social level, to facilitate exports, to raise the rate of employment generation, to increase technological skills, to widen consumption patterns, and to decrease the differences in economic development between the countries.(13) These were clearly very general guidelines, which could be interpreted according to the interests of each country. In hard reality, the CET had to be part of a process that ensured the continuation of import substitution on a more efficient basis than in the past. Both the sectoral and intersectoral spread and the maximum level of effective protection were to be lower than those existing in each country. These provisions were justified by the greater market size, which would guarantee more efficient production; this requirement was in turn included in both the MCETs that were approved.

The Junta and the national representatives began studying how to put these directives into force as part of the common tariff. They adopted a complex approach which, for the first time, used effective production as a criterion, and it included

> criteria which had some basis in the reality of the
> sub-region, which provide answers to common priori-
> ties and are compatible with each other, and which
> can be applied to a unified tariff.(14)

This study does not set out to discuss what goals tariff policies can or cannot achieve. However, it is worth saying something on the subject in order to show that a tariff can produce different effects according to the way it interacts with other policy commitments or because of varying emphases being placed on one or another objective.

The primary effect of the tariff is to erect a barrier between the internal and external market which, in turn, encourages the substitution of imports. Therefore, it influences trade flows and affects the productive structure, the internal availability of goods, and the level of employment. To the structure and level of the tariff is linked the force of the effects it has upon the efficiency of import substitution, the diversification of production and exports, and the extent to which advantage is taken of economies of scale.

Where there is absolute protection of consumer goods, while capital goods enjoy freedom from import duties, there is a tendency for a great increase and spread to take place in the production of consumer products for the internal market. This includes increases in production for very limited markets that militate against possible economies of scale. The "de-protection" or negative effective protection accorded to the capital goods sector aggravates the difficulties in starting domestic production in these sectors and pushes economic activities toward more capital-intensive processes. Excessive protection and diversification in the production of consumer goods makes access to the international market difficult and, therefore, exports continue to be concentrated in those primary products in which an existing comparative advantage is enjoyed. On the other hand, if a tariff structure is chosen that is characterized by a small degree of differentiation in protection levels between sectors and in the dispersion of tariff structures, then this allows countries to obtain more balanced internal growth, and a greater diversity in exports. While excessive protection causes unbalanced development, excessive "deprotection" causes disequilibria that reinforces imbalances between the industrial and monoexport, primary product sectors.

Basic Criteria for Working Out the CET

The allocation of productive resources throughout the sub-region was to be obtained through a tariff scheme drawn up according to the following basic criteria:

i. Efficiency

It should seek social efficiency in the use of productive resources. This would be achieved by having a level of protection that permitted a greater efficiency in the import substitution process than in the past, and promoted exports.

ii. Employment

Apart from its negative impact on the distribution of income, unemployment means an irrational allocation of resources. Therefore, the creation of employment is a goal both of social and economic policies. Greater relative tariff protection had to be given to labor-intensive industries, thereby eliminating discrimination in existing customs duties against the wider use of labor and also of subregional production of capital goods.(15)

iii. Technological contribution

The CET had to produce a technological contribution effect, defined in terms of the value of external economies generated by developing a certain sector within the subregion. Such economies come through the greater use of human resources and the spread of knowledge and also, from the linking of technology with other productive activities.(16)

iv. Infant industry

The CET had to take account of the "infant industry" concept. In general, this meant the granting of extra protection to industry against other sectors. Within industry, it meant more safeguards for products specifically included in sectoral programs, especially those activities assigned within the plan to Bolivia and Ecuador. The use of this concept as a criterion was valid because of inherent factors in the existing levels of development of member countries that tended to hinder the development of the manufacturing sector. Without special protection, such factors as the weakness or lack of an infrastructure or the long gestation period of a project would act against industry as a whole.

There were some additional measures adopted to correct problems arising from the application of the criteria listed above. These dealt with agricultural inputs, traditional exports, products that had social importance, capital goods that were not or could not be produced in the subregion, and those products for which there was a high propensity to import.

Bolivia posed a special problem because it is landlocked. Originally, the Treaty contained clauses allowing for the manipulation of tariffs to take this fact into account. It was amended by the proposal to set up a fund, supported by contributions from member countries and third parties, which would help solve the shortcomings of Bolivian infrastructure through special mechanisms for promoting and financing the country's exports.

Although the criteria for the CET were to be applicable to the whole tariff structure, it was thought that, because of the relative importance of those industrial activities specifically included within sectoral plans, in the application of the criteria, the circumstances of each program should be taken into account. In addition, another criterion was to be used: the balance between redistributive justice and productive efficiency. In other words, the centralized location of industries as laid out in the sectoral plans had to be accompanied by tariff levels sufficient to reinforce the objectives of economy and specialization, to prevent overlapping investments and to ensure the redistribution of the benefits of the programs. All of this would be achieved, in theory, by creating special margins of preference through specific tariff levels and structures. For the reasons given above, the Junta's proposal on the CET referred to 2871 items, which represented 63 percent of the total tariff. This excluded products to be included in the SIDPs.

The Structure of the CET Proposed by the Junta

In applying those criteria discussed, the Junta proposed a tariff structure that contained nominal levels of duty between 0 and 65 percent. These figures were arrived at by finding the maximum levels of effective protection the structure would permit, in terms of the effect on value added necessary to stimulate the desired structure of profitability and thus draw resources to priority sectors as set out by the basic criteria. The detailed provisions of the Treaty were based on a web of Andean industries made up from the technical coefficients of the input-output table for 32 productive sectors, and the criteria already analyzed. Next, the maximum level of effective protection was distributed among the three priorities as follows: 40 percent to employment, 20 percent to the technological factor, and 40 percent to infant industries. Within the last group, there was a split of protection; 90 percent maximum effective protection was to be given to new industries outside the SIDPs and 100 percent for those within the programs (see table 6.5 or the last column of table 6.7).

To arrive at these results, the Junta employed the following method to set up the CET: starting from the basic formula of the concept of effective protection, it is possible to derive a system of linear equations with n equations and n unknowns, in which the unknowns correspond to the nominal tariffs, the effective protection, the input-output coefficient, and the coefficient of value added for each activity being given.(17)

The method was applied in stages, first calculating nominal tariffs for groups of products (such as food products, wood, paper, etc.) and related products, and maintaining a greater degree of aggregation for the other products of the tariff universe. To calculate nominal tariffs for product groups, a pilot aggregate matrix of technical coefficients was derived for a group of 32 sectors of production, by comparing the input-output matrices of Colombia, Chile, and Peru with those of France and the United States. The most adequate coefficient for each sector was selected, accepting those of the United States or France if they did not differ greatly from those of the subregion. In cases such as the mining sector, information from the subregion was used. The pilot matrix was disaggregated for each sector analyzed, the principal products composing the sector in each group were determined, as were their principal inputs, and the other sectors of production were maintained at the same level of aggregation as given in the pilot matrix.(18)

Such then was the methodology followed by the Junta in the drawing up of a project for a CET. The levels presented in tables 6.5 and 6.7, and which constituted their proposal to member countries (which was never approved), are the result of the application of this methodology and of many consultations with national experts. In such consultations, as we explained in Chapter 1,(19) national positions are sounded out, discussed, and integrated by the Junta into its project. In other words, the CET proposed by the Junta was already the result of numerous negotiations, as the Junta began its work on the subject in 1974.

These provisions imply a less diverse tariff structure than that prevailing in each nation. On average, there was a lower level of tariff on a subregional basis, and the protection given to sectors producing for final consumption was lowered, while the level for intermediate and capital goods was raised.

Perhaps the most salient factors, apart from the inclusion of the concept of effective protection which has already been mentioned, were as follows.

i. There was a reduction of negative protection in the agricultural sector. For example, in Chile, the very marked negative protection of agriculture prevailing before the 1975 reforms was eradicated.(20) However, there was some discrimination in tackling employment. When applying this concept, only 30 percent maximum protection was given to agriculture, while 40 percent went to industry. This discrimination was reduced mainly by the reduction of customs duties on inputs for industries that produce inputs to agriculture and on materials of an agricultural nature.

ii. Special treatment was accorded to traditional exports. Fifty-seven items were picked out from the basic exports of the countries. These include minerals, metal, fish, and agricultural products. A zero tariff was set up for minerals, 5 percent for metals, and 10 percent for the remainder. This put Bolivia at a disadvantage by giving its main export sector no protection in other member countries' markets, while intermediate and semifinished goods received a higher level.

iii. The nominal tariff for goods which, for technological reasons or market limitations, could not be produced in the group, was reduced to 25 percent. There were 54 of these products; most were capital goods.

iv. There was an increase to 65 percent in the tariff on goods with a high propensity to be imported, such as tobacco, alcohol, preserves, perfumes, furs, and sweets.(21)

If one compares the old national tariff structures with that put forward by the Junta, it can be seen that there has been an improvement in terms of breaking down excessive discrimination in favor of industry and a lessening of the diversity of the system.(22)   But it tends toward the position held by the less developed countries within the group in appearing to identify the "common needs of sub-regional development" with the necessity to accelerate and regionally to equilibrate the industrial growth.

For the CET to operate properly and in line with the objectives implicit in its structure, other measures related to it have to act in compliance with the policy.   The use of these measures in place of or in conjunction with customs duties can raise the price of imported goods above the levels envisaged in the tariff.   Regulations allowing exemptions reduce or eliminate the effect of the tariff upon imports.   Multiple exchange rates produce discriminatory effects in the cost of imported products, thus changing the relative prices established by the tariff.   An undervalued rate of exchange discriminates against imports.   Therefore, if the CET is to act as an effective allocator of resources, apart from the setting of a tariff structure and levels, there have to be agreements on these other tariff-like measures.   Because of this, the Junta proposed very clearly that the member countries had to unify their policies in these areas, at the same time as accepting the CET.

THE CET AND DIFFERENT LEVELS OF DEVELOPMENT

The debate about the tariff structure and recommendations for unifying paratariff policies(23) clearly show the conflict between our two groups of countries: Colombia and Chile were on one side vis-à-vis the other four.

The differences of opinion appear over the following questions: What should be the effective level of protection given to new subregional industries?   Was the future of manufacturing to be linked only to a substitutive process?   Was the tariff to assume the role of the single allocator of resources, chaneling factors of production from sector to sector and country to country?   Also, differences occur regarding the direction of external trade policy and the readiness to accept some type of measure to unify the approach to the question. The countries that took up more protectionist stances were those that, in the second chapter, we grouped together as the relatively less industrially developed (Bolivia, Ecuador, Peru, and Venezuela).   Chile and Colombia assumed more liberal positions.   This ranking correlated, for obvious reasons, with the preexisting tariff structure, as can be seen in table 6.7.

As we indicated earlier, the general aim or consensus of the countries was to approve a tariff which allowed the promotion of the import substitution process, in a more efficient manner than in the past (it would) reduce discrimination against exports, and reflect the importance of economic activities from the point of view of the net social benefits which may be derived from those activities. (24)

But this apparently represented the limit of the agreement. The first specific area of conflict we will discuss concerns the fundamental role of the CET. Because the Chilean and Colombian governments are committed to the pursuit of the rationalization of their economies, they look for and plan productive structures where the level of costs will be comparable with the international economy. (25) There is also the medium-term goal of evening out the cost of gaining an additional unit of foreign currency, either by substituting imports or increasing exports. The other four countries see the tariff as a planning instrument that allows decisions on what and how to produce at a more centralized level. This ensures that the allocation of productive resources will be made according to the preestablished development strategy. (26)

It is logical that Peru and Venezuela, which are committed to large industrial projects, should prefer a high rate of protection that permits an overvalued exchange rate and hence cheap imported inputs. Venezuela adopted a double position: it maintained its lowest tariffs in the commercial program and sought high tariffs for new industries, in accordance with the high costs derived from the high oil revenue and a raised exchange rate.

Thus the majority of countries and the Junta were concerned with strengthening the young industrialization process in those areas where the subregion had sufficient resources and a relatively wide market. They also sought to create a climate in which industrial activity in the subregion could develop. (27) This position was held by all the countries except Chile and Colombia, who blamed the substitution process as the single cause for slow development, bad income distribution, monopoly power in industry, chronic unemployment, agricultural depression, and fiscal deficits. (28)

By contrast, Chile and Colombia see the tariff as an instrument for bringing the supply and demand for foreign exchange into equilibrium, as an adjunct of exchange rate policy. It is not a tool for promoting industry. Therefore, the optimum tariff would be uniform, would tend toward zero, and would only come into force when the exchange rate does not produce equilibrium. The private sector should be the allocator of resources. Social preferences would be influenced by taxes on consumption, taxes on estimated agricultural income, and other means that would serve as indicators of the relative profitability of sectors and would, therefore, direct the decisions of private investors. The best mechanism for promoting exports is the real rate of exchange.

The various positions of countries within the tariff structure can be seen in table 6.6, which shows the level of their nominal tariffs existing in 1975 in accordance with the International Standard Industrial Classification (ISIC). This type of classification is more useful than the customs classification, because it better illustrates the ranking among productive sectors. The primary sector (Major Division I, agriculture, game, fisheries, forestry, plus Major Division II, exploitation of mines and quarries) has a significantly lower level of duty than products of Major Division III (manufacturing industries). In general, one can say that the official nominal tariff of the GRAN countries in 1975 was 30 percent for the primary sectors and 45 percent for manufacturing. On average, nominal protection is greater for manufactured goods than primary products. Chile, Colombia, and Venezuela have a greater gap (a difference of 50 percent), while Ecuador and Peru have 20 percent and Bolivia 13 percent.

Certainly, national structures were less dispersed compared to those of 1968, because of the MCET and the other reforms mentioned earlier. However, as we have seen, the movement from national schemes to a common scheme was not possible as the countries could not reconcile their interests on specific matters.

The second area of conflict, which follows from the first, was the extent to which the CET should be recognized as an instrument of planning and therefore subordinated to the SIDPs.

Bolivia, Ecuador, Peru, and Venezuela accept that the CET is the "tool to help allocate resources as planned in the sectoral programs."(29) They definitely rank sectoral programming higher in importance than the CET. Therefore, the tariff is constructed to give additional protection to the programs and, in consequence, to allow specified countries to achieve their production targets. The sectoral programs would act to raise the overall level of protection.(30)

In the view of Chile and Colombia, the outlook of the other four countries could create serious distortions in the regional and sectoral allocation of resources. These two countries prefer that the special tariff operating with the SIDPs(31) should be merged with the general tariff; that is, policy should move away from specifying certain products as set out in the commercial program. In this way, they would achieve the elimination of the differentiation between "mature industries," those that can be established through the existing productive structure, and those called "infant industries." The objective of this tariff policy is to stop distortions in a supposedly free competitive market system caused by discrimination between sectors.(32)

A third point of conflict springs from the same basic divisions, manifesting itself in relation to the weighting of different criteria in the structure of the tariff.

All the countries are agreed that their economies have to move toward higher levels of efficiency. For this, a tariff structure should be set up with the minimum amount of dispersion. This will minimize the risk of resources being allocated too far from the optimum situation. However, social efficiency is not an abstract term, and it varies with one's time horizon. In conditions of massive unemployment, the creation of more productive jobs can be more important for some countries than the achievement of efficiency measured in terms of costs and production. For others, the measurement criterion may be shifted to the saving of foreign exchange. Again, the forms may be foreign exchange plus national independence: Peru, for example, stated very strongly its idea of subregional productive social efficiency at the third meeting of the Tercer Consejo de Comercio Exterior. This efficiency has to be measured in the long term as a function of the growth in "basic" industry, which Peru defines as those sectors that are important for achieving a permanent and independent growth of the industrial sector, in such a way that it will insure the independent economic development of the country. Therefore, conditions of underdevelopment in the subregion justify the temporary introduction of distortions that will allow industrial enterprises in such basic industries to grow, even though this may be at the cost of moving away from the hypothetical short-term optimum.(33) Sometimes attempts are made to promote production even of products whose market or productive structure does not guarantee the return of minimum costs even in the long term. In these circumstances, the tariff allows an enterprise to develop which could not do so without special protection. In the long term, growth in these activities would mean a growth at the subregional level.

The conflict emerges clearly in relation to employment, technological contributions, and infant industries. Much depends upon the type of product or the sector and also on the various notions of productive efficiency. For example, the employment criterion seems to contradict the strategy of developing modern industry as planned in Bases para una Estrategia. This policy seeks to raise the modern industrial sector to the same levels as the more developed Latin American countries,(34) or Spain. One aim is to widen the export base to third parties, to be achieved by giving preference to industries such as chemicals and petrochemicals. But even in those industries such as textiles, which traditionally use more labor, international competition has notably increased the capital coefficient. It is clearly stated in Bases para una Estrategia that the accomplishment of the aim of growth in production will

come primarily from increasing the intensity of high productivity enterprises, that is, those that will permit the countries
of the GRAN to compete in external markets: in the first
instance, in LAFTA. The employment problem is shifted to the
agricultural sector, and also to the artisan sector, medium-
sized enterprises, and the tertiary sector.(35)

The Peruvian and Venezuelan position is more consistent
with the Bases than that of the Junta. Peru sees the employment problem as a structural one that cannot be solved by
means of tariffs. There have to be reforms in sectors such as
agriculture in order to alleviate the employment problem.

The Junta's position lies between the Colombian one,
which from the outset pushed for the introduction of the
employment criterion, and that held by the rest of the
countries,(36) which prefer the stimulation of modern
industry.

While accepting the concept of infant industries, Chile
and Colombia demand its extension to the rural sector; they
think that the concept should apply to all infant economic
activities, given the contributions they may make to technological advances.(37) The two countries accept that there are
infant industries that need extra protection. However, this
should be granted over a limited period and has to be the
same for all infant industries without singling out those
included in the SIDPs.

Certainly, the other four countries ask for a greater
weighting in favor of infant industries that are part of a
sector to be specially promoted. Peru and Venezuela go
further and demand extra aid for what they call "strategic
sub-regional industries." They put forward the following
argument: Industrial development has previously been concentrated in light industries or in assembly work, which have
lower levels of transformation and are very dependent upon
imported inputs. It is necessary to have special protection to
develop industries that have high multiplier effects, because of
the low levels of efficiency and small scale of plants.(38)

It is interesting to consider how different levels of
development generate distinct interpretations of concepts such
as efficiency, growth, etc., even among socialist countries,
where conflicts occur even without the intervention of private
interests and within a framework of central planning. In the
CMEA, the split over efficiency and growth also occurred
according to the level of development of the member countries.
The CMEA experience allows us to suggest that the conflict
around the relative weight each country gives to market forms
is not the central one, and that agreement about how much to
plan does not resolve the problems of different levels of
economic development. The relatively more developed countries
tend toward a division of labor based upon the "minimization of
the social cost of labor." The less developed countries, led

by Rumania, criticize this approach on the grounds that it grants too much importance to the law of value in the international market and it does not concentrate enough upon the task of evenly proportioned development. The Rumanians maintain that preference given to the capital goods sector in each country aids the consolidation of the dictatorship of the proletariat by expanding the industrial labor force. Such an argument is very consistent with this country's circumstances: two-thirds of its working population is still tied to agriculture, either directly or indirectly. The criterion advocated by the USSR, East Germany, and Czechoslovakia is the minimization of social costs. Even though some consideration is given to infant industries, by stating that analysis of comparative costs has to be based upon present and future costs, the Soviet approach establishes present profitability as the major determinant. Kaser summarizes the opposing stances on efficiency and growth that come out of the differing levels of economic development of COMECON countries as follows:

> For a variety of reasons the possible non-coincidence of the economic interest of different socialist countries raises the question how, under such circumstances, to approach the evaluation of economic efficiency and the worth of the international division of labour on the one hand from the stand point of the national economy of the separate countries, and on the other hand from the stand point of the entire socialist efficiency.(39)

It is interesting to note the similarities between the positions of the relatively less developed countries in the GRAN and COMECON. They both propose as the basis for economic cooperation principles of pure protectionism, moving away from protection of infant industries while favoring the argument for a balanced external account. The most important points, according to COMECON's less developed countries and expressed most clearly by the Rumanians, can be summed up as follows:

> Only the elimination of disparities in the development of socialist countries can do away with the situation that if international trade is carried on at world prices, developed countries will benefit because they are in the position of exporting goods whose international value exceeds their national value.
> If the criterion of economising social labour were to be made the basis for the international division of labour, this would tend to perpetuate the backwardness of the underdeveloped countries and to conserve the old economic structure inherited from the domination of monopolistic trusts.

Strict respect for the principles of speciali-
sation on the basis of production cost must be replaced by an analysis of natural endowment and of
specific national conditions, which may give rise to
greater future profitability.(40)

The East German and Czech point of view well represents
the position of the more developed countries. They think that
it is imperative to develop industry by assigning the various
production processes to countries with advanced technology,
that is, those that can guarantee the best results in a given
time. They claim that the interests of the socialist system as
a bloc require a productive structure that reflects the
differences in the various countries' productivity levels.(41)

Given the fundamental conflicts traced here, table 6.7 will
come as no surprise. Here we see the countries' positions
with respect to the maximum levels of protection and the
weighting given according to the various corrective criteria.
The maximum level of effective protection varies from 150
percent, which is the Peruvian position, to 30 percent, the
Chilean one.(42)

Given these circumstances, it is not surprising that the
date set for signing the CET, December 31, 1975, passed
without its fulfillment. The impasse was resolved by a
compromise, the introduction of a tariff band which allowed
maximum and minimum levels of protection within which countries could set their own tariffs.(43) This represented the
abandonment of the objective of a common tariff. Besides the
abandonment of the principle of common protection for subregional production, the establishment of the tariff band has
the effect of allowing countries in the lower ranges to
concentrate upon their commercial balances. These countries
give little advantage to imports of goods coming from the
subregion, and, instead, they take advantage of the fact that
the other countries offer greater protection for exports to
them. A second but no less important effect is the increase in
diverted trade, that is, the tendency for imports from outside
countries via member countries with a lower CET to increase.
This creates tensions concerning rules of origin and will lead
to new obstacles to intra-subregional trade.

In principle, the maximum level of protection was set at
60 percent (in a few short-term cases, 100 percent). This low
level of maximum protection was a concession to Chile who had
asked for limits that would vary between 10 percent to 30
percent. However, it was not enough to stop Chile from
leaving the group. Perhaps, as we will see later, this occurred because conflicts within the GRAN were taking on a
more complex nature. Suffice it to say here that the tariff
proposed by the Junta did not affect Chile's competitive
position in terms of its basic export products and, as men-

tioned earlier, it allowed the country to reverse the mathe-
matical sign of protection given to its agriculture.(44)
        The Junta has interpreted its role in studying maximum
and minimum levels of protection to be the coordination of two
tools: the CET and the use of "paratariffs."(45) The former
represents the minimum level and the latter the maximum that
would remain at the discretion of each individual country.
The paratariffs as opposed to tariffs, are to be used in
balance-of-payments crises when the countries do not wish to
change customs levels. Colombia, and up to a point, Peru,
reject this interpretation, while Bolivia, Ecuador, and
Venezuela appear to accept it and seek to unify paratariff tools
in the short term. However, as will be seen in the last
section, the viability of unifying any policy also has its costs
and does not seem to be directly related to the advancement of
the trading program. In the case of paratariffs, the process
of unification will depend on the importance placed upon it by
each country with respect to its use in controlling external
trade. The result is that Colombia has almost dismantled these
systems, has accepted the idea of unification and is looking for
an agreement by December 31, 1979.(46) On the other hand,
Bolivia believes that they should be used at the countries'
discretion and the individual countries should decide the
nature of any agreement according to their own evaluation of
the results of integration in their own economy. Ecuador,
Venezuela, and Peru make unification conditional upon the
agreement and application of a full-scale CET.(47)

THE HARMONIZATION OF FISCAL, MONETARY, EXCHANGE, AND INDUSTRIAL AND EXTERNAL TRADE PROMOTION POLICIES

Although harmonization of those policies was not included in
the Cartagena Agreement as part of the framework of the CET,
we have decided to analyze this aspect here because their
effects upon the CET are immensely important.
        Work carried out in this field has added to the general
knowledge of the different mechanisms used in each country
and has become the basis for proposals made by the Monetary
Exchange Council and for recommendations to the Commission,
the most important of which is the creation of the Common
Reserve Fund. No decisions have so far been approved.
        Harmonization still seems to be a remote goal, partly as a
result of the different economic schemes that have been
adopted by the countries, as epitomized in the shifts to
greater liberalism in Colombia and Chile, and to increased state
control in Peru. It would perhaps be worthwhile emphasizing
the Peruvian case. In its scheme of worker participation (un-

derstood basically as the strengthening of economic pluralism and income redistribution), the government manages changes by means of planning: centralized for the public sector and indicative for the private sector. It would seem that the Peruvian scheme and that of the Treaty of Cartagena are similar. Both reflect the need to overcome the problems of import substitution by means of planning and a coherent policy towards multinational companies. According to Thorp, "The Pact reflected, in a weaker form, the forces appearing in Peru."(48) For Colombia and Chile there could only be harmonization if it were based on the adoption of a single exchange rate with a system of permanent devaluations according to the internal price index, nonintervention in the capital market, a unified rate of interest, the complete dismantling (which can be progressive) of tariff-based import control mechanisms, and the abolition of special systems favoring state imports and specific sectors. Such a view would be considered extreme by other countries, which have implemented a complex industrial promotion program based on the stimuli afforded by precisely those mechanisms which the two larger countries wish to eliminate.(49)

An agreement has also been reached in this area regarding industrial promotion policies, and embodied in Decision 49 (D49), approved in December 1971. That Decision was never enforced by any country(50) and is currently being revised because of its controversial character. Among other things, it fixes a time limit for the harmonization of commercial policies with third-party countries, removes all kinds of regional and sectoral stimuli to industrial development, and fixes a deadline for the ending of provisions for state purchases under special rules.

As an important additional element in the process of forming the common market, the Treaty of Cartagena contemplates the establishment of other mechanisms for the regulation of subregional trade. Those are rules governing competition, rules of origin, and the normalization of the movement of merchandise.

In December 1972 the Junta presented its proposal on the program of harmonization of the instruments and mechanisms for the regulation of foreign trade, establishing the norms for the elimination of distortions in trade competition that could arise from the application of policy instruments relating to foreign exchange, incentives for exports within the subregion or to third countries, and the regulation of imports.(51) The proposal was never discussed in detail by the Commission, and any decision in its respect has in fact been indefinitely postponed.

Regarding the special rules of origin, the countries still have not been able to reach an agreement. Discrepancies arise from the fact that some countries support the idea that the rules should be established after the CET. Everything seems to indicate that, until problems concerning the tariff band are resolved, no progress will be made in this matter. The Junta has made a proposal that has not yet been considered by the Commission.

Similarly, normalization of the transport of merchandise by road has been hindered by the countries lack of interest in putting into effect Decision 56, which deals with international road transport and was approved in 1972. Some countries insist on the transference of goods to vehicles bearing their own license plates. The differences in highway specifications often makes impossible the movement of vehicles accepted in some countries but not in others.(52)

We see therefore that the lack of agreement manifested in the context of the CET was present too in the harmonization of the above-mentioned trade policies. Even as late as 1973, no progress had been achieved in the field, nor is it accorded high priority in the Junta's Action Plan for 1978 to 1980. It has been tacitly recognized that it is prudent to postpone decisions in such sensitive areas.(53)

THE ADOPTION OF THE COMMON
DEVELOPMENT STRATEGIES

From the text of the Agreement it can be deduced that the adoption of a common development strategy is a requisite and a frame of reference for the advancement of the process of integration, as well as a factor that could facilitate the introduction of integration into national development plans and assure its continuity, as much as a common tariff. We have referred already to the document issued by the Junta in 1972 entitled "The Bases of Subregional Development Strategy." This plan, which hinged upon development in the industrial sector, established the subregional growth rates necessary to achieve minimum goals in generating employment, increasing national effective demand, and reducing the external trade gap.

There are two elements that, we will suggest, contributed to make agreement on a common strategy impossible. The first is the strictly substitutive character of the model and the second the political heterogeneity existing in 1972.

Perhaps the most controversial element of the model was the emphasis given to the external trade gap and the ambitious export targets assigned to industry to close the gap. To achieve rapid growth, the Andean subregion would require a rapid expansion of manufactured exports to the rest of the world, so that it could finance the increasing demand for intermediate and capital goods, the production of which might still be insufficient within the subregion. In spite of scale economies and the fact that these help to reduce real costs in some industries, it is very likely, as we have seen, that in many activities unit costs will still be substantially above the international level.

The creation of inefficient intermediate and capital goods industries will induce negative effects throughout the economy. Because no efficiency levels at least comparable with those of major LAFTA countries have been assured, as we will see in Chapter 7, the GRAN will have difficulties in overcoming the obstacle of discrimination which led to the creation of the subregional market.(54) But the dependence of the model on manufactured exports was not its only fragile point: its implications for employment and income distribution were also dubious, given the proposed technology-intensive production structure and the high rate of absorption of investment resources in the industrial sector.

The scant success of the plan can also be attributed to the difficulty in finding points of contact between divergent nationalist policies, and to its lack of realism in attempting to reach compromises in a situation of political pluralism like that of 1972, on matters such as agrarian reform, income redistribution, production structure and interdependence, and employment policy. The Junta suggests that the impossibility of an overall macroeconomic agreement is due to the refusal of the countries to take integration seriously and to include it in their plans.(55) But that can hardly be a cause: it is rather evidence of the impracticability of the idea of regional planning.

In the Andean countries, as in almost all developing countries, the form planning has taken is above all that of ordering public expenditure so as to allow regular control of current commitments by international agencies, with a project approach much in evidence as a result. This factor, added to the lack of continuity in economic policies for both internal and external reasons, leaves little room for optimism concerning the subregional development plan and makes it look like just one more utopian aspect of the Treaty of Cartagena.

The emphasis placed by the Junta on the need to adopt a common strategy reflects above all its fidelity to the spirit of the Treaty and its perception of the need to create a framework that could guarantee the continuance of the integration process, notwithstanding possible changes in individual countries, in order to create a sense of irreversibility and of the indispensibility of integration, rather than a perception of its objective possibility. It also reflects CEPAL's faith in planning (to which they attribute only good qualities) and in the planner as an agent of transformation, as was so fashionable among experts and academics during the 1960s. However, it seems to us a premature aim, given the political conditions of the subregion and the lack of support given to integration, as we have shown in Chapter 4. Now it seems even more difficult to agree on supranational planning because the very idea of planning has lost its momentum, as did integration, social reforms, and so on.

In the "Final Report of the Third Meeting of the Planning Council," it can be seen clearly that the countries and the Junta have abandoned the idea of a subregional development plan, or of any general directives concerning national economies. It is recommended that sectoral studies be undertaken (financing, social policy, agricultural policy). The report also defines the relationship between the Junta and national planning organisms, stating that these should continue to analyze the Junta's evaluation reports and evidence of integration in the national economies, and should furnish the Junta with detailed information concerning the economic and social development of the countries. On the other hand, the projected work on macroeconomic policy is vague, lacking in content and without a fixed date of completion.(56)

In principle many of the problems that beset the integration of underdeveloped countries could be resolved through regional planning. However, experience suggests that such planning would be very difficult if not impossible to achieve, since it involves a great loss of sovereignty, greater than that caused by free-trade schemes. The experiences of COMECON are very relevant to this matter. Greatly increased volumes of trade have been achieved by means of bilateral agreements. Whereas COMECON commissions have brought about a series of industrial specialization agreements with certain common provisions, efforts to deepen the role of the institutions and to obtain a substantial degree of plan coordination between schemes have been defeated by governments unwilling to renounce their sovereignty. For example, at the root of its disagreement with COMECON is the Rumanian government's refusal to renounce its control of planning.(57)

The secretariat of the Economic Commission for Asia and the Far East (ECAFE) notes that in Asia, "if planning is comprehensive, as it is in most of the Asian countries, whether it is indicative or imperative, then comprehensive integration can be adopted only if the development plans of all countries are fully harmonized," but concludes that, "at the moment, this does not seem to be politically feasible in Asia."(58)

Acceptance of the idea of planned economies has not been easy in the EEC either, as can be noted in the clash of French and German positions, the first being liberal and the second in favor of planning. After prolonged discussion they agreed, first, upon the calculation of macroeconomic projections (for four or five years) for the economy as a whole and for major sectors, all within the concept of a market-oriented economy.

Second, they agreed on flexible planning in the areas of public spending, capital and current. The medium-term programs reflect a very restrictive definition of planning and the limited area of agreement on planning possible between countries.(59)

THE HARMONIZATION OF SOCIAL POLICIES

There has been some administrative progress through the creation of Councils responsible for policy formulation in the areas of employment, social security, education, and health. The Councils meet fairly regularly and national delegations are headed by the ministers of the respective departments. Since the Councils are not invested with full power, their decisions are simple policy recommendations made to the Commission. Trade union participation is very limited or nonexistent. Particularly in the case of the Council of Social and Economic Policy, governments have not guaranteed union participation, and employers attend only sporadically. In the 1977 Evaluation Report, there are indications that the "Plan de Accion 1978-80" attempts to make governments aware of the real lack of progress in the harmonization and about the need to accelerate it.(60)

CONCLUSIONS

The following conclusions emerge from studying the definition and setting up of the CET and the harmonization of policies regulating intraregional competition:

A. Doubts arise as to the existence of a common objective for all countries and of the tools to achieve it, because of the relative nature of concepts such as industrialization, growth, and social productive efficiency. The different levels of acceptance or use of these concepts seem to originate from the varying degrees of industrial development within countries. These different levels in turn create conflicts of interest.

B. The conflicts of interest arising from different levels of industrial development were not resolved according to the functionalist model, which would have led to agreements on more integrated policies. In the GRAN, conflicts over the CET were resolved by abandoning the compromise policy of giving common protection to subregional production. This solution demonstrated the fragility of common interests and of the "political decision" to become integrated.

C. The impossibility of reaching an agreement on the CET not only postponed agreements in the field of unifying external and internal trade policies, but also those related to exchange-rate and monetary policies. As was seen in the first chapter, these policies varied greatly from country to country. Their unification is very important for the working of the subregional market.

D. The lack of definition of a common tariff policy especially affects sectoral planning. After the placing of chosen productive enterprises in a centralized system not directly affected by market forces, the tariff structure and levels should ensure that decisions of productive units on what, where, and how to produce would be made according to the objectives and criteria accepted earlier by all member countries. In the absence of a CET, it seems doubtful that long-term industrial specialization, for example, would reduce the differences in levels of industrialization at the same time as making use of economies of scale.

E. The harmonization of macroeconomic policies and the adoption of common development strategy was made impossible by the same elements that prevented the implementation of the CET, and as a result were indefinitely postponed. This means that the creation of the full Common Market now appears very uncertain.

In the following chapter, we shall examine how industrial planning developed. We shall try to establish again what caused the conflicts which, as with the CET, brought about changes in the Treaty.

Table 6.1. National Nominal Tariffs and the
Minimal Common External Tariff
(unweighted sector averages, in %)

Sector	MCET	Bolivia	Chile	Colombia	Ecuador	Peru
Agriculture	29	77	133	45	125	57
Fishing	27	25	150	52	102	86
Mining	11	60	132	20	58	65
Food	50	49	268	92	192	92
Beverages	64	95	388	75	291	208
Tobacco	42	40	186	143	195	117
Textiles	60	72	190	67	101	103
Clothing, shoes	80	76	283	183	184	210
Wood products	47	78	172	115	121	110
Furniture	52	53	152	77	116	85
Paper products	40	52	173	64	83	88
Printing	21	45	160	52	53	71
Leather products	45	76	250	86	124	115
Rubber products	58	62	170	98	98	78
Chemicals	32	34	101	32	52	56
Petroleum	35	31	111	33	57	36
Nonmetallic minerals	42	61	164	72	86	80
Basic metals	27	36	87	31	49	67
Metal products	46	52	149	56	79	76
Nonelectrical machinery	43	27	79	35	45	48
Electrical machinery	55	42	110	40	56	60
Transport products	42	42	183	76	81	58
Other industries	50	47	164	69	93	90
Arithmetic average	40	54	172	70	106	90
Standard deviation	21	19	68	37	58	41

Source: Calculated from national tariff schedules.

Table 6.2. Comparison Between Official Nominal Tariff and Nominal Liquid Tariff of the Andean Countries (1972) and the Nominal MCET (Decision 30, 1973) and MCET (Decision 104, 1976), by NAB Sections of Andean Customs Tariff

Section	Description	Colombia ONT[a]	NLT[b]	Chile ONT[a]	NLT[b]	Peru ONT[a]	NLT[b]	Venezuela ONT[a]	NLT[b]	CMET D30 1971	D104 1976
I	Animal products	38	(25)	39	28	57	39	54	42	26	19
II	Vegetable products	32	(21)	41	31	76	53	48	37	24	18
III	Oils & fats	36	(25)	42	33	62	33	71	43	31	21
IV	Food & drink	55	(28)	73	(37)	144	130	190	150	53	40
V	Minerals & fuels	20	20	39	33	57	29	26	17	14	12
VI	Chemicals	35	33	50	45	55	29	25	16	31	21
VII	Plastics, rubber, & their products	57	52	67	(15)	78	(49)	82	46	31	37
VIII	Hides & leather & their products	49	(17)	64	(19)	157	120	107	66	54	30
IX	Wood, cork, & their products	48	(21)	57	(28)	90	61	68	49	45	33
X	Pulp, paper, & their products	40	(33)	65	45	76	57	70	44	42	25
XI	Textiles & their products	70	(41)	91	46	164	127	180	100	36	42
XII	Footwear	66	19	87	(34)	218	213	75	62	42	40
XIII	Glass, earthenware	51	46	68	49	81	46	73	58	40	40
XIV	Precious stones & metal & their products	48	37	83	66	110	97	46	45	31	31
XV	Nonprecious metals	43	37	54	(34)	70	54	37	(27)	29	29
XVI	Machinery	42	(39)	56	(40)	55	(24)	24	20	43	30
XVII	Transport equipment	48	45	65	44	57	(29)	38	(28)	43	30
XVIII	Instruments	50	(47)	66	(47)	79	59	26	24	31	31
XIX	Arms & munition	56	53	95	47	72	72	40	(20)	54	41
XX	Miscellaneous	55	39	77	(47)	116	116	105	91	44	27
XXI	Art and Antiques	7	0	49	23	32	32	1	1	50	36
	TOTAL	44	34	58	41	86	61	64	48	40	28

Source: Junta, La Situación Arancelaria de los Países Andinos, J/PE/45, Lima, 1975.

Notes: (a) ONT = Official nominal tariff.
(b) NLT = Nominal tariff net of reductions, drawbacks, exemptions.

Table 6.3. Average Nominal Protection and
Average Margins of Preference in the
Minimal Common External Tariff

	Section	No. of items	Average MCET		Margins of Preference %	
			Dec 30	Dec 104	Dec 30	Dec 104
		1	2	3	4	5
I	Animal products	126	26	19	15	9
II	Vegetable products	218	24	18	14	9
III	Oils and fats	49	31	21	21	11
IV	Food and drink	192	53	40	26	15
V	Minerals and fuels	150	14	12	8	6
VI	Chemicals	524	31	21	21	13
VII	Plastics, rubber, and their products	82	54	37	34	15
VIII	Hides and leather and their products	52	45	30	18	7
IX	Wood, cork, and their products	67	42	33	20	11
X	Pulp, paper, and their products	81	·36	25	20	10
XI	Textiles and their products	265	42	67	41	16
XII	Footwear	29	40	59	20	7
XIII	Glass, earthenware, and their products	109	46	31	23	10
XIV	Precious stones and metals and their products	32	38	29	19	11
XV	Nonprecious metals and their products	297	43	30	26	15
XVI	Machinery	309	43	30	33	20
XVII	Transport equipment	43	39	31	30	17
XVIII	Instruments	91	54	41	41	27
XIX	Arms and munitions	16	44	27	21	5
XX	Miscellaneous	86	50	36	21	10
XXI	Art and antiques	6	0	0	0	0
	TOTAL:	2824	40	28	25	13

Source: Junta, Informe de Evaluación, 1976, and national
statistics.

Table 6.4.   Andean Group, Structure of the Minimal
Common External Tariffs, Decision 30, 1970
and Decision 104, 1976

	MCET according to Decision 30 1970			MCET according to Decision 104 1976		
Level	No. Items	%	% Accum.	No. Items	%	% Accum.
0	50	1.8	1.8	43	1.5	1.5
5	36	1.3	3.1	36	1.3	2.8
10	193	6.9	10.0	197	7.0	9.8
15	67	2.4	12.4	514	18.2	28.0
20	246	8.8	21.2	358	12.7	40.7
25	238	8.5	29.7	426	16.3	57.0
30	384	13.7	43.4	76	27	59.7
35	104	3.7	47.1	621	22.0	81.7
40	393	14.0	61.1	39	1.4	83.1
45	36	1.3	62.4	191	6.7	89.0
50	414	14.7	77.1	95	3.4	93.2
55	12	0.4	77.5	-	-	93.2
60	316	11.2	88.7	99	3.5	96.7
65	4	0.1	88.8	2	0.1	96.8
70	119	4.2	93.0	47	1.7	98.5
80	121	4.3	97.3	26	0.9	99.4
90	46	1.6	98.9	10	0.3	99.7
1900	28	1.0	99.0	6	0.2	99.9
110	2	1.0	100.0	2	0.1	100.0
120	1	0.0	100	-	-	-

Source: Junta, Informe de Evaluación, 1976, Jun Di 248,
Lima, 1977.

Table 6.5. The Junta's Proposals on Maximum Levels of Effective Protection (%)

Sector	Employment		Technological Contribution		Infant Industry		Total effective protection a+b+c
	Category	Level of effective protection a	Category	Level of effective protection b	Category	Level of effective protection c	
		(a)		(b)		(c)	
Agriculture	1	30	1	20			50
	2	25	2	15		0	40
	3	15	3	10			25
Industry	1	40	1	20	(1) Products reserved for SIDPs	(1) 40(1a)30	(1)100 (1a)90
	2	35	2	15			
	3	30	3	10	1a Products not reserved	30	90
	4	25	4	0			50
	5	20					40
	6	15					25
	7	0					20
Mining	1	0		15			15

Table 6.6. National Official Nominal Tariffs, 1975, Arithmetical Averages, ISIC Divisions

ISIC	Description	Bolivia	Colombia	Chile	Ecuador	Peru	Venezuela
11	Agriculture and hunting	23	24	38	36	55	48
12	Forestry and timber exploitation	17	21	34	27	68	24
13	Fishing	27	25	51	50	88	61
21	Coal mining	10	10	28	0	47	1
22	Crude oil and gas	36	11	5	0	29	14
23	Metallic minerals	21	8	28	0	41	5
29	Other minerals	17	11	33	12	61	23
31	Food, drink, and tobacco	31	38	57	78	75	131
32	Textiles, clothes, and leather industries	69	62	89	70	161	139
33	Wood and its products	55	47	65	59	96	82
34	Pulp, paper, publishing, and printing	27	31	65	39	78	60
35	Chemical substances derived from oil, rubber, and plastics	14	22	52	12	52	34
36	Nonmetallic mineral products	31	39	64	39	79	73
37	Basic metal industries	13	22	39	15	65	28
38	Metallic products, machinery equipment	18	31	60	32	59	21
39	Various industries	45	48	79	63	105	59
	TOTAL	23	30	58	31	69	49

Source: Junta, Situación Arancelaria En los Países Andinos, J/PE Lima, September 2, 1975.

Table 6.7. Andean Group, The Countries' Positions on the Maximum Levels and Structure of the Common External Tariff in 1976

Structure of effective protection in %	Bolivia	Chile	Colombia	Ecuador	Peru	Venezuela	Junta
Maximum level of effective protection in %	90 for SIDP 80 for the rest	30 for SIDP 30 for the rest	60 for SIDP 60 for the rest	100 for SIDP 80 for the rest	150 for SIDP 100 for the rest	100 for SIDP (90) 100 for the rest (80)	100 for SIDP 100 for the rest
Employment	–	15	30	40	–	40	40
industrial	–	15	30	40	–	40	40
agriculture	–	15	30	40	–	40	30
Technological contribution	–	15	15	20	–	20	20
industrial	–	15	15	20	–	20	20
agriculture	–	15	15	20	–	20	20
Infant industry	–	–	15	40	–	30	40
SIDP	–	–	15	40	–	30	40
the rest	–	–	15	20	–	20	30
Observations:	Greater weighting for infant industry				Greater weighting for infant industry and for strategic industry		Greater weighting for infant industry in Bolivia and Ecuador

Source: Junta, Actas Finales de la Comisión and of Consejo de Comercio Exterior.

Note: the figures in brackets show the position put forward by the countries at the IV meeting of the Consejo de Comercio Exterior in February.

CHAPTER 7

SECTORAL INDUSTRIAL PLANNING

This chapter discusses the case for sectoral planning first in general, and then in the specific context of the Andean Group. It then defines the role assigned to sectoral planning in the Treaty. The third part of the chapter evaluates the experience of sectoral planning, discussing the nature of conflicts that have arisen, and how far they are implicit in intercountry differences, and, then, showing specifically how these conflicts have affected the development of the Sectoral Industrial Development Programs and originated the crisis of 1975, which can still be felt in some aspects. The cost of resolving this crisis is represented by the resignation of one member country and the relaxation of the integration agreements, both in relation to sectoral planning and tariff policies as in the treatment given to foreign capital. In the fourth section, this analysis is used to show up to what point the recent crisis in the GRAN is rooted in these conflicts. Finally, the actual programs achieved are reviewed, to see how far they modify our analysis of conflict and to assess whether or not the gains have in fact been significant.

THE CASE FOR INDUSTRIAL PLANNING

The Need for Regional Equilibrium

Various factors induce a concentration of industrial activity in already established centers; examples of these factors are the relationship between transport and raw material costs and those of the finished product, spread effects and the development of technology, which means that many processes need no longer be located near sources of raw material. New

237

technology tends to be labor-saving, not only in industry, and generates population surpluses in the rural areas.

For economic integration between underdeveloped countries, in addition to the foregoing considerations, the industrial planning is justified in terms of savings in scarce resources vis-à-vis reduced industrial demand for the need for intercountry specialization; to avoid duplication of investments, and to take advantage of economies of scale to prevent further critical trade imbalances between countries and the growing concentration of new industrial enterprises within the relatively more developed countries.

A detailed and sophisticated study made by Martin Carnoy(1) of different industries in Latin America proves that only a few industries, in which the cost of transporting raw materials is a significant part of the total costs and where plants are not located near their sources of material, have higher costs or are less efficient than those near their sources of primary supplies. Examples of these are factories producing dairy products, paper and pulp, and nitrogeneous fertilizers. For the manufacture of tractors, universal lathes, and cars, for example, the developed industrial base and the market are the variables that determine their location.

In the case of industries in which the cost of transporting both raw materials and the finished product is high compared to the value of the product, or when the transport costs are low, the plants have had to locate themselves near the market. The development of technology and transport has freed many industries from location near their sources of primary materials and has given greater importance to the market and to external economies, that is, to the existence of an industrial base and of services.(2)

Until very recently, economic theory paid insufficient attention to the location of productive activities. The optimum location of economic activity was made secondary to the problems of growth or of stability. Aspects such as the transport of merchandise or the economies associated with a better location were handled with traditional analyses, for example, within the general theory of prices or of time saving.

In classical economics the elasticity of wages and prices and the mobility of factors within the country are crucial, so that regional aspects are not problems to be taken into account, because regional differences in prices, costs, wages, and incomes tend to disappear due to the mobility of factors. The only restriction preventing complete equalization comes from transport costs. But, in order to ensure a complete uniformity, transport costs are typically assumed to be zero.

Many authors have attributed the existence of regional differences in returns to the lack of mobility of the factors in response to differences in marginal productivity. But, even if total geographical mobility of factors existed, and trade brought about   equality of prices, differences in per capita income would still persist.   In those regions with lower incomes, there is, in general, a concentration of activities with low productivity and relatively slow growth in productivity. Also, there are differences in natural resources in the regions.

In underdeveloped countries it is in any case unrealistic to allow spontaneous migration from the less developed regions to the more developed because, among other things, of the limited dynamism of the latter regions.   Agricultural development has been achieved through a more intensive use of labor and a higher capital ratio.   Their capacity to generate gainful employment is very restricted, and they are currently typically experiencing rising rates of unemployment.   Even within the developed regions disequilibria are to be found between urban and rural zones, and between various sectors resulting in important migratory movements.

Tangible and intangible capital is more easily moved to the interior of the countries than any other of the productive factors.   But generally movements occur because of the higher marginal productivity of capital (and labor) in the latter areas from the poor to rich regions.

This attraction of capital (and all productive factors) to already developed centers, is related to external economies and the indivisibility of factors.   The growth of an area attracts more growth to itself (polarization) and induces growth in others (dispersion).   The problem of regional disequilibria arises when the effects of polarization cancel out or exceed those of dispersion.   Several authors have emphasized the importance of the concentration and polarization effect in one or more of the members of an economic union.   They also emphasize that the problem is more acute when it is a union(3) among less developed countries.

Through dispersion effects, the growth of one region induces growth in others and increases the total product of the country (or of an economic union of countries).   Among other things, the result of regional specialization can be more rapid growth even in poor areas.   In economic unions of poor countries, however, a large part of income (and even direct investment in the poor regions) will be absorbed by the rich areas.   Demand from the integrated regions will tend to be satisfied by exports from the developed areas because the poorer regions will have problems in expanding supply rapidly, and even in keeping up with the growth of their own demand. All economic unions tend to strengthen the effects of polarization and dispersion across national frontiers because certain restrictions remain on the mobility of capital and especially labor.(4)

Among other factors the transfer of resources within an economic union is more difficult to achieve than at the national level, because the net benefits of integration that provide the rationale for the transfer cannot be easily determined.

If some countries gain from growth while others lose, then the bases for political unification are broken, unless preventative measures at the national and regional level are adopted.

The experience of LAFTA confirms the predictions of many theories as to the strength of polarization effects and the need to take corrective measures before those effects manifest themselves. The creation of the GRAN was the response of the "intermediate" countries to the concentration of the positive effects of trade and new investment in Argentina, Brazil, and Mexico. Thus, it was clear to the drafters of the Treaty of Cartagena that measures should be taken that would favor less developed countries, if they were to create an integrated area with some prospect of success. As we have seen, differences among GRAN countries are greater than those existing in many other integration schemes.

Planning in the Face of Limited Markets

The necessity for programming and allocating industrial investments centers on two important factors: first, the limited market and financial resources, and, second, the different levels of industrial development achieved by the countries and their capacity for future development. The Treaty of Cartagena is based on the fundamental assumption that market forces should be submitted to a certain degree of control, in order to prevent disequilibria between countries and unnecessary damage to companies, but also, as Article 32 says, "in order to move towards an efficient use of factors by taking advantage of available resources and improving productivity."

Chapter 2 studied the size of the real market, concluding that it was limited to 7 million inhabitants. However, it has to take into account the fact that one cannot speak of "one market of 7 million people," but of an aggregate of six national markets with factors such as size, topography, and the lack of adequate transport facilities, all fighting against their integration.

A study carried out by ECLA and LAFTA identified products for which regional demand would be sufficient to obtain levels of efficiency comparable to those found in Europe.(5) The study showed that, in LAFTA, investment per unit would be from 1.6 to 2 times more expensive than in medium-sized plants in developed countries; costs of production would be well above international prices.(6) These products are the subject of GRAN's programming. Transferring these conclusions from LAFTA to the smaller market of the Andean Group, the implications obviously become more serious. The internal demand for manufactured goods in the GRAN is only 16.5 percent (see table 2.13) of that in LAFTA. At the sectoral level the relationship remains the same.

Numerous studies on economies of scale show that they do exist. These studies present evidence of two types. The first is macroeconomic, relating aggregated variables connected with the level of industrialization to some measure of the economic size of countries.(7) The second set of indicators are microeconomic and show the relationship between the volume of output and the unit costs of production in specific plants or industrial processes.(8) These studies give exclusive consideration to the developed countries conditions.

Sutcliffe notes some limitations of the studies on economies of scale which derive from the fact that they are based on market and production conditions in developed countries. There are conditions in less developed countries under which production below the minimum optimum volume is not irrational. Costs and conditions of transport give protection that makes small-scale production competitive.(9) In spite of these conditions, it is possible to conclude that there are a considerable number of industries in which economies of scale exist at levels of production higher than those obtained in underdeveloped countries and higher than the capacity of demand. For those industries integration programs are important.

The Andean Group proposes to advance import substitution policies by concentrating upon those industries reserved for sectoral programming in which economies of scale are significant. We shall demonstrate the importance of economies of scale by examining one such sector: the automobile industry. Apart from being the "horror story" of the Latin American experience of substitution, it plays a central role in the industrial strategy of the GRAN because of its multiplier effects. To extend the analysis to the whole range of activities reserved for programming would require a completely separate study.

i.   Conditions in the Andean motor industry

The industry started as an assembly process; since then, there have been gradual attempts to integrate it nationally. However, the majority of basic components are still imported.

Table 7.1 shows how very limited production was in 1972 in the four GRAN countries that had developed their motor industries. The joint output of these four (Colombia, Chile, Peru, and Venezuela) is below the individual levels of output of Mexico, Brazil, or Argentina. The total production of cars and commercial vehicles in the GRAN is below the optimum volume of output. It has been accepted that there are still economies of scale to be obtained up to levels of output

between 100,000 and 600,000 vehicles per annum, the latter
figure exceeding the production level of even Argentina or
Brazil,(10) and being 4.3 times greater than the 1972 output
of these four Andean countries combined.

Apart from limited demand, the major problem is the large
number of makes and models that each country produces:

1971	No. of Vehicles	No. of Makes	No. of Commercial Vehicles	No. of Makes
Colombia	12,445	4 (5 models)	7,108	2 (7 models)
Chile	20,760	8 (10 ")	2,864	1 (1 model)
Peru	18,151	6 (10 ")	5,666	2 (3 models)
Venezuela	57,295	12 (60 ")	15,823	8 (46 ")

Venezuela produced the greatest number of vehicles per
make, with an average of 4,774, but as this country produces
60 models, the average is reduced to 954 vehicles per model.

ii. Forecast demand up to 1985

The Junta calculated this by taking into account the stock of
vehicles in the country and the projected growth of GNP.(11)
For rates of growth of GDP, figures for 1960 and 1972 were
used, together with the stated aims of the countries' development plans and the aims set out in the Bases Generales para
una Estrategia Subregional de Desarrollo. The results (see
table 7.1) show that, by 1985, the subregion would have a
demand for 400,000 cars, which is still below the optimum level
of 600,000 mentioned earlier. The demand for commercial
vehicles would be far too low. And, further, this demand is
divided among six countries, all of which want to develop the
industry. Until 1972 there were only four producer countries,
but Bolivia and Ecuador are hoping to begin production. By
1985, each of the six countries would be producing an average
of 66,000 cars and 33,000 commercial vehicles.

The demand for cars and commercial vehicles was divided
into categories according to engine size, in the following way:

Cars	Commercial vehicles (trucks)
Category A1 up to 1000 cc	Category B1 up to 4.5 tons
A2 1000 - 1500	B2 4.5 - 9
A3 1500 - 2000	B3 9 - 17
A4 2000 +	B4 17 +
C up to 2700	

Distribution of that demand forecast for 1985 was calculated on the basis of historical data (by country), according to types of vehicle.(12)

The proposals were submitted in March 1974 and suffered a series of modifications because of the pressures exerted by the countries themselves and by the manufacturers already established. As a result, the number of categories of trucks was raised to six and agreements were introduced on assembly, coproduction, and complementarity.(13)

On August 28, 1977, the automobile program was approved, after adjustments had been made because of the withdrawal of Chile. The allocation can be seen in table 7.2, from which it can be concluded that, although the situation is an improvement on that which previously existed, it was still far from exploiting fully potential economies of scale, because there are many assembly and coproduction agreements. The vehicles allocated are those that can be exported to the subregion. There is no agreement on the part of the countries to limit their production to their assigned models, and they can maintain the different existing models for the national market if they so wish.(14) There are only a few exclusive allocations, and production is divided because of the different agreements on coproduction and assembly.

The problems of disequilibrium within the Andean Group are severe, as we have shown in Chapter 2. The initiators of the Treaty were well aware of the need for special measures to induce balanced economic growth and to prevent and correct the action of concentration effects that might threaten the stability of the group. However, the ambiguity of the Treaty's Article 32 has given rise to different interpretations of balanced development and from these conflicts have arisen. The Junta interprets the basic objective of sectoral programming to be the equitable distribution of the benefits of integration and the balanced development of the countries: "The Treaty of Cartagena is an innovation with respect to LAFTA, which makes programming the basic tool for controlling the equity of the system."(15)

The original idea of the national representatives was to give greater emphasis to the free trade program,(16) and to stress that the aim of the sectoral program was to promote the efficient location of industries and savings on capital resources rather than the redistribution of benefits. The change to a strong planning orientation came about because of two elements. First, there was an interest in giving concessions to Venezuela, whose entry to the group was vital and who was demanding both a change of emphasis towards programming and the reduction of the scope of the free trade program. Second, there was the definite support for planning among some technical advisers, who saw clearly that only through planned allocation could the industrial development of the less industrialized countries be stimulated.(17)

Both the positions of the advisers and the Junta's interpretation were reinforced by the fact that the Treaty contained no other measures for distributing benefits in an equitable way - such as sharing out fiscal revenues or financial aid, or the transfer of resources to solve chronic deficits.(18)

All the member countries of the GRAN joined the Pact in the hope that the enlarged demand would lead both to faster growth in the industrial sector and to the establishing of industries that would have been impossible to contemplate previously, given the size of individual national markets, or that could only have operated with excessively high social costs.(19)   However, if maximum efficiency and output were the only goals, then there would be a tendency towards industrial concentration in the relatively more developed countries and a possible increase in disequilibria. But the Treaty's idea of balanced development is that the location of industry should follow a pattern of distribution distinct from that which would lead to minimum costs and maximum output. Only in this way could the less developed close the gap in industrial development.   The contradiction between productive efficiency or the "optimum" location of industry (accelerated regional growth) and the equitable distribution of benefits (preferential growth of the less developed countries) through accelerated industrial production, became evident from the outset of work on the sectoral program. The Junta said that sectoral programming "is, from the practical point of view, the instrument upon which the participation of all the member countries in the development of the integrated zone rests, especially in industrial activities."(20) From this, it is clear that the equitable distribution of the benefits of integration is not simply redistributive but developmental; it is not a simple question of transferring monetary resources, but of the mobilization of productive resources through the planned location of industrial activity.(21)

What the principle of balanced growth as stated in the Cartagena Agreement really means is that the relatively more highly developed countries voluntarily give up part of the industrial growth that would otherwise be concentrated in their area. It also means that they should accept the need to absorb into their own cost structure, the costs of the industrialization induced in the less developed member countries.

SECTORAL PLANNING IN THE TREATY

Sectoral planning is a long-term element in planning industrial integration, an element that the Treaty defines as the fundamental tool for achieving an integrated development combining

both equity and efficiency. Article 32 established the following objectives for the program:

a. to take maximum advantage of the productive resources
   available in the subregion
b. to improve productivity and the effective utilization of
   productive factors
c. to achieve a greater expansion, specialization, and
   diversification of industrial production
d. to take advantage of economies of scale
e. to achieve the equitable distribution of the benefits of
   integration(22)

The policy of integrated industrial development, which
served as the basis for the drawing up of the sectoral
programs, is laid out clearly and in detail in the Bases Generales para una Estrategia Sub-regional de Desarrollo, Chapter
I and III.(23) The minimum goal of this policy was a 7 percent p.a. growth of GDP (the average for 1950-67 was 4.1%
p.a.). This was held to be indispensable for reversing historical trends.

The industrial sector was given the task of growing at $1\frac{1}{2}$
times that of total product, that is, at 10.5 percent p.a. (for
1960-70 it grew at 7.3% p.a.). This means increasing the
degree of industrialization from 21 percent to 34 percent by
1985.(24) The policy seeks to raise productivity by 5.3
percent between 1970 and 1985, compared with only 3.2 percent in the preceding decade. It also gives preference to the
growth of basic sectors such as light engineering, iron and
steel, nonferrous metals, chemicals, petrochemicals, paper and
cellulose, fertilizers, and transport equipment. These sectors
produce goods which in 1970 accounted for 75.8 percent of
industrial imports and which are, in general, capital-intensive.

The goals of the import substitution process represent a
significant impulse toward achieving a coefficient of 86.2
percent of the internal market supplied by domestic industry
(see table 7.3). It also has crucial implications for the
financing of investment, for the balance of payments and for
employment, as we shall see later.

The Part Played by Sectoral Programming in the Integrated Industrial Strategy

Sectoral programming distinguishes between existing industries
and those which, for one reason or another, it has not been
possible to develop nationally, and for which the policy hopes
to create the conditions for joint development.

In the case of the first group of industries - those
already in existence - which often have excess installed ca-

pacity, it was hoped that the liberation of trade would have significant effects upon their level of efficiency and productivity. In some cases, however, it would be convenient to develop programs of "rationalization," which would allow these industries to face the new levels of competition.

For the second group, programming would attempt to "prevent the duplication of investment, the wasting of resources and to stop industrialisation on a scale which would be incompatible with the degree of efficiency necessary to prepare the sub-region for competing in external markets."(25)

In Decision 25 of December 31, 1970, the Commission reserved for the program products that represented about one-third of the total tariff. These goods belong to those sectors with the strongest linkages and which, therefore, play the largest role in determining the productive structure of the subregion. They include the following goods: vehicles, light engineering products, petrochemicals, electronics, iron and steel, fertilizers and pesticides, industrial chemicals, pharmaceuticals, pigments and dyes, photographic and cinematographic equipment, and pulp and paper.

In trying to discover the weight and importance of the programmed sectors in industry as a whole, calculations have to be limited to the use of statistics on value added. This is very much a partial approach because it does not take into account other important indicators (direct and induced employment, backward and forward linkages, etc.). It has not been possible to overcome this problem owing to the lack of sufficiently disaggregated statistics for making a study at the national level, and also because of the difficulty of setting up a comparative analysis using the existing data. Calculations are based upon the long-term (up to 1990) economic projections of the Junta, which were taken from historical trends in each country, and from the policies contained in the development plans, to which the Junta added the best expectations of growth to be gained from integration. The figures are presented in protected prices and in 1968 dollars in order to obtain some degree of comparability between the macroeconomic forecasts and the sectoral programs, which are set out either in international prices or protected prices expressed in current dollars.

The following are some conclusions that are suggested by the data obtained (see table 7.4).

i. By 1990, the programmed sector will generate 17.7 percent of total industrial value added. But if light industry, which is the subject of rationalization programs, is excluded, this proportion increases to 30 percent.

ii. The sectors most affected by the sectoral programs are light engineering and basic metals. Surprisingly, the petrochemical program (a sector in which economies of scale are considerable) only accounts for 12.6 percent of the value-added forecast for 1990. This may indicate that part of the sector is excluded.

    iii. The importance of programming is relatively greater in the case of the two less developed member countries, Bolivia and Ecuador, in which the programs covered 37 percent of heavy industry (only 19% for the other members) and 90 percent of light engineering. This clearly shows the dependence of these two countries upon an enlarged market for the development of new production. For this reason, the Junta stated: "The development strategies planned in Bolivia and Ecuador include a well-defined reorientation of the industrial sector, inspired by the dynamic capacity of the manufacturing sector and the possibilities which may open up for them in the Andean market together with the advantages granted by the Treaty."(26)

    The objective of this list of products reserved for the program is to keep those products covered by Decision 25 outside the free-trade program and the application of the Minimum Common External Tariff (MCET), while the respective development plans are being drawn up for each sector.(27) The Sectoral Industrial Development Programmes are made up of sections on: the location of production, the joint programming of new investments, a common external tariff, a program of trade liberation (the pace of which can vary according to country and product, but which keeps a monopoly of the market for the producer country), the unification of economic policies that have direct bearing on the development plans and, finally, periods during which rights and duties arising from the program should be honored, should the Treaty be cancelled.(28)

    One factor which is not included in Article 34, but which is a part of the program and is very important for the efficacy of allocation, is each government's agreement not to stimulate, in their own countries, production that has been assigned to others.

THE EXPERIENCE WITH SECTORAL PLANNING:

The Nature of the Conflicts

We analyzed the Junta's records of the discussions on the several SIDPs so far presented by the Junta. The discussions took place at technical level first of all, and then at the political level at the Commission's meetings. Our analysis showed that the following were the main problems that arose over how to measure the costs and benefits of integration and over the equitable distribution of benefits.

i. The measurement of the benefits of participating in an integration scheme is no simple task and requires previous common agreements and definitions. It has to take account of changes in income (in terms of social value), changes in the rate of growth, trends in foreign trade, changes in the volume and structure of employment, fiscal revenues, and the "backwash" and "spread" effects of industrial development. From the Junta records it is clear that no agreement has been achieved in this area. The Junta failed in its attempt to get acceptance for the regional strategy of development that might serve as a framework for establishing those criteria (see Chapter 6, section 6). The measurement of the effects over time, especially those related to externalities, is very complex when the available data are unreliable, and when the relative prices upon which the evaluation is made change because of the impact of the increase in investment and the restructuring of the economy under the integration program.(29) The establishing of shadow prices is not a simple matter even at the national level. Further, the definition of "national welfare" - difficult enough in any context - becomes exceedingly problematical when dealing with countries in each of which the social welfare functions may be different. One country may prefer a lower real rate of growth and a better distribution of income or an immediate increase in employment. On the other hand, another country may seek to maximize the rate of growth even at the cost of lower employment or immediate consumption.

The differences tend to be greater when dealing with countries like those of the Andean Group in which factors such as the real and potential dimensions of the internal market, the relationship between the urban and rural population, the productivity of sectors, the capacity of the external sector, and natural conditions or the social and political structures vary significantly from country to country. These variations were demonstrated in Chapter 2 describing the subregion. Countries establish different sets of policy objectives and accord different levels of priority in accordance with their conditions.

ii. The second problem arises in defining the equity of the distribution of benefits. It is possible to argue that distribution is equitable when each member country receives absolute benefits either proportionate to, or equal to its population, or to the gross domestic income, or to income per capita. The final criterion assumed is more political than technical. The Treaty contains no clear definition of equity, but one can gather from the articles that it is held to mean the reduction of the gap between the more and less developed countries.(30)

The existence of large disequilibria between Bolivia and Ecuador and the other four member countries, when measured in terms of GDP, industrial product, or total or per capita foreign trade, seems to justify giving the greatest priority to the consolidation of the union and to the narrowing of the gap between the less developed countries and the rest.

iii. The nature of the program generates repercussions that some countries may regard as very burdensome in terms of employment, the financial load, and exports. Let us take some examples - first, employment. Because industrial growth is to be based on dynamic industries, the employment generated by industry is expected to be small.(31) As a result, agriculture, urban services, and small industry are the sectors that bear the burden of generating new employment. The Junta calculated that, by 1985, industry will account for 17.8 percent of total employment (it was 13.9% in 1970). This means that agriculture will have not only to retain its workforce but to generate new employment at 1.4 percent p.a., in order to reverse the process of spontaneous migration that has affected all the countries. Urban services and construction will have to increase their share of total employment to 45.7 percent; in 1970 they accounted for 33.5 percent. In absolute terms this means the employment of 5.8 million people in 1970 and 13.1 million in 1985. Industry will generate 2.6 million new jobs, of which 1.5 million will be in factory industries and 1.1 million in artisan establishments.

Second, the financial burden: interpreting the macro-targets of the Acuerdo, a 7 percent growth rate means a move to coefficients of internal and external savings of 25.1 percent and 4.6 percent, respectively. The external debt servicing would need 34.4 percent of exports. These figures are consistent if we assume the achievement of Prebisch and Pearson's optimum conditions for indebtedness, paying 2 percent interest p.a. for the first five years, and 5 percent on the remainder.(32) But under the prevailing financial conditions, the model requires an internal savings coefficient of 27 percent and an external savings coefficient of 2.6 percent, which then require 54.3 percent of exports for its servicing.

The third element is the high effort in exports to non-member countries also needed, if the goals of increasing GDP (7% p.a.), industrial GDP (10.5%), and productivity are to be achieved (5.3%). These exports are very important given the limited size of the subregional market and the capital-intensive character of industry. Exports to third world countries would be possible because the integrated market allows for greater levels of efficiency. The objective is to maintain a rate of growth of manufactured exports of 15.4 percent p.a. between 1970 and 1985, a far greater rate than that which historical trends would suggest. This rate means achieving a coefficient of exports to third world countries of 1.7 percent (1970) and 3.1 percent in 1980.(33) In absolute terms, this means raising manufactured exports by $1,000 million by 1985. If previous trends were continued, the increase would only be $480 million.(34) The feasibility of this objective is based upon the new levels of efficiency and "an indicator which points towards the feasibility of this hypothesis is that, historically, some countries have reached these global levels; Spain and Japan for example."(35) Unfortunately this argument did not analyze carefully the historical conditions of the economic and socio-political development of these two countries, nor of the world circumstances that made possible the export of their manufactures.

Besides the above problems, which can be classified under the political economy of integration, others arise, of a technical nature, but no less urgently in need of solution.

i. The scope of the program is too wide. The reserved list includes 1,800 products. Allocating and planning the investments for such a large number is a burdensome task. However, the most important problem regarding the scope of the program is not the number of items, but the lack of differentiation with regard to the complexity of the technological process involved in their production. The Treaty sets 1980 as the date by which total free trade should be achieved in the area. Therefore investors tend to see this date as the limit of the monopoly conceded to them. Whatever the level of technological complexity, the investments have to be undertaken by the countries as quickly as possible, in order that they might have an effective monopoly and reach 1980 with such an advantage that it ceases to be attractive for other countries to set up competitive production. The compulsion to invest and consolidate the advantage granted can result in efficiencies.(36)

ii. While the programs may have been drawn up coherently sector by sector, intersectoral integration is not taken into account. Among others, the reasons for this methodology could be the priorities established by the Commission based upon the importance of the sectors and the lack of prior definition of the subregional industrial policy. Having packages that are negotiated independently has led to interminable discussions as each country tries to obtain the maximum number of allocations in each sector. It also made it difficult to use one sector to compensate another. A country with limited possibilities for developing petrochemicals and which is therefore given a small share of the sector, cannot be compensated with a larger share of another sector in which it may be more efficient. However, while the use of multisector packages is desirable, in practice it creates difficulties. First, there are no means by which the relative importance of each sector in the countries' economies can be evaluated and compared. Little is known about the external economies that come from a given project. Within the national plans, it is difficult to find a classification of industries in accordance with national priorities. Moreover, few adequate analytical tools exist to permit the measurement of the effects of an investment in one sector vis-a-vis another.(37) There is another reason that shows "compensation" to be difficult. There are too few footloose industries and the advantage of the relatively more developed countries is such that almost every sector will be allocated in their territory.

iii. The tendencies that dominated the process of industrialization in previous decades continue. The objective is the substitution of imports over the subregion, such that, by 1980, the group will have a similar productive structure to those of Argentina and Mexico 10 years ago. The system is programmed by starting from the final product and, according to the existing capacity, assuming the rationality of the process used in the past. No corrective elements have been introduced into the system, based, for example, on criteria of the abundance or scarcity of factors, the need to restructure existing patterns of consumption, or the technology employed. As was noted earlier, the industries included in the program tend to be capital-intensive and directed toward the upper segments of the market. It is therefore to be expected that the bottlenecks arising from the exhaustion of the first stage of import substitution will simply be repeated in due course. These include inflationary disequilibria, the marginalization of a large part of the population, the persistent inequality of income distribution, and increasing dependence upon the export sector. The basis for this conclusion is the fact that the size of the market is not an exogeneous variable but a result of historical formation. The only new factor is the enlargement of demand via the aggregation of the top end of the member countries' markets; this has not been accompanied by modifications in the income structure, in the rate of labor absorption, in the inefficiency of the agricultural sector, or in the supply structure.(38)

iv. The criterion of "equilibrium" only considers the size of the designated market, neglecting dynamic concepts like the generation of linkages, external economies, or technological changes: that is, those changes in the productive structure that are the final goal of sectoral programming and of economic integration. Again, the tendency for countries to try to obtain the greatest possible share of the market in each sector is reinforced; thus they lose sight of the long-term effects which may be more important.

The approved programs will suffer from inefficiencies in the form of losses of economies of scale, because market criteria were applied in drawing up the plans, because national industrial priorities have not been defined, and because the prestige of the individual countries tends to be measured in terms of industrial development and diversifications.(39) For example, in the petrochemical sector, each country was per-

mitted to develop a complex petrochemical industry. The level
of efficiency achieved is considered by the Junta as having
been third level.(40)   Similarly, efficiency was sacrificed in
the automobile sector.   There are a large numbers of models:
four for passenger vehicles and seven for commercial vehicles
for a market of 600,000 vehicles to be shared by six producers.(41)   Excessive slowness both in the drawing up of the
programs and their discussion, approval and application on the
part of the governments, has led to the point where the data
used for analyses have become out of date, especially those
referring to the costs of investment and the size of the designated markets.   The petrochemical program was negotiated
over five years, the automobile over three and a half years,
and that in light engineering over two years.   Approval is still
pending for various programs presented three years ago (fertilizers, electronics, paper).   The short period between the
approval of the programs and the termination of the reserved
market means that new investments have to be effected immediately in a very short period of time.   This leads to the need
to resort to extra foreign financing and the transferring of
national funds initially designated for other activities.

The Conflicts as Reflected in National Attitudes

The ambiguity of the Treaty in defining the priorities of
efficiency and equity and the impossibility of agreeing on a
subregional strategy of industrial development that would take
account of the various national stances, meant that conflicts
arose between countries; these became evident during the
negotiation of each national program.   Confronted by these
difficulties, especially by the poor results coming both from
meetings of the Consejo de Planificacion and from the discussions on the Bases,(42) the Junta avoided initiating any
discussion of the contents of the programs, of the definition of
equity, efficiency, and balanced development, or of the common macroeconomic indicators to be used for drawing up and
evaluating the programs.   Thus, the differences had to be
resolved at the level of each individual negotiation.

The only statement of a national position was made to the
Commission by the Colombian delegation in December 1971 in a
document aiming to develop discussion about what each country
understood by efficiency, equilibrium, planning.   This, however, only provoked accusations that it was anti-integrationist,
and it was never discussed within the Commission.(43)   The
most important points in the Colombian stance are as follows.

i.   Above all, sectoral programming is an element of
planning for achieving specialization among the member countries, optimizing the use of resources, and preventing the
duplication of investments.

ii. The reduction of disequilibria between the countries is a policy objective, the achievement of which cannot depend exclusively upon economic integration and, even less, on just one of its tools. The acceleration of the growth of the countries' economies is, above all, an objective of internal policy, and requires the mobilization of all their own resources together with the redrafting of the relations of each country with the world economy.

iii. When distributing benefits, the different levels of development of each country have to be incorporated in a positive way; that is, distribution has to be planned in direct proportion to GDP or to the industrial product. "This level [of development] was gained during a period of national sacrifice. Therefore, a country which contributes more to the sub-region's economies, should not be punished."

iv. The allocation of industries which would guarantee the maximum level of benefits for the subregion is probably unacceptable in political terms. Therefore, the resulting distribution is likely to be far from that optimum. Before making the allocations, the costs of the policy and how they should be distributed should be studied.

v. It could be more economical for the subregion to make some compensatory corrections by transferring resources. The allocation of industries to inefficient countries means losses for the subregional economy and for the country in question because the existence of linkages means that the effects of inefficiencies are felt throughout the structure.

vi. The CET has to be extended to cover the whole range of tariffs before the allocations are made and should be the factor for measuring the maximum acceptable level of inefficiency. (44)

We can see clearly that, especially with regard to those points concerned with productive efficiency, the scope of redistributive measures and the degree of discrimination in favor of industry in general and in favor of SIDPs in particular, comprise in embryonic form the main points of the economic strategy followed by Colombia. All these aspects were analyzed in Chapters 2 and 6.

The Popular Unity government in Chile maintained a "planning" stance within the framework of an import substitution policy. It used its membership of the GRAN to reinforce its industrial policy, especially to argue for additional protection, and for the stimulation and nationalization of those sectors designated as the motors for development: a policy that was in complete agreement with the model implicit in the Treaty. The present absolutist government has moved to the liberal economic model, similar to that of Colombia as described in earlier paragraphs. The two countries' strategy is based on the use of the market as the central mechanism for regulating the economy, a strategy that comprises the opening of

the economy to the international market, and in which efficiency has to be measured in terms of international prices and the
cost of foreign currency. This opening up should also be the
means by which distortions arising from the "indiscriminate
policy of import substitution" are eliminated. In both Chile
and Colombia, the state would only intervene in strategic sectors: mining, oil, the physical infrastructure. The relative
profitability of the different sectors would be determined by
means of tax and tariff policies, and it would be the private
entrepreneur who would decide where, when, and how much to
invest, using the criterion of the maximization of profit. The
direct implications for integration are, among others, the lowering of tariffs and the reduction of investments in leading
industrial sectors.

It is clear that, for Bolivia and Ecuador, sectoral
programming offers an opportunity for them to accelerate and
strengthen their import substitution, since the tariffs in the
respective programs always grant special protection to the
industries allocated to them. Thus the height of the tariff
depends upon the location of industries, and not on the
maximum level of subregional inefficiency previously existing.

These two countries have to mobilize important public
resources in order to finance investment; because private
savings are inadequate, the State becomes the protagonist in
carrying out the industrial development laws.(45) The industrial laws of the two countries show how priority has been
given to a wide selection of basic sectors, all of which are
reserved for the SIDP and toward which the policies of protection and development are directed.(46)

Peru decided to join the GRAN when it embarked upon a
process of social change in which the State was to assume the
responsibility for directing the economy and for allocating
resources from the center according to a development plan.
As in the Chilean case under Frei and Allende, there was
agreement with the criteria of the Treaty: centrally planned
development, a strong state sector that would be increasingly
active in productive investment, and a continuation of the
import substitution process.(47) The government always upheld the Treaty in its declarations, and in its industrial plans
it included the subregional market when drawing up the plans
of key projects.(48) It made its continued membership conditional upon the realization of the sectoral programs.(49) The
present government has made no statements contrary to the
earlier attitude, at least on matters touching on the development of sectoral programming. Some important changes of
policy can, however, be seen, which may lead to the relaxing
of planning mechanisms and the consequent strengthening of
the market. The most important here is the postponement of
the implementation of certain basic industrial projects, as a
part of the stabilization program. These are precisely the

projects for which the expanded market is very important and were the reason for Peru's firm attitude toward the priority to be granted to sectoral programming rather than to the other tools of integration.(50)   In second place, Peru drastically reduced tariffs, imposed a liberal handling of foreign exchange rate policies, and weakened the economic role of the state sector.

Venezuela's industrial policy is of necessity based upon the possibilities of an enlarged market together with the opportunities of specialization provided by sectoral programs. Venezuelan industrial strategy tries to shift the structure of the productive sector toward intermediate and capital goods, to make a more rational use of human and material resources, to use installed capacity more fully, and to create more employment.   These changes are difficult to bring about on the basis of the internal market, despite the high purchasing power of the population.   Venezuela's participation in the GRAN is not justified in terms of solving balance-of-payments problems or of conserving foreign currency - the primary export sector provides the economy with sufficient resources.   The justification is rather in terms of the search for better investment opportunities in the country and the subregion and the better utilization of productive resources.(51)

Thus, we have two positions that emerged as conflicting during the process of elaborating policies.   On the one hand, Bolivia and Ecuador, in agreement with the Junta's point of view, insisted that the distribution of benefits should be ensured by SIDPs, because market forces would lead to a greater concentration of industrial activity in already established centers.   The lack of alternative redistributive mechanisms and the inefficiencies of the preferential treatment granted via the commercial program justified this position and led these countries to single out SIDPs as the most important element in the Treaty.

Peru and Venezuela assumed the same stance, though for somewhat different reasons.   They are pushing forward with a process of accelerating industrialization, in which the State plays a dominant role.   The enlarged market is important for both countries, though to a lesser degree for Venezuela. They also apply a high level of protection because of the characteristics of the modern industries they are developing and their relatively high costs.   These two countries consider it indispensable to pursue the growth of basic and strategic industries in order to achieve independent and self-sustained development.

On the other hand, we have Chile and Colombia, who after 1974 fundamentally changed their development strategies. Both abandoned the emphasis on the industrial sector(52) and sought to develop industry based upon the traditional international division of labor, and not on a process of import substitution. They tried to minimize the State's role as a planner of the sector. Therefore, they are now trying to reduce to a minimum the economic costs of industrialization, and have proposed tariff levels considerably lower than those of the other countries, and without any significant degree of dispersion. They are not interested in the SIDPs, because neither of their new strategies grants preference to the program industries, and because the State is not to be the principal promotor of industrialization, which is vital to the concept of the SIDPs.(53) Thus an element of uncertainty and inefficiency was introduced, which, to say the least, weakens planning.

To sum up, the heart of the conflict lay in the division which, as we have seen, runs right through the whole political economy of the integration movement. On the one hand, there were those countries that wanted to use the SIDPs primarily to reduce disequilibria and to support the protectionist conception of the new phase of industrial development, and the additional intrinsic elements of planning and State intervention. On the other side were those that tended towards greater efficiency, measured in terms of the cost of foreign exchange, and towards a greater role for market forces in their internal economic policies and in their relations with the world and with subregional markets.

Interesting light may be thrown on the roots of this conflict by examining the similar situation that appeared among the COMECON countries at the end of the 1950s, a situation that lasted until the crisis of 1968, when the specialization of the countries and the priorities between accelerated growth and the reduction of disequilibria among the countries were discussed. The CMEA has adopted an integration scheme that has more in common with those of the underdeveloped countries than with the Western European model. It seeks to implement a development strategy that will advance industry and technology. The proposed goal of integration is not the liberation of trade, as in the EEC; rather, it is industrialization itself that is the most important objective of integration among the unevenly developed member countries.(54) Given the existing asymmetry, distributive problems gain great importance.(55) As with underdeveloped countries, high levels of polarization and the varying degrees of development inevitably have consequences both for problems of socioeconomic change and for the distributive aspects of integration.(56)

Since industrialization and the technological revolution are the goals of CMEA integration, policy is directed towards interconnected cooperative forms of intensifying development. The division of labor, scientific research, and development motors were all designed for the maximization of rates of growth and economies of scale at the regional level.(57)

Fear that this strategy, based on high technology development, would lead to the concentration of benefits on the more advanced countries, was shown by the two less developed member countries of CMEA, Rumania and Bulgaria. "These two less industrialized countries have been consistently critical of Soviet-proposed international division of labour within the CMEA, fearing that it would stifle their development, and lock them into a position of being agricultural and primary goods producers for the rest of the region."[58] The more developed countries proposed specialization based on the reduction of the social costs of production, according to the principles of comparative advantage. They also sketched out the idea of "active" industrialization having taken place in the more efficient countries and "passive," or induced, development in the less developed by means of spread effects derived from the former group.[59] Czechoslovakia and East Germany emphasize the principle of comparative advantage, and they think that the different levels of factor costs should be considered in the CMEA's planning.[60]

It is clear that the mere acceptance of planning is not sufficient for solving problems of distribution. If more importance is given by some countries to comparative advantage in the plans, then structural disequilibria will persist because industries will be allocated to the more efficient countries. What is needed is an agreement on the criteria for planning. The conflicts over the division of labor between the member countries led to a worsening of the differences between the USSR and Rumania. The latter was opposed to the projects put forward by the Soviet Union for setting up a central industrial planning body in charge of the formulation of common plans and of solving organizational problems, which were put forward in the "Basic Principles of the International Division of Labour," signed by all the countries in June 1962. The idea was reinforced in August, when Khrushchev published an article in Komunist, in which he asked for new measures to consolidate the group's economic coordination. He proposed the creation of a common investment fund for the member countries: only those countries that cooperated in agreements on centrally directed specialization could obtain finance from it. This proposal was aimed at creating supranational planning organs, ending the dispersion of capital resources, and planning and locating investment in accordance with sectoral plans and projects, which, once accepted, would acquire the status of "common." In the same article, Khrushchev placed great emphasis upon costs and profit as planning criteria.[61]

Rumanian opposition was soon manifested and showed itself in the fields of sovereignty and national defense. The leaders of the Rumanian party stated that the transmission of such levels to the competence of super-state or extra-state bodies would turn sovereignty into a notion without any content. ... The idea of a single planning body for all CMEA countries has the most serious economic and political implications. The planned management of the national economy is one of the fundamental, essential and inalienable attributes of the socialist state.(62)

Thus the party refused to participate in companies that were connected with several countries, giving as a pretext that those companies were not directed in agreement with the principles that rule relations between socialist countries.(63) The leader of the Rumanian Party sent his decision to Khrushchev saying that Rumania would abandon the CMEA if the policy of supranationality were to be imposed.(64) Khrushchev's principles were upheld by the USSR, Czechoslovakia, East Germany, and Poland.

According to Kaser, the possibilities for transforming the COMECON by creating supranational institutions vanished because the initial political homogeneity was not sufficient. He adds that, when the CMEA began, one could think it possible to achieve political integration because there was a general consensus among the Soviet political and economic leadership. By 1963, it had to be accepted that the economic political climate was changing. The new situation was seen in the reaffirmation of national sovereignty and in the less developed countries' preference for bilateral negotiations.(65)

The Comprehensive Program of 1971 attempted to resolve the resulting crisis; it sought to achieve a more centralized level of industrial planning. Until that time, national production plans had only included medium-term bilateral trade agreements, which were far from an ideal integration scheme and the long-term coordination of joint investments designed to shape the complementarity of productive structures, binding the development of matrix sectors to common objectives and goals. It is not yet clear the degree to which the transition from coordination of commercial bilaterality to industrial planning coordination will take place.

Conflict inside CMEA propitiated the organization of economic relations between member countries based on the "structural bilaterality" (commercial bilateral agreements which seek a commercial balance in terms of products or groups of products rather than in terms of countries). The effects on the productive structure and on integration are very important. The first being the reduction of the space for specialization. Each country seeks to expand its foreign trade by means of a diversification of the industrial products offered.(66)

Similar statements to those made by the developed members of CMEA were made by the head of the Industrial Study Unit of the Colombian N.P.D. during interviews held with the author in May 1975. He feels that efficiency should be the philosophy of economic integration. Those goods that are produced more cheaply should be bought in member countries; others have to be imported from third countries.(67) The technological characteristics of Andean industry have to be the result of the relative prices of factors. This philosophy implies a minimum CET and less planning. If industrial plans were to be established with the Colombian criteria, the expectations of Bolivia, Ecuador, Peru, and Venezuela would remain largely unfulfilled.

THE ANDEAN GROUP'S CRISIS

The contradictory nature of the two lines of thought was immediately apparent after the approval of the light engineering program in 1972, and it impeded the approval of new SIDPs for three years, provoking a crisis that was resolved in a way which clearly reflects the positions of the two groups of countries. We studied the records of the Commission meetings and found that the strategy of Colombia and Chile was to prolong the discussions, trying to gain the approval of the CET first,(68) with minimum levels and dispersion. They also tried to have the products reserved for SIDPs included in the CET, in order to reduce the costs of balanced development. As we saw in Chapter 6, the other countries insisted on establishing special tariff structures for each SIDP. In their view, approval of the SIDPs should be accelerated, because they had drawn up their investment plans with the enlarged market in mind, and they needed the allocations and reserved markets defined; for Chile and Colombia this was not the case since they were not interested in industrial planning. Bolivia, Ecuador, Peru, and Venezuela attacked the Chilean/Colombian position, arguing that it meant "a modification of the Treaty which they were not prepared to accept,"(69) because the Treaty states that "each program has to have its own CET and that the approval of SIDPs is not, in any article, conditional upon the approval of the CET."(70) Venezuela, for example, finds it impossible to accept a very low CET, especially for new industries. The high level of protection for the industrial sector is partly a compensation for the overvalued rate of exchange, which is the result of the great volume of oil revenue, leading to a surplus on the trade balance. Thus the negotiation of the defining mechanisms, the CET and the SIDPs, had to be linked, rather than forging ahead with one or the other. This resulted in a general nonfulfillment of the timetable stipulated in the Treaty; by December 31, 1975 neither the CET nor the SIDPs were approved, nor were the modifications made to the light engineering program in order to include Venezuela.

Regarding the negotiation of timetables, the same polarized position arose between the same two groups of countries. On one side, Chile and Colombia hoped that a large proportion, if not all, of the products on the reserved list would be moved on to the automatic reduction lists, thus ending or limiting as far as possible the scope of programming.(71) The other four countries tried to extend periods for all the reserve lists, and to "freeze," or at least, to slow down, the automatic reductions in the commercial program until sectoral programming had been advanced proportionately.(72) The impasse was broken by passing Decision 100, which, apart from extending the period for approving the SIDPs (and the CET) by two years, made it possible to approve SIDPs with the participation of only two-thirds of the member countries. It also sets out the conditions under which the nonparticipating countries can eventually join the SIDPs. For the CET, it introduced the "tariff band" studied in Chapter 6.

The two modifications represent a short-term compromise between the two conflicting camps. Chile and Colombia are able to place themselves within the lower levels of the tariff band and not take part in the SIDPs, which is in line with their policies of allocating resources according to comparative advantage, measured in world market terms. By participating in the SIDPs, the other four countries would withhold a part of their development from market forces and they would use the CET for allocating resources according to the SIDPs and to their economic strategies.

However, this does not appear to be a wise solution. Those countries that place themselves in the lower levels of the tariff band would have favorable balances because they would offer less protection to the products of other member countries, while they would receive from them greater protection for their own exports. Countries with a lower CET would increase their imports from third countries, a factor that would make it more difficult to implement the rules of origin.

This solution is only a passing phase in terms of programming. Article 6 of Decision 100 states that the Commission will fix the terms and conditions for the adoption of the CET by the countries not participating in the SIDPs and decide how they should open their markets to the products of the participants in the SIDPs. Again, such negotiations would present problems concerning efficiency, and the nonparticipant countries would try to gain tariff reductions that would fit in with their own structures and levels of efficiency. For the participating countries this would be unacceptable because they would have been forced to develop their production within a reduced market, implying higher costs and less benefit from economies of scale. This argument is especially relevant because of the proportion of the subregional market which the nonparticipating countries might represent.

It seems unlikely that the problems can be resolved definitively, or that sectoral programming and the philosophy of the Treaty will be saved. In effect, Colombia bases its anti-SIDP position on the argument that the programs do not lower but increase the costs of production. Besides, given that in Colombia there is no political decision in favor of planning the economy at the national level, there could be none for planning it at the regional level - even less so when this would mean the transfer of costs and resources prejudicial to its own position.(73)

These conclusions, drawn in 1979, found full corroboration in the 1980-81 negotiation process which showed the approval of the remaining programs impossible. The Commission meetings of September and October 1981 made the change in the direction of the global strategy for the Agreement clearly evident. The final documents grant full priority to the commercial program. For sectoral programming it recommends shortening the market reserve, that is, practically liberating the market from programmed products before the year 1990 and maintaining only those assignments agreed upon in favor of Bolivia and Ecuador.(74)

ACHIEVEMENTS OF SECTORAL PROGRAMMING

Various programs have been approved: light engineering (September 1972), petrochemical (September 1975), automobile (October 1976), and the iron and steel industry (December 1980).(75) All of these were accepted at a time of crisis and, it could be thought, because the countries concerned wanted to show that neither the impulse toward, nor the faith in integration had been lost.

The light engineering program covers 200 items (machine tools, electrical machinery and equipment, and instruments). It requires a total investment of $450 million and should generate 40,000 jobs. Its annual value of production is calculated to be $500 million (1974), and the demand in 1980 is expected to rise to $800 million.(76)

The petrochemical program was the subject of very prolonged discussions; presented in 1971, it was approved four years later. It requires investments of $2,620 million to generate 8,000 jobs, mainly at the higher levels of technical skill. Optimal efficiency is not guaranteed because of the multiplicity of plants. It covers 56 petrochemical products, some of which are exclusive to one country; others are shared by two or three.

The automobile program was signed in September 1977. On this occasion also there was an element of drama.(77) It was possible to pass Decision 120, after four years of negotiations, in which the external sector played an important role, only because of the firm positions held by Venezuela and Peru, who made their membership of the Group and the continuation of the commercial program conditional on the approval of the remaining SIDPs.(78)

The fact that the program is very flexible suggests that it is probably not very efficient, because it allows a rather large number of plants to exist, and because of the dispersion of plants and assembly agreements.(79)

The signing of the above-mentioned SIDPs does not modify our earlier analysis, for several reasons. First, we would mention the nature of the agreements. All SIDPs were approved during periods of political crisis with the intention of showing that the Treaty was alive. All are flexible enough to permit each country to develop fully its own industrial structure, and in all, the principle of specialization is weakened by numerous shared allocations. Second, the results so far are almost negligible and represent trade in goods from already existing plants.

A rapid evaluation of what has happened to the two programs since they were approved allows us to draw some conclusions regarding trade and investment, but not before noting that the entry of Venezuela after the signing of the light engineering program and the withdrawal of Chile, after the approval of the petrochemical program have meant the reformulation and renegotiation of already approved allocations. We want to suggest that the approval of the respective SIDPs does not necessarily mean their success. We will see that only trade of existing production has grown while the basic agreements involved in programming have not been fulfilled.

Light Engineering Program

Trade in this sector increased because 33 of the 72 units allocated were in production before the signing of the program, at which time Colombia and Peru accounted for the greatest volume of production. For the period 1973-77 investments amounting to 21.4 million dollars were made, basically for expansions in existing production facilities.

Light Engineering Sector Exports

	1969 (US $,000s)	%	1975 (US $,000s)	%	1977 (US $,000s)	%
Bolivia	–	–	–	–	728	8.5
Colombia	659	97.2	4135	56.4	3743	44.0
Chile	11	1.6	2468	3.7	–	–
Ecuador	–	–	3	–	2230	26.2
Peru	8	1.2	725	99.9	1812	21.3
Total	678	100.0	7331	160.0	8513	100.0

Source: Junta, Evaluación 1977, p. II. 2.4.
Evaluación 1969-1979.

The Junta's evaluation documents for 1975-80 showed that no investments had been made in production that did not exist before the signing of the program. According to the Junta, the main cause is that "the member-countries are not convinced that an enlarged market actually exists, which is prejudicial to the taking of investment initiatives.(80)

Uncertainty arises from the nonfulfillment of basic agreements, for example, over the adoption of the CET and the freeing of trade in favor of those countries given allocations,(81) and over Article 33 of the Treaty, which refers to the advantages that could be given to programmed products from preferential public sector purchases. Most important, the agreement not to encourage production allocated to other countries has not been fulfilled. Also, it is important to take into account the difficulties of programming and locating industries in accordance with criteria such as equilibrium between countries, when the private sector is to realize the investment in an economic climate in which, theoretically, subsidies would be eliminated in the near future. Companies export only a small part of their production and they increasingly tend to locate themselves according to market demands.(82) There is also a lack of aggressiveness on the part of exporters. Until now it has been impossible to agree upon the reforms in the light engineering program to include Venezuela.

The Junta notes that, in 1977, there was a stagnation of activity and apart from some expansion of existing production in Colombia and Peru, and one new plant in the latter, the most notable events were the closure of the plant in Bolivia and the difficulties of three Ecuadorian companies due to problems in trading their products.(83) The 1979-80 Assessment Reports confirm that the foregoing problems still remain.

Petrochemical Program

To this date the assessment of the petrochemical program has been centered on verification of existing production and analysis of investment projects.(84) The results obtained have been very slim so far, due to the following factors: Bolivia and Ecuador have not incorporated it into their domestic law, and Peru, in its corresponding law, included a clause requiring "reciprocity" in the elimination of restrictions of any kind upon trade in goods subject to the program, which raises doubts as to how far such a provision is compatible with the program. The Junta has shown that all except Venezuela have fallen behind in making plans for the production of the relevant intermediate goods.

Only Colombia and Venezuela have complied with the free trade program. The degree of nonfulfillment of the CET is difficult to measure because Colombia and Venezuela maintain tariffs below the CET for 139 and 128 products, respectively (the program is made up of 160 products). Peru has higher tariffs but applies rebates and exemptions. Bolivia has stated its decision not to put into operation the petrochemical program, until some solution is found to the problems of its equitable participation in the process of integration (and more especially of its share in the petrochemical sector). As long as Bolivia has not reached levels high enough to permit exports, it will not open its market to the other countries' petrochemical products.(85)

Trade in goods covered by the program has been important because many of the goods allocated in the program were already being produced. In 1975 the total value of imports of petrochemical products with subregional origin represented 5 percent of total imports of these goods.(86) This proportion is relatively constant.(87)

The automobile program described in this chapter, section B, may be considered successful in reducing the number of marks, limiting models, and incorporating regional-made parts. Progress is slow, however, since "technical and political" difficulties arising in the negotiations process have not been overcome.(88)

During the year 1980, Decision 160 on iron and steel SIDP and Decision 162 on fertilizers were approved. In the first case, - the iron and steel SIDP - the projectable space was determined, and a due date of December 1981 was established for reaching agreement with respect to programming mechanisms. In the second case the program includes the mechanisms applicable to nonprogrammable products CET trade liberation problem. The Junta has the responsibility for preparing all necessary studies for the proposals to be made on rationalization of production and sectoral cooperation.(89) These two SIDPs are a big deviation from the programming model described in Article 32 of the Agreement.

CONCLUSIONS

It is the differences in economic development that have made the implementation of SIDPs impossible, because the costs resulting from allocating industries according to equilibrium criteria were considered by the more developed countries to be too high.

Those same differences were the source of conflicts among the less and the more developed countries, conflicts that basically expressed themselves in terms of contradictions between the principles of efficiency and of equity. The contradictions are so acute because of the characteristics of the Andean subregion and because of the nature of the Treaty's economic model.

There is a significant asymmetry in industrial development and effective demand between the lesser and more developed member countries. This makes the policy of balanced development more costly and means that more resources have to be transferred from one country to another. Further, the limited size of the subregional market for the type of industries for which the new stage of substitution is aimed and for the level of national value added expected necessarily makes the subregional policy of industrialization more costly. And, since other compensatory mechanisms are lacking in the Treaty, the whole weight of redistribution problems therefore falls upon the location of industry. It seems that the members are more disposed to transfer taxation revenues or to create compensation funds than to relinquish to another country production that would have been in its own territory were it not for the industrial program.

The parallel with the COMECON experience enables us to suggest that the contradictions between the less and the more industrialized countries are not just those of ideologies. The problem is not just how far the countries are for or against planning, but what will be the extent of planning and which criteria will be applied. Within COMECON disagreement was not about planning itself, but about planning at the supranational level and the extent to which the central criterion of planning should be that of efficiency.

The disagreements among countries delayed approval of the programs, but also reduced the level of specialization among countries, with the consequent loss of economies of scale owing to the multiplication of plants in the three SIDPs so far agreed.

Trade has increased in those goods included in the approved programs, goods that were already being produced before the signing of the Treaty. The progress in new investments is insignificant. It is valid to conclude, as we did in regard to the commercial program, that the industrialists'

main interest is only in exporting surpluses and that investments are based on prospects in the national market. This
indicates the difficulty of programming and promoting industries when the national market is not sufficient. There are
risks implicit in projects directed toward exports, risks that
are greater when there is uncertainty over the stability or
seriousness of the agreements.

Certain aspects of the SIDP policy have not been complied
with. We are referring to the agreements not to promote
competitive production, to respect specialization programs, and
to include allocated projects in national investment and
production plans.

The conflicts over the criteria of equity and efficiency
were apparently resolved by the weakening of the agreement
on industrial specialization and industrial balanced growth.
The solution was largely formal and a resurgence of the
problem can be expected. Meanwhile, there have been no
advances made in regard to the new programs, and the timetable for the approval of the remaining SIDPs ran out in
December 1978, December 1980, and again in December 1981.
One country's opposition to the SIDPs was enough to prevent
the approval of new programs. Later Peru changed its policy
and reinforced the liberal line. The Treaty lost one, if not
more, of its important tools and the problems of redistribution
are still to be resolved.

Table 7.1. Andean Group, Production of Cars and
Commerical Vehicles by 1972 and Projection for 1985

	Production 1972		Projected Production 1985	
	Passenger vehicles	Commercial vehicles	Passenger vehicles	Commercial vehicles
Colombia	12,445	7,108	68,051	45,904
Chile	20,760	2,864	77,727	48,736
Peru	18,151	5,666	81,770	36,884
Venezuela	57,295	15,283	154,576	39,167
Bolivia	–	–	12,162	12,133
Ecuador	–	–	22,823	15,224
Total GRAN	108,941	30,921	417,109	198,048
Argentina	207,623	70,599		
Brazil	408,712	200,273		
Spain	600,559	94,822		
Mexico	163,005	66,761		

Source: Junta, Propuesta de la Junta Sobre Programa Sectorial
de la Industria Automotriz, Documento Jun/prop. 45,
Marzo 7, de 1974, pp. 9-19 and 105-108.

Table 7.2. Andean Group, Automobile Program

Categories[a]	A1 (passenger vehicles up to 1050cc)	A2 (passenger vehicles up to 1050–1500cc)	A3 (passenger vehicles up to 1500–2000cc)	A4 (passenger vehicles up to 2000cc)	C vehicles below 2.5 tons	B1.1 trucks up to 3 tons	B1.2 3.0 to 4.6 tons	B2.1 4.6 to 6.2 tons	B2.2 6.2 to 9.3 tons	B.3 9.3 to 17.0 tons	B.4 17 tons and over
Countries											
Bolivia			Assembly agreement with Venezuela	Assembly agreement with Venezuela	Assembly agreement with Colombia	Allocation of basic model		Assembly agreement with Peru	Allocation of basic model	Allocation by agreement of complementarity with Colombia, Peru, & Venezuela	
Colombia	Allocation of basic model	Allocation of basic model	Allocation of basic model	Allocation of basic model	Allocation of basic model	Assembly agreement with Bolivia		Assembly agreement with Peru		Allocation of basic model	Assembly agreement with Venezuela
Ecuador		Allocation of basic model			Agreement of coproduction with Venezuela		Allocation of basic model			Assembly agreement with Venezuela & Colombia	Assembly agreement with Venezuela
Peru			Allocation of 2 basic models		Agreement of coproduction with Colombia			Allocation of basic model		Allocation of basic model & agreement of complementarity with Bolivia, Colombia, & Venezuela	Allocation of basic model
Venezuela			Allocation of basic model	Allocation of basic model	Allocation of basic model	Assembly agreement with Bolivia	Assembly agreement with Colombia			Allocation of basic model	Allocation of basic model

Source: Junta, Carta Informativa, No. 69, October 1977.

Note: (a) Within each category, the member country receiving the allocation will elect to produce one basic model, according to subregional manufacturing. In the manufacture of subregional vehicles, components of subregional origin will have to be used.

268

Table 7.3. Andean Group, Gross Value of Production of Manufacturing Industry until 1985 and Percentage of Internal Market Supplied

Type of Industry	Gross Value of Production (mil 1960 US$)			Annual Growth Rate		Percent of Internal Market Supplied		
	1960	1970	1985	1960-70	1970-85	1960	1970	1985
A. Nondurable Consumer Goods	2456	4747	16569	6.8	8.7	91.6	92.2	95.2
Food	936	1938	6471	7.5	8.3			
Drink	303	530	1459	5.8	7.0			
Tobacco	97	148	392	4.5	6.7			
Textiles	522	985	3389	6.6	8.6			
Clothes and Footwear	246	491	2173	7.2	10.4			
Wood	61	92	285	4.1	7.8			
Furniture	49	91	310	6.3	8.5			
Publishing	105	224	784	7.9	8.7			
Leather	75	99	364	2.8	9.0			
Miscellaneous	62	149	942	9.1	13.1			
B. Intermediate Goods	1084	2266	12657	7.6	12.2	70.1	73.4	87.1
Paper	101	208	1211	7.4	12.5			
Rubber Products	90	160	1028	5.9	13.2			
Chemicals	323	673	3734	7.6	12.1			
Oil and Coal	222	491	2509	8.2	11.5			
NonMetallic Mineral	191	350	1582	6.2	10.6			
Basic Metals	157	384	2593	9.3	13.6			
C. Light Engineering	373	934	8313	9.6	15.7	33.6	41.8	72.0
Metal Products	159	373	2164	8.9	12.4			
Nonelectrical Mach.	42	152	1885	13.7	18.3			
Electrical Machinery	74	194	1814	10.1	16.0			
Transport Equipment	98	215	2450	8.2	17.6			
TOTAL	3913	7947	37539	7.3	10.9	73.2	76.0	86.2

Source: CEPAL/ILPES-JUNAC. Junta, Bases Generales para una Estrategia Subregional de Desarrollo, Lima, marzo 1972, Chap III, pp. 36-37.

Table 7.4.   Impact of the SIDPs on Manufacturing Industry
(mil. US$, 1968 prices)

I. Light Engineering	Colombia Chile Peru Venezuela	Bolivia Ecuador	Total
Gross production of light engineering SIDP including Venezuela	2,153	591	2,744
Gross production of automobile SIDP	5,478	722	6,200
Gross production of electronic SIDP	166	26	192
1. Subtotal	7,797	1,339	9,136
2. Value added under SIDPs (est. 45%)	3,509	630	4,111
3. Total sector value added	8,700	700	9,400
4. Impact of SIDPs (2/3)	40.3%	90.0%	43.7%
II. Basic Chemical Industry			
Gross production of			
Petrochemical SIDP	1,066	224	1,290
Fertilizer	-	-	1,069
Pharmaceutical	-	-	83
Industrial chemical	-	-	193
Light chemical	-	-	53
Coloring agents	-	-	110
5. Subtotal			2,798
6. Value added under SIDPs (est. 45%)			1,251
7. Value added under petrochemnical SIDP	(480)	(101)	(581)
8. Total sector value added	4,100	500	400
9. Impact of SIDPs (6/8)	-	-	27.4%
10. Impact of petrochemical SIDP (7/8)	11.7%	20.0%	12.6%
III. Basic Metallurgical			
Gross production steel mill SIDP	-	-	3,222
11. Value added under SIDP steel mill industry (est. 45%)	-	-	1,449
12. Total sector value added	-	-	3,100
13. Impact of the SIDP (11/12)	-	-	46.7%
IV. Total Heavy Industry			
14. Total heavy industry value added	20,900	2,000	22,900
15. Impact of SIDPs with locations: (2+7)/(4)	19.1%	36.6%	20.5%
16. Impact of as yet unintroduced SIDPs: 6 + (11-7)/14	-	-	9.3%
V. Total			
17. Total industrial value added	36,000	4,400	40,400
18. Impact of SIDPs adopted 2 + 7/17	11.1%	16.6%	11.6%
19. Impact of as yet unintroduced SIDPs: 6 + (11-7)/17	-	-	5.2%
TOTAL			16.8%

Source: Junta, Documento de Evaluación, 1975, Jun/di 198,
Anexo Técnico II, p. 14.

CHAPTER 8

CONCLUSIONS

The experience of the Andean Group during its first eight years of existence, when it was subject to internal and external political and economic pressures quite different from those expected during the 1960s, allows us to draw certain conclusions about the functioning of integration schemes among underdeveloped, highly dependent countries that attempt to diversify their production structure through industrialization. To be generally valid these conclusions would call for analytical comparison with experience in other continents. Nevertheless they are significant because they stem from the most complex scheme of integration between underdeveloped countries in existence, the theory and practice of which were summarized earlier.

From our quantitative evaluation of the dynamic effects of increased trade on growth, we draw the following conclusions.

1. A considerable increase in intraregional trade was registered for the period under examination. Nevertheless the weight of trade in basic products from the agricultural and mining sectors represented, in 1975, around 68 percent of total reciprocal exports.

2. There has been a considerable measure of success in expanding trade in products the manufacture of which had begun in different member countries under the protection of import substitution, and prior to integration. Such trade represents 32 percent of total intraregional trade. But its real scope has been limited by restrictions on competition, which mean that the potential trade-creation effects have been partially prevented.

3. The dynamic effects of trade, especially the promotion of new areas of production and the mobilization of investment, have been so limited as to be virtually imperceptible. There is no registered trade in products contained in the list of goods

not produced before 1969, although such goods were favored
by the total elimination of duties from February 1971 on. Nor
is there any change in the traditional patterns of investment.
We found that this result can be explained by the size of the
regional market and by the attitudes of industrialists, for
whom the more important variable in decisions on investment is
the size and institutional environment of the national market.
Industrialists start export activity only as a complement to
domestic production and basically prefer to remain within the
framework of import substitution.

In this book we also studied other possible dynamic
effects such as an improvement in installed capacity use, an
increase in industrial employment, or a change in income
distribution and again found the results to be extremely
limited. The explanation lies in the type of enterprise that
takes advantage of the freed market. These are mainly large
enterprises, producing under conditions of monopoly and with
advanced technology. Furthermore the limitations of the
import substitution model have not been removed. The regional market for manufactures continues to be one limited to high
income groups.

4. Finally, the experience of the first years of operation
of the commercial program, which offered special trade concessions to the relatively less developed members, demonstrates
the strength of concentration effects. These less developed
countries are net importers of manufactured goods and exporters of basic products. In general, the special provisions
given to them within the commercial program proved to be
almost totally ineffective.

The above conclusions reinforce the arguments in favor of
stronger forms of integration between LDCs if developmental
objectives are to be obtained. However, the integration
movement entered into crisis while plans for such an agreement
were on the discussion table.

Our conclusions are that the process stagnated because a
"national objective" common to all member countries and centered on the goal of industrialization does not in fact exist,
although its existence and integrating power were presupposed
in the theory of integration and implicitly in the Cartagena
Agreement.

We have argued that there exists a relationship between a
country's level of development and its national policies. A
country's policies tend to follow the import substitution goal
more closely if it is one of the less developed countries; the
more developed among the LDCs tend toward more liberal
models. Those countries with a relatively greater level of
development gain immediate benefits because they have a
greater elasticity of supply of industrial output and can
therefore respond more quickly to the so-called "negative"
stage of integration, that is, the abolition of tariff barriers.

The less developed countries cannot respond so quickly, and therefore stand to gain little from the freeing of the market. Their interests lie mainly in the "positive" stage, that is, the policy that aims at the growth of the country's industrial sector, with the least possible social cost.

The conflict between the two groups remained latent until the moment when the GRAN had to move from the greater relaxation of commercial barriers to agreements and to the application of SIDPs, to a CET and to the formulation of a mutual set of macroeconomic policies. At this point the differing values and conflicting interpretations of concepts became apparent. The concepts questioned were those of industrialization, social efficiency, specialization, costs and benefits and, finally, the very goals of integration. For the more developed countries, efficiency means rationalization of industry to secure the lowest possible costs of production. Therefore they favored a low and nondispersed CET and a regional industrialization policy guided by concepts of efficiency measured in international terms. For the less developed, the concept of efficiency signifies the creation of a structure within which industry can develop more intensively while making the best possible use of productive resources, which in an open economy may remain unutilized. What are benefits for the latter group are long-term costs for the former; while, in reverse, the benefits for the more developed countries are immediate costs for the less developed group because of the opening up of their markets.

The problem is not just that diametrically opposed points of view exist concerning the different stages of integration, but that these attitudes manifested themselves in the form of conflicts, the extent and nature of which changed the orientation of the whole process by making the approval and the implementation of common macroeconomic policies practically impossible.

Further, the small size of the Andean subregional market increases the costs of integration for the wealthier members. This is implicit in the principle of "subregional balance," which set out to accelerate growth in the less developed member countries. This factor weakened the willingness of the more developed partners to participate, especially in the more complex forms of cooperation such as SIDPs or the full unification of policies. The real size of the Andean market is limited by the size of national income and by unequal income distribution. Further, the limitations that reduce the effects of integration reduce the market even more. These limitations stem from the different levels of development and the search for national independence based upon a wholly national industrial structure. Also, transport costs and national patterns of consumption, tastes, and customs further reduce the effective market size.

Yet another element that increases the costs of integration is the constraint deriving from the nature of the historical import substitution process. In the integrated version of the import substitution model we found that the only new element is really the integration of the national markets, which is intended to free industry from those constraints that make it impossible for it to grow within national boundaries. We find no measures that will act upon the supply side (production processes and supply structure) or upon the demand side (increase of agricultural productivity, income redistribution, or employment policies). The costs of the new type of industrial growth increased the costs implied in the loss of national sovereignty and weakened the ability to act of those political leaders and industrialists in principle interested in integration. It is obviously unlikely that the aim of regional industrial- ization will be accepted by the different national pressure groups, if they perceive themselves as assuming the costs of other countries' industrialization.

These are some of the economic elements that come together to explain the general lack of political support for integration and the limited possibilities that politicians (and, consequently, technocrats) have of enforcing an integration agreement nationally. That lack of support made it impossible to reach the higher levels of integration required to fully integrate the Andean countries.

To these factors it is important to add another element: the changes in the international context that contributed to diminish the interest in integration. Especially important was the declining interest of the United States and the interna- tional development agencies in promoting socioeconomic reforms to counteract the political effects of the Cuban revolution. Also, changes in the world scene moved countries even further away from the planned development model, and from centralized decisions on the location of productive resources. And perhaps most important, they abandoned the definition of industry as the strategic sector for development, to which end the remaining sectors should be adjusted. Today they are moving toward a more "classical" economy and seem more inclined to accept, in the international division of labor, their vocation as natural providers of primary materials, foodstuffs, and light manufactured goods and as importers of those products that cannot be produced nationally at a level of efficiency greater than or equal to the international level. The need to create productive employment for millions of urban settlers is still unsatisfied, as is the need to relocate the great number of underemployed in more profitable activities. The development of a true urban services sector and the accumu- lation of the resources necessary for the modernization of the rural sector seem unlikely without an efficient industrial sector. That remains true even after integration.

Many of the contradictions between the two groups of countries, in the fields mentioned above, were in part the expressions of problems concerning the transference of productive resources among the member countries, which was considered vital for the stability of the GRAN. It was assumed that because of the identity between regional and national interests those conflicts would be progressively resolved by upgrading the level of integration, that is, by the adoption of agreements and commitments at a high political level, after which it would be impossible for any country to withdraw.

Such "spillover" action failed to occur. Conflicts in four main fields of positive integration have been resolved instead by a combination of compromises which have weakened the level and the extent of integration. In effect, the CET has been abandoned, as was the obligation on all countries to participate in each SIDP. Decision 24 was greatly weakened and the harmonization of macroeconomic policies indefinitely postponed. In addition, the most industrialized member country withdrew.

The experience of the Andean Group, in common with that of other integration schemes among LDCs, shows that there exists a margin within which an integration process can develop more or less smoothly and trade can increase, without this necessarily creating the conditions for progress towards a higher level of integration. What interest there is in integration among national groups seems to be satisfied by limited immediate gains from exports of marginal production.

The apparent impossibility of agreements at the political level entails great risk to the GRAN's stability, which depends upon the successful solution of the problems originating in the difference in economic development. But, as we have seen, the very differences in economic development made the envisaged solutions politically impossible.

POSTSCRIPT

The most recent evaluation(1) published by the Junta at the end of 1979, on the occasion of the tenth anniversary of the approval of the Treaty, confirms the conclusions we have drawn from our analysis. Despite the undeniable increase in reciprocal trade, this continues to be marginal to the economies of the member countries, and its contribution to their growth is considered to be insignificant. The growth of reciprocal trade is negatively affected by the lists of exceptions, the policies of tariff discounts and exemptions, and official purchases. The negative effect of concentration on Ecuador, and especially on Bolivia, continues to be plainly manifest, which has led to new frictions between these two countries and

the other three.   There has been no advance whatsoever in
the manner intended in the field of harmonization of policies
with regard to foreign trade, industrial development, and
fiscal affairs.   The Junta sees this as a potential brake on the
growth of trade.

With regard to sectoral programming, the document points
out that there has been growth in trade, but that there is a
serious lag in the presentation of studies and the making of
investments and that the governments are backward in observ-
ing commitments undertaken under the programs.   To date
only the three programs agreed to by September 1977 have
been approved, and there has been no notable advance in
programming the remaining sectors: iron and steel, fertilizers,
electronics, pharmaceuticals, and chemicals.   The reason for
the failures lies in the impossibility of agreement on location
and on levels of protection.

Member countries, continues the document, have not
begun to build integration into their own planning and
economic policy making, nor have important decisions been
incorporated into domestic legal systems.

All of this means that at the end of 1979 they find a
persisting climate of uncertainty and lack of confidence on the
part of the private sector.

Some important political actions were undertaken by the
Andean Group during 1979-1981 such as the pronouncement in
favor of human rights in Nicaragua and the negotiations to
diplomatically isolate Somoza;   later contacts with Carter
government representatives preparing bilateral United States-
GRAN operations and trade agreements; talks sustained with
the EEC to formulate the first general bilateral agreement.   In
the region meetings took place with Argentine, Brazilian, and
Mexican commissions, and finally the four GRAN member countries exercised pressure upon the Bolivian military regime.
These actions projected to the outside world the picture of a
consolidated group, nevertheless they prove to be rather dis-
ruptive.

NOTES

INTRODUCTION

1. Many authors agree on integration as the best alternative for LDCs as a means of achieving economic development. Economic planning, investment, and all import substitution policies should be considered at a regional level. In other words, there has to be a certain degree of coordination of economic policies. See B. Balassa, The Theory of Economic Integration (London: Allen and Unwin, 1962), pp. 231-252; and, for more detail, B. Balassa, El Segundo Decenio de la Integración y el Desarrollo Económico en America Latina (Buenos Aires: BID-INTAL, 1970), pp. 21-23; H. Kitamura, "Economic Theory and Economic Integration of Underdeveloped Regions," in M. Wionczek, ed., Latin American Economic Integration, (New York: Praeger, 1966), pp. 59-63; R. Mikesell, "The Theory of Common Markets as Applied to Regional Arrangements Among Developing Countries," in D. Harrod and C. Hague, eds., International Trade Theory in a Developing World, (New York: Macmillan, 1963); Sidney Dell, "Regional Integration and the Industrialization of Less Developed Countries," Development Digest, Vol. 3, No. 3. October 1965.

2. H. Kitamura accepts that the trade effects are limited and suggests that to make integration effective it is necessary to act upon the productive process itself, with a view to changing the components and scale of investment (Kitamura, "Economic Theory," p. 59). Similar arguments may be found in Mikesell, "Theory of Common Markets"; in Harrod and Hague, eds., International Trade Theory; and Balassa, Theory of Economic Integration, pp. 191-210.

3. B. Balassa, Economic Development and Integration (Mexico City: Centro de Estudios Monetarios, 1965; "El segundo decenio para el desarrollo y la integración económica regional," in BID-INTAL, La Integración en America Latina en una etapa de Decisiones (Buenos Aires: BID-INTAL, 1970), pp. 21-23; D. McClelland, The CACM: Economic Policies, Economic Growth and Choices for the Future (New York: Praeger, 1972); E. Lizano, "A Second Thought on Central America: The Rosenthal Report," JCMS, Vol. 13, 1975, p. 296.

4. A. Hazlewood in his well-known article, "Economic Integration in East Africa," suggests that because "the relative backwardness of East African countries cannot be blamed on the Common Market and withdrawal from the Common Market would not neutralize the disadvantages under which they labour," it will not be convenient for countries to do so. The reason is that the small national market made industrial development impossible, and new industries in which economies of scale are important "will be attracted to East Africa only on the basis of guaranteed tariff-free access to the whole EACM." And logically he concludes that "a break-up of the Common Market would set back the industrial development of East Africa by many years." He follows up with the suggestion that even the relatively less developed countries (Tanzania and Uganda) will not see their relative backwardness intensify. See Hazlewood, ed., African Integration and Disintegration (London: Oxford U.P., 1967), pp. 110-114. S. Dell, in "Early Years of LAFTA," suggests that, because integration is a second-best solution and because no country wants to experience once again the recession and crises of the sixties, they will solve the problems implicit in integrating (Dell, "Regional Integration"; Wionczek, ed., Latin American Economic Integration, p. 120).

5. Hazlewood, Africa, p. 167.

6. H. Kitamura states that "the task of negotiated, rather than spontaneous, co-ordination and harmonization of economic policies will be enormously facilitated by the fact that almost all underdeveloped countries have adopted the planning approach to the problem of economic development," ("Economic Theory," pp. 59-60). A similar view is held by P. Garcia Reynoso, "Problems of Regional Industrialization," in Wionczek, ed., Latin American Economic Integration, p. 161; and by Tinbergen, J. On the Theory of Economic Integration, (Amsterdam: North Holland, 1950) p. 1972, and idem, International Economic Integration, (New York: Elsevier, 1965), p. 94 and chap. 10.

7. Pointing to the availability of such studies, and their usefulness in reducing the scope for divergences of judgment as to the differential effects of integration on member coun-

tries, an UNCTAD Group of Experts considering a report by Professor Edwardo Lizano concluded that, once provided with such technical data, "since it is not possible for all countries to achieve all their objectives simultaneously, each country has to evolve its own hierarchy of priorities and such different national objectives may be mutually accepted by the grouping as a whole when devising the scope and measures of co-operation." See UNCTAD, The Distribution of Costs and Benefits of Integration Among Developing Countries, TD/B/413, September 1972, p. 5. Tinbergen (On the Theory... 1950, pp. 173), believes that the existence of technical sectoral studies will serve governments and will be accepted by them to orient their own economic activity and that of the private sector in order to achieve regional specialization. Morawetz blames the lack of accurate allocation studies for the failure of the Andean Group SIDPs. If those studies were available, he argues, it would be possible to solve what are in his opinion the two main problems in industrial planning: the length of negotiations and multisectoral programming (Morawetz, The Andean Group: A Case Study in Economic Integration Among Developing Countries [Cambridge, Mass.: MIT Press, 1975], chap. V and pp. 90-92). And, for a similar view, see R. Ffrench- Davis, "The Andean Pact: A Model of Economic Integration for Developing Countries," World Development, Vol. 5, Nos. 1-2, 1976, p. 143; D. Scnydlovsky, "Allocating Integration Industries in the Andean Group," JCMS, Vol. 9, 1971, pp. 299-307.

8. See Hazlewood, Economic Integration: the East African Experience (London: Heinemann, 1975). He considers that jointly owned companies are a "complete answer to the industrial location problem" (p. 124). See as well, M. Kuczinsky, Planned Development in the Andean Group, Industrial Policy and Trade Liberalization (London: Latin American Publication Fund, 1973).

9. For the differences between these three approaches, see J.S. Nye, Peace in Parts, (Boston: Little, Brown, 1972), chap. 2.

10. See E. Haas, "The Uniting of Europe and the Uniting of Latin America," JCMS, Vol. 5, 1967, p. 327.

11. E.B. Haas and P.C. Schmitter, "Economics and Differential Patterns of Political Integration," Davidson W. P. ed., in International Political Communities (New York: Praeger), p. 262.

12. See R. Hansen, "Regional Integration: Reflections on a Decade of Theoretical Efforts," World Politics, Vol. 21, No. 2, 1969, pp. 251-256; and our Chapter 4, Section 2 for a detailed discussion of European experiences and their theoretical implications.

13. S.J. Nye, "Comparing Common Markets," International Organization, Vol. 24/2, 1970, p. 816.

14. M. Wionczek, "Latin American Integration and U.S. Economic Policies," in R. Grieg, ed., International Organization in the Western Hemisphere (Syracuse, N.Y.: 1968).

15. See A.J. Tayseer, "Relevance of Traditional Integration Theory to Less Developed Countries," JCMS, Vol. 9, March 1971, p. 256; L. Mytelka, "The Salience of Gains in Third World Integration Systems," World Politics, Vol. 25, January 1973, pp. 240-241; I.C. Orantes, Regional Integration and Industrialization in Central America (Mass.: Lexington Books, 1972), pp. 13-17.

CHAPTER 1

1. This point is discussed in Business International Corporation, The Andean Market (New York: BIC, 1970), pp. 12-13.

2. To date the following councils have been created: Planning, Monetary and Exchange, Finance, Fiscal Policy, and Foreign Trade (Decisions 22 and 53 of December 30, 1970), Tourism (Decision 36 of March 10, 1971), Social Affairs (Decision 39 of July 17, 1971), Health (Decision 68 of November 17, 1972), and Physical Integration (Decision 71 of June 1, 1973).

3. The members of the first Junta elected by the Commission for the period 1970-72 and reelected for the following period were men of great prestige, representatives of their own countries in LAFTA, and active participants in the Mixed Commission in the past. Their experience and prestige lent the Junta authority on matters of integration. Particularly from 1970 to 1972 it happened that many if not all of the national representatives before the Commission were friends and colleagues of the three members of the Junta, which increased their influence. The three men were Salvador Lluch (Chile), Germanico Salgado (Ecuador), and Felipe Salazar Santos (Colombia).

4. Bolivia was present for the first time, as an observer, at the Third Meeting of the Mixed Commission, held on August 16, 1967, and as a full member from the Fourth Meeting, held in November of the same year. See Junta-INTAL, Historia Documental del Acuerdo de Cartagena (Buenos Aires: Junta-INTAL, 1974), pp. 273-288.

5. The CAF was created at the Fifth Meeting of the Mixed Commission, which took place February 5-10, 1968. See "Acta Final de la 5ª Reunión de la Comision Mixta," in Junta-INTAL, Historia, pp. 289-297.

6. See "Actas Finales" for the Second and Third Meetings of the Mixed Commission (July 1967), the Fourth Meeting, First Session (July-August 1967), and Second Session (May 5-25, 1968), in Junta-INTAL, Historia, pp. 273-279, 299-313.

7. See Junta, Documento de Evaluación del Proceso de Integración Subregional Andina 1969-1975, Jun/di 195, Annex III, Lima 1976.

8. See Decision 103 (November 1976) and our Chapter 5, Section 1.

9. See Chapter 4, Section 4.

10. See Chapter 4 for a detailed discussion of the role played by different social actors.

11. The Executive Committee of LAFTA declared the compatibility of the Treaty of Cartagena and the Treaty of Montevideo in Resolution 179 at the Extraordinary Session held July 4-9, 1969.

12. The author was a member of the Colombian delegation during 1971 and 1972, as chief of the office responsible for the studies on the SIDP in Colombia.

13. See Junta, Documento de Evaluación, 1969-75, Annex III.

14. See Junta, Situación del Acuerdo Luego de los Cambios Introducidos en 1976 (Evaluación 1977), Jun/di 295, Lima, March 1978.

15. See Jorge Mario Eastman's Speech, in the noted Agreement Commission meeting, Thirtieth period of extraordinary sessions. Final Act, Annex No. 1-5. For the first time in the official GRAN documents, the "Andean Free Trade Zone" term appears.

16. See, Junta, Elementos de un plan de acción destinado a reactivar el Proceso de Integración Economica Subregional. Jun/dt 172, Lima, July 10, 1981.

17. The guiding ideas of the ECLA school are most easily accessible in the works of Raul Prebisch, the best known of which are El Desarrollo Económico de America Latina Y Sus Principales Problemas, ECLA, 1950; "Commercial Policies in the Underdeveloped Countries," American Economic Review, Papers and Proceedings, May 1959; United Nations Conference on Trade and Development, Report by the Secretary-General, New York, 1964.

18. Prebisch's theses have naturally aroused a considerable polemic among economists, the majority of whom feel that there is not sufficient empirical evidence to show a tendency for the terms of trade to deteriorate, and that there is no reason to suppose that they should do so in the future. See H. John-

son, Economic Policies Towards Less Developed Countries, (New York: Praeger, 1967); Flanders, "Prebisch on Protectionism: An Evaluation," American Economic Review, May 1950, pp. 472-479; Morgan, "Trends in Terms of Trade and their Repercussions on Primary Producers," in Harrod and Hague eds., International Trade Theory in a Developing World, New York, 1965; G. Haberler, "International Trade and Economic Development," in National Bank of Egypt, Fiftieth Anniversary Commemoratory Lectures, Cairo, 1959. Viner has vigorously criticized another key aspect of ECLA thinking. that which asserts the intrinsic superiority of industry over agriculture. See J. Viner, International Trade and Economic Development, Glencoe, Ill.: The Free Press, 1952). Kindleberger is somewhat more cautious, and calls for more historical investigation. See Kindleberger, "The Terms of Trade and Economic Development," in The Review of Economics and Statistics, Supplement, February 1958. Few Latin American authors, curiously enough, have entered the debate. For two contributions that defend and develop the ECLA argument, see H. Singer, "The Distribution of Gains Between Investing and Borrowing Countries," American Economic Review, May 1950; and E. Bacha, "Un Modelo de Comercio Entre Centro Y Periferia en la Tradicion de Prebisch," Trimestre Económico, No. 162, 1974.

19. Economists such as Balassa, Tinbergen, Hazlewood, Rosenstein-Rodan, Hirschmann, and others participated along with functionaries of UNCTAD and the GATT in the elaboration of studies to develop such important areas of the Treaty of Cartagena as the removal of tax barriers, the CET, the Sectoral Programmes for Industrial Development, and Policy Harmonization.

20. CEPAL, El Pensamiento de la CEPAL, Santiago, 1969, p. 22.

21. Ibid., p. 26.

22. Illustrative of faith in the transformative qualities of planning and the planner is Kaplan's article "Aspectos políticos de la planificación en America Latina." The author proposes for the planner a strategy of alliances with "the proletariat, the rural work force, intellectuals, professionals, small and medium national businessmen, and soldiers who are not resigned to being mere oppressors and occupying forces in their own countries...." The planners should at the same time be on their guard against the danger of being converted into a "privileged elite alienated from the people.... and promoting some variant of bureaucratic state capitalism which distorts the objectives sought." In this way, Kaplan concludes, a high degree of consciousness and participation would be stimulated in the majority; he argues that "the state can become an effective agent of planned development, without favouring its

tendency to limit and oppress social life; this would permit the recuperation of liberty in a social and not merely political sense, and promote the deliberate and rational expansion of all human potentiality." He goes on to warn planners of the "legitimate and illegitimate violence which the old order uses against those who threaten or question it. In Revista de la Sociedad Interamericana de Planeación, No. 15, September 1970, pp. 43-63.

23. CEPAL, El Pensamiento, p. 37.

24. Ibid., p. 37.

25. "Declaración de Bogota," in Junta-INTAL, Historia Documental del Acuerdo de Cartagena, p. 25.

26. For analyses of LAFTA and the CACM, see BID-INTAL, La Integración en América Latina: realizaciones, problemas y perspectivas, 1968; and El proceso de integracion en América Latina, various issues.

27. Ffrench-Davis, "The Andean Pact: A Model of Economic Integration for Developing Countries," Corporación de Investigaciones Económicas para America Latina, mimeo, 1976, p. 5. The same effect was observed in CACM. See Rosenthal Report, BID-INTAL, 1973, Nota Resumen.

28. J. Viner, The Customs Union Issue (New York: Carnegie Endowment, 1950). J.E. Meade, The Theory of Customs Unions (Amsterdam: North Holland, 1955) R.J. Lipsey, "The Theory of Customs Unions: A General Survey," Economic Journal, Vol. LXXI, June 1961.

29. N. Lundgren, "Customs Unions of Industrialized West European Countries," in E.R. Denton, ed., Economic Integration in Europe (Weidenfeld and Nicholson), World University, London, 1971, p. 25.

30. B. Balassa, Economic Development and Integration, (México City: Centro de Estudios Monetarios Latinoamericanos, 1965), p. 16.

31. Trade creation is Viner's term to describe a shift from high cost domestic production to lower cost production in a partner country. Trade diversion involves a shift from the lower cost producer outside the union to a higher cost source of supply within it.

32. R.G. Lipsey, "The Theory of Customs Unions: Trade Diversion and Welfare," Economía, February 1957, p. 41.

33. H.G. Johnson, "An Economic Theory of Protectionism, Tariff Bargaining, and the Formation of Customs Unions," Journal of Political Economy, Vol. LXXIII, June 1965.

34. C.A. Cooper and B.F. Massell, "Toward a General Theory of Customs Unions for Developing Countries," Journal of Political Economy, Vol. LXXXV, October 1965.

35. T. Scitovsky, Economic Theory and Western European Integration (Stanford: Stanford University Press, 1958), p. 10.

36. R. Allen, "Integration in Less Developed Countries," Kyklos, Brazil, Vol 14, 1961, p. 319. The net static effect of a customs union depends on a number of factors which have been discussed in the context of developed countries. See Balassa, Theory of Economic Integration, pp. 29-48; Meade, Theory of Customs Unions, pp. 107-115; Johnson, "An Economic Theory," p. 57.

37. However, there is still confusion as to the meaning of the terms complementarity and competitiveness as defined, for example, in Viner, Customs Union Issue, p. 15, or G. Haberler, The Theory of International Trade (London: Hodge, 1936), p. 389-391. "That confusion makes it 'difficult' to treat the problem as a problem separated from the size of the Union (share of total trade carried on with members) and height of tariffs, reflecting differences in comparative costs." Lundgren, "Customs Unions," p. 38.

38. Mikesell, "Theory of Common Markets," in Harrod and Hague, eds., International Trade Theory, p. 212.

39. It is generally said that "a customs union is more likely to increase welfare the higher is the protection of trade (with the country's union partner) and the lower the proportion with the outside world." Lipsey, "Theory of Customs Unions," p. 273.

40. For a discussion of the possibilities, see T.A. Jaber, "The Relevance of Traditional Integration Theory to Less Developed Countries," JCMS, Vol. IX, 1970, p. 264.

41. S. Dell, Trade Blocks and Common Markets (New York: Knopf, 1963), pp. 242-250, argues that the CET may have to be higher than national levels. This would be justifiable during the first few years of the union. It is preferable that a union should pursue the philosophy of integrating its member-countries' markets rather than protecting them from other nations.

42. Lipsey, "Theory of Customs Unions," pp. 496-515.

43. Mikesell, "Theory of Common Markets," in Harrod and Hague, eds., International Trade Theory, p. 175.

44. Hazlewood, "Problems of Integration among African States," in Hazlewood, ed., African Integration and Disintegration, p. 10.

45. See Morawetz, The Andean Group, pp. 11-24.

46. C.A. Cooper and B.F. Massell, "General Theory of Customs Unions," p. 462.

47. See Balassa, Economic Development and Integration, p. 35. Mikesell, "Theory of Common Markets," p. 213; and Cooper and Massell, "General Theory of Customs Unions For Developing Countries," Journal of Political Economy, October 1965, p.462. See also Bird, Kitamura, and Linder. All agree that a common market with planning policies is a better form of integration for less developed countries than a Free Trade Area.

48. In 1959 the secretary of ECLA stated in his report that "the common market would offer each and all the Latin American countries equal opportunities of expediting their economic growth. The common market could play a leading role in mitigating the Latin American countries' vulnerability to external contingencies and fluctuations" (UN/ECLA, The Latin American Common Market New York, 1959), pp. 5-6.

49. P.C. Schmitter, "The Progress of the CACM," JCMS, IX, September 1970.

50. This stance is reflected in the timetable of the Treaty of Cartagena's programmes. They predicted the unification of policies by 1973 and the completion of the process of freeing intraregional trade by 1980:

> The programme of policy unification policies occupies a place in the institutional arrangements of the Treaty of Cartagena. The objective is to set up the juridical conditions which will allow the exact fulfilment of the goals of the other programmes of sub-regional integration, without creating distortions affecting the basic aims of the Treaty. Therefore, the various instruments for achieving unifications were given priority in the timescale. [Junta, Informe de Evaluación del Proceso de Integración Subregional Andino, 1977, Jun/di,295, March 1978, pp. 11-61]

51. Members of an integration scheme agreed on some collective goals for a variety of motives but unequally satisfied with their attainment of these goals, attempt to resolve their dissatisfaction either by resorting to collaboration in other related sectors (expanding the scope of the mutual commitment) or by intensifying their commitment to the original sector (increasing the level of mutual commitment) or both. [P.C. Schmitter, "Three Neo-functionalist Hypotheses about International Integration," International Organization, Vol. XXIII, No. 1, Winter 1969, p. 166]

52.   Integration can be conceived as involving the gradual politization of the actors' purposes which were
initially considered "technical" or "non-controver-
sial".   Politization implies that the actors, in
response to the initial purposes, agree to widen the
spectrum of means considered appropriate to attain
them.   This tends to increase the controversial
component, i.e. those additional fields of action
which require political choices concerning how much
national autonomy to delegate to the Union.   Politization implies that the actors seek to resolve their
problems so as to upgrade common interests and in
the process, delegate more authority to the center.
It constitutes one of the properties of integration,
the intervening variable between economic and political union along with the development of new
expectations and loyalties on the part of organized
interests in the member nations.   [Hass and Schmitter, "Economic and Differential Patterns of Political
Integration: Projects about Unity in Latin America,"
in W.P. Davison, ed., International Political Communities (New York: Praeger, 1966) pp. 261-262.

53.   See pp. 19-23 of this chapter and Chapter 4, p. 156,
section 4.   Ex-President Lleras Restrepo is well versed in the
details of integration in Europe.   See his article, "Los Aspectos Politicos y Sociales de la Integración en America Latina," in Wyndham-White, ed., La Integración Latino-Americana
en una Etapa de Decisiones, BID-INTAL, 1970, pp. 60-94.

54.   See also Chapter 4, section 1, and Chapter 6 and 7.

55.   For the resolutions in question see Junta-INTAL, História
Documental del Acuerdo de Cartagena, Buenos Aires, 1974,
pp. 351-360.

56.   Ibid., p.351 (Article 2).

57.   Ibid., p.352 (Article 5).

58.   Ibid., Acta de la séptima sésion extraordinaria del CEP, 4
a 9 de Julio 1969, pp. 53-120.

59.   See Articles 16 and 17 of the Treaty of Montevideo, and
Chapter IV, Articles 32-40, of the Treaty of Cartagena.

60.   LAFTA is described and analyzed in detail in S. Dell, A
Latin American Common Market? (New York: O.U.P., 1966);
Wionczek, ed., Latin American Economic Integration; E.B. Hass
and P.C. Schmitter, The Politics of Economics of Latin
American Regionalism, Monograph Series in World Affairs,
Denver University Press, 1965; M. Wionczek, "The Rise and
Decline of Latin American Economic Integration," Journal of
Common Market Studies, Vol. IX, No. 1. pp.49-66.

61. In the first part of this chapter and in Chapter 4 we discuss the role of politicians in the genesis of the GRAN; it contrasts with their role in LAFTA and the CACM, where the ideas and first projects came from technical quarters.

62. This list was approved on 31 December 1970. It included goods which were produced in sufficient quality and quantity to satisfy sub-regional demand, or those which only required relatively low levels of investment to achieve this. Within this group were goods which were the subject of frontier trade and basic mineral and agricultural products, programming for which would be impracticable because of natural conditions.

63. The common list comprises products on which all LAFTA countries agreed to the complete elimination of duties, changes and other restrictions by 1973. It was to be negotiated in 4 parts, 1967, 1970 and 1973. Each of the first 3 parts was to be composed of products representing 25% of the aggregate value of intra-LAFTA trade during the last 3 years. So far, only the first part has been negotiated.

64. The most important goods in this group are those not produced because of the lack of a large national market, even though production does not need high levels of investment. Also included are goods that need a higher level of technology than the group possesses to make production feasible in the medium term (such as computers and very sophisticated capital goods).

65. In order to fix the number of items on the lists of exemptions, the level of industrial development of each country was taken into account. The only limitation was to ban the inclusion of goods which were, or could be, staple exports from Bolivia and Ecuador. The figures for each country were: 600 items for Bolivia and Ecuador; 450 items for Peru; and 250 items for Colombia, Chile, and Venezuela.

66. Treaty of Cartagena, Article 63.

67. Ibid., Article 65, section (a).

68. See Tinbergen, West European Economic Integration (New York: Elsevier, 1965) chap. 10 and p.94.

69. R. Ffrench-Davis, "The Andean Pact," p.20.

CHAPTER 2

1. For an analysis of the ECLA model and its lack of applicability to relatively less developed countries, see A. Bianchi, America Latina, Ensayos de interpretación Económica, (Santiago: Tiempo Latinoamericano, 1969), pp. 11-25. The predomi-

nant interpretation of Latin American economic development
associated with ECLA presents problems in the "inward-look-
ing" model. Subject of discussion are ECLA's views on the
duration of the determinant role of the export sector and the
undervaluing of the internal sector as the characteristics of
the "outward-looking" model.

2. See M. Kaser, COMECON: Integration Problems of the
Planned Economies, (London: Oxford University Press, 1967),
pp. 201-213; and Nye, Comparing Common Markets, International Organization, Vol. 24, 1970, pp. 814-15.

3. The ratio between per capita GDP in Venezuela and in
Ecuador (the country with the second lowest values) is also
inferior to those registered in other integration schemes. In
1975, for example, the ratio was 2.5:1, while the corresponding
ratio for global GDP was 4.3:1.

4. Junta, Imagen Agropecuaria Dentro del Marco de la Inte-
gración Andina, J/PR/31 October 1973, p.30. See also CEPAL,
El Desarrollo Economico y Social y las Relaciones Economicas
Externas de America Latina E/CEPAL/1061/January 1979.

5. See Departamento Nacional de Planeación, Para cerrar la
Brecha - Plan Nacional de Desarrollo 1975-1978, Bogotá, 1975.

6. Economically Active Population, Urban and Rural,
1975 ('000)

	Urban	Rural		Urban	Rural
Bolivia	746	1,117	Ecuador	884	1,115
Chile	2,664	720	Peru	2,891	1,606
Colombia	5,013	2,846	Venezuela	2,729	729

Source: ECLA, Tendencias y Prayecciones a Largo Plazo del
Desarrollo Economico de America Latina, E/CEPAL/
1027/Rev., May 1977, p.99.

7. The following is the ranking of the Andean countries,
taking the index of real "liquid" wages in manufacturing in
December 1970, and using the LAFTA average as a base:

Country	Index
LAFTA	100
Ecuador	63.2
Bolivia	67.6
Colombia	70.6
Chile	109.6
Peru	111.0
Venezuela	140.4

("Liquid" salary is equivalent to nominal salary less social security contributions. See F. Salazar, "Las Diferenciales Salariales en ALALC," in ECIEL, Industrialización y Empleo en el Contexto de la Integración Latinoamericana, Rio de Janeiro, 1976, p.76.

8. The location quotient can be calculated as follows:

> Numerator: the country's percentage share of total value added (or employment) in industry.
>
> Denominator: the country's percentage share of total regional value added (or employment) in industry.

Dividing the numerator by the denominator gives the location quotient. See J. Alden, and R. Morgan, Regional Planning: A Comprehensive View (London: Leonard Hill Books, 1974), chap. VII; and W. Issard, Methods of Regional Analysis (Cambridge, Mass.: MIT Press, 1960); chap. 12.

9. Alden and Morgan, Regional Planning, p.231.

10. The method of calculation of the coefficient of specialization is as follows:

> Numerator: ratio of employment in industry x in the country to industry in the same country
>
> Denominator: ratio of employment x in the region to employment in the industry.

The numerator is subtracted from the denominator without regard to the sign, yielding values between 0 and 1. See Alden and Morgan, Regional Planning, chap. VII.

11. Maizels suggests that industrialization, for the majority of LDCs, is the key to economic development, because it raises physical output per capita in the economy. See A. Maizels, Industrial Growth and World Trade (London: Cambridge University Press, 1963), chap. One.

12. Kaser, COMECON; p.205.

13. The level of import substitution is measured as follows:

$$a = \frac{X - E}{X + I - E}$$, where X = production, E = exports, and I = imports. See S.C. Chu, "Industrialization in Colombia," Rand Papers, Series PJOIJ.

14. See Junta, Bases Generales para Una Estrategia Subregional de Desarrollo, Lima, 1972, Vol. 1, p.123.

15. Ibid., pp.120–130.

16. There is no clear definition of the metal-mecánica sector, which we have described as "light engineering." It includes the following ISIC divisions:

371 Basic iron and steel industry
381 Metal products
382 Nonelectrical machinery
383 Electrical machinery
384 Transport materials
385 Manufacture of equipment for professional and scientific purposes.

See UNCTAD, Definicion de Productos Básicos, Semimanufacturados y Manufacturados, UNCTAD, TD/B/C.2/3.

17. See Chapter 1, section 1, and Chapter 7, section 3.

18. See Chapter 6, section 4 and Chapter 7, sections 1 and 3.

19. For further details see Chapter 2, section 4, and Chapter 7, section 5.

20. In Colombia, with an average income of $281 per capita, only 1.56% ($4.4) per capita is spent on consumer durables and 5.37% ($15.1 p.a.) on clothing and footwear. See ECIEL, Distribución de Ingresos y Estructura del Consumo, Junta, J/PR/68, March 15, 1976.

21. In its study Integración y Substitución de Importaciones en América Latina, ECLA maintains that the population earning less than $500 has no effect upon investment decisions: "This population," it says, "in practical terms, does not exist." ECLA, Integración y Substitución de Importaciones en América Latina, Santiago, 1974, p.60. The Junta del Acuerdo de Cartagena calculates that "$800 per capita p.a., is the minimum income level for having a house, a family, car and essential domestic equipment." See Junta, La Población Andina y su Capacidad de Compra, J/PR/70, April 19, 1976, pp.16-17.

22. In Santiago, the 50% of the population whose per capita average income is $533 p.a. spends 7.4% ($39) on domestic consumer durables and is unable to buy cars; 58% goes on food and housing. In Ecuador, it is only the top 20% that has an income of $600 p.a. This level still does not allow for the purchase of cars, and only 4.8% goes on domestic consumer durables and 8.3% on clothes and footwear; 70% is accounted for by food and housing. Junta, La Población Andino, pp.46 and 53.

23. This is the level that ECLA considers to be the basis for industrial integration in Latin America. See ECLA, Intergración, p.63.

24.   Population ('000) in 1978 According to
                     Income Scale (in US$ 1968)

Scale	US dollars	Bolivia	Chile	Colombia	Ecuador
1	0-300	4,375.9	4,657.7	18,903.1	5,672.3
2	301-500	702.9	2,640.1	3,944.5	875.0
3	501-1,000	142.7	2,318.1	2,049.2	799.6
4	1,000-1,500	63.5	568.8	384.2	120.7
5	1,501-2,000	-	171.7	281.8	75.4
6	2,000 and over	-	375.6	51.2	-
	TOTAL	5,285.0	1,073.2	2,561.4	7,543.0

Scale	US dollars	Peru	Venezuela	GRAN
1	0-300	10,546.7	4,644.3	49,110.2
2	301-500	2,556.8	2,154.3	13,037.4
3	501-1,000	2,825.9	4,476.5	12,397.5
4	1,001-1,500	420.5	1,454.8	2,877.8
5	1,501-2,000	151.5	685.4	1,279.7
6	2,000 and over	319.6	573.6	1,279.7
	TOTAL	16,821.0	13,989.0	79,984.0

Source: CELADE, Boletin Demografico, No. 22 July 1978,
         Junta, La Población Andina y su Capacidad de Com-
         pra.

25.   Distribution of the Subregional Market Before and After
Venezuela's Entry (Population with Income Above $1,000 p.a.)

	Distribution without Venezuela %	Distribution with Venezuela %
Bolivia	1.9	0.9
Chile	39.3	22.9
Colombia	25.1	12.2
Ecuador	5.9	2.9
Peru	27.8	16.9
Venezuela	-	44.2

Source: Calculated from Junta: La Población Andina y Su Ca-
         pacidad de Compra, J/PR/70, April 1976, Table 11.

26. See Acta final de la Tercera Reunión del Consejo de Comercio Exterior, Lima, 1975. For Bolivian statement on the
significance of the subregional market for the development of
its own industrial sector, see Documento CEE/111, final report.
See also Salvador Galo, Estratégia y Política de Fomento Industrial del Ecuador, Junta de Planificación del Ecuador, Quito,
May 1976.

27. In Junta del Acuerdo, Bases para una Estrategia de Desarrollo Subregional, growth of the manufacturing market at
the national level is planned only as a result of greater
employment. This will be gained by enlarging subregional
trade and discarding other actions designed to amplify national
demand, such as income redistribution. See Junta, Bases,
pp.106-116.

28. See, UN ECLA, Integración, Substitución de Importaciones
y Desarrollo Económico de América Latina, Santiago, April
1974, pp.67-75.

29. Subregional and national studies seem to indicate that the
share of the salaried sector in total GDP has not changed.
See Anibal Pinto, La distribución del ingreso en América La-
tina, New York, 1970; Ricardo Webb, "The Distribution of
Income in Peru," in A. Foxley, ed., Income Distribution in
Latin America, (New York: Cambridge University Press, 1976),
pp.11-26; Alejandro Foxley and Oscar Muñoz, "Income Redis-
tribution, Economic Growth and Social Structure: the Case of
Chile," in Foxley, Income Distribution, pp.135-162; and Robert
Berry and M. Urrutia, Income Distribution in Colombia (New
Haven: Yale University Press, 1977), chap. 12; and our Chap-
ter 3, section 2D.

30. Junta, La Población Andina y su Capacidad de Compra.

31. R. Webb, La Distribución del Ingreso en Peru, Instituto
de Estudios Peruanos, Lima, 1975.

32. Bogota, Quito, and La Paz are over 2,500 meters above
sea level and at a considerable distance from the nearest
seaport (an average of 1,000 km.). The important Colombian
cities, Medellin and Cali, both with one-million-plus populations, are also in the interior, but not so far from ports
(about 300 km.).

33. R.T. Brown, Transport and Economic Integration of South
America (Washington D.C.: Brookings Institution, 1969), p.36.

34. Brown says that there are "relatively good inter-country
routes between Chile, Bolivia, Chile-Peru, Colombia-Venezuela
and Peru-Ecuador." Ibid., pp.37-38. However, with regard
to the conditions of the routes between Colombia-Ecuador and
Bolivia-Peru which this author also calls good, one can see
that these roads are of limited use. Nevertheless, those

bordering countries do have some type of existing communications.

35. David Morawetz, "Problems of Transport and Communication in the Andean Group," Revista de Integración, No. 2, Santiago, 1972, pp. 63-78. Calculations based on AVIANCA's information (the Colombian Airline) show that to transport 500 kgs. from Bogota to Santiago costs $5.4 p.kg., over a distance of 2,704 air miles. From Bogota to New York the same cargo would cost $2.3 kg. or 2,487 air miles and $2.6 p.kg. from Bogota to Caracas over 638 air miles.

36. Morawetz, "Problems of Transport"; he studied the internal transport costs of Colombia in greater detail and found that a ton of goods moved from the Pacific port of Buenaventura to Bogota was charged only 25% less than for the same goods to move from Guayaquil, Ecuador, to Buenaventura, including port and ocean freight charges.

37. Dell found, for example, that in 1963 the freight rate for lumber shipped from Mexico to Venezuela was $24 per ton, against $11 from Finland to Venezuela, even though the distance is three times greater. S. Dell, A Latin American Common Market? (London: Oxford University Press, 1966), p. 101.

38. Brown made a list of 28 factors that play an important role in determining freight charges. Above all, the conferences take into account the volume of trade distance, the possibility of getting return cargos, the condition of ports, and the estimates of ship owners of "what the trade will bear." Since the owners do not use scientific methods to calculate the elasticities of prices, rate making is an extremely contentious subject. Brown, Transport and Economic Integration, p. 118.

39. It costs 1.1¢ per ton to transport unroasted coffee from Buenaventura to Valparaiso (2,600 miles). From Buenaventura to New York for the same goods it cost 0.90¢ per ton (2,400 miles). To transport coffee and wood from Guayaquil to Valparaiso (2,000 miles) costs 1.87¢ and 1.72¢ respectively per ton per mile. To New York (2,600 miles) the same figures are 1.4¢ and 1.5¢. Ibid., p. 66.

40.

Andean routes	Distance (miles)	cost per ton ($)
Lima-Quito	1,125	30.35
Lima-Santiago	1,613	30.35
Bogota-Santiago	3,512	60.60
EEC routes		
Rome-Amsterdam	1,084	47.70

Source: Morawetz, "Problems of Transport," p. 20.

41. Junta, Imagen Agropecuaria Dentro del Marco de la Integración Andina, J/PR/31 October 1973, chap. I. See also our
Chapter 2, section 2.

42. Junta, "Bases Para una Estrategia Subregional de Desarrollo," Lima, 1972, Vol. I, pp. 6-7.

43. See R. Nurske, Patterns of Trade and Development
(Stockholm, 1959), pp. 41-50.

44. That percentage represents rural population with a yearly
income over US$500. If we move the limit up to US$1,000 it
would cover only 0.07% of the total rural population.

45. For more detail on market size and economies of scale, see
our Chapter 7, section 1B.

46. Germánico Salgado, "El Grupo Andino y el Poder de Acción Solidario," in Bid-INTAL, La Integración Latinoamericana
en una Etapa de Decisiones, Santiago, 1970, p. 131.

47. See R. Prebisch, "El Desarrollo Económico de America
Latina," chap. 1.

48. The terms of trade became especially favorable to the
oil-exporting countries, Venezuela, Ecuador, and Bolivia, and,
to a lesser degree, to Colombian coffee exports. The evolution
of terms of trade is different depending on the products exported. In Bolivia, for instance, the recovery after a fall in
1971 occurred only in 1974, while in Colombia improvements can
be observed since 1970. But, in summary, it is from the
energy crisis that the terms of trade show a better tendency
for Andean countries, excepting only Chile and Peru.

49. From 1975 to 1980, international reserves which had risen
to US$10,291 million, in 1975 fell to US$8,048 and 9017 million
in 1978 and 1980, respectively and were distributed as follows:

	1975	1978	1980
Bolivia	156	197	137
Colombia	521	250	536
Chile	-1,104	1,149	4,087
Ecuador	286	653	1,030
Peru	467	432	226
Venezuela	8,861	6,516	7,088

See Junta; Jun/di/248/1977, Anexo Tecnico, p. 40. The
fall in Chilean reserves was caused both by the fall in copper
prices and the international reaction to the political situation
after 1971.

1978-1980= IMF, International Financial Statistics, No. 11,
November 1981.

50. This is the expression used by Serra when he refers to the Brazilian experience after 1967. In this case, there was also an increase in the import coefficient of industrial goods. J. Serra, "El Estilo de Desarrollo en América Latina," El Trimestre Económico, Vol. XLIV (2), Mexico, 1977, pp. 442-447.

51. In countries like Chile and Colombia the proportion of imports to satisfy internal industrial demand for capital and intermediate goods has remained relatively static over the last 6 years.

In 1975, the rise in external resources in Colombia led it to take antiinflationary measures which included the reform of the tariff structure, the elimination of deposits, and the abolition in practice of import licenses.

Chile, for the opposite reason, fell back on devaluing the escudo and, because of the size of the country, "the opening of the market to foreign trade was seen as the mechanism for allocating resources."

In Peru, the government resorted to foreign loans to finance the deficit on current account, which, by 1975, had risen to US$1,567 million. These credits, however, did not reach the required levels. The reserves fell to a minimum equal to the requirements to cover 3 months of exports.

52. The evolution of total Andean imports and exports can be seen in detail in Chapter 3. The weight of each country in the total foreign trade of the GRAN has varied, which indicates again the enormous asymmetry of the subregion. In 1968, total Venezuelan exports were worth US$2,849 million and those of Bolivia were US$169.6 million. By 1974, the figures were US$15,748 million and US$592.8 million, respectively.

53. The balance on current account (in US$ millions at current values) was as follows for the period 1969-1979:

	1969	1970	1974	1975	1977	1978	1979
Bolivia	-27	-24	108	-167	-185	-313	-465
Chile	229	-95	-187	-587	-470	-715	----
Colombia	-144	-330	-382	-97	411	209	97
Ecuador	-28	-122	23	-334	-365	-300	-585
Peru	-185	-146	-752	-1573	-957	-327	618
Venezuela	-213	-51	5729	2236	-2003	-4120	-287

Source: ECLA, El Desarrollo Económico y Social y las Relaciones Externas de América Latina, E/CEPAL1064, March 1979.
1979, Junta: Indicadores Socio-economicos de la Subregion Andina, Jun/di/277 Rev.3, April 3, 1980.

54. Payments of debt service and amortization, and remittance of profits on foreign investment, expressed as a percentage of the value of exports, is as follows:

	1970	1974	1976	1977	1978	1979
Bolivia	22.6	17.8	24.1	28.8	66.9	41.5
Chile	30.0	38.2	48.8	52.4	67.9	57.0
Colombia	32.0	27.5	20.2	17.8	20.8	19.0
Ecuador	22.0	24.6	21.4	27.1	31.7	60.4
Peru	27.8	33.1	59.7	53.2	97.1	80.5
Venezuela	22.6	10.9	10.9	8.0	11.1	18.1
Latin America	29.6	25.6	31.5	17.2	19.6	20.4

Source: ECLA, El Desarrollo Económico y Social y las Relaciones Externas de América Latina, p. 69.
1978-1979, ECLA, Estudio Económico de America Latina 1980.

55. Consumer Retail Prices (1970 = 100)

	1969	1970	1971	1972	1973	1974	1975	1978	1980
Bolivia	96.2	100	103.6	110.3	145.1	236.3	266.6	333.7	587.4
Chile	75.0	100	119.0	211.0	959.0	5797.0	85835.0	719667.2	438908.6
Colombia	93.0	100	109.0	124.6	153.0	190.3	280.9	531.1	837.4
Ecuador	95.2	100	108.4	117.0	132.2	163.0	208.1	291.3	362.3
Peru	95.2	100	107.1	114.5	125.4	146.5	181.1	527.0	1398.1
Venezuela	97.6	100	103.2	106.1	110.5	119.9	142.0	176.5	241.4

Source: IMF, International Financial Statistics.

56. Percentage Rates of Growth of Imports and Exports of Goods, 1974-78

	Imports				Exports			
	1974	1975	1977	1978	1974	1975	1977	1978
Bolivia	24.3	13.0	11.0	8.0	98.4	-10.2	17.6	10.0
Chile	32.5	8.9	11.0	8.0	40.1	-27.4	-0.5	3.2
Colombia	32.6	4.1	10.0	9.0	19.9	-5.8	58.5	-15.0
Ecuador	29.7	15.0	15.0	6.0	128.3	-12.7	12.3	-8.0
Peru	24.1	12.0	6.5	8.0	46.6	-4.9	9.0	-4.0
Venezuela	24.2	16.0	10.2	10.0	166.7	6.8	11.9	n.a.

Source: Junta, Estadísticas de Comercio Exterior para el Grupo Andino, 1969-1979. Jun/di 365, March 30, 1980.

57.   Andean Group Import/Export Price Index, 1970

YEAR	BOLIVIA		COLOMBIA		ECUADOR		PERU		VENEZUELA	
	M	X	M	X	M	X	M	X	M	X
1974	156.0	218.0	157.5	159.1	160.0	267.6	156.3	193.3	162.0	498.5
1975	176.3	195.7	163.9	149.9	184.0	244.5	175.0	183.9	188.0	532.4
1976	183.5	209.5	173.0	225.0	194.9	280.4	178.5	183.9	225.8	564.4
1977	203.7	246.3	189.2	356.6	214.4	339.3	190.1	197.3	205.2	631.6
1978	220.0	270.9	206.2	303.1	227.3	312.2	205.3	189.4	248.4	631.6

Source: Junta, Estadísticas de Comercio Exterior de los Paises del Grupo Andino 1969-1979, Jun/di 499, September 9, 1980.

58.   Public Sector Deficit as % of GDP

	1969	1975	1979		1969	1975	1979
Bolivia	6.9	4.1	18.8	Ecuador	2.3	1.7	5.4
Colombia	0.9	0.1	25.6	Peru	3.0	10.0	21.7
Chile	2.4	3.4	67.0	Venezuela	5.7	0.8	50.3

Source: World Bank, World Tables 1976, N.Y., 1977; and IMF, International Financial Statistics, 1977 and 1980.

59. Public investment in Bolivia for 1971-1975 increased as follows:

1971-72:	3%
1972-73:	34.4%
1973-74:	60.3%
1974-75:	26.9%

Source: Report prepared by Fedesarrollo in Coyuntura Andina, October 1976, Fedesarrollo, Bogotá, p. 244.

60. The financial results of COMIBOL (Mines and YPBF - petroleum) can be seen from the following figures (in millions of Bolivian pesos).

	1971	1972	1973	1974	1975
COMIBOL	27.3	-33.2	-50.8	-54.6	-906.9
YPBF	-	105.5	548.3	1001.4	-643.4

Source: Ibid.

61. Peru: Consolidated Government Finances (% of GDP)

	1970	1972	1974	1975
Current revenue	23.6	24.2	25.5	24.9
Current expenditure	19.2	21.7	24.0	24.0
Public savings	4.6	2.7	1.5	0.9
Public investment	4.3	4.9	7.4	8.0
Deficit	-1.4	-3.1	-7.2	-10.0

Source: World Bank, World Tables 1976, N.Y., 1977.

62. For a detailed analysis of the stabilization policies negotiated between the Peruvian Government and the IMF, see Thorp, "The Stabilisation Crisis in Peru 1975-1978," in Thorp and Whitehead, eds., Inflation and Stabilization in Latin America (London: Macmillan, 1979).

63. The lowest level of income subject to taxation in Venezuela is $4,673 p.a. which has a marginal rate of tax of 4.5%. In Argentina the respective figures are $200 p.a. and 7%, while in Colombia, they are $667 p.a. and 10%. The lowest level of the highest scale in Argentina is $12,000 p.a., taxed at 46%. In Venezuela, the highest scale is $1,869 p.a. bearing a rate of 45%. "Informe sobre Venezuela" in Coyuntura Andina, No. 1, Bogotá, October 1976, pp. 196-197.

64. See Chapter 7, sections 2 and 3.

65. See D.N.P., Para Cerrar la Brecha, Plan de Desarrollo Economico de Colombia, 1975-78, Bogotá, 1975.

66. The Chilean development strategy, seen more clearly after 1975 when stabilization policies were introduced, identified the causes of slow growth in GNP over the previous 40 years as the allocation of resources according to the import substitution scheme and the mechanisms adopted to push industrialization ahead: high and dispersed tariffs, overvalued exchange rates, distortions in relative factor prices caused by price controls, subsidies, and import licenses.

67. The only exception is the motor vehicle industry.

68. Sergio de Castro, El Mercurio, August 28, 1976.

69. In 1975, Venezuelan steel sold for US$402 per ton above the average world price; its cars were 45% more expensive; see Coyuntura Andina, October 1976, p. 179.

70. "Planning in our country is to become the tool of national policy called upon to overcome progressively our dependent character and to replace it with a pluralist one, centred on the

sector given priority as social property; this is not necessarily the industrial sector." El Peruano, November 18, 1974.

71. By the end of 1973, 3,332 industrial communities had been set up, covering more than 200,000 workers. In 1974, their share of companies, social capital was 8.8%. On average, the legal maximum share of 50% was expected to be achieved after 20 years.

72. S. Galo, Estrategia y Política de Fomento Industrial del Ecuador, Junta de Planificación del Ecuador, Quito, May 1976.

73. See Chapter 6.

74. Sergio de Castro, "El Esquema Proteccionista Fracasó en Chile," El Mercurio, August 28, 1976.

75. Ibid. Also, the Colombian President fully accepted this idea in his speech of September 10, 1976; see El Espectador, September 11, 1976.

76. The Chilean position is clearly stated in Decree No. 600 of 1975, which we discuss in Chapter 6, section C.

77. See Chapter 6, section 2 and 3.

78. During 1977 Peru devalued its currency from 65 soles per dollar to 130 soles per dollar. The devaluation process was pursued until a rate considered real of 450 soles per dollar was fixed in September 1981.

79.   Foreign Exchange Rates, Annual Averages,
                   Measured Against the US$.

	1969	1970	1972	1974	1975	1978	1979	1980
Bolivia	11.88	11.88	13.23	20.00	20.00	20.00	24.5	24.5
Chile	9.09	11.65	43.10	593.00	13,273.00	32,690.00	39.0	39.0
Colombia	17.21	18.34	22.10	27.10	34.97	38.80	44.0	50.9
Ecuador	18.00	20.40	25.00	25.00	25.00	25.00	25.0	25.0
Peru	38.70	38.70	38.70	38.70	57.40	165.70	250.1	341.3
Venezuela	4.50	4.50	4.40	4.30	4.30	4.30	4.3	4.3

Source: IMF International Financial Statistics, various issues.

80. Colombian government spending included in the budget has evolved as follows:

Annual increase

1971	–
1972	-4.4%
1973	18.8%
1974	13.8%
1975	19.6%
1976	-13.3%

See Coyuntura Económica, October 1977, p. 62.

81. For 1976 and 1977, the 1975 level of public spending was maintained, but resources were reallocated between the various sectors. For example, in current expenditure, interest payments rose fastest, while on the capital account loan repayments were frozen.

Expenditure in Foreign Currency for 1974 to 1976

	1974	1975	1976
Current expenditure	57.2%	45.9	45.9
Wages and salaries	5.4	3.3	3.3
Purchases of goods	25.7	7.9	7.9
Family allowances	0.02	0.01	0.01
Transfers to private sector	9.3	0.1	1.4
Transfers to public sector	6.4	0.09	0.09
Interest	10.2	32.1	32.0
Capital expenditure	42.7	54.0	54.1
Direct investment	2.7	1.3	1.3
Transfers	7.0	2.7	2.7
Loan repayments	33.0	50.0	50.0
Others	–	–	–
Total	100.0	100.0	100.0

Sources: Coyuntura Andina, October 1975; Chile; informe Elaborado por el Departamento de Economía de la Universidad de Chile, Fedesarrollo, Bogota, 1976; pp. 111-114.

82. See "Analisis de la Incidencia del Proceso de Integración Andina en la Economía del Peru," Documento Presentado por la Delegación Peruana a la 3a Reunión del Consejo de Planificación del Grupo" Andina, Jun/di/276, January 4, 1978.

83. Junta, Informe sobre la coyuntura de los paises miembros, first semester 1981, J/PR/133, August 1981, pp. 51-54.

CHAPTER 3

1. These are the criteria put forward by Germánico Salgado. They are the same as those espoused by many politicians and economists connected with the process of integration in under-developed countries. See G. Salgado, El Grupo Andino y el Poder de Acción Solidaria, Bid-INTAL, 1970, p. 31; and Balassa, Economic Integration and Economic Development, 1965.

2. Junta, Evaluación del proceso de integración, 1969-1975, Jun/di 195, Lima, 1976, p. 11.

3. For details see Chapter 1 pp. 27-28.

4. Lipsey, Theory of Customs Union, p. 261.

5. B. Lambri, "Customs Union and Underdeveloped Countries," Economia Internazionale, May 1962, p. 245.

6. For the effects of economic integration in countries with excess labor, see W.G. Demas, The Economics of Development in Small Countries, with Special Reference to the Caribbean (Montreal: McGill University Press, 1965), and his article, "The Economics of the West Indies Customs Union," Social and Economic Studies, March 1960, p. 15.

7. Viner's argument, that a customs union between underde-veloped countries has a negative effect because it can reduce the proportion of external trade as a result of the diversion of trade, is refuted, by, among others, Balassa, Economic Integration and Economic Development, pp. 13-14; Kitamura, "Economic Theory," p. 38 and Mikesell, "Theory of Common Markets," pp. 205-210.

8. A.R. Allen, "Integration in Less Developed Areas," Kyklos, 1967, p. 331.

9. T. Scitovsky, Economic Theory and Western European Integration, (London, George Allen and Unwin, 1958). Nils Lundgren follows the same line as Scitovsky, saying that "as long as their basic approach is accepted the quantitative results will remain small, so small that they would not be measurable in the present system of national accounts and so small that it would hardly seem worth while to devote so much of the attention of economists, statisticians, politicians and newspaper editorials to the problem of removing tariffs between industrialized countries" (N. Lundgren, "Customs Unions of Industrialized West European Countries," in G.R. Denton, ed., Economic Integration in Europe; World University London, The Graduate University of Contemporary Studies, 1971], p. 25).

10. "I believe, however, that the theoretical analysis of customs unions should be directed more towards the problem of their impact on the direction of investment in the developing countries for future output rather than limited to an analysis of the welfare implication of shifting existing patterns" (Mikesell, "Theory of Common Markets," p. 206).

11. "Substitution within countries will increase the availability of foreign currency needed to buy from the rest of the world capital goods which are essential for development. Therefore, supposing that any capital goods originate from outside the region, this supply of those goods and the volume of investment can be increased considerably with economic integration" (H. Kitamura, "La Teoria Económica y la Integracion Economica de las Regiones Subdesarrolladas," in M. Wionczek, ed., La Integración Económica de América Latina: Experiencias y Perspectivas [Mexico: Fondo de Cultura Economica, 1964], p. 35).

12. This conclusion on the effects of a customs union in underdeveloped countries is reached by Kitamura, ibid., p. 38; and Meade, Theory of Customs Unions, p. 345.

13. K.B. Griffin, Underdevelopment in Spanish America (London: Allen and Unwin, 1969), pp. 241-242.

14. Lyzano, "A Second Thought on the Central American Common Market," JCMS, Vol. 13, 1975, pp. 280-307.

15. Also, the effect of world inflation on the value of total trade has to be taken into account. With 1968 as the base year, the following unit value index of external trade is obtained for the Andean Group:

	1968		1975		1978	
	IMP**	EXP**	IMP***	EXP***	IMP**	EXP**
Bolivia*	283	187	176	195	220	270
Colombia	180	172	163	149	206	303
Chile	142	202	-	-	-	-
Ecuador*	266	193	184	244	227	312
Peru	299	177	175	183	205	189
Venezuela*	630	203	188	532	248	631

*Oil Exporting Countries
**Reference year 1968 = 100
***Reference year 1975 = 100

Source: Junta, Estadísticas de Comercio Exterior de los países del Grupo Andino 1969-1979, Jun/di 499, September 9, 1980, pp. 6-7.

16. Peru devalued its currency in 1975, for the first time since 1968.

17. If Venezuela is included, the annual growth rate since 1967 is 29.0%.

18. See Chapter 6 on the CET. 1968 tariffs varied on average by 50% in Bolivia and up to 150% in Chile.

19. The existence of extensive contraband between Colombia and Ecuador, Colombia and Peru, Peru and Bolivia, and Colombia and Venezuela proves that there is a potential for great amounts of trade, given that illicit traffic has been continued under very tight restrictions. In Bogotá Ecuadorian woolens and sweets can be found openly and Colombian pharmaceuticals are sold openly in the Quito City Market. See C. Díaz-Alejandro, "The Andean Common Market: Gestation and Outlook", Yale University, Economic Growth Center, Discussion Paper No. 85, May 1970.

20. From the SIDP in light engineering only.

21. Fedesarrollo, "El Comercio Exterior de Colombia en el Marco del Acuerdo de Cartagena, 1969-1976," mimeo., Bogotá, May 1978, p. 30.

22. Junta, Evaluación de las Empresas Exportadoras de los Paises Miembros al Grupo Andino, Jun/di 297, March 22, 1978, pp. 40-41.

23. Of those 110 companies, 84 said they had received permanent fiscal aid, 60 had credit preference, 12 took advantage of foreign exchange regulations, and 53 benefited by administrative provisions, Junta, Evaluación, p. 4.

24. See subsection ii, below.

25. A. Musalem, "Las Exportaciones Colombianas, 1959-69," mimeo., Bogotá, 1970, pp. 16-17; and J. Sheahan and S. Clark, "La Respuesta de las Exportaciones Colombianas a las Variaciones en las Tasa Efectiva de Cambio," Fedesarrollo, Bogotá, 1970.

26. Given an effective protection of 130% for industrial sales in Colombia, there would be negative effective protection for sales outside the country (-48%). By applying the Plan Vallejo, this level can be raised to +39% of effective protection (unpublished calculation made by the Departamento Nacional de Planeacion de Colombia, used by Díaz-Alejandro in, "Las Exportaciones de Mercacias Colombianas," Trimestre Económico, Vol. XLIII, No. 171, 1976, p. 720.

27. For example, Peru set up two types of forced financing of imports to be borne by the seller. For capital goods, 80 percent of the price is payable between 2 and 5 years. For other goods, the total value is due within 180 days.

28. The Peruvian national register of manufactures prohibits imports of goods when the same national products are registered. Rules on state purchases also favor national products and consider sub-regional goods to come from third parties.

29. Exports are marginal to production. Only in Colombia did exports rise to significant levels. For example, in 1974, an extraordinary year for exports of Colombian textiles, they represented 10% of production. But even then, their market is not in the GRAN. See Coyuntura Económica, March 1975.

30. Members of the Asociación Nacional de Colombia blame the loss of dynamism of sales in 1975 on the ending of drawbacks for exports to the GRAN.

31. Colombia reduced nominal tariffs for any capital goods to 5%, hoping to stimulate investment. Such a low tariff for outside countries makes the purchase of capital goods produced by member countries impossible.

32. In his study on trade policies and economic development in Colombia, Díaz-Alejandro concludes that a new breed of industrial entrepreneur, the exporter, has still not been created. On the contrary, those who export are taking advantage of both export promotion and import substitution policies, selling marginal quantities under the provisions of the various schemes. See Díaz-Alejandro, Trimestre Economico, p. 720; and idem, "Efecto de las Exportaciones no Tradicionales en la Distribución del Ingreso," Trimestre Economico, Vol. LLIV (2), No. 174, p. 425.

33. In 1975, a record year for manufactured exports, intraregional trade of manufactures amounted to 24% of the total.

34. Within a given industrial sector, those firms considered large tend to use less labor and more capital goods, or less raw materials, per unit of output, and/or more imported inputs.

35. In Colombia, those sectors where exports represent more than 10% of total output have their markets outside the GRAN and only export limited amounts to the GRAN, and that without the benefits of tariff reductions. This is the case with Colombian textiles. Products such as batteries and hydraulic valves, which have their principal market within the group (i.e., the group receives more than 25% of the total exported of the good), represent very little in terms of total production. By contrast, Mexico has had a systematic export promotion policy since 1961, and manufactured export grew at an annual rate of 23% during 1970-74. Taking manufacturing industry as a whole, exports represented 9.9% of output in 1974. Thanks to special promotion policies, in sectors such as chemicals or cars the figure was over 30%. In nondurable consumer goods it was 4.8%. See CEPAL, "La Exportación de

Manufacturas en México y la Política de Promoción," CEPAL/ MEX/76/10/revl Dic 1976, pp. 7-13.

36. Many arguments about the possibilities of taking advantage of economies of scale are put forward, including those by Balassa, Economic Integration, p. 103; P. Streeten, Economic Integration: Aspects and Problems, Leyden, A.W. Sybhoff, 1961, p. 128; and T. Scitovsky, Economic Theory and Western European Integration (London: Allen and Unwin, 1958), pp. 110-130. All of these writers accept the importance of these economies, but, while accepting that there are limits to these economies in Europe, they think they are of greater relevance in underdeveloped groups of countries.

37. R. Allen, Economic Journal, LXIX, 3954; and H. Johnson, "The Gains from Freer Trade," Manchester School of Economic and Social Studies, September 1958, pp. 247-255. Hazlewood found for the EACM countries a small improvement in the use of industrial capacity; see Hazlewood, Economic Integration. In the Central American Common Market the Rosenthal Report found a decrease rather than an increase in the use of install- ed capacity; see G. Rosenthal, La Integración Centroamericana en la Década de los Setentas (Buenos Aires: Bid-INTAL, 1973), Vol. 1, Appendix 3.

38. H. Johnson, "Gains."

39. See our Chapter 7, section 1, for discussion on economies of scale of new investments in the case of the Andean group.

40. Allen takes up the point of view that few results can be expected from the opening of trade on the use of economies of scale in underdeveloped groups. The experiences of the GRAN tend to confirm his skepticism, especially with reference to the intensification of competition among countries with different levels of development. See R. Allen, "Integration in Less Developed Areas," Kyklos, 1967, pp. 327-329.

41. Scitovsky, Economic Theory, p. 115, thinks that econ- omies of scale in new investments are of more importance because of their relationships with specialization in the countries.

42. Colombia has been chosen because of the availability of detailed information on the use of industrial capacity. We prefer to study the impact of total manufactured exports, rather than those sent to GRAN countries, which only repre- sent 20% of total manufactured exports and are very diverse, thus making a satisfactory study at sector levels very diffi- cult.

43. These sectors are:

31	Food, drinks, and tobacco	35	Chemicals, petroleum by-products, and plastics
32	Textiles, clothing, and leather goods	36	Nonmetallic minerals
33	Timber and furniture	37	Basic metals
34	Paper and printed material	38	Machinery and transport equipment
		39	Others

44. Recent figures on utilized capacity indicate that Ecuador achieved a level of 74.2% and 69.9% in 1975 and 1976, respectively. The figure for Chile was 69.1% in 1976. See Coyuntura Andina, No. 1, Bogota, 1976, pp. 88-136.

45. F. Thourmi, "La Utilización de la Capacidad Instalada en Colombia," Bogotá, Fedesarrollo, 1974.

46. G. Rosenthal, La Integración Centroamericana, Appendix 3, Table 9. Hazlewood concludes for the EACM that the growth of excess capacity has not been avoided. See Hazlewood, Economic Integration, p. 122.

47. Linder, An Essay on Trade and Transformation (New York: Wiley, 1961).

48. C. Díaz-Alejandro says that, with Colombia's trade policies, lower exports did not change the employment situation. See Diaz-Alejandro, Colombian Foreign Trade Policies and Development (New Haven: Yale U.P., 1976), pp. 239-246.

49. Lizano arrives at the same conclusion in his analysis of the effects of increased trade upon manufactures in the CACM. See Lizano, "A Second Thought," p. 289 and Rosenthal, La Integración Centroamericana, Appendix 6, sections II and III.

50. C. Díaz-Alejandro, "El Efecto de las Exportaciones no Tradicionales en la Distribución del Ingreso," Trimestre Económico, Vol. XLIV (2), No. 174, 1976, p. 411.

51. One finds that only oil production uses more technology than sectors producing final consumption goods, food, tobacco, and drinks. Capital goods production is less capital-intensive. V.E. Tokman, "Distribución del Ingreso, Technología y Empleo un Análisis del Sector Industrial del Ecuador, Perú y Venezuela," Trimestre Económico, Vol. XLI (4), No. 164, 1974, pp. 750-751.

52. M. Urrutia and A. Berry, La Distribución del Ingreso en Colombia (Bogota: La Carreta, 1975).

53. Studies on Chile and Peru show that the income situation has not improved over the last 20 years. See Estudios de Extrema Pobreza en Chile. (Chile: U. Catolica, 1975); and R.

Webb: Distribución de Ingreso en Perú, Lecturas No. 7, FCE, 1974. Figueroa has done a detailed study for the Junta on the incomes pyramids for the Andean countries. He concludes that at best the situation has remained stationary from the 1960s to the present. See A. Figueroa, Visión de las Piramides Sociales: Distribución del Ingreso en America Latina, Junta, J/PR/45, April 17, 1974.

54. W. Corden, The Theory of Protection (Oxford: Oxford U.P., 1971), pp. 2-18.

55. Total subregional trade in 1975 was 1.4% of GDP; manufactured exports were 0.3% of GDP.

56. Junta, Evaluación de las Empresas Exportadores de los Paises Miembros al Grupo Andino, Jun/di, 297, March 1978.

57. DANE, Boletín Mensual de Estadistica, No. 307, pp. 69-23.

58.   i)   Banco de la República, Encuesta a 260 Empresas Extranjeras, January 1974.
      ii)   Las Exportaciones Manufacturadas Colombianas, Fedesarrollo, Coyuntura Económica, 1976.

      iii) "Las Exportaciones Manufacturadas al GRAN," 1969-1976, mimeo, Fedesarrollo, 1978.

      iv)   "Las Inversiones Extranjeras en la Industria Colombiana", DANE, Boletín, No. 302, Bogota, 1976.

59. G. Misas, "Estudio de la Concentración Industrial en Colombia", DANE, Boletín, No. 266.

60. Junta, Evaluación de las Empresas Exportadoras de los paises Miembros al Grupo Andino, Jun/di, 297, March 1978, pp. 37-38. An inquiry made in 1975 by the Instituto Mexicano de Comercio Exterior found in a survey of 599 firms that 14 (2.3% of the total) were responsible for 42% of the exports of the group, with an average value per firm of 315 mil. pesos. At the other extreme they found that 88% of the firms were responsible for 27% of total exports, at an average value per firm of 3 mil. pesos.

61. Banco de la República, Revista Mensual, January 1974; and DANE, Boletín Mensual, Nos. 302-303. The detailed studies of foreign participation in Colombia based on the experience of 260 firms differ in their conclusions from the Junta's document cited above (note 60). The latter gives companies with foreign capital a secondary role in exports. In the Junta's study, the share of foreign companies in exports is less than their share of production. The study finds that 73% of Colombian exporting companies have 75-100% national capital.

This conclusion is significantly different from the studies cited above, which can in part be explained by the fact that the Junta studied only 20 enterprises, while the other works used a survey of over 260 firms.

62. For example in the following sectors, foreign participation was:

		Share of Production	Export Share
369	Nonmetallic minerals	56.6	96.7
355	Rubber goods	82.0	95.1
351	Industrial Chemicals	79.5	86.1
381	Metal goods, except machines	42.7	82.3
341	Paper and related goods	79.3	61.0
383	Machinery and electrical equipment	67.2	87.7

For more details see DANE, Boletín Mensual, No. 266, p. 116. The Mexican experience corroborates the suggestion that it is the firms linked to foreign capital who have the best opportunities of expanding exports. In 1974 it is estimated that 55% of Mexican manufacturing exports emanated from transnational enterprises. In the metal mecánico sector this figure was 78%, 85% in transport equipment, and 91% in chemicals. See CEPAL, La Exportacion de Manufacturas en México, pp. 80-82.

63. Fedesarrollo, Estudio de la demanda de factores de las exportaciones al GRAN, 1978.

64. See Junta, Indicadores Económicos, 1976, Lima, 1977.

65. See Junta Indicadores Socio-Económicos 1980. Jun/di 777/Rev. 3, April 21, de 1981.

66. See Banco de la Republica, Cuentas Nacionales 1970-1975. 1975 was a year of low investment because of the world recession and balance of payments difficulties. The share of gross domestic fixed investment in GDP fell in real terms, from 20.3% in 1970 to 18.1% in 1975.

67. I would like to thank A. Villate for the supply of a great part of the information utilized in this section and for long discussions held in 1976 which contributed to make the conclusions clearer.

68. These are the divisions used for studies of income elasticity of demand, grouping together the standard international industrial classification industrial branches:

i) Traditional industries:

20 Foodstuffs	25 Wood-using industries
21 Beverages	26 Wooden furniture
22 Tobacco	28 Printing
23 Textiles	29 Leather and related
24 Footwear	industries

39 Various

ii) Intermediate industries:

27 Paper and related	31 Chemical products
products	32 Petrol derivatives
30 Rubber goods	33 Nonmetallic minerals

34 Basic metals

iii) Mechanical industries:

35 Metal products,	37 Electrical machinery
except machinery	38 Transport equipment and
36 Nonelectrical	machinery
machinery	

69. See C. Díaz-Alejandro, Colombian Foreign Trade Policies (New Haven: Yale U.P., 1976), chap. 1.

70. See Chapter 3, section 3 on SIDPs, in which an almost total absence of investments in the approved SIDPs was detected.

71. The production of some of these goods was allocated exclusively to Bolivia and Ecuador. By 1975, when interviews of the author with representatives of the industrial private sector took place, no investment had taken place in either country. Worries about the lack of interest in making use of these advantages were expressed in the Junta's analysis in the Junta's evaluation for 1976, Junta, op. cit., Indicadores Económicos, 1977.

72. These previous observations can be found in the 4th annual evaluations elaborated and published by the Junta between 1976 and 1979 and are also evident in more recent documents: Junta, Consideraciones sobre la Programación Industrial en el Grupo Andino dt. 3, July 7, 1981; and Junta, Elementos de un Plan de Acción destinado a reactivar el Proceso de Integración Económica, Jun/dt 172, July 10, 1981.

73. A.O. Hirschman, "Devaluation and the Trade Balance: A Note," Review of Economics and Statistics, No. 31, 1949, pp. 50–53.

74. C. Díaz-Alejandro, "A Note on the Impact of Devaluation and its Redistributive Effect," Journal of Political Economy, No. 71, 1963, pp. 577–580.

75. For an analysis of the contractionary effects of devaluation in semi-industrialized countries, on output and

employment via redistribution of income in favor of profits, see P. Krugman and L. Taylor, "Contractionary Effects of Devaluation," Journal of International Economics, No. 3, August 1978, pp. 445-456. Similar conclusions for a number of countries are suggested by A. Krueger, Foreign Trade Regimes and Economic Development, National Bureau of Economic Research, 1978.

76. Prebisch has produced a great amount of evidence in favor of protection to industry in underdeveloped countries. Streeten has done the same for Europe. See R. Prebisch, The Economic Development of Latin America and its Principal Problems, UN, 1950; and, "Commercial Policy in Underdeveloped Countries," AER Papers and Proceedings, May 1969. Also P. Streeten, Economic Integration: Aspects and Problems, (Leyden: Sytthof, 1969), pp. 53-67. On the concentration effects in the EEC and on problems derived out of it, see D. Seers and C. Vaitsos, Integration and Unequal Development, The Experience of the EEC (London: Macmillan & Co., 1981).

77. Articles 91 and 92 and Section III of the Agreement give the details of advantages granted to Bolivia and Ecuador within the commerical programme.

78. For example, in groups 1 to 3 we find fruit and vegetable products, oxides, and oils; in 4 to 6, alcohol and its derivatives, simple manufactures, and yarn; and in 7 to 9, woven goods, complex glass products, consumer durables, and capital goods.

79. In 1976, Colombia exported to the subregion a total of 2,175 items, for an amount of US$175 million, and to Venezuela only exported 1,684 different products.

CHAPTER 4

1. A detailed analysis of this aspect of economic integration can be found in B. Balassa, "El Segundo Decenio de la Integración y el Desarrollo Económico en América Latina," in Bid-INTAL, La Integración Latinoamericana en Una Etapa de Decisiones, Buenos Aires, 1970, pp. 21-23.

2. See MacClelland and Grunwald, "Industrialización e Integración Económica en América Latina," ECIEL, Rio de Janeiro, 1976; and W.R. Cline, Benefits and Costs of Economic Integration in Central America (Washington, D.C.: The Brookings Institute, 1975).

3. See B. Balassa, "El Segundo Decenio," p. 26; Junta, "Bases," chap. 1, pp. 133-135; E. Lyzano "A Second Thought on the CACM," JCMS, Vol. 13, No. 4, 1975.

4. See Chapter 1, section 2C; Stages One to Four below; and Notes, Chap. 1, note 51.

5. Haas was able to substantiate the functioning of a "spill-over effect" on the basis of his study of the role of political and economic links in the ECSC since the Schumann Plan (1950), which proposed the Coal and Steel Community and the establishment of Euratom and the EEC (E.G. Haas, The Uniting of Europe [Stanford: Stanford University Press, 1958]). An analyst such as Haas would argue that such political ideals as peace and union in Europe and the avoidance of confrontation with the USSR and the East European Bloc would have to be achieved through the deepening of economic relations to the point where political integration is reached. Haas argues that, given certain conditions, "the progression from a politically inspired common market to an economic union, and finally to a political union among states is automatic." See Haas, "The Uniting of Europe and the Uniting of Latin America," JCMS, Vol. 5, 1967, p. 327. It is possible to accept Haas's view if one bears in mind that European cooperation derived from expressed political ideals, but proceeded and took the form it did because there were real economic advantages to be gained.

6. The Declaration of Bogota stressed the need to perfect LAFTA by converting it into a customs union and harmonizing national economic policies. At the same time the declaration did have utopian elements, proclaiming the formation of a "Latin American Economic Community" as essential in order to achieve the substantial reforms "in institutional, economic and social structures in order to satisfy the demands of our peoples." See "Declaracion de Bogota," in Junta-INTAL, His-toria Documental, pp. 246-250, esp. p. 246. A detailed scheme for a Latin American Economic Community is not ad-vanced, but it appears from this and other documents that it was to feature the delegation to a supranational body a number of macropolitical policy areas. A discussion of schemes of this kind can be found in J. Binder, "Problems of European Inte-gration," in G.R. Denton, ed., Economic Integration in Europe (London: World University Press, 1971), pp. 144-145.

7. See Junta, Documento de Evaluación 1969-75, Jun/di 195, Lima, 1976, pp. 15-16. References to the same process, see Junta, Evaluación del Proceso 1977, Jun/di 295, March, 1978.

8. J. Pinder suggests that "the motives for joining economic groupings such as free trade areas, Customs Unions or eco-nomic Unions usually have more to do with political orientation than with calculations of economic gains. This was certainly the case with the European Communities; and it was also the case with the British application to join the communities, announced in May 1967, when the forecasts about net gains had been very discouraging." See Pinder, "Problems of Euro-pean Integration," p. 154.

9. Thus opponents of the EEC can be found on the left of the Labour Party and on the right of the Conservative Party, as well as on the left in Scandinavia and on the right in the Iberian Peninsula. The Communist Parties have not taken a united line, for while the French party has wavered regarding France, it is at odds with the Spanish party over the entry of Spain.

10. The volume of intra-subregional trade in 1979 represented only 6.4% of total imports and 4.7% of total exports of the member countries. A further reflection of the marginal nature of the GRAN is that it does not play any role in national development plans, which ignore the question of integration. See Junta, Documento, Jun/di 195, Annex IV, pp. 3-5. Only by one in all the evaluation studies this same complaint appears. These themes are taken up in greater detail in Chapter 3.

11. The second meeting of the Ministers of Foreign Affairs of the member countries agreed that "an element of profound importance in our integration process is the respect for ideological diversity which is implied by the collaboration on which we are engaged, which observes fully the principles of non-intervention and the right of all peoples to self-determination." See "Acta de la Segunda Reunion de Ministros de Relaciones, marzo 13, 1971," in Junta-INTAL, Historia Documental, p. 419; this statement contrasts with LAFTA resolutions 36 and 37 of September 1962, which described as a condition required for LAFTA membership "compatibility" of the candidate with the "spirit" laid down in the Montevideo Treaty. In consequence, Cuba's application for membership was rejected. LAFTA, Resoluciones de la Conferencia de los III, IV períodos de Sesiones, Montevideo, 1963.

12. Junta, Elementos de un plan de acción destinado a reactivar el proceso de Integración Economica Subregional, Jun/ dt 172, July 10, 1981.

13. The opponents of entry argued that Bolivia's traditional trading partners were countries outside the group, and that there was no reason for this to change. See E. Camacho, La Integración Andina (Fundamentos Políticos y Perspectivas), La Paz, 1974, pp. 20-24.

14. Chile's interest in the GRAN was "the way to prevent Bolivia's development by keeping her land-locked." J. Escobari, "La integración y la diplomacia Chilena en la cuestion portuaria," in Bolivia y los Problemas de la Integración Andina (La Paz, Universidad de San Andres, 1970), p. 176.

15. See Chapter 7; and Junta, Documento de Evaluacion 1976-77, Jun/di 295, Lima, March 1978, pp. 1-11. y Elementos de un plan de acción destinado a reactivar el proceso, Jun/dt 172, July 10, 1981, pp. 5.

16. The author derived from interviews with representatives of the industrial sector in 1975 a clear impression of their skepticism regarding benefits from Bolivia from the GRAN.

17. See Junta, Documento de Evaluación 1969-75, Annex 1, p. 5. Chile took 4 months to implement the first stage of the tariff reduction program, and 4 and 15 months, respectively, to implement the second and third stages. It also took 12 months to implement the first step toward a minimum common external tariff; Peru delayed 37 months before adopting the same measure.

18. FEDECAMARAS believed that Leoni pressed for entry to LAFTA for fear of being left in isolation from regional groups. See FEDECAMARAS frente a la Decisión del Gobierno Nacional de Adherir al Tratado de Montevideo, Caracas, 1965.

19. Presumably Chile left the GRAN in order to disassociate itself from any kind of economic nationalism, completely breaking away from Popular Unity policies.

20. Resolution 11 of 1976, concerned with the "Colombianisation" of industry, is discussed in further detail in Chapter 5. As regards the banking sector, Pastrana's government had excepted it from the provisions of Decision 24 through Decree 2719 of 1973; despite Lopez's public statements that foreign capital should not be discriminated against, his government reversed Decree 2719 in 1975 by issuing Decree 795, which obliged foreign banks to convert themselves into national banks by reaching a position in which 80% of capital was nationally owned.

21. Interestingly, Chile's withdrawal from the GRAN coincided with approaches from the military rulers of Argentina sufficiently persistent to provoke press reports that an application for entry was imminent; see Comercio Exterior, Vol. 28, No. 5, 1978, p. 610. As for Colombia's view of the direction in which the GRAN was heading, an internal memorandom from the adviser to the Council for the Conduct of foreign Trade to the Minister of Economic Development gave the following blunt appraisal:

> In synthesis, a summary of the position is that four countries (Bolivia, Ecuador, Peru, and Venezuela) do not appear willing to make revisions of substance to the original scheme of import substitution, in which industrialisation is conceived as a goal, and not as an instrument of economic policy. In the case of Colombia, the adoption of the strategy proposed by the block of four would imply fundamental revisions in our recent development plan, and a return to the scheme of indefinite protection for the modern sector of the economy. This could be the principal

cost of participation in the process of Andean integration.... We must find a strategy for which the benefits are greater than the costs, or assume the political cost of abandoning the Pact.

The strategy suggested was to link the Sectoral Programmes for Industrial Development and Common External Tariff negotiations to each other and to accelerate the tariff reduction program, rather than to withdraw altogether. See Memorando del Asesor del Consejo Directivo de Comercio Exterior, Bogota, December 16, 1975.

22. In this context, narrow nationalism as distinguished from the concept used on pp. 157, refers to the policies that seek national advantages over neighboring countries rather than those that aspire to political union vis-à-vis the industrialized countries.

23. "One of the most important effects will be precisely that which is produced in the manufacturing sectors of the member countries, for it is there that we shall see tangible results in the form of factories, products, employment and new currents of trade within our countries." See exposition of Jorge Valencia V., coordinator of the Mixed Commission to the Extraordinary Session of the Permanent Executive Committee of LAFTA, July 4, 1969.

24. In Chapter 3 we showed the marginal participation of intraregional market in the GDP, and found that the effects of trade on growth were negligible.

25. The fact that a number of Decisions have been signed which involve a degree of ceding of sovereignty (such as numbers 46, 49, and 84, and those concerning technology policy and industrial property) is no guide to the real willingness of member countries to cede sovereignty. In the 21st Extraordinary Meeting of the Commission, the Junta presented the Documentary Report for Restricted Circulation Only from the Junta to the Commission on Compliance with the Treaty and the Decisions (COM/xxi/di 3/rev 1) of November 25, 1976, in which evidence was given of a general failure to comply with agreements, and immediate measures to resolve the problem were requested. Nevertheless, the Documento de Evaluación 1977 reports that noncompliance continues and predicts negative consequences in the future. In that Document, the Junta declared that some decisions had been premature, as there was neither the will nor the political conditions for them to be executed. See Junta, Documento de Evaluación 1977, Jun/di March 1978, pp. I 5-6, I 16, and II 1-5. Apreciaciones sobre la situación actual del Proceso de Integración Económica y del Acuerdo de Cartagena, Lima, dt 1, July 7, 1981.

26. Similarly contradictions have emerged within the CMEA. Countries such as Rumania have openly opposed the creation of supranational planning organizations, arguing that to cede sovereignty on the point is to destroy the very essence of the socialist state. Here, as elsewhere in integration schemes among less developed countries, the state has grown in stature rather than declined, and its saliency has increased as industrialization has remained a major goal. We analyze the CMEA in greater detail in Chapters 6, 7, and 8.

27. Salgado, El Grupo Andino, BID-INTAL, 1970, p. 31.

28. Acuerdo, Article No. 25.

29. Acuerdo, Article No. 26.

30. See letter from Frei to Prebisch in J.A. Mayobre et al., Hacia la Integración Acelerada de América Latina, CEPAL, Santiago, 1965. R.C. Lleras, Speeches in Santiago, June 22, 1967, in Lima June 27, 1967, and in Quito June 30, 1967, in El Tiempo, Bogota, June 23, June 28, and July 1, 1967; Declaración de Bogotá, August 16, 1966 and Declaración de las Presidentes de América.

31. "Politization" is used in this context to signify agreements that involve a loss of sovereignty, as such agreements could only be made at a political level. See Chapter 1, section 2C for a definition of "politization" in the neo-functionalist framework.

32. See M. Weber, Económia y Sociedad (2 Vol.), F.C.E., Mexico 1944, Vol. 1, p. 639ff.

33. The political scientist F. Cepeda, political advisor to the Colombian president Lopez Michelson, refers to the founders of the GRAN as the "select club of friends." In his view, the Presidents of Chile, Colombia, and Venezuela carried on the process at a purely personal level, without seeking the support of their parties, partly because they were unsure that they would receive it, and partly because they sought international prestige for its internal advantages. Interview by the author, May 1975. In the same way, M. Urrutia analyzes the active role played by the liberal Minister of Economic Development, J. Valencia, in pushing forward the D. 24 and the SIDP. M. Urrutia "Diversidad Ideológica e Integración Andina," Coyuntura Económica. Vol. X, No. 1, 1980.

34. We don't find extremely convincing the hypothesis discussed by Urrutia about Pastrana's position towards integration. First, his government was far less enthusiastic than Llera's; second, a great amount of imagination is required to define Pastrana as "anti-imperialist"; third, the anti-imperialist speech of Anapo did not evolve into action, nor even after the 1970 elections, when they had an important share in the legis-

lative and administrative bodies, which failed to prevent the Pastrana's accelerated foreign debt policy in the eurodollar market. M. Urrutia, "Diversidad Ideológica e Integracion Andina," Coyuntura Económica, Vol X, No. 2. Julio 1980, pp. 180-203.

35. Pastrana was succeeded in 1974 by A. Lopez Michelsen, a member of the Liberal Party.

36. When interviewed, Cepeda explained Lopez's change of position with respect to the GRAN in terms of rivalry among the leaders of the Liberal Party. Lopez himself, as Foreign Affairs Minister under Lleras, had been an enthusiastic supporter of Andean integration.

37. R.E. Bernales, "Perú, actores y agentes políticos internos del proceso de integración andina," in Variables políticas de la integración andina, Nueva Universidad Catolica de Chile, 1974, pp. 201-231; UNDAT, Perú, su situación económica y social y sus perspectivas immediatas, mimeo., Lima, 1976, p. 52; speech by Presidente Velasco, "Mensaje a la Nación," La Voz de la Nación, in Colección documentos revolucionarios, Publicaciones SINAMOS, Lima, 1972.

38. See C. Vaitsos, Crisis en la co-operación económica regional: la integración entre paises subdesarrollados, Instituto Latino Americano de Estudios Transnacionales, Mexico, 1978, p. 27.

39. See R.D. Bond, "Business Associations and Interest Politics in Venezuela: The FEDECAMARAS and the Determination of National Economic Policies," (Ph.D. thesis, Vanderbilt University, May 1975), p. 268. This author presents a well-documented account of the negotiations and the opposition of FEDECAMARAS to integration.

40. J. Valencia J., the Colombian representative and coordinator of the Mixed Commission, states emphatically that the industrial sector "is for us the heart or the motor that will drive us to accelerated development." He later defines it as the dynamo of development, for this reason and because "in it in fact are the immediate and most important prospects for progress and development." See Junta, INTAL, Historia Documental, pp. 73-74.

41. On this aspect of the program, see Chapters 6 and 8.

42. In December 1971 the Treaty was declared unconstitutional in Colombia. The Liberal members of Congress were the ones who strove hardest to limit the plenipotentiary powers of the representative to the Commission, and insisted on ratification by Congress of decisions affecting the institutional order. See Law 8 of 1973, which ratified the treaty while limiting the powers of the executive with regard to it.

43. The elements that make up the "integrative potential" according to the neo-functionalist school are:

A. Structural conditions: Symmetry of units
The capacity of member states to adapt and respond
Pluralism (Modern Associational Groups)
Elite Value Complementarity

B. Perceptual conditions: Perceived equity of the distribution of benefits
Perceptual external cogency
Low visible costs

44. See Nye, "Comparing Common Markets," International Organization, Vol. 27, 1970, p. 821.

45. There was little will to implement the plans made, and national planners were out of touch with their own budget offices, ministers, and private sectors. This led them to seek a solution by internationalizing the problem and the agreements, by planning for integration. A.O. Hirschmann, Ideologies of Development in Latin America (New York: 1961), p. 15.

46. See the interview of Christopher Mitchell with R. Almedia, First Secretary of LAFTA, in C. Mitchell, "The Role of Technocrats in Latin American Integration," Inter-American Economic Affairs, Vol. 21, No. 2, in which the latter states that "the formation of LAFTA was not a decision of the governments but a conspiracy of some governments' officers - the governments would tell these officers 'we will agree to what you think advisable, but you'd be wise not to compromise too much.'"

47. In many countries, the technical teams that worked on the constitution and negotiation of the Treaty of Cartagena were made up of the same men who had negotiated the Treaty of Montevideo, or trained by ECLA.

48. "The political costs of such assistance, however, could be high. The planners' proposals, especially those advocating tax reform and land reform or the programme of organising bureaucracies on a merit system threatened an important area of presidential patronage and source of support." The presidents considered the cost to be too high and isolated the planners. See David Browing, "The Rise and Fall of the Central American Common Market," Journal of Latin American Studies, May 1974, pp. 161-8.

49. The change of government in Colombia in 1970 did not lead to the replacement of the plenipotentiary representation before the Commission (the Director of INCOMEX) or of the team of experts charged with the related studies. Even so,

both had to accept the new policies of the President and the Ministry of Economic Development, which modified the Colombian position substantially.

50. S. Dell, "Regional Integration and the Industrialisation of Less Developed Countries," Development Digest, Vol. 3, No. 3, October 1965, p. 45; and Nye, "Patterns and Catalysts in Regional Integration," International Organisation, Vol. 19, pp. 878–884.

51. The problem is clearly illustrated in the Colombian document on sectoral programming and the distribution of benefits. See the discussion here in Chapter 3, part B.

52. The term is used in the sense defined earlier.

53. For example, within the first year of the Treaty, the MCET was to be approved, after two years, the common foreign capital policy, and after six years all the SIDPs. For more details, see Chapter 1.

54. See Orantes, "Regional Integration" p. 84, and Nye, "Central American Regional Integration," International Conciliation, No. 562, March 1967.

55. See E. Lyzano, "Second Thoughts on the CACM," JCMS, Vol. 13, 1975, p. 289.

56. The only sectors lending support in Argentina, Uruguay, and Paraguay were the wine producers. The most recalcitrant was the Brazilian textile sector. See Mikesell, "The Movement Toward Regional Trading Groups," in Hirschmann, Latin American Issues: Essays and Comments (New York: Twentieth Century Fund, 1961), pp. 121-151.

57. Studies have been made of the attitude of Brazilian and Argentinian industrialists to integration. See Ianni, "La crisis de LAFTA y las corporaciones transnacionales," Comercio Exterior, Mexico, 1971, pp. 1119-1126; on Argentina, see Oneto Gaona's article in La Prensa, September 9, 1966 (quoted in Vaitsos, Crisis, p. 17); and Cardoso and Ianni, Las Ideologías de la Burguesia Industrial, Siglo XXI, Mexico, 1970.

58. Interviews held in 1975 when the author was engaged in evaluating the Andean integration program as a member of the U.N. Advisory team to the Junta. See 71-76 below.

59. In a meeting held in Chile in December 1974, representatives of Trade Chambers of the member countries opposed the Andean Group policies on foreign capital and the SIDPs; see Boletín de la Integración, No. 109, January 1975, p. 109.

60. See the following articles: "El sector privado apoya la integracion de comunidades Latino-Americanas," El Tiempo, January 6, 1968, p. 2; "ANDI define su posicion ante la integracion andina," El Tiempo, March 26, 1968, pp. 1, 21,

which can be considered as very cautious expression of support mainly for the trade program. As head of the office responsible for carrying out the studies of SIDP in Colombia (1971-1972), I had contacted many different industrial associations, and no major differences in attitudes towards the Andean Group were detected. About the negative attitude of Colombian Industrialists, see also Comercio Exterior, Vol. 26, No. 5, April 1976, p. 594.

61. See El Tiempo, November 11, 1970, p. 7 (the Banks criti-
                                    cize D24)
     "   14,   "   p. 6 (the Banks oppose
                                    the statute)
     "   17,   " pp. 1-7
     "   29,   "   p. 21 (increasing opposi-
                                    tion)
          December 19, 1971, pp. 1-8
     "   18, 1975, p. 14A (companies back
                                    the government)

The Colombian Chamber of Trade made public its opposition to D24 in October 1975. See Boletín de la Integración, No. 108, November-December 1975.

62. See El Tiempo, February 7, 1973, pp. 1-8A (ANDI rejects
                                         the admission
                                         of Venezuela)
          September 8, 1973, pp. 8-9A (ANDI asks
                                         for equality).

63. See El Tiempo, July 13, 1972, pp. 13-2A (protest by
                                         petrochemicals)
          May 12, 1973, pp. 11-13 (light engineer-
                                         ing - metalme-
                                         canica - + GRAN)
          June 2, 1975, p. 10D (Fedemetal not happy
                                         with planning).

64. From interviews with union representatives and from personal experience during the two years from 1970 to 1972, when the author was engaged in studying sectoral planning as a member of the staff of INCOMEX.

65. Vaitsos quotes G. Fernandes and accepts his interpretation; see Vaitsos, Crisis, p. 21. Both authors assume that the experts and political leaders represent the class interests of the industrial group. On Colombian and Chilean protectionism in the GRAN, see Comercio Exterior, Vol. 26, No. 2, February 1976, pp. 345-47.

66. Gomez B. Hernando: "Los Grupos Industriales y el Desarrollo Colombiano. Conjecturas e Interpretaciones," in
Conjuntura Económica, VI, 4, 1976, p. 110. The author adds
that Colombian development has placed many diverse actors on
the political scene, so that "in the medium and long term the
representation of the industrial groups has proved to be
comparatively small" (p. 114). Furthermore, the author
believes the managerial class to be scattered, conservative,
and indecisive.

67. G. Madeiros, "El sector privado y la integracion subregional Andina," in Universidad de San Andres, Bolivia y los
problemas, pp. 103-105.

68. Based on interviews conducted by the author in 1975 with
representatives of the private sector, and on the 1975, 1976,
and 1977 Evaluacion de la Junta reports.

69. See El Tiempo, July 10, 1968, p. 15, Ecuador puts forward its objections to the Andean Group; El Tiempo, April 29,
1969, Ecuador states conditions of entry; El Tiempo, October
17, 1970, in Bolivia the private sector asks to withdraw from
GRAN. Although Ecuador had benefited more than Bolivia
from regional exports, on many occasions the private sector
criticized the lack of adequate special guarantees. See Junta,
Evaluacion, 1968, March 1969.

70. See El Tiempo, June 11, 1968, p. 25, and El Tiempo,
August 2, 1968, p. 14. During the negotiations within the
Mixed Commission the Peruvian private sector supported the
opposition stance of FEDECAMARAS and adopted similar protectionist positions. The Peruvian industrialists received the
support of the fishmeal exporters and of elements of the
National Mining and Petroleum Societies. These groups felt
that integration would not be to their advantage. See Cale,
p. 17.

71. Vaitsos, Crisis, p. 29, quotes several statements made by
the president to the National Society of Peruvian Industry
(SNIP) in 1969. During her stay in Lima as a member of the
Advisory Group of the United Nations, the author did not find
within the private sector opinions favorable to the subregional
Andean model.

72. See Concenso de Lima, February 1973, for modifications to
the Agreement for the admission of Venezuela. For a chrono-
logical, well-documented review of FEDECAMARAS' opposition
to Latin American integration see Robert D. Bond, Business-
Associations and Political Interests in Venezuela: The Fedecamaras and the Determination of National Economic Policies
(Ph.D. Thesis, Vanderbilt University, 1975), chap. VII and
Conclusions.

73. Junta, Evaluación de las Empresas Exportadoras en los Paises Miembros del Grupo Andino, Jun/di 297, May 22, 1978.

74. See Special information from IPS, from July to December 1981.

75. Alicia Puyana, Alternativas de vinculación entre Panama y los Esquemas Latinoamericanos de Integración, BID-INTAL, Buenos Aires, 1982, pp. 178-180.

76. See Junta, Apreciaciones sobre la Situación Actual del Proceso de Integración Económica del Acuerdo de Cartagena, dt. July 7, 1981, Anotaciones sobre la Formación del Mercado Ampliado en el Grupo Andino, dt 2, July 7, 1981; Consideraciones sobre la Programación Industrial Conjunta en el Grupo Andino, dt 3, July, 1981, y Elementos de un Plan de Acción Destinado a Reactivar el Proceso de Integración Económica Subregional, Jun/dt 172, July 10, 1981.

77. See Chapter 3, section 2.

78. An evaluation of Colombian exporting experiences, for example, reveals that there are, strictly speaking, no exporting companies. The companies appear to have struck an ideal balance between an adequately protected internal market and an external market that absorbs fluctuating surpluses, sold if necessary at marginal costs. See C. Díaz-Alejandro, "Efecto de las Exportaciones no Tradicionales en la Distribución del Ingreso," Trimestre Económico No. 174, 1977, p. 425.

79. In 1971 and 1972 we found that Colombian industrialists were specially concerned with the possibility of subsidizing the industrialization of the Chilean and Peruvian regimes.

80. "We don't wish socialism to be introduced in Colombia through the integration programmes" was frequently heard in meetings of industrialists in Bogota. (Meetings and interviews with the author).

81. We discuss the effects of Venezuela's entry in Chapter 2, section 2.

82. From personal interviews of the author with leaders of Fedemetal (Federation of Managers of the Colombian Light Engineering - metalmecanica - Industry), a sector with good prospects in the Andean Group. It became clear that the admission of Venezuela changed Colombia's perspectives because Venezuelan production, in spite of high costs, is very modern and efficient. C. Lleras Restrepo, ex-president of Colombia and integrationist leader, suggested in an interview with the author (April 1978) that the admission of Venezuela altered the existing balance and introduced new elements (advanced technology and an abundance of resources) and suggested a revision of strategy, which was never carried out.

83. Nye suggests that economic integration is not solely the politics of cooperation, but also "the politics of status" between traditionally rival states: "what matters is how decision-makers perceive that they have gained or lost status or rank in relation to their neighbours. This is not always predictable from the hard data of economic changes." Nye, "Comparing Common Markets," International Organisation, No. 24, 1970, p. 819.

84. See El Tiempo, relevant statements by ANDI and Fedemetal made during CET negotiations, January to October 1976.

85. These are conclusions on the participation of the agrarian sector in the CACM according to Lyzano JCMS, Vol. 13, 1975. They coincide with Christopher Mitchell's remarks on LAFTA, in "The Role of Technocrats in Latin American Integration," Inter-American Economic Affairs, Vol. 21, No. 2, Summer 1967.

86. When the Treaty of Cartagena came into force, the projects for frontier integration which were in progress, financed by BID and World Bank, were allowed to lapse.

87. Miguel Wionczek has pointed out that presidential agreements in Latin America have not always been binding upon nationalized industries, let alone government or societies. See Wionczek, "Latin American Integration and US Economic Policies," in R. Greig, ed., International, Organization in the Western Hemisphere (Syracuse, New York: 1968).

88. See. N. Grundwald, M. Wionczek, and M. Carnoy, Latin American Economic Integration and US Policy (Washington, D.C.: Brookings Institute, 1972); F. Perroux, "Quién integra? En beneficio de Quienes se Realiza la Integración?" Revista de la Integración, No. 1 (Buenos Aires) November 1967, pp. 9-39. For the French position regarding African integration, see R.H. Green and K.G.V. Krishna, Economic Co-operation in Africa. Retrospect and Prospect (London: Oxford U.P., 1967), and Mytelka, "Foreign Aid and Regional Integration: The UDEC case," JCMS, Vol. XII.

89. Grundwald, Wionczek, Carnoy, Latin American Economic Integration, pp. 55-65.

90. P.C. Schmitter, "Autonomy or Dependence as Regional Integration Outcomes: Central America," Research Series No. 17, Institute of International Studies, University of California, Berkeley, 1972, p. 21.

91. United States - US Aid "A report on CACM and its Economic Integration Movement," 1966, quoted in Vaitsos, Crisis, p. 36.

92. I. Cohen, Regional Integration in Central America (Lexington, Mass.: 1972), pp. 49-50.

93. H. Brewster, "The Central American Programme for Integrated Industrial Development," Public and International Affairs, Spring 1966.

94. Vaitsos, Crisis, p. 41.

95. In 1960 North American investment in Central America was $350 million. Ten years later it had risen to nearly $900 million; see Vaitsos, Crisis, pp. 54-55.

96. For example, in 1960 total remittance payments by foreign firms were $14.1 million, and in 1971 $138.5 million, having increased at a rate of 23% per annum. Ibid., p. 56.

97. See Wionczek, "La reacción norteamericana ante el Tratado Común a los Capitales Extranjeros en el Grupo Andino," Comercio Exterior, Mexico, May 1971; and our Chapter 5 in which we discuss in more detail the external opposition to D24.

98. A more detailed discussion of the attitude of external actors to the GRAN is found in Chapter 5.

99. Ibid., p. 48. In his analysis, Vaitsos suggests differentiating between "integration" and "effective integration." The first may be achieved by liberalizing trade in the absence of policies governing foreign capital and industry. In this case, the CET would be higher than national average. "Effective integration," besides the liberalization of trade, requires some degree of policy harmonization, industrial rationalization and specialization, and a CET lower than previous national averages.

100. J.N. Behrman, The Role of International Companies in Latin American Integration, (Mass.: Lexington Books, 1972), p. 81.

101. Of 513 North American subsidiaries (1969), 362 had affiliated companies in at least one other member country and 258 in at least two. In Bolivia during the same year there were only four industrial companies financed by North American capital, all with affiliated companies in the rest of the countries. In Colombia 50% of the companies with IED had affiliates in two or more countries. Dow Chemicals and Exxon had five subsidiaries; Chrysler three; Squip, Pfizer, and Sydney Ross four subsidiaries. See Tironi, Economic Integration, chap. 6.

102. This material is drawn from our own experience during negotiations regarding the proposals for the automobile industry. Chrysler's role in attempting to prevent planning in the automobile sector is worthy of analysis. The reason for this action was the significant size of Chrysler's production before integration.

103. Tironi, Economic Integration, p. 239; and Wionczek, "La reacción norteamericana."

CHAPTER 5

1.   Furnish considers Decision 24 "as something more than an isolated attempt to solve a unique problem.... It is a piece of legislation which will serve as a point of reference and perhaps as a milestone in an area of vital importance to the development of the international economy." See D.B. Furnish, "El régimen común del Gran para las inversiones extranjeras," Derecho de la Integracion, No. 14, 1973. According to A. García, revolutionary changes in Bolivia, Peru, and Chile allowed the introduction of new elements (active state participation, the formation of Andean multinationals, SIDPs, and the common treatment of foreign capital) which went ideologically far beyond LAFTA's liberal scheme and led to the redefinition of the development and integration models. See Antonio García, Integración Andina, (Bogota: Fundación F.F. Neumann, 1974), pp. 63-64.

2.   Germánio Salgado. "El Grupo Andino o la Fuerza de Acción Solidaria" in La Integración Latinoamericana en una Etapa de Decisiones, BID-INTAL, Buenos Aires, 1972.

3.   A. García, "Industrialización y Dependencia en América Latina," Trimestre Económico, No. 38, 1971, pp. 731. F.E. Cardoso y Falleto, "Dependencia y Desarrollo en América Latina," Al Hirschmann "Porque Desinvertii en América Latina," Trimestre Económico, 1971, No. 3.

4.   The light engineering (metalmecanica), petrochemical, automobile, and electronics programs alone would demand, until 1985, investments in the order of $3,800 million, a sum equal to the net foreign contribution for the period between 1950 and 1960.

5.   We need foreign investment. We are prepared to offer access to a new, dynamic market and to assure a stable agreement which would allow foreign investment to know exactly what opportunities are available to it.   Naturally we are speaking of a new formula, a formula which has been much discussed but never formulated in legal terms. Perhaps for this reason it has been ill-received in some business circles, although in the present situation it is undoubtedly a formula which reconciles national interests with those of foreign companies. It thus creates a climate of peaceful coexistence propitious to a receptive attitude to foreign capital at times when, given the profound political changes occurring in Latin America, hostile, emotional reactions are very likely.

Germánio Salgado (founder-member of the Junta del Acuerdo de Cartagena until 1976), pp. 145-147. "El Grupo Andino." Vol. XXIII, Mexico 1973.

6. See D. Huelin, Investment in the Andean Group, Latin American Publications Fund, London 1973; and D. McClelland, Central American Common Market, pp. 89-94.

7. Tironi, "Tratamiento del Capital Extranjero en Procesos de Integracion," Coyuntura Economica, August 1977, p. 228.

8. E. Tironi, Economic Integration and Foreign Direct Investment. The Andean Case, (Ph.D. Thesis, M.I.T., 1976), chap. V; G. Misas, "Contribución al Estudio del Grado de Concentración en la Industria Colombiana," DANE Boletín, 266, Bogota, 1973.

9. For a detailed analysis of the articles and policy of Decision 24, see M. Guerrero, "El regimen Común de la Inversión Extranjera en el Grupo Andino," in Derecho de la Integración No. 14, 1973; and Furnish, "El regimen común del Gran."

10. M. Wionczek, "La Reacción Norteamericana ante el Trato Común a los Capitales Extranjeros en El Grupo Andino," Comercio Exterior, May 1971; and R.M. Swansborough, "The American Investor's View of Latin American Economic Nationalism," Interamerican Economic Affairs, Vol. XXVI, No. 3.

11. See El Tiempo, December 11, 1970, p. 7; December 17, 1970, pp. 1-7; December 19, 1970, p. 11; December 30, 1970, p. 14; January 16, 1971, pp. 1-18. See also "Declaraciones del Presidente de la Asociación Bancaria Colombiana," El Siglo, April 19, 1971; "Diez enmiendas propuestas por la Andi al Estatuto de Capitales Andino," El Espectador, November 29, 1972; and Algunas observaciones a la Política del País con Relación a la Inversión Extranjera, National Planning Department, Bogota, September 1971.

12. M. Urrutia analyzes the opposition to Decision 24 on the part of the Colombian private sector but he assumes that in this opposition there was a complete lack of external influence and suggests only nationalistic sense, because according to him, the first project of the Decision constituted a norm intended to discourage foreign investment in the industry and appeared to have been formulated "in order to limit said investments in Colombia"; by excluding the mining sector "the exception gave the impression that Decision 24 was a strategy adopted by the Junta to harm Colombia." M. Urrutia, Diversidad Ideológica e Integración Andina. [Ideological Diversity and Andean Integration], Coyuntura Económica Andina, Vol. X N_2, July 1980, p. 193.

13. Bond, "Business Associations," p. 239.

14. In August 1974, ANDI published its alternative industrialization policy, demanding greater flexibility in the common agreement on the treatment of foreign capital. See ANDI; "Colombia y la Integración Sugerencias para la Definición de una Política," Bogota, August 1974.

15. See R. Junguito and C. Caballero, Situación de la Economía Colombiana en Relación al Proceso de Integración, Jun/ S1,PL/I dt 4, Lima, 1974. The authors are, respectively, the former director and researcher of FEDESARROLLO, Bolivia.

16. Interviews by the author with the head of the Private Investment Unit of the National Planning Department, in Bogota, 1975 and 1978.

17. See Junta, Documento de Evaluación, 1975, Jun/di 195, Anexo II.

18. Junta, Evaluación del proceso de Integración 1969-1979, Jun/di 360, March 30 1979, Anexo Técnico No. 4; Evaluación de la Inversión Directa Extranjera en el Grupo Andino y de la Administración de la D. 24; pp. 3-4, 23-26; 147-168. Junta, Desarrollo del Proceso de Integración durante 1979, Jun/di 444, January 29, 1980. Cumplimiento de los Compromisos Derivados del Acuerdo de Cartagena y de las Decisiones de la Comisión. Jun/di 478, June 26, 1980. Apreciaciones sobre la Situación Actual del Proceso de Integración Económica del Acuerdo de Cartagena, dt 1, July 7 1981, Elementos de un Plan de Acción Destinado a Reactivar el Proceso de Integración Económica Subregional, Jun/dt 172, July 10, 1981. Comisión Resumen de las Situaciones de Incumplimiento y Reclamos por Materias. Com/XXXI/dt 3, November 14, 1980. Trigésimo Período de Sesiones Extraordinarias. Acta Final, Bogotá, September 1-4, 1981.

19. About direct foreign investment, see Junta, Evaluación del Proceso de Integración Económica 1969-1979, Jun/di, Lima, March 1970; Anexo IV and Evaluación de la Inversion Extranjera Directa en el Grupo Andino y de la Administración de la D. 24, Jun/di 360, March 30 1970, pp. 23-26.

20. We are not including Venezuela because it entered the Pact later (1973).

21. Wionczek, "La Reacción Norteamericana," p. 98.

22. During this new orientation Colombia emerged as the most attractive country, not only because of the size of its internal market, but also because it was a country that did not participate in the policy of recovery of natural resources exercised by Chile, Peru, and Bolivia. See M. Wionczek, El GRAN y la Inversión Privada Extranjera, Junta, Lima, 1970, p. 5.

23. Wionczek, El GRAN y la Inversión Privada, p. 67.

24. Junta, Documento de Evaluación 1975, Jun/di 195, Anexo Tecnico III, p. 12.

25. For example, Decree 444 allowed companies to repatriate profits amounting to 10% of net registered capital. Decision 24 allowed up to 14%.

26. See R. Junguito and C. Caballero, Situación de la economía Colombiana en Relación al Proceso de Integración; a study presented in the first Interregional Seminar on Integrated Planning, November 1974; and DANE, Boletín Manual de Estadistica, No. 239, June 1971.

FDI after decree 444 in Colombia (million US$)

	1967	1968	1969	1970	Total
Foreign Direct Investment (FDI)	18.3	13.3	18.3	7.6	57.6

Source: DANE, Boletín, No. 239.

Junguito and Caballero and Planning Officers agreed that this represents the "normal" flow of foreign capital.

27. See C. Díaz-Alejandro, Foreign Trade Regimes and Economic Development (New Haven: Yale University Press, 1976), p. 299.

28. Junta, Evaluación 1975, Anexo Técnico, III, pp. 16-18; and Evaluación 1977, Jun/di 295, March 1978, pp. II64-65.

29. See Junta, Evaluación de la IED en el Grupo Andino y de la Administración de la Decision 24, Jun/di 360 Marzo 30 de 1979, Anexo Técnico IV pp. 28-42.

30. See Junta, Documento de Evaluación 1975, Jun/di 195, Anexo Técnico III, p. 14. The same complaint is repeated in the document Evaluación 1977, p. II-64; and in Informe de Evaluación 1969-1979, op. cit., Table II-6. The Junta notes that the mechanisms are permanently renovated pp. 147.

31. The "Agreement on Conversion into Mixed Enterprises." Our analysis of this point is based on unpublished data provided to the author in the National Planning Department in April 1978. It is important to clarify that the signing of the "Convenio" does not mean that the transfer has been completed, it is only a document "of intention."

32. Based on the analysis of unpublished data of the "Junta Monetaria" and Banco de la República. The amount approved represents about 3% of the total North American assets in the manufacturing sector in 1975.

33. I am indebted to Ricardo Plata who supplied me with valuable information without which the present section could not have been written. The analysis is only approximate because only 211 out of the 761 registered foreign enterprises supplied required information to the "Oficina de Cambios" at Banco de la República.

34. "Capitales en el limbo": profits without the right of transfer and which cannot be reinvested.

35. It is important to note that 78% of total profits of foreign investment were generated in the manufacturing sector, mainly in the chemical, oil, rubber, and plastic industries.

36. U.S. Direct Investment in the manufacturing sector in Colombia:

Stocks	1970	1971	1972	1974	Stocks
1969					1974
220	9	27	50	69	375

Source: Study of Current Business, Department of Commerce USA. Sept. 1976, Vol. 56, No. 59.

37. See Junta, Evaluación del Proceso de Integración Económica 1969-1979, op. cit. pp. 40-43.

38. For a detailed study of Decree 600 see F. Granel, "La retirada del Pacto Chile. La crisis del Grupo Andino," Comercio Exterior, Vol. 27, No. 1 (Mexico), January 1977.

39. Decision 24, article 37.

40. Decision 103, article 10.

41. Taking 14% as the limit of profit transfer, it can be calculated that in 1985, if foreign investment continues to enter according to historical trends, profit remittances will constitute 11% of total exports. Junta, "Bases," chap. I, p. 80.

42. Decision 24, agreement I, point 2; and Decision 103, enclosure J.

43. These modifications are above all the result of a proposal made by the Colombian delegation that the countries should have complete liberty in managing internal savings resources. INCOMES, "Conclusiones del Grupo de Trabajo," on the Junta's document, "Bases para un reglamento del al D.24," Bogota, October 28, 1975.

44. M. Kuczynski, Planned Development in the Andean Group. Industrial Policy and Trade Liberalisation (London: Latin American Publication Fund, 1973).

45. Huelin concludes that in the CACM the impact of the entry of foreign producers of consumer goods under protective "regional" status has been extremely negative for national producers of the same products, and may have contributed to the suspension of trade liberalization in Central America. D. Huelin, Investment in the Andean Group, (London: Latin American Publications Fund, 1973).

46. A. Hazlewood, Economic Integration, 1975, p. 124.

47. Junta, Evaluación 1975, Jun/di 195, Anexo III, p. 21; and Junta, Evaluación 1977.

48. A. Vidales, "Dificultades e Inconvenientes Constatados en la Aplicacion de la D. 46, Aspectos Principales a Considerar en su Modificacion," en Revista, No. 13, Lima 1980, pp. 107-128.

49. A. Vidales, "Definicion de las Empresas Multinacionales Andinas," Revista No. 13, p. 57.

50. Junta, Documentos de Evaluación 1975, p. 24, 1976, II.1,3; and 1977, p. II.6.

CHAPTER 6

1. Victoria Curzon concludes that a simple free-trade area is not sufficient for countries that have great disparities between their tariff levels for inputs. To avoid the adverse effects on the allocation of resources that come from tariff differences, there has to be a strict system controlling origin. V. Curzon, The Essentials of Economic Integration: Lessons of EFTA Experience (London: Macmillan & Co., 1974), pp. 147-150.

2. For a wider discussion of the effects of tariff differences upon specialization in countries belonging to a customs union, see B. Balassa, El II decenio para el desarrollo y la integracion en América Latina Bid-INTAL, 1971, p. 20.

3. Ibid., p. 30.

4. See table 6.1.

5. ECLA, Integración Económica, p. 35.

6. S. de la Cuadra, "La estructura de la proteccion en Chile," Universidad Catolica de Chile, 1970, quoted in M. Selowsky, Política Campiaria y asignación de recursos, Universidad Catolica de Chile, CIE, 1972, and ECLA Integración Económica, p. 35.

7. ECLA, Integración Económica, p. 35.

8. M. Bruno, "Protection and Tariff Changes under General Equilibrium," Journal of International Economics, 1972, iii, pp. 205-235.

9. See Junta, Evaluación 1976, Jun/di 248, Lima, 1976; and Situación Arancelaria de los Países Miembros, J/PE 45, Lima, September 1975, pp. 15-18.

10. See Junta, Evaluación 1976, Jun/di 248, Lima, 1975, p. 9; C. Boloña in his work, Las compras estatales, Peru, 1977, calculates that between 1971 and 1976 the state accounted for 51% of Peru's imports.

11. See Junta, Proyecto de Bases para la Elaboración del AEC, Document CCE/11/dt 14, p. 2.

12. Tacitly Garay accepts the Junta's criteria and assumes the possibility of achieving those regional goals if a technically correct tariff structure is adopted and fully implemented and if member countries give up political national positions which depart from the economic optimum. See L. Garay, Grupo Andino y Proteccionismo, Contribución o un Debate Ed. Pluma, Bogota, 1979.

13. See Junta, El Proceso de Elaboración del AEC, J/PE/62, 1973.

14. Ibid., p. 4.

15. Junta, Proyecto de Bases para la Elaboración del AEC, CEE/11/dt, April 14, 1975, pp. 8-9.

16. Ibid., p.9-10.

17. Starting with the basic formula for effective protection:

$$Zj = \frac{tj - \Sigma aijti}{VAj}$$

it follows that tj = ZjVAj + Σ aijti, and from this we can derive a set of linear equations with the form

$$t_1 = Z_1 VA_1 = a_{11}t_1 + a_{21}t_2 + \cdots\cdots a_{n1}t_n$$

$$t_n = Z_n VA_n + a_{1n}t_1 + a_{2n}t_2 + \cdots\cdots a_{nn}t_n$$

in which Zj, VAj and aij are known and tj can be obtained.

Zj = effective protection for product j
tj = Nominal tariff on product j
aij = Value of input i necessary to produce one unit of value
of product j
ti = Nominal tariff on input i

See Junta, Método de Estimacion del CET, CCE/II/dt13, May 1975, p.1, and L. Garay, in Grupo Andino y Proteccionismo, presents a detailed analysis of the Junta's methodology and shows its inconsistency with the basic principles.

18. For more details on the methodology used to calculate the CET, see Junta, Aplicación del Criterio Empleo en el CET, CCE/II/dt9, May 1975; Aplicación de la Contribución Tecnologica en el CET, CCE/II/dt10, June 1975; Aplicación del Criterio de la Industria Incipiente en el CET, CCE/II/dt11, May 1975; El Nivel del CET, CCE/II/dt12, May 1975; Método de Estimación del CET, CCE/II/dt13, May 1975; Coeficiente de Insumo Producto Y de Valor Agregado para la Elaboración del CET, J/PE/40, rev. 3; Proceso de Elaboración del CET, J/PE/63, March 1976.

19. See Chapter 1.

20. See Sebastian Edwards, "El efecto de un CET en la balanza de Pagos y en el tipo de Cambio: El caso de Chile" in El Trimestre Económico, Vol. XLIV, No. 3, pp. 677-683. This article concludes that the Junta's proposal on Chile's tariff structure not only served to raise the agricultural sector's efficiency, but that it would also aid its exports by changing the sector's protection from negative to positive.

21. For greater detail of the application of the various criteria for constructing the CET, see Junta del Acuerdo de Cartagena: Proyecto de Bases para la Elaboración del AEC, CCE/11/dt 14, 1973. Orientaciones generales para la Elaboración del AEC, J/PE/13/Rev, October 1, 1973. Applicación del criterio de la industria incipiente en el AEC, CCE/11/Dt, May 11, 1975. Applicación del criterio de empleo en el AEC, CCE/11/dt, May 9, 1975. Applicación del criterio de la contribución technologica en el AEC, CCE/11/dt, May 10, 1975. El Nivel del AEC, CCE/11/dt, May 12, 1975.

22. 66.9 percent of products are to be found in the range of 0-60 percent effective protection while only 3.1 percent are above the 90 percent level.

23. For example, import licenses, import deposits, tariff rebates, and exemptions.

24. Junta, Proceso de Elaboración del AEC, J/PE/63, Lima, 1976, p.4.

25. In 1977, Colombia reduced the tariff on capital goods to 5% in order to stimulate investment and to discourage their production. The Junta proposes a level of 25% for those that cannot be produced because of their technological complexity or market limitations; for the rest of the CET it can rise to 100%.

26. See Junta Situación Arancelaria de los Países Miembros, J/PE 45, September 1975, pp. 15-18, for the discussions of government representatives about the nature of the CET. Also, see the various Actas Finales of the Consejo de Comercio Exterior, especially numbers III and IV.

27. The substitution model of the Treaty of Cartagena is clearly outlined in a document produced by the Junta called the Bases generales para una estrategia subregional de desarrollo, which was never discussed or approved by the Commission. It describes the emphasis of the model of integration as being one that "would place its main emphasis upon those sectors of basic and heavy industry whose development would provide opportunities to substitute imports." (Vol. I, p.37). "Integration will make it possible to undertake activities, which, without it, would not be feasible because of the limitations on the size of national markets. These initiatives are a prerequisite for giving new life to the economy through modernization and strengthening of the industrial development pattern and by opening new horizons in diversified areas," ibid., p.3.

28. High Chilean government officials, interviewed in May 1975, maintained that only an integration policy that set itself apart from the substitution process could be acceptable for Chile. Its economic stabilization and rationalization policy was incompatible with the Junta's model. Chile's new approach was going to "pull a face" at 50 years of mistaken economic policies.

   The Colombian president clearly stated his country's position in a speech delivered in September 1976: "This is the fundamental shortcoming of the CET, when there are countries which have still not passed the stage of import substitution. Can a country like Colombia, which has rediscovered its agricultural and livestock vocation as has no other in the subregion, retrace its steps over the years and return to the dropping of protection in favour of intrazonal industry?" El Tiempo, September 17, 1976, p.1.

29. See Informe final de la 3 reunión del Consejo de Comercio Exterior Lima, November 3, 1975.

30. "The relative importance of the different economic activities included in sectoral programming should be evaluated, as far as the CET is concerned, on the basis of the same criteria used to assess other productive activities. The remaining definitions corresponding to the SIDP's, such as the distribution of production, the programme of internal liberation and other commitments, are completely valid within the limits of the community decision to protect those sectors to a certain degree with regard to external competition." Junta, Projecto de Bases Para la Elaboracion del Arancel Externo Común, CCE/II/ dt14, Lima, April 1975, p.7.

31. The treaty states, however, that for each program there should be a corresponding CET, taking into account the characteristics of each sector. This allows for the interpretation that the SIDPs are excessively favored. See Acuerdo, article 65.

32. The Chileans and Colombians maintained that the CET should be "a neutral instrument which does not discriminate between productive sectors," established before the approval of the SIDPs. See Acta Final del XVL Periodo de Sessiones Extraordinarias de la Comisión, February–April 1976, p.3. The stance approved in Colombia by the Consejo Directivo de Comercio Exterior concerning the CET states very clearly that "to accept this situation of buying subregional industrial products above the world market price would be to accept a strategy in which Colombia would be subsidising the development of the countries belonging to the Pact." INCOMEX, Ejercicios Cuantitativos Para la Elaboración del Arancel Externo Común, C.D.C.E. A-1Z, October 1975. On the Colombian position, see also Comercio Exterior, Vol 26, No. 5, May 1977.

33. See Acta de la Tercera Reunión del Consejo de Comercio Exterior, CE/III, 1975.

34. Bases para una Estrategea, pp. 3-44, chap. 3.

35. See Bases, pp.86-96, chap. 1; and our Chapter 7, section 3.

36. See Acta de la Tercera Reunión del Consejo de Comercio Exterior, CCE III, 1975, p. 13.

37. Ibid.; and CCE/IV/Informe Final 25 January 1978, p. 3.

38. See "Declaración del Delagado Peruano," at 3rd Consejo de Comercio Exterior, Lima, 1975.

39. Kaser, Comecon, p. 25.

40. See J. Montias, "Background and Origins of the Rumanian Dispute with Comecon," Soviet studies, Vol. XVI, No. 2, p. 132; J. Vánek, Economický a Politický Význám Vyovoju Strojirenských Výrobků (Prague: 1960), p.197; and D. Máchová: CSSR V Socialisticke Delbé Práce, (Prague: 1962), p.135.

41. The development of discussions about social efficiency between COMECON countries and plans supported by the developed countries is well presented in J. Novozansky, "Jednotne Hosopodarstvi socialisticke soustavy," Nová Mysl, No. 10, 1962, pp.1165-1166 and 1169; Vyrovngni Economické Urovne Socialistickych Zemi, Nova Mysl, No. 4, 1962.

42. The Bolivian delegation said clearly in the third and fourth meeting of the Consejo de Comercio Exterior (1975 and 1978) that any tariff that did not take Bolivia's landlocked position and lesser relative development into account would discriminate against the country. Therefore, it was proposing a general raising of the customs level. It was only in 1978 that Bolivia stated the levels it considered not to be harmful to its interests.

43. The modifications to the Treaty of Cartagena for extending the term for adopting the CET are included in the Protocolo de Lima, 1976.

44. For an analysis of the external tariff proposed by the Junta and its relation with the possible causes of Chile's withdrawal, see Intereconomicas, 1977, March-April 3/4, pp. 72-78.

45. "Para tariffs" were defined in section 4 of this chapter.

46. See CCE/IV, Informe Final, 1978, pp. 5-7.

47. Ibid.

48. See R. Thorp, "The Post-Import-Substitution Era: The Case of Peru," World Development, 1977, Nos. 1-2, p.125.

49. See Actas Finales del Consejo de Comercio Exterior, March-April 1976.

50. See Documento de Evalucación 1977, Jun/di 295, Lima 1978, pp. II-6.

51. See Junta, Propuesta No. 36, December 1, 1972. The Foreign Trade Council subsequently presented a project of its own, which suffered the same fate as that of the Junta. See Projecto de Esquema de la Política de Comercio Exterior, CCE/II/dt8, March 1975.

52. Ibid., p. II-4.

53. See Junta, Informe Final de la Tercera Reunión del Consejo de Planificácion, CPL/III/Informe, Final rev. 1, November 1977, Annex III, pp. 19-23.

54. During interviews held in 1975 by the author with planning officers of the Andean group, the Chileans and Colombians were skeptical about the convenience of linking their economies to long-term regional import-substituting plans that were after all inefficient.

55. Junta, Documento de Evaluación 1975, Anexo Técnico IV, p. 2.

56. Informe Final de la Tercera Reunión del Consejo de Planificación, CPL/III/Informe Final/4/1977.

57. For more details, see John Montias, "Background and origins of the Rumanian dispute with Comecon," Journal of Soviet Studies, Vol. 16, 1964, pp. 151-52.

58. Nye, "Comparing Common Markets: A Revised Neofuncionalistic Model" International Organization, Vol. 27, 1970 p. 835.

59. For more details see G.R. Denton, "Planning and Integration. Medium-term Policy as an Instrument of Integration," in G.R. Denton, ed., Economic Integration in Europe (London: World University, 1971, pp. 330-56.

60. Junta, Informe de Evaluación del Proceso de Integracion Subregional Andina: 1977, Jun/di 295/March 20, 1978.

CHAPTER 7

1. Martin Carnoy, Industrialisation in a Latin American Market (Washington, D.C.: Brookings Institution, 1972.

2. See Mikesell, "The Theory of Common Markets," pp. 221-24.

3. See Perroux, "Note sur la Notion de Pole de Croissance," Economie Appliquée, No. 8, pp. 307-320. For the regional problems within the EEC, see Bird, "The Need for Regional Policy in a Common Market," S.J. and P.E., Vol. 12, 1965, pp. 225-242. E. McCrone argues in favor of regional policy in the EEC on the bases of (a) political cohesion, (b) the possibility that the Common Market may aggravate the regional problem, and (c) national regional policies must be coordinated. E. McCrone, "Regional Policy in the European Communities," in E.R. Denton, ed., Economic Integration (London: World University, 1971). See A.J. Brown, "Economic Separatism Versus a Common Market in Developing Countries," Yorkshire Bulletin of Economic and Social Research, 1961, No. 13, pp. 13-14 and 88-96.

4. Countries have restrictions on the free movement of capital and labor that may be removed only at the later stages of integration. See Balassa, Theory of Economic Integration, pp. 191-210 and 231-252.

5. UNECLA, Integración, Substitución de Importaciones y Desarrollo Económico en América Latina, 1974. p. 67.

6. Ibid., pp. 72-86.

7. Chenery and Taylor studied the relationship between the level of industrial protection and market size. They showed how industries with significant economies of scale produce about 40% of the manufactured product when per capita income is $300 p.a. If income is increased to $600, these industries would create 57% of total output. If the population increases from 2 to 50 million people, while incomes stay at US $300 (1960) dollars, then per capita industrial product would double, and in those sectors with significant economies of scale, it would be tripled. At this income level, which is very similar to that of the GRAN, economies of scale are significant in determining the level of per capita industrial product up to a population of 100 million. The study identifies the following sectors as having significant economies of scale: petroleum products, paper, rubber, metals, and textiles. Printing, chemicals, machinery, and transport equipment also have these economies on a significant scale, though less than the previous list. H.B. Chenery, "Patterns of Industrial Growth," American Economic Review, September 1960.

8. For an analysis of the different studies and methodologies on economies of scale and their significance for underdeveloped countries, see R.B. Sutcliffe, Industry and Underdevelopment (London: Addison-Wesley, 1971), chap. 6, pp. 198-243.

9. Ibid., pp. 225-6.

10. J. Baranson, "Automotive Industries in Developing Countries," International Bank for Reconstruction and Development, Staff Occasional Papers, No. 8, 1969, p. 20.

11. For an analysis of the methodology used to calculate the demand for vehicles and to draw up the proposed program see Junta, Propuesta de la Junta Sobre Programa Sectorial de la Industria Automotriz, Proposal 45, March 7, 1974, chap. II, III, and IV; and ECLA, La demanda de vehículos motorizados en América Latina, Santiago, 1971.

12. The regional distribution of cars and commercial vehicles (trucks) for 1985 is:

A1	16%	B1	52%
A2	29%	B2	15%
A3	29%	B3	29%
A4	26%	B4	4%

The distribution by country for cars is as follows:

	Bolivia	Colombia	Chile	Ecuador	Peru	Vene- zuela	Total
A1	620	13786	31583	2268	8261	7944	64,462
A2	4989	23778	30218	8144	36487	28102	121,718
A3	3520	19913	18250	7865	25070	46751	121,369
A4	3033	10457	7676	5441	11952	71779	109,444
TOTAL	12162	67934	77727	22824	81770	154576	416,993

Source: Junta, Propuesta 45, chap. III, pp. 54-60.

13. The B1 and B2 truck categories were each divided into subcategories:

B1.1 trucks and similar vehicles up to 3 tons
B1.2 trucks and similar vehicles from 3 to 4.6
B2.1 trucks and similar vehicles from 4 to 6.2
B2.2 trucks and similar vehicles from 6.2 to 9.3

The assembly agreements allowed a country that was allocated the production of a model to pass the assembly to another country. Coproduction allowed countries with a shared allocation to interchange necessary parts as a condition of national manufacture. Complementarity meant that countries could agree to specialize in the production of components of any vehicles allocated to them. These agreements gave greater flexibility to allocation, and in fact they allowed countries that had not been given allocation to assemble or produce components. See Grupo Andino, Carta Informativa, Junta, Lima, October 1977, No. 69, pp. 8-13.

14. In the National Planning Dept. in Colombia it is agreed that the automobile SIDP is not a production program but an assembly and coproduction one. This is the reason why Colombia signed it. (Interview with the head of Macroeconomic Planning in April 1978, by the author).

15. Junta, Appreciación General del Acuerdo, Luego de los Cambios Producidos en 1976, Jun/di 248, Lima, 1977, p. 10.

16. In an interview in April 1978, the Colombian ex-President, R. Carlos Lleras, said to the author that the intention was to create an integrated zone with great freedom for reciprocal trade and commercial concessions to other underdeveloped countries, which would have the capacity to negotiate with and act as a block against the US and Europe. In the scheme, programming would be limited to a very select group of industries which would be allocated according to criteria of efficiency. Other mechanisms, such as fiscal transfers, should be tried in order to achieve balanced development.

17. See, Junta-Intal, Historia Documental del Acuerdo de Cartagena, 1974, discussions of Comisión Mixta on the Cartagena Agreement.

18. The rules favoring the less developed countries are contained in the following articles of the Treaty: No. 93 grants priority to Bolivia and Ecuador in the granting of the allocation of industries. Nos. 100-194 give Bolivia and Ecuador a generous time period in which to eliminate intra-subregional trade barriers and to set up the CET. No. 55 gives these two countries a greater number of exemptions for products. No. 50 gives immediate entry to the other four markets, to a list of specific products coming from these countries. No. 106 gives Bolivia and Ecuador priority in financial activities and the technical assistance on the CAF (Corporación Andina de Fomento).

19. Hazlewood suggests that the economic integration of underdeveloped countries becomes meaningful when they face a major industrialization project, because if investments do not count upon a market any larger than the national one, industrial development will suffer restrictions. A. Hazlewood, ed., African Integration and Disintegration, pp. 11-16; and for socialist countries, see J.M. Bravant, Essays on Planning, Trade and Integration in Eastern Europe (Rotterdam: UP, 1964), pp. 43-63.

20. Germánico Salgado, "El Grupo Andino y el Poder de Acción Solidaria," in Bid-INTAL, La Integración Latino-Americana en una Etapa de Decisiones, p. 141. This author also recognises that programing has to stimulate efficiency. However, while the stability of the treaty depends on ensuring the real participation of each member country, it is important to give priority to the principle of equilibrium. Also see Junta, Evaluación del Proceso de Integración, 1976, Anexo II, Bases para una Estragia, chap. III; and G. Salgado, Informe a la Segunda Reunión de Cancilleres, 1972.

21. On the importance of giving preference to industrial development in the relatively less developed members of an economic union because of the polarizing effects of market forces, see R. Ffrench-Davis, "The Andean Pact: A Model of Economic Integration for Developing Countries," World Development, No. 1-2, 1977. In this article he fully accepts the equilibrating nature of programming; "The SIDP mechanism was designed to correct injustices and inefficiencies that would be provoked by unregulated functioning of the economy when the merging of markets took place among countries with both insufficient and different levels of development. The instrument is of a particular importance in avoiding the danger of benefits polarising with regard to investment programmes designed for the expanded market." Also Wionczek, Latin American Econom-

ic Integration: Experiences and Prospects (New York: Praeger, 1966), pp. 9-10; Morawetz, Andean Group, chap. 5; A.J. Brown, "Economic Separation versus a Common Market in Developing Countries," Parts I and II, Yorkshire Bulletin of Economic and Social Research, No. 3, 1961, pp. 13-40. and 88-96. The Junta clearly states, "The Treaty of Cartagena innovates with respect to LAFTA and institutes planning as the basic tool to control system equilibrium." Junta, Evaluación, 1969-1975, p. 10.

22. It can be seen that in fact there are only two objectives: a and e; the objectives listed in b, c and d are the ways in which objective a can be achieved.

23. Bases Generales para una Estrategia Sub-regional de Desarrollo, Junta del Acuerdo de Cartagena, Lima, March 1972, 3 vols.

24. Ibid., p. 89.

25. Ibid., chap. 3, p. 46. Jan Tinbergen argues for regional planning as opposed to competition in the heavy industry field on the grounds that free entry and competition in these industries are not likely to produce optimal development. He gives several reasons why free entry and competition would not achieve optimum patterns of heavy industry development; (a) long construction periods required for profits, (b) large amounts of capital required to establish plants of optimum size, (c) failure of free enterprise to establish heavy industry in option locations. J. Tinbergen, "Heavy Industry in the Latin American Common Market," Economic Bulletin for Latin America, UNECLA, Santiago, March 1960, pp. 2-4.

26. Junta, Bases, chap. 1.

27. Initially the Treaty set December 31, 1973 as the date for incorporating reserve products in the programs, but the period could be extended for 2 years.

28. Acuerdo, article 34.

29. Morawetz analyzes the technical difficulties of measuring the benefits to be derived from integration. The use of shadow prices is problematical, even if they have been passed on already in cost-benefit analysis in the use of a single country. Morawetz, Andean Group, p. 74.

30. See Acuerdo, articles 1 and 2. Article 2 especially defines balanced and unified development as the reduction of the differences in the development existing between the more and less developed countries. By setting up study programs, too, it says that macroeconomic elements, such as capital formation, the generation of new employment, and the expansion of global exports to be gained from integration should be studied, and studied from the viewpoint of reducing the differences between countries.

31. Bases: "Finally, it has to be considered that the industrial sector will not be able to reduce by itself the
sub-region's need for new jobs. The direct generation of
employment coming from industries reserved for the sectoral
programme for industrial development will in general be scarce.
Therefore, these sectors should have as their priorities efficiency and technological progress." Chap. III, p. 20

Regarding the criteria for choosing technology Bases
says, "Although technology in the manufacturing sector can be
considered as a function of an optimum criterion with regard to
the generation of employment, this ought not to be an objective per se in the region's industrial policy, but rather a
complement to other actions and measures which can be cul-
tivated in other economic sectors in which the proportion of
labour is substantially higher." Chap. I, p. 89.

32. Past trends have shown that the internal coefficient was
only 16%. The proposed aim means that the marginal propensity to save of the Andean population, measured against gross
income, must rise from 18% to an average of 30% between 1979
and 1985. Bases, chap. I, pp. 66-84. External savings will
have to rise faster than in the last two decades. The light
engineering, petrochemical, automotive and electronic programs
alone would need investments of about $3,800 million by 1985,
a sum similar to the net external credit contribution between
1950 and 1969 and greater than direct foreign investment in
the same period. See Bases, chap. I, p. 69.

33. Bases, chap. I, pp. 44-49.

34. Ibid., p. 44.

35. Ibid., p. 133.

36. Marglin found different social costs according to the time
when production was begun. See S.A. Marglin, Approaches to
Dynamic Investment Planning (Amsterdam: North Holland,
1963).

37. Morawetz suggests that the negotiation of allocation by
separate sectors could have led to a multiplicity of plants, and
that there should be internally balanced multisectoral packages. However, because of the points made here and especially because of the lack of national priorities and of elements
that allow for the delicate intersectoral (intercountry) balance,
it is unrealistic to recommend these intersectoral packages.
See Morawetz, Andean Group, pp. 92-93.

38. We have discussed in chapter 2 the size of the market
and how and why the integration model does not resolve the
problems derived from the small market size.

39. The Junta has recognized that major elements exist which
mean that "national aspirations have to be satisfied at the

price of efficiency." Junta, Evaluación del Proceso de Integración, 1975, Anexo 2, p. 4. Ffrench-Davis argues that the
negotiations by individual sectors and the tendency for countries not to give concessions, bring losses in efficiency, of
economies of scale and external economies. As a solution, he
suggests that the countries should negotiate allocations among
themselves after the signing of the programs, in order to
interchange allocated industries. The programs agreed by the
national Plenipotentiaries would only be a basis for bilateral
negotiations, not an agreement for subregional specialization.
This author does not explain how these negotiations would
become common agreements. This strategy would lead countries to try to gain the maximum number of allocations in order
to increase their bargaining powers. It also supposes that the
resulting structure would be more efficient than if negotiations
took place at the level of the five countries. See Ffrench-
Davis, The Andean Pact, p. 21. Interviews held by the author with officials of the national planning agencies in Colombia
and Chile in April and May 1975 took up criticisms that the
Junta had violated article 32 of the Treaty, creating "white
elephants" by allocating industries inefficiently and by dividing
production. Examples were quoted for petrochemicals, automo-
biles, and tractors.

40. See Junta, Propuesta de la Junta sobre el Programa Sectorial de Desarrollo Industrial de la Petroquímica, Lima, 1974;
and Anexos Tecnicos al Documento de Evaluación de la Marcha
del Proceso de Integracion, Jun/di 196, Lima, March 25, 1975.

41. Junta, Propuesta No. 45, and Decision 120, 1976.

42. See Junta, Informe del Primer Seminario Interregional
sobre la Planificación Integrada de los Paises Miembros, Jun/si
PL/I Informe Final, 1974.

43. See Bases y Criterios Para la Evaluación de los Programas
Sectoriales de Desarrollo Industrial, Doc COM/UI-E/II, Lima,
December 1971. This Colombian document is, so far, the only
explicit national position on the SIDPs.

44. The above criteria were formulated by the Colombian
delegation to the Commission during the 6th period of extraordinary sessions in Bases y Criterio para la Evaluación de los
Programas Sectoriales de Desarrollo Industrial Doc COM/VI-
E/II, December 1971. After 1973, the Chilean position became
virtually identical with the Colombian one.

45. See Ministeriode Planeamiento y Co-ordinación, Plan de
Desarrollo Económico y Social, La Paz, June 1976; and Junta-
UNDAT, Situación Económica y Social del Ecuador 1976, pp.
20-22 and 40-41.

46. See Junta Nacional de Planificación y Coordinacion
Económica, Lineamientos Fundamentales del Plan Integral de

Transformación y Desarrollo, 1973-1977, Quito, 1972; and idem, Plan Integral de Transformación y Desarrollo, Quito, 1972.

47. The Ley General de Industrias, legislative decree No. 18350, sets out the Peruvian scheme for import substitution. Besides the rules on protection according to the nature of various industries, it establishes reforms for the distribution of income and the transformation of the system of property holding, and reserves for State ownership, companies producing inputs for production.

48. The Peruvian government has taken the new market into account when elaborating its development projects, and it was the first country to implement the metalmecánico program. This sector is considered to be of the greatest priority. In carrying out the program, studies were made on all the allocated sectors and the projects were advanced for the following: heavy machinery, steel and cement, naval and fishing shipbuilding, and irrigation equipment for agriculture. The principal project is the machinery and heavy equipment complex at Arequipa, which is made up of 22 plants. Similarly, petrochemical projects have been implemented, based upon the size of Andean demand. Peruvian government investment projects rose to $8,900 million, of which 22% was to go to hydrocarbons, 20% to industry, 12.3% to mining, and 12% to agriculture. See Junta, Situación Económica y Perspectivas Immediatas, Lima, 1976, pp. 14-32, which gives an extensive list of projects now in operation, related to the Andean market.

49. On several occasions in the first half of 1975, the president Morales Bermudez, stated his concern that the sectoral program was stagnating. He said that Peru would reconsider its membership if the approval of the programs was not speeded up. At the 14th period of extraordinary sessions of the Commission, the Peruvian representative announced Peru's decision not to take part in any more meetings of the Commission. It was going to study other themes until "a positive decision may have been made on the programming proposals which we came to talk about." Anexo I al Acta Final del XIV, Periodo de Sesiones Extraordinarias, Lima, May 1975; and Exposición del Representante Titular Peruano ante el XIX Período de Sesiones de la Comisión, Documento COM/XIX/de 10, December 12, 1975.

50. To compare the Peruvian Position, see: Oficina Central de Planificación, Plan Nacional de Desarrollo 1971-1975, Lima, 1972; and idem, Analisis de la Incidencia del Proceso de Integración en el Desarrollo Nacional, Junta, Lima, 1977.

51. For more details of Venezuela's interest in the GRAN and its preference for programming see: Bacha, "Venezuela y el Grupo Andino," El Trimestre Económico, 37 (1), 1970; De

Blanco Iturte Eglee, "La Estrategia de Desarrollo y la Integracion: el Caso Venezolano," Junta SI.PL/I/dt 5, No. 5, 1974,
p. 24; and "Exposición de R. Figuereo Planchart, representante titular de Venezuela ante la XIX Comision," December 10,
1975, Documento COM/XIX/di e. Public investment is decisive
in básic industry and hydrocarbons. The country is proceed-
ing with projects that will make Venezuela the most industrialized nation in the subregion, enlarging iron and steel
capacity to 5 million tons p.a., and aluminum to 400,000 tons
p.a. State investment for 1976-1980 in the manufacturing
sector will rise to $10,000 million, a figure approximately equal
to the GDP of Colombia. See, "Segundo mensaje del cuidadano
Presidente Carlos Andrés Perez al Congreso," March 1976; and
Oficina Central de Coordinación y Planificación, Cuarto Plan de
la Nación 1970-1974, Caracas, 1971.

52. An important part of their economic policy is to alter the
terms of trade between agriculture and industry, which, within
the substitutive model, favor the latter.

53. In the Colombian development plan, "Para Cerrar la Brecha," it is stated that "the responsibility for Colombian
industrial development will fall upon the private sector, except
in the case of exploiting metallic resources and the setting up
of certain companies which supply basic primary materials, and
in the development of those industries allocated in the SIDPs
of the GRAN. ..." Later, the Plan adds that "the majority of
the allocated industries should be developed by the private
sector, but the State may feel it is necessary to help some of
the basic industries assigned to Colombia, which may need a
large amount of additional investment." See DNP, Para Cerrar
la Brecha, Bogotá, 1976.

54. See J.M.P. Van Brabant, Essays on Planning, Trade and
Integration in Eastern Europe (Rotterdam: Rotterdam University Press, 1974), pp. 43-63; and Kaser, Comecon, p. 29.

55. "The economic integration of the socialist countries is an
objective process regulated in a balanced manner in which
their national economic structures are brought together, mutually adapted and optimized in an international economic
complex, in which deep and stable cooperation ties are shaped
in the leading sectors of production, science and technology,
in which their international market is expanded and consolidated through the creation of the corresponding political,
economic, technological and organizational conditions." Among
these organizational conditions, it is considered that a common
plan "will apparently require new forms for joint forecasting
and planning, including the possible establishment of international planning bodies." Alampieu O. Bogomolov and Y.
Shiryaev, A New Approach to Economic Integration (Moscow:
Progress Publishers, 1974), pp. 27, 28, 83, and 84.

56. Mytelka Lynn, "The Salience of Gains in the Third World Integrative Systems," World Politics, No. 25, January 1973, pp. 240-241.

57. Van Brabant, Essays, p. 163.

58. A. Abonyi and Sylvain, "CMEA Integration and Policy Option for Eastern Europe: A Development Strategy of Development States," JCMS, No. 15, 1977, p. 144.

59. Kaser, COMECON, p. 205.

60. Rumania always criticized Czechoslovakia and East Germany for giving too much importance to the Law of Value and for not concentrating on proportional development, which should be the first priority; efficiency should take second place. Ibid., p. 206; and Soviet Studies, Vol. XVI, pp. 130-158.

61. For a discussion of Khruschev's article, see J.B. Thomson, "Rumania's Struggle with COMECON," East Europe, June 1964, p. 7.

62. Statement on the Stand of the Rumanian Workers' Party Concerning the Problems of the World Communist and Working Class Movement, Supplement to Anger Press, April 1964, p. 28.

63. Ibid., p. 29.

64. Kaser, COMECON, p. 108.

65. With the same vehemence, the Rumanians held back the creation of the "District of the Lower Danube," another supranational project of Khrushchev's, which aimed at managing and exploiting the region's oil resources. Again the Rumanians placed national sovereignty above the efficiency and utility of the bloc.

66. J.M. Brabant, Socialist Economic Integration. Aspects of Contemporary Economic Problems in Eastern Europe (Cambridge, London: Cambridge U.P., 1980), chap. 3.

67. In an interview in May 1975, the subdirector of the Colombian National Planning Department stated very clearly that this principle should be the only one used when drawing up the SIDPs. In this way, he continued, Bolivia would achieve the greatest efficiency in mining, Venezuela in petrochemicals, and so on.

68. The Chilean representatives, backed by Colombians, put forward the thesis that "the CET should be approved before the SIDPs. To back up this position, it used technical-economic arguments, particularly that the tariff should be a neutral instrument, which does not discriminate between the various productive sectors." Junta, Acta final del XVI periodo

de sesiones extraordinarias de la Comisión, February 28-April 9, 1976, p. 6.

69. Ibid., p. 6.

70. In 1976 when the deadline for the approval of SIDPs ended, Chile and Colombia were prepared to extend the terms for approving the SIDPs by 18 months, if and when a list was drawn up to exclude many products from the reserve and if the Junta were to put forward the remaining programs within 9 months. They did not include in their planning the delaying of the free trade program nor the additional period for the CET, which was a de facto prerequisite for the adoption of the CET. Junta, Documento de evaluación, 1976, Jun/di 248, June 22, 1977, p. 1.3.

71. Ibid.

72. See Acta de la XVI Sesion Extraordinaria de la Comisión, February-April 1976, pp. 92-98; Documento de Evaluación, p. 1.3; and La Exposición del Representante Titular Peruano ante el XIX Periodo de Sesiones de la Comisión, Documento, COM/XIX/di, December 10, 1975, p. 2.

73. This was substantiated in an interview held by the author in April 1978 with the head of the Unidad de Planeación Global del Departamento Nacional de Planeación de Colombia, in which he stressed that Colombia is only interested in the commercial aspects of integration and that the country will prevent the approval of, or its participation in, other programs. But as Colombia is an important member this means that there is little hope for more SIDPs to be approved.

74. Comisión, Trigesimo Periodo de Sesiones Extraordinarias, Acta Final, September 1-4, 1981, Bogotá-Paipá; and Junta, Reactivación del Proceso.

75. Approval of these SIDPs has induced some authors to conclude that the Andean Group has successfully resolved the problems of allocating industries efficiently. See Ffrench-Davis, The Andean Pact; Guerrero, Programación de la Industria Metalmecánica.

76. A detailed study of this program is M. Avila, "Programación de la industria metalmecanico en el Acuerdo de Cartagena," Revista de la Integración, INTAL, Buenos Aires, May 1973.

77. During the meeting of the Presidents of the Andean countries held in Washington in September 1977 on the occasion of the signing of the Panama Agreement, they manifested the "political will" to approve the automobile SIDP immediately. See "Declaración Conjunta de las Presidentes de los Países Miembros del Grupo Andino," Washington, September 7, 1977.

78. See Finals del XIV perio de la Comisión, May 1975; and Acta Final del XIX perio sesiones de la Comisión, December 1975.

79. According to the Jefe de Planeacion Global del Departamento Nacional de Planeacion de Colombia, Colombia changed the position it had maintained against the program for four years, when its meaning was changed and it was converted into a program of coproduction and assembly and not one of production. Interview, with the author, April 1978. For definition of the various agreements, see p. 0410, note No. 13.

80. Junta, Documento de evaluación, 1975, Jun/di 198, 196, Lima, March 25, 1976, Anexo VII, p. 13. This is confirmed in Junta, Evaluación del Proceso de Integración 1969-1979, Lima, Marzo de 1979, Anexo Técnico No. 3, Jun/di 359 pp. 303-305. COMISION, Resumen de las Situaciones de Incumplimiento y Reclamos por Materias, COM/XXXI/dt3 Nov. 14, 1980; Junta, Desarrollo del Proceso de Integración Andina Durante 1980, Jun/di 444/Enero de 1989, pp. 17-19. Junta, Apreciaciones de la Situación Actual del Proceso de Integración Económica del Acuerdo de Cartagena, Jun/dt11/ 7 de Julio de 1981, pp. 10-13.

81. A detailed study of the fulfillment of the agreement on the CET and tariff reductions in favor of those countries receiving allocations makes it possible to say that the basic points have not been put into operation, and that the members strongly resist the opening of their markets. Bolivia was 32 months late, Colombia 12, Chile 18, and Ecuador 33; only Peru complied on time. See Junta, Documento de evaluación, 1975, p. 15. El documento de evaluación, Jun/di/248, June 1977, shows erratic behavior in the application of the margins of preference, apart from the fact that 50% of designated production had no margins of preference (pp. 11-28).

82. R.L. Allen suggests that countries are more or less attractive to investors according to their general attitude and economic policies, "so that in fact, the location of investment is not indifferent to the specific country and it is the market of that country which is regarded as of primary importance in making the investment decision." R.L. Allen, "Integration in Less Developed Areas," in Kyklos, 1967, p. 325.

83. Junta, Informo de Evaluación del Proceso de Integración Subregional Andino, 1977, Jun/di 295, March 20, 1978, p. II, 7-10.

84. In the Documento de Evaluación de 1977, the Junta verified new petrochemical production in Venezuela, and expansion of existing production in Colombia. Bolivia, Ecuador, and Peru have carried out feasibility studies on projects that would need investments of US$549.3 million, 502 million, and 737

million, respectively. In general, the State assumes the responsibility for investment in petrochemicals, because the sector is very closely linked to national programs: it is considered to be a strategic sector and therefore there is more activity here than in the light engineering program.

85. Junta, Informe de Evaluación, 1976, Jun/di 248, p. II, 2.19.

86. Ibid.

87. Junta, Evaluación del Proceso de Integración 1969-1979, Anexo técnico No. 3, Jun/di 359, May 30, 1979, pp. 185-190.

88. Ibid. pp. 298-305; Junta, Desarrollo del Proceso de Integración Andina durante 1979, Jun/di 444, Enero 1980. p. 16.

89. Junta, Apreciaciones sobre, dt/Julio de 1980 pp. 10-14.

CHAPTER 8

1. Junta, Informe de Evaluación del Proceso de Integración 1969-1979, Lima, 1979.

BIBLIOGRAPHY

PRIMARY SOURCES

Periodicals and Statistical Publications

Banco Central de Bolivia, Cuentas Nacionales, La Paz, 1969-1974.

Banco Central del Ecuador, Cuentas Nacionales del Ecuador, No. 7, Quito, March 1977.

Banco de la República, Cuentas Nacionales 1970-1975, Bogotá, 1976.

Banco Central de Chile, Memoria Anual, Santiago, 1970-1975.

Banco de Reserva del Perú, Memorias, Lima, 1970-1976.

Banco Central de Venezuela, Informe Económico, 1976.

Balance of Payments Yearbook, IMF, Washington, D.C.: Vols. 15, 20, 21 and 28.

Boletín de Comercio Exterior, Dirección General de Estadísticas y Censos Nacionales, Caracas, 1972-1976.

Boletín Mensual, Banco Central de Chile, Santiago, 1972-1976.

Boletín del Banco Central del Ecuador, Quito, 1972-1976.

Boletín del Banco de Reserva del Perú, Lima, 1970-76.

Boletín de la Integración, INTAL, Buenos Aires, 1969-1975.

Boletín Demográfico, CELADE, Santiago, various issues.

Boletín Estadístico, Banco Central de Bolivia, various issues.

Boletín Mensual, Banco Central de Venezuela, 1970-1976.

Boletín Mensual de Estadística, DANE, Bogotá, various issues.

Coyuntura Andina, Fedesarrollo, Bogotá, 1976-1978.

Coyuntura Económica, Fedesarrollo, Bogotá, 1969-78.

Carta Informativa, Junta, Lima, 1970-78.

Comercio Exterior, mimeo., 1970-79.

Derecho de la Integración, INTAL, Buenos Aires, 1967.

Economic Survey of Latin America, ECLA, Santiago, 1966-1974.

El Comercio, Lima, Perú, 1975.

El Espectador, Bogotá, 1972-1975.

El Informador Andino, Bogotá, 1974-1975.

El Mercurio, Santiago de Chile, 1975.

El Tiempo, Bogotá, Colombia, 1965-1975.

Información Estadística, Banco Central del Ecuador, various issues.

Información Económica, Banco Central de Venezuela, various issues.

Informe Anual del Gerente, Banco de la Republica, Bogotá, various issues.

Integración Latino-Americana, INTAL, Buenos Aires, 1976-1978.

Revista de la CEPAL, ECLA, Santiago, 1976-1978.

Revista de la Integración, INTAL, Buenos Aires, 1968-1977.

Statistical Yearbook, United Nations, New York, various issues.

Yearbook of Trade Statistics, United Nations, New York, various issues.

Yearbook of Industrial Statistics, United Nations, Vols. I, J, K, L, 1974-1976.

B. Official Publications

ALALC (publicaciones en orden cronológico)

General aspects.

Tratado de Montevideo, Montevideo, 1961.

Resoluciones del Comité Ejecutivo Permanente, Montevideo, 1963.

Resoluciones de la Conferencia de las Partes Contratantes, Montevideo, 1963.

Declaración de Bogotá, Bogotá, 1966.

Declaración de los Presidentes de América, Punta del Este, Uruguay, 1967.

Latin American Concensus of Vina del Mar, Organization of American States, OEA/Ser H/X14 CIES/1403, June 16, 1969.

Publicaciones del Acuerdo de Cartagena (en orden cronológico).

Bases Generales para una Estrategia Subregional de Desarrollo, Lima, 1972.

Informe Final de la Primera Reunión de Expertos Gubernamentales de Oficinas de Planificación, ONP/1 Informe Final, June 1974.

Informe del Primer Seminario Inter-regional sobre Planificación Integrada de los Países Miembros, Jun/S1 PL/1 Informe final, Dic. 1974.

Bolivia, Desarrollo e Integración, Jun/S1 PL/1 dt 6 rev. J., November 23 1974.

Colombia Situación y perspectivas de la Economía Colombiana en relación con el Proceso de Integración Andina, Jun/S1 P1/Idt, 4 November 1974.

Ecuador Integración Andina y Desarrollo Economico: el caso ecuatoriano, Jun/SI PL/Idt, 3 November 1974.

La Estrategia de Desarrollo y la Integración Economica: El caso Venezolano, Jun/S1 PL/Idt, 5 November 1974.

Elementos para una Futura Estrategia Subregional Andina, considerando especialmente la incorporación de Venezuela, November 1974.

Características Económicas de Venezuela y su relación con el Grupo Andino, November 1974.

Indicadores Socio-Económicos de la Subregion Andina, J/PR 46, 1975.

Analisis y Perspectivas de la Balanza de Pagos de los paises del Grupo Andino, J/PR/58 add, 1 January 1975.

Acta Final del Cuarto Período de Sesiones Ordinarias del Comité Asesor Económico y Social, 22 May 1975.

La Subregión Andina, UNCTAD, Junta, January 1976, 3 vols.

Informe de Evaluación de la Marcha del Proceso de integración 1968-1975, Jun/di 195, March 1976.

Anexos Técnicos al Documento de Evaluación de la Marcha del Proceso de Integración, Jun/di 196, March 1976.

Indicadores Socio-Económicos de la Subregión Andina, J/PR50 rev., 3 March 1976.

Distribución de Ingresos y Estructura del Consumo-Area Urbana, J/PR 68, 15 March 1976.

La Población Andina y su Capacidad de Compra, J/PR 701, 19 April 1976.

Situación Económica y Social de Venezuela y sus Perspectivas, UNCTAD and Junta, Lima, 1976.

Perú su situación económica y social y sus perspectivas immediatas, UNCTAD and Junta, Lima, 1976.

Situación Económica y Social del Ecuador y sus perspectivas, UNCTAD and Junta, Lima, 1976.

Situación Económica y Social de Colombia y sus perspectivas, UNCTAD and Junta, Lima, 1976.

Situación Económica y Social de Bolivia y sus perspectivas, UNCTAD and Junta, Lima, 1976.

Evaluación de la Marcha del Proceso de Integración, Jun/di 195, 25 March 1976.

Informe de Evaluación de la Marcha del Proceso de Integración Andina 1976, Jun/di 247, 1977.

Anexo Técnico al Informe de Evaluación del Comercio Subregional 1971-1975, J/DS-E/44, 1977.

Grupo Andino Comercio Global e Intra-Subregional 1971-1975, J/DS-E/44, 1977.

Programa Especial de Apoyo a Bolivia, Jun/Prop 82, 1977.

Incidencia de la Integración en el Desarrollo de Bolivia, Ministerio de Planeamiento y Coordinación, Junta, Lima, 1977.

Evolución de la Economía Colombiana, Departamento Nacional de Planeación, Junta, Lima, 1977.

Informe final de la tercera reunión del Consejo de Planificación, CPL/111/informe final rev., 1 November 1977.

Análisis de la Incidencia del Proceso de Integración en el Desarrollo Económico y Social de Venezuela, Oficina Central de Coordinación y Planificación de la Presidencia de la República, Junta, Lima, 1977.

Indicadores Socio-Económicos de la Subregión Andina, Jun/di 277 add, 1 March 1977.

Apreciaciones sobre el Sistema Generalizado de Preferencias y el Grupo Andino. Jun/di 262, 31 August 1977.

Análisis de la Incidencia del Proceso de Integración Andina en la Economía de Venezuela. Jun/di 276.5, 21 November 1977.

Análisis de la Incidencia del Proceso de Integración Andina en la Economía de Bolivia. Jun/di 276.1, 16 November 1977.

Declaración de los Presidentes del Grupo Andino. Jun/di 265, 20 September 1977.

Protocolos de Arequipa, Decisión 128, April 1978.

Apreciación general del Acuerdo luego de los cambios producidos en 1976 (Informe de evaluación de la marcha del proceso de integración 1977), Jun/di 295, March 1978.

Evaluación de las Empresas Exportadoras de los Países Miembros del Grupo Andino, Jun/di 297, March 1978.

El Grupo Andino y los Medios de Comunicación Social. Jun/di 310, 29 May 1978.

Informe de la Junta sobre la Quinta Reunión de Directores de Promoción de Exportaciones. Jun/di 318, 13 June 1978.

Informe de Evaluación del Proceso de Integración Subregional Andino: 1977. Jun/di 295, 20 March 1978.

Declaración de los Presidentes de los Países Andinos. Jun/di 331, 10 August 1978.

Conclusiones Generales del Programa de Promoción Comercial entre las Comunidades Económicas Europeas y los Países del Grupo Andino. Jun/di 348, 7 December 1978.

Resumen, Comentario y Análisis del Documento Jun/di 297 Jun/di 305, 5 May 1978.

Indicadores Socioeconómicos de la Subregión Andina. Jun/di 277/Add. 1, 15 March 1978.

Indicadores Socioeconómicos 1970-1979. Junta del Acuerdo de Cartagena Lima, 26 May 1981.

Mandato de Cartagena. Jun/di 401, 29 May 1979.

Tratado que crea el Tribunal de Justicia del Acuerdo de Cartagena. Jun/di 402, 29 May 1979.

Tratado Constitutivo del Parlamento Andino. Jun/di 493, 20 August 1980.

Personalidad, Autonomía y Duración del Acuerdo de Cartagena. Jun/dt 107/Rv. 1, 4 May 1979.

Documentos relacionados con el Apoyo Latinoamericano al Proceso de Reconstrucción de Nicaragua. Jun/di 424, 30 August 1979.

Relaciones del Grupo Andino con los Estados Unidos y las Comunidades Europeas. Jun/dt 104/Rev. 1, 8 June 1979.

Anexo Técnico No. 7. Evaluación de la Situación y el Ecuador en el Proceso de Integración Subregional. Jun/di 363, 30 March 1979.

Anexo Técnico No. 10. Indicadores Socioeconómicos de la Subregión Andina. Jun/di 366, 30 March 1979.

Declaración de los jefes de Estado de los Países del Grupo Subregional Andina. Jun/di 407, 29 May 1979.

Anexo Técnico No. 9 Estadísticas de Comercio Exterior para el Grupo Andino: 1969-1977. Jun/di 365, 30 March 1979.

Comunicado Final de la Reunión entre la Junta del Acuerdo de Cartagena y la Secretaría General de la Comunidad Económica del Africa Occidental (CEAO). Jun/di 446, 31 January 1980.

Discurso del Señor Doctor Diego Uribe Vargas, Ministro de Relaciones Exteriores de Colombia en nombre de los Signatarios del Acuerdo de Cartagena, en la sesión solemne de la Junta, en Honor de los Señores Ministros de Relaciones Exteriores del Grupo Andino, de la República Federativa del Brasil y de España. Jun/di 442, 18 January 1980.

Desarrollo del Proceso de Integración Andino durante 1979. Jun/di 444, 29 January 1980.

Compromisos que han asumido los Países Miembros y que deberán cumplirlos a partir de 1980. J/PR/102, 8 April 1980.

Evaluación y Perspectivas del Perú en el Proceso de Integracion Andina. Gustavo González Prieto, Consultor. J/PR/103, 8 April 1980.

Perspectivas del Desarrollo Económico Venezolano en la Decada de los ochenta y su participacion en el proceso de Integración Andino. J/PR/104, 8 April 1980.

Incidencia del Proceso de Integración en el Desarrollo Económico y Social del Ecuador. J/PR/105, 8 April 1980.

La Problemática Social en la Integración Andina. Ponencia Presenta da al Seminario Pacto Andino, Sindicalismo y Democracia, Caracas, J/PR/106, 24 al 27 December 1980.

Lineamientos de Orientación del Proceso de Integración Andino. Anexo I: Indicadores Socioeconómicos; Previsiones a 1990. J/PR/107.1, 11 November 1980.

Lineamientos de Orientación del Proceso de Integración Andino. Anexo 2: Grupo Andino; Proyecciones nacionales de las principales variables económicas y sociales. J/PR/107.2, 11 November 1980.

Lineamientos de Orientación del Proceso de Integración Andino. Anexo 3: La Política de Desarrollo en la Subregión. J/PR/107.3, 11 November 1980.

Perú: Diagnóstico Nacional con énfasis en el proceso de integración. J/PR/108, 20 November 1980.

Incidencia del Proceso de Integración Económico y Social de Bolivia. J/PR/109, 23 January 1981.

Organización Institucional Monetaria y Financiera de los Países del Grupo Andino. J/PR/129, 17 April 1980.

Desarrollo del Proceso de Integración Andino. Durante 1979. Jun/di 444, 29 January 1980.

Elementos para la Definición de la Posición Andina respecto a las relaciones comerciales entre el Grupo Andino y los Estados Unidos: Sistema Generalizado de Preferencias y Medidas para Promoción del Comercio Recíproco. J/PE/130, 29 April 1980.

Las negociaciones Comerciales Multilaterales del GATT y el Grupo Andino. J/PE/131, 30 April 1980.

Elementos para la Definición de la Posición Andina respecto a las relaciones comerciales entre el Grupo Andino y los Estados Unidos: Sistema Generalizado de Preferencias y Medidas para la Posición del Comercio Recíproco. J/PE/130/Add. 1 2

Importaciones del Grupo Andino de Productos no producidos realiza dos en 1977 y 1978. J/PE/132, 26 August 1980.

Orientaciones para la armonización de los incentivos tributarios a las exportaciones no tradicionales. J/PE/133, 23 September 1980.

Análisis del artículo 105 del Acuerdo de Cartagena en lo que se refiere a las franquicias para el mercado interno de Bolivia y el Ecuador, Contemplados en los artículos 37, 13 y 47 de la propuesta 96/MOD. 1 J/PE/134, 5 November 1980.

Elementos de un plan de acción, destinado a reactivar el proceso de interpretación económica subregional. Jun/dt 172, 10 July 1981.

Anotaciones sobre la formación del Mercado Ampliado en el Grupo Andino. dt 2, 7 July 1981.

Informe sobre la Coyuntura de los Países Andinos. J/PR/113, 30 August 1981.

Resumen de las situaciones de incumplimiento y reclamos por materias. COM/XXXI dt 3, 14 November 1980.

Cumplimiento de los compromisos derivados del Acuerdo de
 Cartagena y de las decisiones de la comisión. Jun/di 478,
 .26 June 1980.

Bases para la Revisión de la Decisión 46. Jun/dt 138, 18 July
 1980.

Informe de la Junta sobre Revisión de la Norma de Reserva.
 Jun/dt 129/Rev. 1, 11 August 1980.

Consideraciones de la Junta del Acuerdo de Cartagena respecto
 a la elaboración del "Planteamiento de orientación general
 del proceso de integración hasta 1990." Jun/dt 132, 31
 January 1980.

Harmonization of macroeconomic policies.

Decisión 24 sobre el régimen de tratamiento común a los capitales extranjeros y sobre marcas, patentes, licencias y
 regalías, Junta, Lima, 1971.

Informe Final de la Tercera Reunión del Consejo Monetario y
 Cambiario, CMC/111/Informe Final, Dic. 1974.

Bases para la Armonización de las Políticas Monetaria y Cambiaria de los Países Miembros de Grupo Andino, Jun/dt 54
 17 dic. 1974.

Acta final de la Segunda Reunión del Consejo de Comercio
 Exterior de Mercaderias, CCE/11/dt, 2 March 1975.

Bolivia: Instrumentos y Mecanismos de Regulación del Comercio
 Exterior de Mercaderías, CEE/11/dt, 3 March 1975.

Colombia: Instrumentos y Mecanismos de Regulacion del Comercio Exterior de Mercaderias, CEE/11/dt, 4 March 1975.

Chile: Instrumentos y Mecanismos de Regulación del Comercio
 Exterior de Mercaderías, CEE/11/dt, 4 March 1975.

Ecuador: Instrumentos y Mecanismos de Regulación del Comercio Exterior de Mercaderías, CEE/11/dt, 5 March 1975.

Perú: Instrumentos y Mecanismos de Regulación del Comercio
 Exterior de Mercaderías, CCE/11/dt, 6 March 1975.

Venezuela: Instrumentos y Mecanismos de Regulación del Comercio Exterior de Mercaderías, CEE/II/dt, 7 March 1975.

Acta Final de la Tercera Reunión del Consejo de Comercio
 Exterior. CEE/III/Informe Final, November 1975.

Estudio sobre Compras Estatales en Colombia, J/PR/59, 1975.

Informe Final de la Quinta Reunión del Consejo Monetario y
 Cambiario, CMC/V/Informe Final, 21 November 1975.

Orientaciones Generales para la Armonización de la Política
 Fiscal, J/PE/51, November 1975.

Normas vigentes sobre Inversión Extranjera en el Ecuador. Jun/di 188, 22 December 1975.

"Análisis y perspectivas de la Balanza de Pagos de los paises del Grupo Andino", J/PR/72, July 1976.

Informe Final de la Sexta Reunión del Consejo Monetario y Cambiario, CMC/VI/Informe Final, 3 September 1976.

Informe de la Junta a la Comisión sobre Cumplimiento del Acuerdo y las Decisiones: COM/XXI/di 3 Rev. 1, November 1976.

Acta final de la Cuarta Reunión del Consejo de Comercio Exterior, CEE/IV/Informe Final, 25 January 1978.

Anexo Técnico No. 4. Evaluación de la Inversión Directa Extranjera en el Grupo Andino y de la Administración de la Decisión 24 Jun/di 360, 30 March 1979.

Sectoral industrial programming.

Consideraciones para la programacion del sector metalmecánico, Junta/dt II, Lima, 1971.

Bases y Propuestas Generales para la elaboración de los Programas Sectoriales de Desarrollo Industrial, Representacion de Colombia, COM/VI-E/December 1971.

Propuesta de la Junta sobre Desarrollo del Sector Petroquimico, Prop. No. 44, corrig 1, 1974.

Propuesta de la Junta sobre Desarrollo del Sector Automotriz, Prop. No. 45, corrig 1, 1974.

Propuesta de la Junta sobre el Programa Sectorial de Desarrollo de la Industria Electronica y de Telecomunicaciones, Jun/prop 69, dic. 1975.

Política Tecnológica Andina: Un caso de Investigación conjunta. Jun/di 178, 11 August 1975.

Propuesta de la Junta sobre el Desarrollo de la Industria Siderúrgica, Jun/prop 66/Rev 4, November 1976.

La Racionalización Industrial en el Grupo Andino. Jun/dt 69/Rev. 1, 18 October 1976.

Anexos Técnicos al Documento de Evaluación de la marcha del Proceso de Integración. Jun/di 196, 25 March 1976.

Programas Andinos de Apoyo a Bolivia Proyecto 1 Identificación de Oportunidades para la Instalación de Complejos Industriales. Análisis respecto de los complejos Industriales Metalmecánicos para Bolivia. J/PAB/8/Rev. 1, 22 November 1978.

Informe de la Junta sobre el Avance de las Producciones Asignadas en el Programa Sectorial de la Industria Metalmecánica. Jun/di 194/Rev. 5, 31 March 1978.

Reglamento del Intercambio Compensado. Jun/dt 99, 2 August 1978.

Identificación de Oportunidades para la Instalación de Complejos Industriales en Bolivia. Jun/dt 98/Rev. 1, 15 May 1978.

Anexo Técnico No. 8. Los Aspectos de la Integración y la coordinación con los Convenios Andres Bello, Hipólito UNANUE y Simón Rodríguez.

Diagnóstico de la Industria de Bicicletas y Componentes en el Grupo Andino: Antecedentes y Análisis Preliminar. Jun/dt 115, 24 August 1979.

La Evaluación del Programa Petroquímico Resumen, Conclusiones y Recomendaciones Jun/di 374, 25 March 1979.

Bases para la propuesta de la Junta sobre el Desarrollo de la Industria Siderúrgica. Jun/dt 120, 30 October 1979.

Informe del avance en la Evaluación del Programa Petroquimíco. Jun/dt 114, 23 August 1979.

Informe sobre la comprobación de producciones en países miembros que no qozan de la asignación correspondiente en la decisión 57 y relevamiento de las producciones en Venezuela, vinculadas con la propuesta 100. Jun/di 375, 3 April 1979.

Programa Sectorial de Desarrollo de la Industria Automotriz Proyecciones de Demanda de Vehículos Estudio Preliminar. C. AUT. DEC. 120/IX/dt 4/Rev. 1, 24 November 1979.

Anexo Técnico No. 3. Evaluación de la Programación Industrial Jun/di 359, 30 March 1979.

Anexo Técnico No. 5 Evaluación de la Política Tecnológica Jun/di 361, 30 March 1979.

Términos de referencia para el Estudio de la Racionalización de la Industria Textil en el Grupo Andino. Jun/dt 128, 17 January 1980.

Caracterización de Sectores Industriales para determinar prioridades de Racionalización Industrial. Jun/dt 126, 16 January 1980.

Maquinas herramientas en Bolivia. Proyecto Integral de Desarrollo. Jun/di 475, 18 June 1980.

La Subcontratación Internacional Industrial. Jun/dt 497, 30 August 1980.

Caracterización de Sectores Industriales para determinar prioridades de Racionalización Industrial Jun/dt 126, 16 January 1980.

Bases para la propuesta sobre el tratamiento de los programas industriales de los sectores electrónico y de telecomunicaciones, farmoquímico y químico. Jun/dt 140, 13 August 1980.

Bases para el Programa Sectorial de Desarrollo de la Industria de Fertilizantes. Jun/dt 125/Rev., 23 May 1980.

Bases para la Revisión de la Decisión 46 Jun/dt 138, 18 July 1980.

Términos de referencia para el estudio de la racionalización de la Industria Textil en el Grupo Andino. Jun/dt 128, 17 January 1980.

Informe de la Junta sobre la elaboración de Programas Sectoriales e Intersectoriales de Desarrollo Industrial Jun/dt 127, 17 January 1980.

Máquinas Herramientas en Bolivia. Proyecto Integral de Desarrollo. Jun/di 475, 18 June 1980.

Información sobre el Programa Sectorial de Desarrollo de la Industria Metalmecánica. Jun/di 462/Rev. 1, 16 June 1980.

Informe sobre el Programa Sectorial de Desarrollo de la Industria Automotriz. Jun/di 461/Rev. 1, 16 June 1980.

Consideraciones sobre la Programación Industrial conjunta en el Grupo Andino. dt 3, 7 July 1981.

Common external tariff.

Orientaciones para la Elaboración del Arancel Externo Común, J/PE/13/Rev. 1, Lima, October 1973.

La Armonización Aduanera y el Arancel Externo Común en el Grupo Andino, J/PE/29, Lima, 1974.

Proyecto de Bases para la Elaboración del AEC, CCE/It/dt, 14, May 1975.

Aplicación del Criterio de Industria Incipiente en el AEC, CEE/II dt 11, May 1975.

Aplicación del Criterio Empleo en el CET, CCE/11/dt, 9 May 1975.

Aplicación del Criterio de Contribución Tecnológica en el AEC, CEE/11/dt 12, May 1975.

La Situación Arancelaria delos Países Miembros del Grupo Andino, J/PE/45, 1975.

El Proceso de Elaboración del AEC, J/PE/63, 1976.

Propuesta de la Junta sobre Modificación al Arancel Externo Mínimo Común, Jun/Prop 77, November 1976.

Antecedentes sobre el Arancel Externo Común, J/PE/86 rev. 1, 1978.

Indicadores Generales y Estructura de la Protección Nominal del Arancel Externo Minimo Comun de la Decisión 104, J/PE/80, 1978.

Anexo Técnico No. 1. Evaluación de la Armonización de Políticas Económicas y de la Aplicación del Arancel Externo y del Programa de Liberación. Jun/di 357, 30 March 1979.

Informaciones Complementarias a la propuesta 96 de la Junta sobre Arancel Externo Común y Armonización de los Instrumentos de Comercio Exterior. Jun/dt 96/Rev. 1, 26 November 1979.

Análisis Comparativo de los Aranceles Nacionales de Colombia, Perú y Venezuela con los niveles del Arancel Externo Común correspondiente a 1983. Jun/di 454, 25 March 1980.

Ambito de aumento de los aranceles nacionales como consecuencia de la aproximación del Arancel Externo Común. Jun/ di 453/Rev. 1, 24 June 1980.

Información sobre el Programa Sectorial de Desarrollo de la Industria Petroquímica. Jun/di 460/Rev. 1, 16 June 1980.

Criterios correctivos utilizados en la Propuesta 96/Mod. 1 de la Junta sobre Arancel Externo Común y armonización de los Instrumentos de Comercio Exterior. Jun/dt 136, 14 May 1980.

Propuesta de la Junta sobre Arancel Externo Común y Armonización de los Instrumentos de Comercio Exterior. JUNTA-Prop. 96/Mod. 1, 17 May 1980.

Información Estadística sobre los Niveles Mínimos de la franja del Arancel Externo Común para 1983 y 1990 y aranceles nacionales vigentes. COM/XXV-E/dt 4, 5 March 1980.

Agricultural policy.

Lista de productos agropecuarios para los efectos de la aplicación de los artículos 72, 73 y 99 del acuerdo. Decisión 16, 14-20, October 1970.

Primeras medidas para incrementar el comercio de productos agropecuarios. Decisión 43, 9-18 December 1971.

Sistemas de estadísticas e informaciones de mercados.   COM
    AGR/5, 4 August 1971.

El comercio de productos agropecuarios de los países de la
    subregión y la acción de los organismos estatales de co-
    mercialización. JUN/COM. AGR/di/03, August 1971.

Lista de productos agropecuarios para los efectos de la apli-
    cación de los artículos 72, 73 y 99 del acuerdo expresada
    en términos de Nabandina. Decisión 66, 4-9 September
    1972.

Addendum, características de la oferta y demanda de aceites y
    grasas comestibles de los países de la subregión. Jun/
    Reg. OAG/Idt 1/Add. I, 13 June 1972.

Características de la oferta y demanda de aceites y grases
    comestibles de los países de la subregión.   Jun/Reg.
    OAG/I/dt 1, 9 June 1972.

Informe sobre la situación y perspectivas de los aceites y
    grasas en los países del Pacto Andino.   Jun/Reg. OAG/
    I/di 1, 19 June 1972.

Informe sobre la situación y perspectivas del trigo, arroz y
    maíz en los países del Grupo Andino.   J.PR/16, 9 Novem-
    ber 1972.

Programa subregional de grasas y aceites comestibles.   Jun/
    Reg. OAG/I/1, 21 June 1972.

Situación actual y perspectivas de la oleaginosas en Colombia.
    Jun/Reg. OAG/I/2, 21 June 1972.

Situación de la industria oleaginosa.   Jun/Reg. OAG/I/3, 21
    June 1972.

Situación de la industria de acietes y grasas comestibles en
    Chile. Jun/Reg. OAG/I/4, 21 June 1972.

Informe sobre la situación y perspectivas del trigo, arroz y
    maíz en los países del Grupo Andino.   J.PR/16, 9 Novem-
    ber 1972.

Imagen Agropecuaria dentro del marco de la integración an-
    dina. J/PR/31, Lima, October 1973.

Planteamientos de acción para el Sector Agropecuario en el
    Marco de la Integración Andina.   Jun/dt, 24 Dec. 1973.

Creación del Consejo Agropecuario. Decisión 76, 29 April to 2
    May 1974.

Lista de productos agropecuarios para los efectos de la apli-
    cación de los artículos 72, 73 y 99 del acuerdo expresada
    en términos de Nabandina.   Decisión 80, 29 April to 2
    May 1974.

Propuesta de la Junta sobre Desarrollo del Sector Fertilizantes.
    Prop. No. 47, 1974.

Comercialización Agropecuaria.   Decisión 93, 22 to 25 October
    1975.

Propuesta de la Junta sobre el Sistema Andino de Sanidad
    Agropecuaria. Jun/Prop 62, January 1975.

Propuesta de la Junta sobre Servicio Subregional de Informa-
    ción de Mercados y Precios de Productos Agropecuarios.
    Jun/Prop 63, January 1975.

Sanidad Agropecuaria. Decisión 92, 22 to 25 October 1975.

Primera reunión del grupo de trabajo de programación agrope-
    cuaria. GT. AGR/I, 17 November 1975.

Consumo histórico y perspectivas de demanda de fertilizantes
    en la subregión andina. Jun/dt 30 y Jun/dt 30 Rev. 1,
    19 October 1972 and 28 April 1975.

Modelo de convenio de cooperación técnica recíproca entre
    países del Grupo Andino. Jun/RE.CTOSA/I/2, 5 August
    1975.

Sistema subregional de información estadística-sector agrope-
    cuario. J/DS-E/21, 24 April 1975.

Modificación a la decisión 92 Sanidad Agropecuaria.   Decisión
    106, 25 to 30 November 1976.

Bases para un primer programa andino de fomento agroindus-
    trial. J/DA/2, 26 October 1976.

Proyecto de bases para un programa de fomento agroindustrial
    en la subregión andina. Jun/dt 74, 23 November 1976.

Bases para la implantación de servicios de información de
    mercados y precios de productos e insumos agropecuarios.
    Sistemas nacionales, sistema subregional.   Jun/Reg.
    CA/Idt 1, 28 April 1976.

Indices comparados del costo de vida. J/DS-E/26, 20 January
    1976.

El proceso de integración en el desarrollo agropecuario sub-
    regional. J/DA/1, 15 September 1976.

Reunión de Ministros de Agricultura de los Países Miembros.
    Decisión 121, 12 to 16 December 1977.

Esquema para un plan indicativo agropecuario de la subregión
    andina. C.AGR/III/dt 3, 4 July 1977.

Diagnóstico agroindustrial de los productos trigo, carne
    bovina, coche, maíz-sorgo y oleaginosas. Términos de
    referencia. Jun/R. JOP. SA/II/dt 2, 18 October 1977.

Propuesta para la iniciación y desarrollo del sistema andino de planificación agropecuaria. C.AGR/IV/dt 3, 28 December 1977.

Modificación de la decisión 92 sobre Sanidad Agropecuaria. Decisión 122, 12 to 16 December 1977.

Informe final de la primera reunión de jefes de oficinas de planificación del sector agropecuario de los países miembros del Acuerdo de Cartagena. Jun/R. JOP. SA/I/ Informe Final Rev. 1, 12 April 1977.

Informe final de la segunda reunión de jefes de oficinas de planificación del sector agropecuario de los países miembros del Acuerdo de Cartagena. Jun/R. JOP. SA/ II/Informe Final, 18 November 1977.

Proyectos específicos de integración agropecuaria. C.AGR/ III/dt 4, 4 July 1977.

Términos de referencia. Proyecto trigo. Jun/R. JOP.SA/II/dt 3, 25 October 1977.

Acta Final del XX Período de Sesiones Ordinarias de la Comisión, COM/XX/Informe Final. October 1976.

Acta Final del 20th Período de Sesiones Ordinarias de 12 Comisión. October 1976.

Acta Final del 21 Período de Sesiones Ordinarias de la Comisión. 25 to 30 November 1976.

Plan de Acción del Grupo Andino 1977-79. COM/XXII/di 1.

Comisión del Acuerdo de Cartagena Trigésimo Período de Sesiones Extraordinarias. Acta Final. 1 to 4 September 1981. Bogotá-Paipa (Colombia).

SECONDARY SOURCES

Books

Alden, J., and Morgan, R. Regional Planning: A Comprehensive View. London: Leonard Hill Books, 1974.

Andic, Fuat A., and Suphan Dosser, Douglas. A Theory of Economic Integration for Developing Countries: Illustrated by Caribbean Countries. London: George Allen and Unwin, 1971. (Studies in economics; 6).

Aragao, J.M. Seminario interno sobre teoría y estrategia de la Integración. 2. Buenos Aires, 29-30 May 1968. Elementos para una estrategia de integración del espacio y de los sistemas económicos concretos en América Latina. Buenos Aires: INTAL, 1968. INTAL SEM. 8/DT. 1.

Balassa, B. The Theory of Economic Integration. London: Allen and Unwin, 1961.

_____. Economic Development and Integration. Mexico: Centro de Estudios Monetarios Latinamericanos, 1965.

_____. Tariff Protection in Industrial Countries. New Haven: Yale University Press, 1966.

_____. The Structure of Protection in Developing Countries. Baltimore: Johns Hopkins Press, 1971.

_____. Economic Integration among Developing Countries. Washington: IBRD, 27 September 1974. (Bank Staff Working Paper; 186).

_____. Types of Economic Integration. Washington, D.C.: IBRD, 1974. (Bank Staff Working Paper; 185).

Barzanti, Sergio. The Underdeveloped Areas within the Common Market. Princeton: University Press, 1965.

Behrman, J.N. The Role of International Companies in Latin American Integration. Mass.: Lexington Books, 1972.

Berry, A., and Urrutia, M. Income Distribution in Colombia. New Haven: Yale University Press, 1977.

Bianchi, A. America Latina. Ensayos de Interpretación Económica Tiempo Latinoamericano. Santiago, 1969.

Bogolonov, A., and Shiryaev, Y. A New Approach to Economic Integration. Moscow: Progress Publishers, 1974.

Brabant van, I.M.P. Essays on Planning, Trade and Integration in Eastern Europe. Rotterdam: U.P., 1974.

Brown, R.T. Transport and Economic Integration of South America. Washington, D.C.: Brookings Institution, 1966.

Camacho, E. La Integración Andina Fundamentos Políticos y Perspectivas. La Paz, 1974.

Carnoy, M. Industrialization in a Latin American Common Market. Washington, D.C.: ECIEL-Lexington Books, 1972.

Centro Interuniversitario de Desarrollo Andino, ed. Variables Políticas de la Integración Andina. Santiago: U. Católica, 1974.

Cline, W.R. Benefits and Costs of Economic Integration in Central America. Washington, D.C.: Brookings Institution, 1975.

Cizelj, Boris. Ekonomska integracija medju zemljama u razvoju: neki teorijski i praktiani aupekti. (prepared for) Savetovanje "Jugoslavija i novi medjunarodni ekonomski poredak." Dubrovnik, 1979.

Cohen Orantes, I. Regional Integration and the Industrialization in Central America. Mass.: Lexington Books, 1972.

Colombia Departamento Nacional de Planeación. Planes y Programas de Desarrollo 1969-1972. Bogotá, 1969.

_____. Las Cuatro estrategias. Bogotá, 1972.

_____. Para Cerrar la Brecha. Bogotá, 1975.

Cooperación e integración económica y financiera. México: CEMLA Centro de Estudios Monetarios Latinoamericanos, 1970.

Corden, W. The Theory of Protection. Oxford: Clarendon Press, 1971.

Córdova, Armando, and Araujo, Orlando. Sobre integración latinoamericana. Caracas: Síntesis Dosmil, 1972. (Libros para desarrollo).

Curzon, V. The Essentials of Economic Integration: Lesson of EFTA Experience. London: Macmillan & Co., 1974.

Dell, S. Trade Blocks and Common Markets. London: Alfred A. Knopf, 1963.

_____. A Latin American Common Market? London, New York: Oxford U.P., 1966.

_____. Problemas de un Mercado Común en América Latina. Mexico: CEMLA, 1959.

Demas, W.E. The Economics of Development in Small Countries with Special Reference to the Caribbean. Montreal: McGill University Press, 1965.

_____. Essays on Caribbean Integration and Development. Kingston: University of West Indies, 1976.

Denton, G.R. Economic Integration in Europe. London: World University, 1971.

Díaz-Alejandro, C. The Andean Group in the Integration Process of Latin America. Standford, 1968.

_____. Colombian Foreign Trade Policies and Development. New Haven: Yale University Press, 1976.

Dosser, Douglas Andic, and Rivat Andic, Suphan. A Theory of Economic Integration for Developing Countries. London: G. Allen and Unwin, 1971.

ECIEL. Industrialización y Empleo en el Contexto de la Integración Latinoamericana. Rio: ECIEL, Brookings Institution, 1975.

Economic Commission for Latin America (ECLA). Exposición en la Comisión Económica para América Latina. E/CN 12/IX/ DI. 6, J May 1961.

_____ . The Latin American Common Market (UNSA-les No. 59 II 6.4.).

_____ . El Proceso de Industrialización en América Latina. (E/CN 12/716 rev. 1), New York, 1965.

_____ . El Pensamiento de la CEPAL. Santiago: Editorial Universitaria. 1969.

_____ . El Proceso de Industrialización en América Latina. Santiago, 1970.

_____ . La Demanda de Vehiculos Motorizados en América Latina. Santiago, 1971.

_____ . Integración Económica, Sustitución de Importaciones y Desarrollo Económico de América Latina. Santiago, 1974.

_____ . La Industrialización de América Latina en los Anos Setenta. SF/CEPAL/con 51/L2, Santiago, 1975.

_____ . La Exportación de Manufacturas en México y la Política de Promoción. México, 1976.

_____ . La Dimensión de la pobreza en América Latina. E/CEPAL/L 180, Santiago, 1978.

_____ . El Desarrollo Económico y Social y las Relaciones Económicas Externas de América Latina. E/CEPAL/1061, January 1979.

Ecuador. Lineamientos Fundamentales del plan integral de Transformación y Desarrollo, 1973-1977. Quito: Junta Nacional de Planificación y Coordinación Económica, 1972.

_____ . Plan Integral de Transformación y Desarrollo, 1973-1977. Quito: Junta Nacional de Planificación y Coordinación Económica, 1972.

Erbes, Robert. L'intégration économique internationale. Paris: Presses Universitaires de France, 1966.

Fekete, Judit. The Necessity of Economic Groupings and Their Main Features: Forms of Cooperation among the Countries of Asia and the Far East. Budapest: Institute for World Economics, 1974. (Studies on developing countries, 65).

Ffrench-Davis, Ricardo. Distribución de los Beneficios de la Integración Económica Entre Países en Desarrollo. Santiago de Chile: CIEPLAN. October, 1976.

Foltyn, J. Mezinárodni ekonomická integrace rozvojouych zemi. (Teoreticky nastim). Prague, 1973.

Foxley, A. Income Distribution in Latin America. New York, London: Cambridge University Press, 1976.

Fregerio, Rogelio. La Integración Regional: Instrumento de Monopolio. Buenos Aires: Hernández, 1968.

Friedrich, G. Gemeinsamer Markt in Ostafrika und Zentralamerika: ein Verguich. Hamburg: Hamburger Gesellschaft für Volkerrecht un auswartige Politik, 1975. (Verfassung und recht in ubersee. beihefte; 6.)

García, A. Integración Andina. Bogotá: Fundacion F. Nauman, 1974.

Green, R.H., and K.E.V. Krishna. Economic Cooperation in Africa. Retrospect and Prospect. London: Oxford University Press, 1967.

Grieg, R., ed. International Organization in the Western Hemisphere. Syracuse, 1968.

Griffin, K. Underdevelopment in Spanish America. London: Allen and Unwin, 1969.

Grunwald, J.; Wionczek, M.; and Carnoy, M. Latin American Economic Integration and U.S. Policy. Washington, D.C.: Brookings Institution, 1972.

Haas, Ernst B. The Obsolescence of Integration Theory. Berkeley, Cal.: University, Institute of International Studies, 1975. (Research Series, 25).

Haberler, E. The Theory of International Trade. London: Hodge, 1936.

Harrod, R., and Hague, eds. International Trade Theory in a Developing World. London: Macmillan & Co., 1963.

Hazlewood, A., ed African Integration and Disintegration. London: Oxford University Press, 1967.

_____. Economic Integration. New York: St. Martin's Press, 1976.

_____. Economic Integration: The East African Experiences. London: Heinemann, 1975.

Herrera, F. Hacia la Integración Acelerada de América Latina. Santiago: ECLA, 1960.

Hirschmann, A. The Strategy of Economic Development. New Haven: Yale University Press, 1958.

_____., ed. Latin American Issues, Essays and Comments. New York: The Twentieth Century Foundation, 1961.

_____. Ideologies of Development in Latin America. New York, 1965.

Hodges, M., ed. European Integration. London: Penguin Books, 1972.

Huelin, D. Investment in the Andean Group. London: Latin American Publications Fund, 1973.

IBRD. Economic Integration among Developing Countries. Washington International Bank for Reconstruction and Development, 27 September 1974. (Bank Staff Working Paper, 486).

Integración económica: trabajos de F. Andic, S. Andic, S.W. Arndt, Bela Balassa. y ostros. sel. de Suphan Andic y Simon Teitel. Mexico: Fondo de Cultura Economica FCE, 1977, (El Trimestre Economico. Lecturas, 19).

Instituto de Estudios Internacionales. Bolivia y los Problemas del Grupo Andino. La Paz: Universidad de San Andrés, 1970.

Johnson, H.E. Economic Policies Towards Less Developed Countries. New York: Praeger, 1967.

Junta-INTAL. Historia Documental del Acuerdo de Cartagena. Lima, 1974.

Kahnert, Friedrich et al. Economic Integration among Developing Countries. Paris: Development Centre/OECD, 1969.

Kansu, Gunal. Some Issues of Planning and Industrial Integration Among Developing Countries. Geneva: UNCTAD, 1974.

Kaser, M. COMECON: Integration Problems of the Planned Economies. London: Oxford University Press, 1967.

Kindleberger, P. Economic Development New York: McGraw Hill, 1958.

_____, ed. International Corporation, Cambridge, Mass.: MIT Press, 1970.

Krauss, Meluyn B., ed. The Economics of Integration: A Book of Readings. London: G. Allen and Unwin, 1973.

Kuczynski, M. Planned Development in the Andean Group Industrial Policy and Trade Liberalization. London: Latin American Publication Fund, 1973.

Labarca, León de, and Ivonne, Alba. La Integración Económica y sus Limitaciones en el Ambito de los Países Subdesarrollados. Maracaibo: Universidad del Zuila, Facultad de Derecho, 1976.

Linder, S. An Essay on Trade and Transformation. New York: John Wiley and Sons, 1961.

Lindberg, Leon N., and Scheingold, Stuart, A., eds. Regional Integration: Theory and Research. Cambridge, Mass.: Harvard University Press, 1971.

Lipsey, Richard G. The Theory of Customs Unions: A General Equilibrium Analysis. London: School of Economics and Political Science, 1970. (LSE research monographs; 7).

Lortie, Pierre. Economic Integration and the Law of GATT. New York: Praeger, 1975.

Machlup, Fritz, ed. Economic Integration: Worldwide, Regional, Sectoral. Proceedings of the International Economic Association held at Budapest, Hungary (from 19-24 August 1974). London: Macmillan & Co., 1976.

_____. A History of Thought on Economic Integration. London: Macmillan & Co., 1977.

Marchal, A. L'intégration Territoriale. Paris: Presses Universitaires de France, 1965.

Maizels, A. Industrial Growth and World Trade, Cambridge, Eng.: C.U.P., 1963.

Machova, D. CSSR y Socialisticke Delbe Prace. Prague, 1962.

Marglin, S.A. Approach to Dynamic Planning. Amsterdam: North Holland, 1963.

McClelland, D. The Central American Common Market, Economic Policies, Economic Growth and Choices for the Future. New York: Praeger, 1972.

_____, and Grunwald, J. Industrialization and Economic integration in Latin America. Washington, D.C.: Brookings Institution, 1975.

Meade, J.E. The Theory of Customs Unions. Amsterdam: North Holland, 1955.

Meade, J.G. Problems of Economic Union. Chicago: The University Press, 1953.

Morawetz, D. The Andean Group; A Case Study in Economic Integration Among Developing Countries. Cambridge, Mass.: MIT Press, 1974.

Morera, Batres, P. Seminario Sobre Perspectivas que Ofrecen los Procesos de Integración de América Latina a Los Paises de Menor Dimensión Económica de la Región. Buenos Aires, 8-26, octubre 1973.

Myrdal, G. Economic Theory and Underdeveloped Regions. London: University Paperbacks, 1975.

Murray, Tracy. Trade Preferences for Developing Countries: Problems of Economic Integration. New York: John Wiley & Sons, 1977.

Mytelka, Lynn Krieger. Regional Integration in the Third World: Some Internal Dimensions. Proceedings of the 5th International Conference of the Institute for International dimensions of regional integration in the Third World. Ottawa: University Press, 1975.

OECD. Economic Integration among Developing Countries. Paris: OECD, 1969.

Perroux, Francois. La integración y el Fracaso de la Teoria Tradicional de los Intercambios Exteriores: Un Método Propuesto para Interpretar la Integracion Europea y Latinamericana. Lima: Instituto de Planteamiento, 1968.

Peru. Plan de Desarrollo Económico y Social 1967-1970. Instituto Nacional de Planificación, Lima, Peru 1966.

_____. Lineamientos de la Política Económica-social del Gobierno Revolucionario. Oficina Nacional de Información, Lima, 1969.

_____. Plan Nacional de Desarrollo, 1971-1975, Oficina Nacional de Planificación, Lima, 1972.

Nye, J.S. Peace in Parts. Little, Brown and Co., 1972.

Prebisch, R. El Desarrollo Económico de América Latina y sus Principales Problemas. CEPAL, Santiago, 1950.

_____. Towards a Dynamic Development Policy for Latin America. New York: United Nations, 1963.

_____. Change and Development, Latin America's Great Task. New York: Praeger, 1971.

Ponce, Mario J. Expansion of Agricultural Trade in Grouping of Developing Countries. (current problems of economic integration). Geneva: UNCTAD, 1971.

Robson, Peter, ed. International Economic Integration. London: Penguin Books, 1971.

_____. Current Problems of Economic Integration: Fiscal Compensation and the Distribution of Benefits in Economic Groupings of Developing Countries. Geneva: UNCTAD, 31 July 1970.

Rosenthal. El Desarrollo Integrado de Centroamerica. Buenos Aires: Bid-Intal, 1973, Vols. X.

Rosenstein, R. Multinational Investments in the Framework of Latin American Integration, Interamerican Development Bank, Bogota, 1968.

Rothchild, Donald S., eds. Politics of Integration. Nairobi: East African Publ. House, 1968.

Salgado-Pena Herrera, Germánico. Reunión Interna de Consulta Sobre Integración Económica de América Latina, Santiago de Chile, 5-7 enero, 1977.

Salvador, G. Estrategia y Política de Fomento Industrial del Ecuador. Junta de Planificación del Ecuador, Quito, 1976.

Scitovsky, T. Economic Theory and Western European Integration. London: Allen and Unwin, 1958.

Seminario Sobre Teoría y Estrategia de la Integración. Buenos Aires, INTAL, 27 enero- 25 febrero, 1967. Teoria y estrategia de la integracion: esquema provisorio.

Streeten, P. Economic Integration: Aspects and Problems. Leyden: A.W. Sythoff, 1964.

_____, ed. Trade Strategies for Development, London: Macmillan & Co., 1973.

Sidjanski, Dujan. National Decision-making Processes and Regional Integration. Geneva: UNCTAD, 1975.

Simai, Mihaly, and Garam, Katalin, eds. Economic Integration: Concepts, Theories and Problems. Budapest: Akadémia Kiadó, 1977.

Sutcliffe, R.B. Industry and Underdevelopment. London: Addision-Wesley, 1971.

"The theory of integration and the Caribbean Community process: ten years on." Paper presented at Conference on Contemporary Trends and Issues in Caribbean International Affairs. Port of Spain, May 1977.

Tinbergen, J. On the Theory of Economic Integration. Amsterdam: North Holland, 1950.

_____. International Economic Integration. Amsterdam: Elsevier Publishing Company, 1965.

Tironi, E. "Economic Integration and Foreign Direct Investment Policies: The Andean Case." Ph.D. dissertation, Massachusetts Institute of Technology, 1976.

_____. La integración y el desarrollo nacional de los países andinos. IEP, Lima, 1977.

Thoumi, F. La Utilización de la Capacidad Instalada en Colombia. Fedesarrollo, Bogotá, 1974.

Tomasini, Luciano. Elementos Para un Estudio Sobre los Procesos de Integración y Otras Firmas de Cooperación en América Latina. Buenos Aires: INTAL, 1976.

UNCTAD. Current Problems of Economic Integration: The Distribution of Benefits and Costs in Integration among Developing Countries. New York: United Nations, 1973.

UNCTAD. Current Problems of Economic Integration: The Problems of Distribution of Benefits and Costs and Selected Corrective Measures. New York: UNCTAD, 1975. (Conference: Guatemala City, 10-19 December, 1973).

Unger, Ladislav. Intégration Économique entre Pays en Voie de Développement: analyse générale des problems théoretiques et pratiques. Geneve: Institut des Hautes Estudes Internationales, 1974.

Urquidi, V. Free Trade and Economic Integration in Latin America. Los Angeles: University of California Press, 1964.

Urrutia, M., and Berry, A. La Distribución del Ingreso en Colombia. Bogotá: La Carreta, 1975.

Vaitsos, C. Crisis en la Cooperación Económica Regional: La Integración entre Países Subdesarrolloados. Mexico: ILET, 1978.

Vanek, V. Economicky a Politicky Uyznam Uyvozu Strojirenskych Vyrobku z CSSR. Prague, 1960.

Velasco, A. La Voz de la Revolución. Vol 2. Oficina Nacional de Información, Lima, 1972.

Venezuela, Cuarto Plan de la Nación 1970-1974. Oficina Central de Coordinación y Planificación, Caracas 1971.

Viner, Jacob. The Customs Unions Issue. New York: Carnegie Endowment for International Peace, 1950.

Viner, V. International Trade and Economic Development. Glencoe: The Free Press, 1952.

Webb, R. Distribución del Ingreso en Perú, Lima: Instituto de Estudios Peruanos, 1975.

Weber, M. Economía y Sociedad (2 Vols.). Mexico: F.C.E., 1944, Vol. 1 p. 639.

White, Eduardo. Cuestión de la Propiedad Industrial en América Latina y su Papel en el Proceso de Desarrollo e Integración Económica. Buenos Aires: INTAL, 1976.

Wionczek, M. La Integración en América Latina. México: F.C.E., 1964.

_____. Problemas Involucrados en el Establecimiento de un Trato Común Para la Inversión Extranjera. Lima: Junta, 1970.

_____. El Grupo Andino y la Inversión Extranjera Privada. Lima: Junta, 1970.

Articles

Abangwu, George C. "Systems approach to regional integration in West Africa." Journal of Common Market Studies (Oxford) Vol. 13, Nos. 1-2, 1975, pp. 116-135.

Arndt, S.W. "On Discriminatory versus Non-Preferential Tariff Policies." In Robson, P. International Economic Integration. London: Penguin Books, 1972.

Abonyi, A., and Sylvain, I.J. "CMEA Integration and Policy Options for Eastern Europe: A Development Strategy of Dependent States." JCMS, Vol. 15, 1977.

Allen, R. "Integration in Less Developed Countries." Kyklos, Brasil, Vol. 14, 1961.

Anger Press. "Statement on the Stand of the Rumanian Workers' Party concerning the Problems of the World Communist and Working Class Movement." Supplement, April 1974.

Arline, W. Andrew. "Underdevelopment, dependence, and integration: the politics of regionalism in the Third World." International Organization 31, Winter 1977.

Asociación Nacional de Industriales. "Colombia y la Integración. Sugerencias para la Definicion de una Política." Bogotá, August 1974.

Avila, M. "Programación de la Industria Metalmecánica en el Acuerdo de Cartagena." Revista de la Integración, May 1973.

Bacha, E. "Venezuela y el Grupo Andino." Trimestere Económico, No. 37 (1), 1970.

_____. "Un modelo de Comercio entre Centro y Periferia en la tradición de Prebisch." Trimestre Económico, No. 162, 1974.

Baer, W. "The Economics of Prebisch and ECLA." Economic Development and Cultural Change. Enero 1962.

Baerresen, D.W. "A Method for Planning Economic Integration for Specific Industries." JCMS, Vol. 6, 1967.

Bhagwati, J. "Trade Diverting Custom Unions and Welfare Improvement: A Clarification." M.I.T. Working Paper, 1970.

Balassa, Béla. "Regional integration of trade: policies of less developed countries." In Trade Strategies for Development. Papers of 9th Cambridge Conference on Development Problems, September 1972. Edited by Paul Streeten, London: Macmillan & Co., 1973. pp. 176-186.

_____. "Tipologia dell 'integrazione economica." Economia Internazionale (Genova) Vol. 29, agosto-novembre 1976.

_____. "Towards a theory of economic integration." Kyklos (Basel) vol. 14, 1961. fase 1.

_____. "Hacia una Teoría de la Integración Económica." In Wionczek, M. La Integración de América Latina. FCE, mimeo., 1964.

_____. "Tariff Protection in Industrial Countries." Journal of Political Economics, No. 73, December 1965.

_____. "El Segundo Decenio para el Desarrollo y la Integración Económica Regional." Revista de la Integración, No. 11, November 1972.

_____. "Aranceles y Política Comercial en el Mercado Común Andino." Revista de la Integración, No. 16, May 1974.

Baranson, J. "Automotive Industries in Developing Countries." IBRD, Staff Occasional Papers, No. 8, 1969.

Barandiaran, L. "Antecedentes Políticos de la Decisión 24." International Seminar on Foreign Investments Regulations in the Andean Group. Caracas, March 1974.

Barrera, C. "Subdesarrollo, bloque e integración." Revista de la Integración. Buenos Aires, May 1970, pp. 90-122.

Bechler, Ekkehard. "Integration for Development: Hopes and Problems." Intereconomics. Hamburg, 8, 1976, pp. 218-221.

Bhambri. "Customs Unions and Underdeveloped Countries." Economia Internazionale. No. 15, March 1962.

Bernales, R.E. "Peru: Actares y Agentes Políticos Internos del Proceso de Integración Andina." Variables Políticas de la Integración Andina. U. Catolica de Chile, 1974.

Brewster, Havelock R. "Industrial Integration Systems." In UNCTAD: Current Problems of Economic Integration. New York: United Nations, 1971, pp. 67-126.

Bird, R. "The Need for a Regional Policy in a Common Market." Scottish Journal of Political Economy, No. 12, November 1966.

Boddewyn, J., and Kapoor, A. "The External Relations of American Multinational Enterprise." International Studies Quarterly, No. 16, Dic., London, 1972.

Bogomolov, D. "Dos Tipos de Integracion Internacional." Ciencias Sociales, No. 4, 1975.

Bond, R.D. "Business Associations and the Interest Politics In Venezuela: The Fedecamaras and the Determination of National Economic Policies." Ph.D. thesis, Vanderbilt University, May 1975.

Brewster, H. "The Central American Programme for Integrated Industrial Development." Public and International Affairs, Spring 1966.

_____. and Thomas C. "Aspects of the Theory of Economic Integration." JCMS, Vol. 8, No. 2, December 1969 pp. 110-132.

Brioner, A. "Crisis del Pacto Andino y Opciones de Desarrollo en América Latina." Comercio Exterior, Vol. 26, No. 6, México, 1976.

Brown, A.J. "Economic Separatism Versus a Common Market in Developing Countries." Yorkshire Bulletin of Economic and Social Research, No. 13, 1961.

_____. "Customs Union vs. Economic Separatism in Developing Countries." I. II. Yorkshire Bulletin of Economic and Social Research Vol. 13, Leeds, England, May 1962.

Browing, D. "The Rise and the Fall of the Central American Common Market." Journal of Latin American Studies, June 1974.

Bruno, M. "Protection and Tariff Change under General Equilibrium." Journal of International Economics, 1972.

Burnet, B.L. "The Role of Foreign Investment in the Andean Common Market." AID, Lima, 1972.

Chenery, H.B. "Patterns of Industrial Growth." American Economic Review, September 1960.

Comercio Exterior, "Grupo Andino; La crisis se agudiza." Comercio Exterrio, Vol. 26, No. 7, México, 1976.

_____. "La escision parece inevitable." Comercio Exterior, Vol. 26. Mp' 8. 1976.

Cooper, C.A., and Massell, B.F. "A New Look at Customs Union Theory." In Robson, P. International Economic Integration. London: Penguin Books, 1972.

_____. "Towards a General Theory of Customs Unions for Developing Countries." Journal of Political Economy, No. 73, October, 1965.

_____. "A New Look at Customs Union Theory." Economic Journal, no. 75, Dec. 1965.

Cuadra de S. "La Estructura de la Protección en Chile." Mimeo. Santiago: Universidad Católica, 1970.

Chiappe-Lemos, Ignacio. "La integración económica como instrumento del desarrollo." Universitas (Bogotá) Junion 1974, no. 46.

Cline, William R. "Beneficios y costos de la integración económica en Centroamérica." En SIECA beneficios y costos de la integración centroamericana. Guatemala, 1977.

Cohen - Orantes, Issac, and Rosenthal, Gert. "Reflections on the Conceptual Framework of Central American Economic Integration." CEPAL Review (Santiago) first sem. 1977, p. 21.

Corden, Max W. "Customs Union Theory and Nonuniformity of Tariffs." Journal of International Economics (1) Amsterdam, 1976.

_____. "Economics of Scale and Custom Union Theory." Journal of Political Economy Chicago, June 1972.

Curzon, Gerard and Victoria. "European Integration: Lessons for Developing World." In Trade Strategies for Development. pp. 189-197. Papers of the 9th Cambridge Conference on development problems, Sept. 1972. Edited by Paul Streeten. London: Macmillan & Co., 1973.

DANE. "Las inversiones extranjeras en la industria colombiana." Boletín, No. 302, Bogotá, 1976.

Dell, S. "Apreciaciones sobre el Funcionamiento del tratado de Montevideo." Wionczek, M. (ed.), Integración de América Latina; Experiencias y perspectivas, FCE, México, 1964.

_____. "Regional Integration and the Industrialization of Less Developed Countries." Development Digest, Vol. 3, No. 3, October 1965.

_____. "The Early Years of LAFTA." Wionczek, M., Latin American Economic Integration, New York: Praeger, 1966.

_____. "Regional Groupings and Developing Countries." In Trade Strategies for Development. Papers of the 9th Cambridge conference on development problems, Sept. 1972. Edited by Paul Streeten. London: Macmillan & Co., 1973.

Demas, W.E. "The Economics of West Indies Customs Unions." Social and Economic Studies, March 1960.

Denton, G.R. "Planning and Integration: Medium-Term Policy as an Instrument of Integration." Chatham House/PEP European Series, No. 5, September 1976.

Díaz-Alejandro, C. "The Andean Common Market Gestation and Outlook." In Analysis of Development Problems, eds.

Eckhaus & Rosenstein Rodan. Amsterdam: North Holland, 1973.

_____. "Las Exportaciones de Mercancías Colombianas." Trimestre Económico, Vol. XLIII, No. 171, 1976.

_____. "El efecto de la Exportaciones no tradicionales en la Distribución del Ingreso." Trimestre Económico, Vol. XLIV (2), No. 174, 1977.

Dosser, Douglas. "Customs Unions, Tax Unions, Development Unions." In Modern Fiscal Issues: Essays in Honour of Carl S. Shoup, eds. Richard M. Bird and John G. Head. Toronto: University Press, 1972.

Dragomanouíc, Uladimir. "Les formes de l'intégration des pays en voie de développement." Revue internationale (Beograd) 27 (627) mai 1976.

Dutta, A. "Domestic Distortions and Customs Union: a Geometrical Analysis." Journal of Development Studies (London) 1969.

Edel, Matthew. "Regional Integration and Income Redistribution: Complements or Substitutes." In The Movement toward Latin American Unity, ed. R. Hilton, pp. 185-202. New York: Praeger, 1969.

Edwards, S. "El efecto de un CET en la balanza de pagos y en el tipo de cambio: El Caso de Chile." Trimestre Económico Vol. XLIV, No. 3, 1977.

El-Shagi El-Shagi. "The Relevance of the Predominant Theories of Economic Integration for Development Strategy." Economics (Tübingen). Vol. 17, 1978, pp. 81-109.

Elkan, Peter G. "Measuring the Impact of Economic Integration Among Developing Countries." Journal of Common Market Studies 14 (Oxford) September 1975, pp. 56-68.

Flanders, J. "Prebisch on Protectionism: An Evaluation." American Economic Review, May 1950.

Ffrench-Davis, R. "La Integracion Andina." Revista de la Universidad Técnico del Estado, Nos. 11-12, Santiago, 1973.

_____. "La Planificación en el Pacto Andino y el Arancel Externo Común." Revista del la Integración, No. 17, September 1974.

_____. "The Andean Pact: A Model of Economic Integration for Developed Countries." World Development, Nos. 1 and 2, 1976.

Fedesarrollo, "El Comercio Exterior de Colombia en el Marco del Acuerdo de Cartagena, 1969-1975," Bogotá, May 1978.

Fernández, G.   "El Regimen Uniforme de la Empresa Multina-
cional en el Pacto Andino." Derecho de la Integración,
November 1972.

Figueroa, A.   "Estructura Social, Distribución de Ingresos e
Intergración Economica en el Grupo Andino." Tironi, E.,
ed. Pacto Andino, Caracter y Perspectivas, América
Problema 9, IEP, Lima, 1978.

Fldystad, Gunnar.   "Non-discriminating Tariffs, Customs
Unions and Free Trade." Kyklos (Basel) Vol. 28, No. 3,
1975.

_____.   "Trade-diverting Customs Unions, Welfare and
Factor   Market   Imperfections."   Weltwirt-schaftliches
Archiv. (Kiel) Bd 111, 1975, H. 2, pp. 243-252.

Foxley, A., and Munoz, O.   "Income Redistribution, Economic
Growth and Social Structure: The Case of Chile." Fox-
ley, A., ed., Income Distribution in Latin America,
London: Cambridge University Press, 1976.

Furnish, D.B.   "El Regimen Común del Grupo Andino para las
Inversiones Extranjeras." Derecho de la Integración, No.
14, 1973.

Garay, L.J., and Perry G.   "Algunos Interrogantes sobre las
Perspectivas del Grupo Andino." Coyuntura Andina, No.
1, Bogotá, Octubre, 1976.

_____.   "La Estrategia de Desarrollo Implícita en el
Acuerdo de Cartagena: ¿Una Alternativa de Desarrollo
Autónomo para los Países del Grupo Andino?." Coyuntura
Económica Vol. VII, No. 4, Diciembre, 1977.

García, R.P.   "Problemas de la Integración Regional."   In
Wionczek M.   Integración de la América Latina; Experiencias y Perpsectivas, FCE, México, 1964.

Glade, William.   "The Role of Public Sector Firms in the
Integration of Latin American Industrial Structure: Some
Preliminary   Observations."   In Economic   Integration:
Concepts, Theories and Problems, edited by Mihaly Simai
and Katalin Garam, pp. 255-284. Budapest: Akademia
Kiado, 1977.

Gilbert, G.C.   "Investment Planning for Latin American Economic Integration." JCMS, No. 11, Oxford, June 1973.

Gómez, B.H.   "Los Grupos Industriales y el Desarrollo Colombiano." Coyuntura Económica, Vol. VI, No. 4, 1976.

Granel, F.   "La retirada del Chile.   La Crisis del Pacto
Andino." Comercio Exterior, Vol. 27, No. 1, México,
1977.

Guerrero, M. "El Regimen Común de la Inversion Extranjera en el Grupo Andino." Derecho de la Integración, No. 8, 1973.

Haas, Ernst. "International Integration: The European and the Universal Process." In International Organization, Vol. 15, No. 4, 1961.

_____. "The Uniting of Europe and the Uniting of Latin America." Journal of Common Market Studies, Vol. 5, 1967.

_____. "The Study of Regional Integration: Reflections on the Joy and Anguish of Pretheorizing." International Organization, Vol. 24, 1970.

_____. "Turbulent Fields and the Theory of Regional Integration." International Organization. Madison, Wisc., Vol. 30, 1976, No. 2.

_____. and Schmitter, P.C. "Economics and Differential Patterns of Political Integration." In Davison, W.P., ed. International Political Communities. New York: Praeger, 1966.

Hague, D.C. "Integration: Worldwide, Regional and Sectorial." Journal of World Trade Law (London) 9, Jan-Feb. 1975, pp. 103-111.

Hansen, R. "Regional Integration: reflections on a Decade of Theoretical Efforts." World Politics (Princeton, N.J.) Vol. 21, 1969, pp. 242-272.

Harborth, Hans-Jürgen. "Transferability of Integration Models." Intereconomics (Hamburg) No. 5, May 1972, pp. 139-141.

Hazlewood, A. "A Common External Tariff for the Andean Group." Bolsa Review, No. 8, 1973.

Herrera. Felipe. "Polos de crecimiento e integración regional." Boletín de la integración (Buenos Aires) (22) 1967, pp. 467-176.

Hirsch, Seev. "The Impact of European Integration on Trade with Developing Countries: Empirical Evidence and Policy Implications." In Trade Strategies for Development. Papers of 9th Cambridge Conference on Development Problems, September 1972. Edited by Paul Streeten. London: Macmillan & Co., 1973.

Hirschmann, A. "The Political Economy of Import Substitution." Quarterly Journal of Economics Vol. LXXXII, 1968.

_____. "Cómo y porqué Desinvertir en América Latina," Trimestre Económico, No. 147, Vol. XXXVII, 1970.

Hofman, S. "Obstinate or Obsolete? The Fate of the Nation State and the Case of Western Europe." Dedalus, No. 95, 1966.

Ianni, C. "La Crisis de LAFTA y las Corporaciones Transnacionales." Comercio Exterior, México, 1971.

Iturbe, E. de Blanco. "La Estrategia de Desarrollo y la Integración: El Caso Venezolano." Junta, Lima, 1974.

Jaber, T.A. "The Relevance of Traditional Integration Theory to Less Developed Countries." JCMS. Vol. 9, No. 3, Oxford, March 1971, pp. 254-267.

Jarrett, R. "Disincentives: the Other Side of Regional Development Policy." Journal of Common Market Studies, No. 4, Oxford, 1975, pp. 379-390.

Johnson, H.G. "The Gains from Freer Trade with Europe: An Estimate." Manchester School of Economics and Social Studies, Vol. XXVI, No. 3, 1958.

_____. "An Economic Theory of Protectionism, Tariff Bargaining and the Formation of Customs Unions." Journal of Political Economy, Vol. LXXIII, Lima, 1965.

Junguito, R., and Caballero, C. "Situación de la Economía Colombiana en relación con el proceso de integración." Junta, Lima, November 1974.

Kafka, A. "Regional Monetary Integration of the Developing Countries." Mundell, R. and Swoboda, A., eds.: Monetary Problems of the International Economy. Chicago: University of Chicago Press, 1970.

Kaiser, Ronn D. "Toward the Copernican Phase of Regional Integration Theory." Journal of Common Market Studies (Oxford) Vol. 10, September 1971 No. 1; No. 3, 1972, pp. 207-233.

Kamara, L. "Intégration Fonctionnelle et Développment Accélère en Afrique." Revue du Tiers-Monde (Paris) 1971, No. 48, pp. 729-750.

_____. "Intégration Territoriale et Conflicts Institutioneels en Afrique." Revue du Tiers-Monde (Paris) decembre 1970, No. 44, pp. 701-732.

Khalil, K.H. "The Conventional Theory of Economic Integration and the African Conditions." L'Egypte Contemporaine (Caire) 62, April 1971, No. 344, pp. 169-188.

Kaplan, M. "Aspectos Políticos de la Planificación en América Latina." Revista de la Sociedad Interamericana de Planificación. Vol. IV, No. 15, September, 1970.

Krauss, M.B. "Recent Developments in Customs Unions Theory: An Interpretative Survey." JEL, Junio 1972.

_____. "Customs Union Theory: Ten Years later." Journal of World Trade Law (London) 1972, nr. 6, pp. 284-293.

_____. "Recent Development in Customs Union Theory: An Interpretative Essay." Journal of Economic Literature. (Washville, Tennessee) June 1972, pp. 413-436.

Kindleberger, C. "The Terms of Trade and Economic Development." The Review of Economics and Statistics, Supplement, February 1958.

_____. "European Integration and the International Corporation." In Courtney, C.B., World Business: Promise and Problems, New York: Macmillan & Co., 1970.

Kitamura, Hiroshi. "Economic Theory and the Economic Integration of Underdeveloped Regions." M. Wionczek, ed. Economic Integration in Latin America. New York: Praeger, 1966.

Kortansky, A. "Theory and Practice of Regional Integration: The Case of COMECOM." International Organization, Vol. 25, 1970.

Kozma, F. "Some Theoretical Problems Regarding Socialist Integration and the Levelling of Economic Development." Trends in World Economy, No. 6, Budapest, 1966.

Krugman, O., and Taylor, L. "Contradictory Effects of Devaluation." Journal of International Economics, Vol. 8, 1978.

Kük, Gert. "Economic Co-operation and Integration: The Case of the Developing Countries." In Economic Integration: Concepts, Theories and Problems, edited by Mihaly Simai and Katalin Garam pp. 285-292. Budapest: Akademia Kiadó, 1977.

Lambri, B. "Customs Unions and Underdeveloped Countries." Economia Internazionale, May 1962.

Lewis, Vaughan A. "Concept and Analysis in the Study of Third World Regional Integration." Social and Economic Studies. (Mono, Jamaica) 26, March 1977, pp. 1-77.

Linder, S.B. "Uniones Aduaneras y Desarrollo Económico." Wionczek, M., Integracion de la América Latina; Experiencias y Perspectivas, FCE, México, 1964.

Liesner, H.H. "Policy Harmonization in the EEC and EFTA." Denton, E.R., Economic Integration in Europe, London: World University, 1971.

Lipsey, R. "The Theory of Customs Unions, Trade Diversion and Welfare." Economica, February 1952.

_____. "The Theory of Customs Unions." Economic Journal, Vol. LXX, No. 279, September 1960.

Little, Ian. "Regional International Companies as an Approach to Economic Integration." Journal of Common Market Studies. (Oxford) Vol. 5, No. 2, December 1966, pp. 181-186.

Lizano, Eduardo Fait. "The Distribution of Costs and Benefits in Economic Integration among Developing Countries." In UNCTAD: Current Problems of Economic Integration, New York, 1973, pp. 25-101.

_____. "Comentarios acerca de la idea integracionista en cuatro autores Centroamericanos." Revista de la integración. (Buenos Aires) septiembre 1973, No. 14. pp. 191-225.

_____. "Integracion económica y nivel de empleo: notas para una investigación." Integración Latinoamericana. (Buenos Aires), 1° December 1976. pp. 6-17.

_____. "Integration of less developed areas and of areas on different levels of development." In Economic integration worldwide, regional, sectoral, edited by Fritz Machlup. London: Macmillan & Co., 1976.

Loehr, W. "Notes on Lipsey's Theory of Customs Unions." Journal of Common Market Studies. Nos. 1-2, (Oxford), 1975, pp. 87-89.

Lundgren, Nils. "Customs Unions of Industrialized West European Countries." Denton, J.R., ed. Economic Integration in Europe, London: World University, 1971.

Magarinos, G. "Los instrumentos de la integración y la experiencia de la ALALC," Wionczek, M., ed. Integración de la América Latina: Experiencias y Perspectivas, FCE, Mexico, 1964.

_____. "Evaluación del Proceso de Integración de la ALALC." LAFTA, Montevideo, 1969.

Makhlouf, Farouk, H. "Comparative Study on the Theory of Economic Integration in Relation to Developing Countries." L'Egypte contemporaine. (Le caise) 65, Juil 1975, pp. 301-324.

Marcy, Gérara. "How Far Can Foreign and Customs Agreements Confer upon Small Nations the Advantages of Large Nations." In Economic Consequences of Size of Nations, pp. 265-281, edited by E.A.G. Robinson. London: Macmillan & Co., 1960.

Macarios, S. "Protectionism and Industrialization in Latin America." Economic Bulletin for Latin America, ECLA, March, 1964.

Mantel, R. "Integración Económica, Distribución del Ingreso y Consumo: Una racionalidad para la integración." Trimestre Económico, XLII, 1975.

Marsh, P. "The Integration Process in Eastern Europe, 1968 to 1975." JMCS, Vol. 14, June, 1976.

McCrone, G. "Regional Policy in the European Communities." Denton, E.R., ed. Economic Integration in Europe, London: World University, 1971.

Mariscal, Nicolás. "Integración y el proyecto de tratado marco." Estudios centroamericanos. (San Salvador) 32, enero gebrero 1977, pp. 57-82.

Martínez-Martínez, Osvaldo Mendez-Cruz, and Armando Alvarez-Figueroa, Oneida. "Some Ideas on Latinamerican Integration and Economic Development." In Economic Integration.... edited by M. Simai and Katalin Garam, pp. 303-312. Budapest: Akademia Kiado, 1977.

Maximová, Margarita M. "O pojětí a typech integrace." Politická ekonomie. (Praha) 22 No. 11, 1974, pp. 991-993.

Mayes, D.G. "The effects of Economic Integration on Trade." Journal of Common Market Studies (Oxford) (197), September 1978, nr. 1.

Maza-Zavala, Domingo F. "La economía política de la integración latinoamericana." Desarrollo (Santiago) Vol. 5, marzo 1971, pp. 39-45.

Mead, D.C. "The Distribution of Gains in Customs Unions Between Developing Countries." Kyklos, No. 21, 1968.

Melvin, J. "Comments on the Theory of Customs Union." Manchester School of Economic and Social Studies, junio, 1969.

Mikesell, Raymond F. "The Movement towards Regional Trading Groups in Latin America." A. Hirschman, ed. Latin American Issues, Essays and Comment, New York: Twentieth Century Fund, 1961.

_____. "The Theory of Common Markets as Applied to Regional Arrangements Among Developing Countries." Harrod and Hague, eds. International Trade Theory in a Developing World, New York: Macmillan, 1963.

_____. "El Financiamiento Externo e Integración en América Latina: Experiencias y Perspectivas." Wionczek, M., Integración de la América Latina: Experiencias y Perspectivas, FCE, México, 1964.

_____. "The Theory of Common Markets and Developing Countries." In International Trade Theory in a Developing World, eds. Roy Harrod and Douglas Hague. Reproduced in Robson, 1971.

Misas, C. "Contribución al Estudio del grado de concentración en la Industria Colombiana." Boletin Mensual de Estadística, DANE, No. 266, Bogotá, 1973.

Mitchell, C. "The Role of Technocrats in Latin American Integration." InterAmerican Affairs, Vol. 21, No. 1, Summer 1967.

Montias, J.M. "Background and Origins of the Rumanian Dispute with COMECOM." Soviet Studies, Vol. XVI, No. 2.

Morawetz. "Problemas de Transporte y Comunicaciones en el Grupo Andino." Revista de la Integración, No. 11, November 1972.

_____. "Harmonization of Economic Policies in Customs Unions: The Andean Group." JCMS, No. 11, June 1973.

Morgan, Harrod. "Trends in Terms of Trade and their Repercussions of Primary Producers", Harrod and Hague, eds. International Trade Theory in a Developing World, New York: Macmillan, 1963.

Mundell, R.A. "Tariff Preferences and the Terms of Trade." In Robson, P. International Economic Integration. London: Penguin Books, 1972.

Musalem, A. "Las Exportaciones Colombianas 1959-1969, Bogotá, 1970." mimeo., Bogotá, 1970.

Mycielsky, J. "A Model for Regional Harmonization of National Development Plans." Economic Bulletin for Asia and the Far East, No. 18, 1967.

Mytelka, L. "The Salience of Gains in Third World Integration Systems." World Politics, Vol. 25, January 1973.

_____. "Foreign Aid and Regional Integration. The UDEC Case." JCMS, Vol. XII, No. 2, Dec. 1973.

_____. "Regional Integration, Dependence and Development." mimeo., Kingston, Ontario: Queen's University, January 1976.

Novozansky, J. "Vyrovnani Economicke Urovne Socialistickyck zemi." Nova Myl, No. 4, 1962.

_____. "Jednotne Hospodarstvi Socialisticke Soustavy." Nova Mysl, No. 10, 1962.

Nye, J.S.F. "Patterns and Catalysts in Regional Integration." International Organization, Vol. 19, 1965.

_____. "Central American Regional Integration." Inter-national Conciliation, March 1967.

_____. "Comparing Common Markets: A Revised Neofunc-tionalistic Model." International Organization, Vol. 27, 1970.

Odell, P. "Economic Integration and Spatial Patterns of Economic Development in Latin America." Journal of Com-mon Market Studies, No. 4, (Oxford) March 1968.

Pazos, Felipe. "La integración regional del comercio entre países de menor desarrollo". Revista de la integración economía, política, sociología No. 14, (Buenos Aires) septiembre 1973, pp. 119-151.

Penaranda, C. "Integración Andina: Dimensionamiento del Mercado Subregional y Distribución del Ingreso." mimeo., Lima, 1976.

Pérez, C.A. "Segundo Mesaje al Congreso." Caracas, 1976.

Perroux, Francois. "Notes sur la notion de la Pole de Crois-sance." Economie Appliquée, Vol. 8, 1955, translated from the French in I. Livingston, ed. Economic Policy for Development. London: Penguin, 1971.

_____. "Quién se integra? En beneficio de quien se realiza la integración?" Revista de la Integración, No. 1. November 1967.

Pilicĺ Vera Vojnovĭc, Milán. "Integration in Developing Countries and the Realization of the Scientific-techno-logical Revolution." In Economic Integration: Concepts, Theories, and Problems, edited by Mihaly Simai and Kata-lin Garam, Budapest: Akademia Kiadó, 1977, pp. 347-358.

Pinder, J. "Problems of European Integration." The World Today, March 1968.

_____. "Positive and Negative Integration." World Today (London) March 1968, pp. 88-110.

Pirec, Dusan. "Traktat o procesu internacionalizacijé kapitale, integraciji i nacionalnoj druzavi." Marksizam u svetu. Jun 1977, br. 6, pp. LI-LVI.

Prebisch, R. "Los Obstáculos al Mercado Común Latinoameri-cano." Wionczek, M., ed. Integración de la América Latina, FCE, México, 1964.

_____. "Commercial Policies in the Underdeveloped Coun-tries." American Economic Review, May 1965.

_____. "Críticas al Capitalismo Periférico." Revista de la CEPAL, No. 1, 1976.

_____. "Estructura Socioeconómica y Crisis del Sistema." Revista de la CEPAL, No. 6, 1978.

Robson, Peter. "Regional Economic Cooperation among Developing Countries: Some Further Consideration." World Development (London) No. 6, June 1978, pp. 771-777.

Sakamoto, J. "Industrial Development and Integration of Underdeveloped Countries." JCMS, No. 7, June 1969.

Salazar, Santos, Felipe. "El Sistema de Nacionalización Progresiva de las Empresas Extranjeras y la Orientación Selectiva de la Inversión Extranjera en el Grupo Andino." mimeo. Junta, 1975. Lima.

_____. "El problema de las desigualdades en la integración". Derecho de la integración (Buenos Aires) Nos. 22-23, jul-noviembre 1976, pp. 13-41.

_____. "Solución de conflictos en organizaciones interestatale para. la integración económica y otras formas de cooperación económica". Derecho de la integración. Revista jurídica latinoamericana. (Buenos Aires). Vol. 11, No. 28/29, November 1978, pp. 11-33.

Salgado, G. "El Desarrollo y la Integración de América Latina." O. Sunkel, ed. Integracion Política y Económica, Editorial Universitaria, Santiago, 1970.

_____. "Informe a la Segunda Reunión de Cancilleres." Lima, Junta, 1972.

_____. "El Grupo Andino y el Poder de Acción Solidaria." Wyndham-White, E., La Integración Latino-Americana en una Etapa de Decisiones. Buenos Aires: Bid-Intal, 1973.

_____. "El Grupo Andino y la Inversión Extranjera." Comercio Exterior, Vol. XXIII, Mexico, 1973.

Schmitter, P.C. "Autonomy or Dependence as Regional Integration Outcomes: Central America." Research Series, No. 17, Institute of International Studies, U. California Berkeley, 1972.

_____. "Three Neo-functional Hypotheses about International Integration." International Organization (Madison, Wisc.) Vol. 22, Winter 1969, pp. 101-166.

Scitovsky, T. "International Trade and Economic Integration or a Means of Overcoming the Disadvantage of a Small Nation." Robinson, E.A., Economic Consequences of the Size of the Nations, London: Macmillan & Co., 1964.

Schydlowsky, D. "Asignación de Industrias de Integración en el Grupo Andino." Revista de la Integración, November 8, No. 8, May 1971.

Segal, A. "The Integration of Developing Countries, Some Thoughts on East Africa and Central America." JCMS, No. 5, May 1967.

Selowsky, M. "Política Cambiaria y Asignación de Recursos." Santiago: Universidad Católica, 1972.

Serra, J. "El Estilo de Desarrollo Reciente de la América Latina, Notas Introductorias." Trimestre Económico, Vol. XLIV (2), No. 174, México, 1977.

Sheaham, J. and S. Clark. "La respuesta de las exportaciones Colombianas a las variaciones en la tasa efectivas de cambio." Fedesarrollo, Bogotá, 1970.

Singer, P. "The Distribution of Gains Between Investing and Borrowing Countries." American Economic Review, May 1950.

Sloan, J.W. "The Strategy of Development Regionalism: Benefits, Distribution, Obstacles and Capabilities." Journal of Common Market Studies, (Oxford). Vol. 10, No. 2, December 1971, pp. 138-162.

Swansborough, R.M. "The American Investors; View of Latin American Economic Nationalism." Interamerican Economic Affairs, Vol. XXVI, No. 3, 1972.

Tavares, M.C. "El Proceso de Sustitución de Importaciones como Modelo de Desarrollo reciente en América Latina." ECLA Boletín Economico de América Latina, Vol. IX, No. 1, Marzo, 1964.

Tayseer, A.J. "Relevance of Traditional Integration Theory to Less Developed Countries." JCMS, Vol. 9, March 1979.

Thorp, T.R. "The Post-Import Substitution Era: The Case of Peru." World Development, Nos. 1, 2, 1976.

Tinbergen, J. "La Industria Pesada y el Mercado Común Latino Americano," Wionczek, M., ed. La Integracion de la América Latina: Experiencias y Perspectivas, FCE, Mexico, 1964.

Tironi, E. "Aspectos Teóricos del Comportamiento de Corporaciones Transnacionales frente a un Proceso de Integración." Revista de la Integración, Nos. 19, 20, 1975.

Tokman, V.E. "Distribución del Ingreso, Tecnología y Empleo." Trimestre Económico, Vol. XLI, (4), No. 164, Mexico, 1974.

Tomasini, Luciano. "Elementos para un estudio de los procesos de integración latinoamericana." Intergración Latinoamericana (Buenos Aires) No. 2, abril 1977, pp. 22-42.

Unger, Ladislav. "Advantages potentiels de l'intégration économique." Mondes en Développement (Paris) 23, 1978, pp. 606-627.

Vaitsos, Constantine. "Crisis in Regional Economic Cooperation (integration) among Developing Countries: A Survey." World Development (Oxford) 6, June 1978, nr. 6. p.719.

_____. "The Process of Commercialization of Technology in the Andean Pact: A Synthesis." mimeo., Junta, Lima, 1971.

Valder, S. "Obstáculos políticos a la integración latinoamericana." Revista de la Integración, Vol. VII, No. 17, 1974.

Van Ginderachter, J. "Economic Integration and Regional Imbalance." Lijdschrift voor Economie on Management (Louvain) No. 1, 1975, pp. 47-62.

Warnecke, Steven J. "American Regional Integration Theories and the European Community Integration." Review of Western Immigrants, Residents and Tourists (Tel Aviv) no. 1, 1971.

Waters, W.G. "International Transport Costs and Regional Industrialization among Developing Countries." Journal of Common Market Studies. (Oxford) Vol. 9, No. 2, December 1970, pp. 151-169.

Webb, R. "The Distribution of Income in Peru." In A. Foxley, ed. Income Distribution in Latin America, Cambridge, Eng.: CUP, 1976.

Williams, Maurice J. "Customs Unions: a Criterium for Welfare Gains in the General Case." Manchester School of Economic and Social Studies (Manchester) 1972, pp. 385-386.

Wionczek, Miguel. S. "Condiciones de una integración viable." Introducción a Miguel S. Wionczek, Integración de América Latina, Experiencias y perspectivas, México: Fondo de Cultura Económica, 1972. 381 p.

_____. "La integración económica latinoamericana y la inversión extranjera." Comercio Exterior (México) Vol. 20, septiembre 1970, pp. 748-757.

_____. "Integration and Development." International Journal (Toronto, Can). Vol. 24, No. 3, Summer 1969, pp. 449-462.

_____. "Multinationals and the LDCs." In The Nation-State and Transnational Corporations in Conflict: with Special Reference to Latin America, edited by Jon P. Gunnemann, New York: Praeger, 1975, pp. 16-20.

_____. "Requisities for Viable Integration." In Latin American Integration, New York: Praeger, 1966, pp. 3-18.

_____ . "La Reacción Norteamericana Ante el tratado común a los Capitales Extranjeros en el Grupo Andino." Comercio Exterior, México, 1971.

_____ . "Hacia el Establecimiento de un tratado común a la Inversión Extranjera en el Mercado Común Andino." Trimestre Económico, LXXVIII, No. 150, México, June 1971.

INDEX

ABOUT THE AUTHOR

ALICIA PUYANA DE PALACIOS received two degrees in Economics from the University of Prague and her PhD in Economics from Oxford University. As a United Nations adviser her research activities focused on economic integration particularly within the Andean Group. She has authored many articles in professional journals and books with the National Department of Planning of the Columbia Institute of External Trade.